Industrial Imperialism in Italy

INDUSTRIAL IMPERIALISM IN ITALY

1908-1915

R. A. WEBSTER

UNIVERSITY OF CALIFORNIA PRESS
Berkeley   Los Angeles   London
1975

University of California Press
Berkeley and Los Angeles, California

University of California Press, Ltd.
London, England

Printed in the United States of America

Acknowledgments

The author acknowledges with thanks the financial assistance of the American Council of Learned Societies, the Guggenheim Foundation, and the Institute for International Studies (Berkeley). In his researches he was helped by Professor C. Cipolla of Berkeley and Pavia. At the Italian foreign ministry Professor F. Valsecchi was of great help: the director of the Historical Archive, Professor R. Mori, was generous with time and assistance. At the Bank of Italy Professor Masera and Dr. M. Borghese found valuable documentation concerning railroad projects. The Banca Commerciale Italiana, at both Milan and Parma, offered untapped sources: the author received special help from the late Professor R. Mattioli and Dr. I. Monti of Milan, as well as from Commendatore Favaro and Mr. Gessi of Parma. Professor A. M. Ghisalberti offered useful advice concerning military journals. The Biblioteca Nazionale Centrale of Florence was always of good service, and the author owes special thanks to the librarian, Mr. I. Baglioni. The author profited from the special knowledge of Professor Y. T. Kurat as well as from the encouragement of Professor T. Von Laue. The present volume is a shortened version of the original work, published at Turin by the Casa Einaudi; the abridgements, done by Mrs. E. Strainchamps, left the author's thoughts and wording substantially intact.

R. A. W.
Berkeley, 1974

Contents

Part I: The Economic Foundations   I

Prologue   3

1. The Predicament of Italian Industrialization:
   The Steel Trust   41

2. The Nontrust Industries:
   Entente versus Alliance Influences   76

3. The Shipping Industry   106

4. Italian Industrial Financing
   and the Banca Commerciale   126

Part II: The Politics of Italian Imperialism
    on the Eve of the War   165

5. Industrial Labor
   and Management Conflicts   167

6. Italy's Drive to the East   191

7. Italian Imperialism on the Eve
   of the First World War   244

8. The End Play in the Balkans,
   1913–14   310

Conclusion: The View from Trieste   333

Notes   341

Index   379

THE
ECONOMIC
FOUNDATIONS

Prologue

When she finally achieved unity and independence, Italy was the embodiment of a nineteenth-century ideal—a nation-state, secular and parliamentary, evolving toward universal suffrage. In the ensuing seventy years of democracy, secularism and nationality turned out to be no easy combination. The Risorgimento synthesis never really worked. The new nation, far from being a model state in the liberal European family, constituted a source of worry and nuisance for decades. Always a maverick, by 1911 Italy was becoming a threat, and her assault on Turkey in that year set off a train of events leading straight to Sarajevo.[1]

In both her domestic and her foreign performance, Italy provided a refutation of the previous century's liberal optimism. In the early twentieth century she became an aggressively expansionist state, eventually sacrificing parliamentary government and secularism to achieve a monolithic national unity and contributing two new terms —fascism and totalitarianism—to the political vocabulary.

Though the Fascist dictatorship did not materialize until nearly four years after the First World War, the turning point in Italy's fatal course seems to have been reached between 1911 and 1915. These were the years during which the parliamentary system faltered, while the national establishment—the monarchy, the armed forces, and the concentrated economic interests that identified themselves with the permanent nation—pressed forward with plans of foreign expansion that the Chamber of Deputies was unaware of. In the nineteenth century the critics of constitutional government could set the "legal" limited-suffrage chamber against the "real" nation—the still disenfranchised masses. But in the early years of the twentieth century, the

3

situation was reversed. Nationalist theorists like Alfredo Rocco could convincingly set the "legal" nation represented by parliament, now elected by universal male suffrage, against the "real" Italy—the productive, managerial, and professional elites that alone knew and furthered the lasting interests of the nation.

This was not just phrase making. There was a real divorce between parliament, which—however imperfectly—had begun to represent the social aspirations of the masses, and the country's ruling oligarchies, which could no longer make their will prevail through parliament. Soon they began to bypass it; the crisis of the parliamentary system took place between the universal-suffrage elections of 1913 and the intervention crisis in the spring of 1915.

These are the years that count. The Fascist coup of October 1922 would have been unthinkable if the deputies had not already been discredited in May 1915. And the Fascist regime, once in power, turned out to have few ideas that did not come from the National-Liberal and Nationalist programs of 1911–15. The prolonged postwar crisis merely gave the coup de grace to parliamentary politics; parliament was moribund by 1915, when the deputies proved incapable of making the most important decision in Italian history till then —whether to enter the First World War.

The years 1911–15 form the center of this study. In those pivotal years Italy's essential dilemmas as a nation-state came to light, provoking a series of crises and wars that did not really end until the mid-1950s, when Italy, joining the great economic communities of Western Europe, entered upon an entirely new course of development.

Since in this study imperialism will be treated as the central, dominant fact of Italian political life in the early twentieth century, the term should be defined. As I shall show, Italy's drive to the East in 1911–15, however lilliputian when compared with Germany's, had the same fundamental cause—industrial-financial imbalance—and the same objective—what Rudolf Hilferding called economic space. Italy was an imperialist country in the same sense that Germany was.

That fact has often been obscured by the elusive and deceptive nature of Italian public life. Italy's industries were not gigantic in statistical terms, and the expansionism of 1911–15 was attributed to

Italy's tragic overpopulation. But an examination of the real aims of Italian expansion will show that the "population-outlet" claim amounted to no more than propaganda and window dressing. True demographic imperialism was dead with Crispi. The imperial schemes of Crispi and the *Africanisti*, disastrously foiled at Adowa in 1896, actually did provide for peasant settlements in the highlands of East Africa. That is why North Italy, with its nascent industrial interests, showed such little interest in Africa's "burning sands" and let Crispi fall.

The new imperialism emanated from the North fifteen years later. It was essentially industrial, concerning itself with ports, railways, and mining projects in the Balkans and the Ottoman Empire. The population-outlet gambit was still useful because it appealed to the unindustrialized South and to the general middle class, which was ashamed of the impression that mass immigration made abroad. But the appeals to injured national pride disguised a policy that actually posed very different national priorities.

A retrospective account of Italy's political and economic power structures, in the shape that these took after the Risorgimento, will substantiate this thesis.

From 1861 to 1876 Italy was managed by a patrician parliamentary oligarchy, most of whose members were a little appalled by the revolutionary violence and unscrupulous diplomacy that had led to Italy's unification: now that they had an Italian state, they had seen enough change in their generation. They were far from being unenlightened, but they saw that the new nation was burdened by its turbulent past and by the huge debts that had been run up in the course of the struggle. Cavour's successors were concerned above all with avoiding revolt or bankruptcy, with establishing the new kingdom's political and financial credit in Europe. Most of them were landowners and professional men, often men of distinction and integrity, but few of them knew very much about the new industrial society emerging in Europe and America; the only industry in Italy with some members in the ruling class was textile manufacturing. Heavy industry, universal suffrage, and mass politics were regarded as things to be feared rather than desired. Italy's immediate development required solvency, foreign capital, and political stability: 1861–76 is one of the least adventurous periods in the history of modern Italy.

The parliamentary oligarchies of the Right reached two minimum goals: international recognition and solvency, though Italy had to pay heavily for both. By dint of crushing land and consumption taxes, the Italian government escaped the fate of Spain, Mexico, and Egypt. Italy became one of the world's elite states, solvent and gold paying on the Paris bourse.

Another need of the new state, a unified national transportation system, presented special problems. By moving skillfully between the rival Rothschild and Pereire investment banks of Paris, North Italian financiers and politicians managed to get financial backing for a national railway network. But the terms were onerous, committing the Italian treasury to guarantee the new rail firms a certain minimum return per kilometer of line in operation, as well as interest on the capital spent in construction. The new rail firms were largely foreign in management and bought most of their equipment abroad. Hence rail construction was not the stimulus to industrial development in Italy that it had been elsewhere.[2]

It would be unfair to blame this state of affairs on foreign financing or domestic chicanery. It is hard to see how a nation burdened with an inefficient peasant economy and inherited debt, malnutrition and illiteracy, could have afforded the luxury of a national rail industry in the 1860s or 1870s: existing rail operators failed to make money on their new lines and survived by grace of the state treasury. Under such circumstances, to have created a unified domestic market at all was a great achievement; domestic heavy industry remained in the future.

Nevertheless, Italy's failure to take off industrially in the first decade of her unity had grave consequences. Italy became independent at perhaps the last moment when it might still have been possible to industrialize on the basis of small, developing units. In the 1860s industrial technique leaped forward, and thereafter Italian industrialization would require large-scale financing and planning, with political guarantees or subsidies.

The reasons for the missed opportunity were partly geographic.

The principal cheap energy available was the waterpower in the northern mountain valleys, so enterprisers had to place their mills at an inconvenient distance from the centers of commerce until the advent of hydroelectric power two decades later.

Italian politics compounded the disadvantages. The liberal oligarchies naturally assumed that Italy would remain fundamentally agrarian and that free-trade legislation and liberal commercial treaties would stimulate the peninsula's latent economic energies with salutary blasts of foreign competition.

These short-run disadvantages were compounded by the long-range, intrinsic fallacies of the free-trade system as it applied to Italy. In the nineteenth century industrial nations were few, and industrial prices remained high, while agricultural prices sank in the latter part of the century because of newly accessible and abundant sources of foodstuffs throughout the world. Only efficient, large-scale cultivation could be a real source of wealth. A nation attempting modern competitive agriculture, however, needed capital investments, equipment, and scientific methods that only industrial development could supply. Finally, a nation with a rising population either had to employ its new labor force in urban industry or let it languish in deepening misery on the farm, dragging down the nation's per capita income and weighing heavily on the home market. Another possible way out, mass emigration, had its own economic disadvantages.

It was natural enough that a ruling class that conceived of income and prosperity in terms of land rent should have been reluctant to come to grips with the problems of industrialization. In the late 1860s small industrial groups were beginning to bring before the Italian educated public the real lines along which Italy would have to proceed: huge, irreversible initial investments would be necessary, with special tariffs and subsidies. Italy had iron ore and chemicals, labor was abundant and cheap, and industries could rise on such a foundation. However, in the new dimensions of late nineteenth-century industrial systems, it was no longer a question of the talent or diligence of an individual enterpriser, as the prevailing economic orthodoxy held. Orthodoxy of this sort had persistently ignored the effects of rising population, as well as technological progress, to concentrate instead on rent and commercial balance as the only indices of prosperity. The battle against that prevailing attitude was long and uncertain, and it was a tragedy for Italy that the winning argument that almost surely led to the final victory of protectionism in the 1880s and 1890s was military rather than economic.

There were good reasons for Italy's rulers to fear the growth of an industrial society. First, the prevalent orientation toward Britain and France led the Italian ministries to accept Italy's subordinate role, both politically and economically, in a world order managed by those two powers: the commercial treaty with France in 1863, which gave France advantages not fully reciprocated by concessions from the senior power, marks the high point in this combined policy of free trade and western political leanings. The most that Cavour himself had conceived of for industrial Italy in this system was a set of machine shops and textile mills: steel production was excluded, even as a possibility, and Italian iron ore might as well be sold abroad. The regional examples of Lombardy and Piedmont, which by 1860 had already achieved a degree of agrarian modernization and development of the textile industry through coordination with the western European markets, were taken to be mandatory for the whole nation after unification; and no attention was given at first to the new possibilities offered by a great national market. And after 1866 the Italian government was dependent on the Paris money market for credit and was therefore in no position to do anything to alienate French lenders.

There were other reasons why Italy hesitated to plan industrialization. The growth of heavy industry would do more than disrupt her tacit partnership with the senior states of the West. It would also tear up the network of paternalistic relations that still prevailed in much of North Italian textile manufacturing, in which home-weaving and putting-out systems meshed well with a peasant society. Few well-to-do Italians wanted at home what they saw with alarm abroad, a great urban proletariat without any sense of restraint or obligation toward the traditional ruling class. Moreover, much of the peninsula's middle class was provincial or rural in origin: its education was humanistic and juridical, and the rhetoric of classical patriotism was nearer to its heart than the hard, prosaic requirements of modernization. There were more lawyers than engineers in the Italian parliamentary class. Indeed, it was a class that served its apprenticeship in law faculties and courts rather than in offices and workshops: the coffeehouse was more familiar than the big-city bank or factory.

These considerations did not lose all their force even after 1870. To be sure, the German, rather than the western European, model of economic development came to seem suitable for Italy: here military success was the determinant. Nevertheless the Commune of 1871 clearly showed the dangers latent in the growth of big cities and confirmed the Italian middle class in its fear of mass societies of any sort. The last traces of the Risorgimento's democratic optimism disappeared, and modernization took place in an atmosphere of pessimism and power politics. Development of heavy industry was undertaken as a dangerous and expensive project but—alas—a military necessity.

The peculiar way in which Italy edged into the modern industrial world cannot be understood without taking into account the fact that the Italian state was a dyarchy, in which power was shared, in an undefined way, between a parliamentary middle class and a traditional military monarchy.

Arriving in power under unfavorable skies, the peninsula's middle classes could not enjoy a 1789 of their own, much less a 1792. The new state had to be founded on a compromise with the House of Savoy and its military establishment. Without even changing its denomination—Victor Emmanuel II of Sardinia became Victor Emmanuel II of Italy—the old dynasty continued to play a decisive role behind the scenes in shaping both the foreign and the military policies of the new state. The parliamentary system "covered" the sovereign while actually allowing him a wide range of choice in military ministries and promotions; the king's constitutional "irresponsibility," far from reducing him to a figurehead, screened him from public scrutiny and allowed him to play the part of supreme arbiter in any situation in which the chamber could not express a clear majority mandate: three times, in 1915, 1922, and 1943, the king decided Italy's political fate.[3]

There was something strange in the spectacle of an adventurous line of border princes, known more for its soldiering and wenching than for any true national feelings, maintaining itself at the head of

the Italian state; characteristically, it took a military disaster to pry
the monarchy loose from its hold on Italy. When the dynasty deserted
Rome and left the army without leadership in the face of the Germans
in World War II, Italy could finally move toward becoming a republic, the abiding aspiration of Risorgimento patriotism. After 1943
even the most conservative Italian found it hard to champion a prince
who had gone AWOL.

The Italian liberal bourgeoisie could no more disestablish the
Church than it could eliminate the monarchy. Here, too, the parliamentary middle class could arrive at only shifting, eclectic compromises. The process of national unification had swept away the Pope's
temporal power and dissolved ecclesiastical land tenure, but a genuine separation of church and state never took place, either in law or
in fact; Italian society and politics never became truly secular. If
much of Italian city life developed outside the orbit of the Church,
the most progressive and prosperous countrysides of North Italy
stayed Catholic, with local clerical credit banks, newspapers, and
labor unions. The old papal aristocracy and administrative classes of
Latium did not lose their grip. On the contrary, they began moving
into the new world of real estate dealing and banking with remarkable
adaptability. A torrent of papal anathemas from one side and a spate
of anticlerical jeers from the other only served to conceal an effective
convergence between the new bourgeois and the old Catholic Italy.

The fundamental reason for the failure of the Risorgimento to
end with the establishment of a true bourgeois political order lay in
the deep diversity of Italy's middle classes.[4] Until the parliamentary
system began drawing the various provincial bourgeoisies together
in a common set of interests and concerns, even the most modern,
European-oriented Italian bourgeois remained regional in his interests and attitudes. The Italian bourgeoisie might be national in its
goals, but it remained regional in its power bases; it had no center
comparable to Paris or London. The situation gave rise to a duality
between Rome, regarded as a parasitic and clerically tinged bureaucratic capital, and Milan, regarded as Italy's moral capital—the real
propulsive center of the nation's economy and culture.

Of all the various regions, Lombardy had the most forward-
looking middle class. The Lombard bourgeoisie, mixed with older

patrician classes, owed its wealth to two sources: large-scale agriculture in the Po Valley and textile manufacturing. Lombardy's agriculture required constant irrigation and land reclamation—from the mid-eighteenth century on, Milan had facilities for training hydraulic engineers, an educational effort that culminated in the founding in 1863 of the famous Reale Politecnico di Milano, the seedbed of many of Italy's future industrial engineers. The Politecnico was more than a state engineering school: it profited from private endowments, industrial education societies, gifts from the municipality, and even grants from Milan's principal savings bank.

Lombardy's textile enterprises, which began taking on large-scale dimensions during the last oscillating years of Napoleonic rule, constitute, together with parallel developments in Piedmont, nineteenth-century Italy's only important "natural" industry. With the great innovations of the 1860s and 1870s, the textile industries began to need mechanical engineers, a need that further stimulated the region's growing technological culture.[5]

The bourgeoisies of Rome and the South performed no similar function. They had grown up in the interstices of an older social order—as lawyers, notaries, money lenders, estate managers, bailiffs. With the dissolution of feudal tenure and common-land rights and the decay of the old spendthrift, mortgage-ridden noble houses, these middle classes emerged as a legally full-fledged bourgeoisie. For them the overthrow of the old regime and its land system meant the chance to become landlords in fee simple.

But their rise to economic independence and political control was not justified by any modernization of agriculture, which geography and climate made far harder in the South than in upper Italy. Only a few favored coastal areas achieved even relative agrarian progress in the nineteenth century.

The Italian bourgeoisie, then, in its national manifestations was an uneasy, shifting coalition of disparate social classes. It lacked the unity of outlook and purpose, as well as the collective integrity, required for a genuine bourgeois revolution. The political system of liberal Italy was eclectic and insecure; its economics took the form of a convulsive effort to combine progress with special privileges. The whole structure was capped by a concept of overriding national interest that lent itself increasingly to nationalistic, rather than to liberal, interpretations and political practice.[6]

Thus, southern and northern statesmen played very different roles in the development of the liberal political system. The southerners, keenly aware of the shaky marginal society from which they came, provided the archconservatives as well as the apostles of national greatness and the profoundest revolutionaries: in this connection, it is enough to cite Salandra, the great conservative premier of the intervention and the coiner of the phrase "*sacro egoismo*"; the Sicilian Crispi; and the Neapolitan-Sardinian Antonio Gramsci, founder of the Italian Communist Party. From the North, on the other hand, came the parliamentary managers and fixers, the great administrators and engineers of the ministerial-parliamentary system, Agostino Depretis and Giovanni Giolitti. Northern and southern statesmen tended to differ in the very content of their patriotism: the southerners aspired toward African-Mediterranean empire and a prestigious role in the concert of Europe, while the northerners gave more thought to the concrete imitation and overtaking of the achievements of other European powers in the industrial and military spheres.

The history of bourgeois politics in Italy in the later part of the nineteenth century is in large part an account of the effort to overcome these intrinsic weaknesses and divisions. The "parliamentary revolution" of 1876 removed Cavour's aristocratic successors at the very moment when Italy's budget finally balanced: the historic Right had accomplished its great objective, though at the cost of unpopularity and defeat at the polls. The Left that succeeded was an agglomeration of Risorgimento democrats who had passed from Mazzini to Victor Emmanuel during the conclusive years of unification, and its political victory was due in large part to the Italian public's discontent with consumer taxes.

Disappointment clouded the years of the Left. The democratic ministers of 1876–96, aging ex-revolutionaries, came to power too late and had to face problems that their early training in conspiracy and insurrection did not prepare them for. Still obsessed with questions of national independence and status, they tried to set a new course for Italy, to follow great-power policies that would confer upon the new nation a less ancillary and marginal role in European affairs. At the same time the democratic ministries of the Depretis-Crispi era were committed by their past ideals to an extension of the suffrage. All this amounted to taking risks at home and abroad simultaneously.

It was the particular misfortune of the Left ministers to govern during twenty years of intermittent depression, with dips in agricultural prices that had especially sad consequences for the economy. Hence their efforts at fostering heavy industry suitable to a great power led to costly and parasitic dead ends, their electoral reforms opened the door to what looked like revolutionary socialism, and their great-power aspirations turned out to be tragically premature. The era of the old Left ended in a squalid decade of bank crashes, colonial defeats, and semirevolutionary tumult from Sicily to Milan. Between 1893 and 1900 the very survival of the Italian parliamentary system seemed in doubt.

Nevertheless, the rule of the democratic Left laid the foundations for the whole political and economic order that was to work so well from 1900 to 1915. In spite of its turbulent and confusing character, there are certain fundamental developments in the Depretis-Crispi era that led to the liberal apogee of 1900–1914, the age of equilibrium presided over by Giovanni Giolitti.

The Left was unable to achieve a genuine democratic state in Italy. But between 1876 and 1896 it did work out a new political system based on a coalition of interests on a peninsular scale and thereby overrode the old, deep-seated regionalisms of the Italian people and attained, however partially, the goal of national unity set by the Risorgimento movements.

The term *coalition* applies to both the political and economic spheres. Indeed, one of the most constant guidelines of the post-1876 system was precisely the integration of political and economic interest groups. Economically, these policies resulted in a complex network of protection and subsidies thrown around the whole peninsular market;[7] politically, they led to transformism.

Transformism is an ugly term, and its primary meaning is negative. It refers to the absence of political parties representing different ideas and methods with alternating terms of power and constitutional opposition. Instead of working through the classic two-party system, the mass of parliamentary deputies form ad hoc groupings to back this or that ministerial combination. Any successful and lasting parliamentary majority group in a transformist system must be held together by a carefully balanced and wide distribution of available political offices, by a generous and broad-based awarding of public works, and by election making.

In a transformist system the real art of a prime minister consists in thus managing a parliamentary majority group. The deputies themselves become brokers or agents, little inclined to look into the higher matters of state. The king, through the veto and the pressure that he can exercise at decisive moments, can guarantee long-term diplomatic, military, and colonial policies. In a sense, he is the guardian of the enduring, traditional interests of the nation. A transformist system gives the monarchy a new lease on life, a new function of power and prestige.

The worst side of transformism is election making or, in extreme cases, election fixing. It characteristically takes the form of a cyclical action between deputy, ministry, and prefect. A deputy supports a given ministry, which in turn instructs its prefect and police to insure the reelection of the loyal deputy. In some constituencies public works and similar favors may turn the trick; in others the prefect may have to resort to corruption or police methods to get the government candidate elected—abuses particularly current south of Rome. All this tended to discredit the whole parliamentary system, and a parliamentary majority returned by such means provided poor material for future cabinets. The transformist system allows for little circulation and few new alternatives in the class of political managers and tends to stagnate in the course of time. Even the greatest architect of transformism, Giolitti, was eventually undone by the intrinsic flaws of the system.

Nevertheless, it is hard to believe that a two-party system would have worked at all in that particular time and place. Italy has always been one of the most regionally unbalanced nations in Europe and has been very late in developing mass parties on a national scale: any really democratic political party in the late nineteenth century would probably have been regional—either papal-reactionary or revolutionary—and destructive of both parliament and Italy's hard-won and fragile national unity. Under these circumstances, transformist politics had one great historical merit: they worked to prevent the appearance of regional parties, with all the disruptive consequences that would have followed.

Although it must be put down to the credit of the transformist politicians of the Left that they achieved a national political system by fragmenting any regional parties or groupings, the means by which they did so actually deepened the basic differences between North and South. Northern constituencies were influenced by public works, while southern constituencies were often coerced into political conformity. An imposing facade of modern parliamentary national politics hid painful regional inequality and disaffection, and the gap between the real and the legal nation has never been bridged.

The most enduring achievement of the transformist system was the creation of a bloc of national economic interests held together by protective-tariff legislation: after 1888 landowning interests upheld industrial tariffs, much to the detriment of most Italian agriculture, while the industrialists of the North voted for duties on grain in spite of their evident unfavorable effects on food prices, which, from an industrialist's point of view, should have been held as low as possible. The omnibus tariff system of 1888 guaranteed a reserved domestic market to steelmakers, textile manufacturers, sugar beet growers and refiners, and, last but not least, wheat growers. Even the most backward and inefficient southern landlord got his cut of the protectionist pie, though the chief beneficiaries were the capitalists of the North.

The effect of such legislation was the establishment of a peninsular economic community, however artificial and rickety, to parallel and uphold the transformist ministerial majorities in the Chamber of Deputies. But the post-1876 governments had higher aims. A goal of military and industrial self-sufficiency and eventual competitiveness lay behind much of what the Left tried to do in those years: Italy was no longer to be a mere political and economic adjunct of western Europe. That goal was never really reached, but the effort produced a real community of interests and aims between the monarchical-military establishment, the nascent industries of the North, and the maze of ministries at Rome. The constitutional Italian state thus achieved the principal goal of the Risorgimento movement, however distorted and costly the result was.

The economic underpinning of transformism had the same defects as the political system: in the short run, protectionist tariffs served to stimulate home industries and to strengthen a sense of national unity based on interest as well as ideals. But over a longer period, the economic settlement proved as damaging as the political devices and failed to serve the Italian people's enduring interests. In other words, the protectionist system fostered certain forms of enterprise that then began to stagnate in the closed conditions that the same tariffs created.

In Italian agriculture grain and beet protection benefited a few hundred thousand large producers and *latifondisti*, landlords who could harvest in the spring and store their produce until the fall, when prices rose. The small peasant had to sell grain immediately and then buy flour in the fall at the high prices that the tariffs insured.[8] Nor were peasants the only damaged party: in the years before the First World War, food cost more in Italy than in other industrial nations, and wages were lower than in the industrial nations of the West. The agricultural tariffs insured a rapid development of milling and sugar refining with eventual export possibilities, but they also perpetuated a chronic state of underconsumption in Italy's laboring classes.

There were other negative effects that weighed for decades on the peninsula's economy. Much arable land that could have been devoted to more productive and variegated uses was left to low-yield grain cultivation or low-quality beet growing, since the national tariff system guaranteed a market for these crops.

Much the same held true for industrial tariffs. The prices that steelmakers obtained from the state for armaments and rails were so high that some economists thought that it would be better if the state made its own steel, in spite of the notorious inefficiency of government enterprise. Machine industries, which suffered from the high cost of metal and enjoyed no similar protection, got other costly favors from the state in the form of special contracts and subsidies. Finally, in the years just before the War, some canning and mechanical industries were allowed to import metal duty-free on condition that the finished product be exported. Thus, even as a source of fiscal revenue, the industrial tariff had its faults. There could be no doubt as to its long-range depressing effects on the domestic consuming public.

Perhaps the worst effects of the protectionist system were political. Pareto shrewdly observed that the Italian political class tended to divide into two groups: ministers and ministerial aspirants, and the spokesmen for special-interest groups. The ministers were rarely personal profiteers, but they needed the support of special interests and their political representatives to get and keep public office. Tariff legislation tended to coalesce special-interest groups on a national level, to fuse political and economic power into single coalitions or blocs: the big bank, the nationwide industry, the newspaper, and the parliamentary group all took the same cues when it came to protectionist legislation and special-interest measures in the military, transport, and shipping spheres.

Italy's banking system was slow to centralize, and it served the nation's economy poorly. Transformist ministries were reluctant to touch local privileges and interests, yet their work of political and economic unification remained premature and incomplete without a stable banking system responsive to the country's credit needs.

The sickness of the Italian banks had its roots in the peninsula's unevenness and backwardness. The note-issuing banks, authorized by law and theoretically under ministerial supervision, had the great advantage of having their notes credited as legal tender—indeed, for many years acceptance was compulsory. However, the banks' dependence on the state was not just a matter of law; they were really subjected to the wishes of the government. A bank director could profit from a minister's willingness to close one or both eyes, allowing his bank to engage in risky credit operations and print more notes than assets would justify or the law permit. Likewise, a minister needing election funds, favors for friendly newspapermen, and other forms of fast credit could find it convenient to turn to a banker with flexible standards.

Mobile-credit banks, engaging in medium- and long-term loans, also led an unhealthy and often feverish existence. The free and sometimes compulsory circulation of bank notes in the peninsula discouraged foreign investment except in state gold bonds payable internationally. This meant that Italian real estate and urban-development projects went ahead with largely domestic capital at tempting but artificially high interest rates. Bankers and speculators built paper-credit castles in the early 1880s that blew away in the bad times between 1887 and 1894. Unfortunately, much of the money that was threatened or lost belonged to private depositors, some of them influential. Their influence, in turn, impelled the government to engage in "salvage."

Why did the investment banks resort to real estate speculation, the riskiest and shadiest of activities? Because in Italy, still fundamentally an agrarian country behind its new great-power facade, public works and urban-development projects were running far ahead of concrete, sound industry building. Nonindustrial, semiparasitic Rome and Naples offered returns that were not to be found in the still lagging industrial world of the North. Not until the development of hydroelectric power in the late 1890s opened up new prospects for Italian industry did this situation change for the better. Meanwhile, Italian investment bankers had to seek out opportunities: the biggest investment firm, Credito Mobiliare, found it expedient to tie up bond money and personnel in undertaking tax collection for big Italian municipalities. This kind of contract was good for the bank's prestige, giving it a notable position among merchants and landlords, but net profits were slow and unimpressive. Investment capital needed higher returns.

To make matters worse, there were too many investment banks for the peninsula's constricted financial market, and they competed fiercely for depositors, compelling each other to offer interest rates and other advantages that were possible only with fast, speculative gains. Many Italian savers or investors were wary; even with this feverish and ultimately disastrous promotion, Italian investment banks never succeeded in mobilizing more than a fraction of the peninsula's available savings. The banks funneled some Milanese, Turinese, and Genoese capital into the quicksands of Roman real estate and Neapolitan urban renewal, but until failure overtook them between 1885 and 1893, they remained regional, like the note-issuing banks. A truly national credit institution, with peninsula-wide perspectives and plans, was lacking.

In its shaky condition Italy's banking system soon became as dependent on the state as its industries and its large-scale agrarian establishments were. However, the government's tie to the banks did not take the form of public law, as it did in the case of protective tariffs. It started as a matter of political makeshifts and expedient ministerial decisions that soon hardened into a line of policy that the state has followed ever since. In the late 1880s the government became alarmed over the plight of various North Italian banks that had plunged over their depth into Roman real estate. In the early 1890s the government had to bring order into the note-issuing banks by finally establishing a central bank of emission. In 1907, after a world-wide panic, the government sponsored a consortium to save the Società Bancaria, a northern bank badly overextended in credits to the cotton industry. Only once, in 1921, did the government refuse to save a tottering bank, and it is not unreasonable to see therein one of the principal reasons for the ensuing fall of the liberal system in Italy.

In 1922 Fascism brought with it guarantees that liberalism could no longer offer, but the original link between government and banks had been forged by the parliamentary managers of liberal Italy a full generation before. The term *liberal* in this connection is, to be sure, peculiar: Italian statesmen, liberal in their view of parliament and its powers, held implicitly that the interests of any great Italian economic enterprise paralleled those of the nation as a whole. Between 1887 and 1915 the Italian parliamentary world remained genuinely liberal in its politics, but its economic assumptions—its conception of what constituted a valid national interest—were already nationalistic in the twentieth-century sense of that word.

The Italian state began to intervene in the Italian banking world to salvage the Banca Tiberina in 1889. That institution, in which the noted industrialist Senator V. S. Breda was heavily committed, had so much backing from the Turinese bank Sconto e Seta that the Tiberina's collapse would have dragged down the Turinese bank as well. At stake were not merely the jobs of thousands of

Roman construction workers, as the government claimed in self-justification, but also the funds of the Savoy dynasty itself, which the influential minister of the royal house, Urbano Rattazzi, had invested at Turin in these enterprises. Little wonder, then, that Premier Crispi grew apprehensive or that his treasury minister, Giovanni Giolitti, worked out a salvage scheme whereby the leading note-issuing bank, the Banca Nazionale, would be permitted to print an extra 50 million lire in legal-tender notes as a credit to the hard-pressed Tiberina. In this fashion the public would pay for the salvaging "painlessly," that is, by inflation, and Rattazzi would be let off the hook. Rattazzi, in turn, became Giolitti's patron at court and seems to have been instrumental in hoisting him into the premiership in 1892, at a moment when even bigger salvage operations were the order of the day. (By then Crispi and Giolitti had parted political company.)

Giolitti thus arrived in power as a technician, expert in mediating interests, and his great achievement during his first term in power was the partial solution of Italy's banking problems. Though Giolitti intended to move slowly, dramatic circumstances compelled him to make a frontal attack. Matters were precipitated by the Banca Romana affair.

The weakest of the peninsula's note-issuing institutions, the Banca Romana had a bank-note circulation vastly exceeding any legal coverage, and its situation became critical after the real estate slump of the late 1880s. The scandal, momentarily deferred by scared ministers, finally broke early in 1893. Some of the Banca Romana's notes were actually fraudulent—duplicates secretly ordered from London and put into circulation by the president in clandestine midnight operations.

Although government and journalistic circles knew all about the Banca Romana's desperate situation, no one wanted to break the charmed circle of complicity that surrounded it. Too many had received favors, discounts, and instant credit from the bank's president, Bernardo Tanlongo, who seems to have been unable to say no to any political figure or newspaperman with money problems. Premiers had found the Banca Romana especially useful at election time, and Giolitti seems to have been no exception.

But Giolitti had the merit of moving fast once the scandal broke.

By the end of 1893 Italy finally had a unified, state-regulated, central note-issuing bank, the Bank of Italy, which had as its nucleus the old Banca Nazionale. Thus refurbished, the new central bank took on all the dubious debts and real estate holdings of its faltering predecessors and later managed to make the best of them as depreciated but still genuine assets; residual losses were indirectly absorbed by the Italian public. The parliamentary system had shown its capacity for basic reform, if only at the last moment and at the prompting of an able manager.

This legislative achievement, evidence of the talent for administration that Giolitti had shown as a government official in the old days of the Right, did not suffice to establish him immediately as a statesman or national leader. During his first term in office, he had shown a rare knack for unscrupulous election fixing, a fact that opponents were always able to seize upon: it ruined any reputation as a reformer that he might otherwise have gained. Worse, Giolitti had none of the colorful, gregarious traits that may make a politician's sins seem venial. He was phlegmatic and matter-of-fact, with a visible contempt for the characteristic rhetoric of Italian political and social life; his wit was laconic and biting. Beneath an impassive professional exterior, Giolitti was capable of vindictiveness and grudge bearing, as events were to show. Except for a small circle of friends, which seems to have included no southerners, he was a man feared rather than loved.

What brought Giolitti down in 1893 was a moral issue. During the confusion, the arrests, and the house searchings of the Banca Romana scandal, Giolitti seems to have set aside for private use a certain number of documents that incriminated the Crispi family, while Crispi got from Tanlongo's son evidence that tended to implicate Giolitti as one of the politicians that had milked the Banca Romana to meet election costs.[9] Giolitti's papers damaged the whole Crispi menage, while Crispi's counter merely tarnished the premier's public credibility—in his personal and family life Giolitti was unassailable. The resulting uproar worked to discredit both men eventually, though Giolitti, who, unlike Crispi, had no background of Risorgimento battles, was harder hit. It took him eight years to reach the top again.

During the years 1893–1900, with the country plagued by revolutionary tumults and strikes at home, at war in East Africa, and seemingly threatened internationally by France, Russia, and the Papacy, much of the Italian political world became convinced that some sort of authoritarian government, drawing on monarchical and military prestige, would have to replace transformist parliamentary ministries, which were losing their grip. In his last ministry Crispi attempted to combine a drive for empire in Africa with the repression of socialism at home, only to quit after the disastrous defeat at Adowa. Successive governments, faced with the economic crisis of 1898, resorted to rule by martial law, with cloture rules for a troublesome opposition in the chamber. Their failure was even more dismal than Crispi's. His regime was at least enlivened by a few sparks of Risorgimento patriotism, while his successors acted only out of conservative panic. The end-of-the-century crisis showed clearly that great-power politics, repression, and efforts to gag parliament did not amount to a viable solution. Rather than take the final step toward some sort of military regime, the monarchy chose to pass the initiative back to the parliamentary politicians, and Italy missed the recurrent fate of Spain.

The return to the chamber prepared the way for a new, updated edition of the transformist system that Crispi had tried to supersede during his last, dramatic years in power. The needed mediator, election-fixer, and parliamentary ringmaster was Giolitti, less thin and contemptuous in public than he had been in his first incarnation. But there was more to Giolitti's reincarnation than a refurbished political following and a touched-up image. He came back with new transformist solutions.

Though both aimed to make centralized parliamentary monarchy viable in Italy, there were some fundamental differences between Crispi and Giolitti. Crispi, the Sicilian, saw politics as a tangle of plots and conspiracies. In his eyes any serious opposition harbored the seeds of treason, and he made no distinction between respectable, middle-class Socialists and anarchist bomb-throwers: he had learned politics in the revolutionary broils of the 1840s and 1850s, and he never outgrew that background. Crispi's last program rested on an appeal to patriotism and social order, and his domestic policy combined police measures with paternalistic land reform. As he saw it, what was legitimate in the new-Left claims could be satisfied by improvements granted from above; independent, far-Left mass parties were intolerable.

Giolitti, the Piedmontese, who had entered political life as a tax administrator, regarded politics as largely a mechanical operation, a system of impersonal forces that a public-spirited parliamentary engineer could understand and control. The far-Left parties and labor leagues could not be broken up with resort to military dictatorship, but they could be domesticated—brought into the parliamentary system step by step. A government that respected the far Left's civil rights could induce it to shift into the area of legality. Thence the opposition, now on the government's own ground, could be brought to vote with transformist majorities and eventually with transformist ministries.

The result would be the same: the liberal parliamentary oligarchy would go on governing Italy. It would simply assimilate its opponents, co-opting one opposition group after another instead of resorting to police repression and gag laws in the style of Crispi.

Both statesmen were democratic in the ultimate sense in that they conceived of government as *for* the people. Neither was democratic in the modern sense—government by mass parties lay completely beyond their ken. When Crispi caught a mere glimpse of approaching mass democracy in the 1890s he resorted to force; when Giolitti saw a system of popular parties replacing the old parliamentary-caucus systems in 1919–22, he finally decided to leave the door open to Mussolini rather than risk government by representatives of the Italian masses. These events of a rancid old age reflect adversely on the meaning of a whole political career—indeed, of a whole system. Italian liberalism, even in its prewar apogee under Giolitti, implied the *mediation* of popular will through a restricted parliamentary elite.

In spite of such limitations, the passage from Crispi to Giolitti meant a great deal to Italians at the turn of the century. Many citizens were nostalgically old or romantically young in their politics. They regretted the disappearance from the premiership of the kind of high drama and idealism that Crispi had represented. Giolitti's prosaic, piecemeal policies put them off; and after the War, he found himself cut off, able to command the loyalty and respect of professional parliamentarians only. Outside Piedmont he was always a stranger to the people he governed. Of all the judgments that have been hazarded of Giolitti, the aptest is perhaps Riccardo Bacchelli's phrase, "a stoic servant of the state."

Like its forerunner of the 1880s, Giolitti's new transformism functioned on both political and economic levels, integrating the two whenever possible. He strove to bring into the ministerial system all the outsiders who could bring votes and influence with them: radicals, republicans, socialists, and Catholics of varying provenance. Orthodox constitutional liberalism was no longer an indispensable requirement; acceptance of the legal parliamentary game was good enough. Only anarchists and syndicalists were permanently frozen out—they explicitly advocated violence.

Giolitti's opening toward the Left was paralleled by one toward the right wing of organized Catholicism, now in the ascendency with the election of Pius X. The premier's method was to use individual Catholic leaders and groups as makeweights to counterbalance the Socialists. One of his key prefect-ministers, Tommaso Tittoni, served as a liaison with the Catholic notables, whom Giolitti never knew personally.[10] Toward the monarchy he was cautious and deferential, offering satisfaction in the field of colonial policy, a field essential to the House of Savoy.

The economic policies of Giolitti's decade closely followed the new transformist political pattern. The old structure of tariffs, preferential contracts, and subsidies not only remained intact but was greatly broadened. To his prospective allies on the Left, Giolitti offered a new government policy toward strikes. Instead of the old repressive tactics, the premier enforced neutrality; when the state did intervene, it was often to proffer arbitration favorable to labor. In the regions where heavy industry and modern large-scale agriculture had begun to flourish, a labor aristocracy enjoying collective-bargaining advantages unknown elsewhere in the country developed alongside a privileged business class. If Piedmont, Lombardy, and Liguria became the showcases of the new labor-union elite, Emilia's "red cooperatives" also benefited heavily. Giolitti allotted them public-works contracts on favorable terms and eventually even set up a special bank to furnish them credit.

These highly publicized and controversial benefits to the Left diverted attention from Giolitti's fundamental concern with industrial-capitalist growth. With a new period of prosperity and technical innovation after 1890, Italian industry leaped forward. However, government aids to industrialization were slight in some areas; the tariff system protected steel but not machinery, and military contracts did not entirely make up for that gap. Here Giolitti's plan for direct state operation of the rail system in 1905 (initiated by him, though executed by Fortis), as well as his successive subsidy programs for the merchant marine and for bus lines, had a fundamental effect.[11] Even more impressive were the salvages sponsored by the Giolittian regime: the Società Bancaria in 1907, the Sicilian sulphur producers, and the steel trust in 1911, all had reason to see in Giolitti an enlightened defender of "national" economic interests in spite of his suspicious softness toward the reds.

There were other links between private capital and the Giolitti regime. The shaky regional banks had been replaced in the 1890s by investment banks that began attracting deposits on a truly peninsular scale; in Giolitti's first years they constituted an important element of Italy's new prosperity. However, these institutions needed government backing for many of their operations, since short-term comercial credit and discounts were controlled by the Bank of Italy. The director of that bank, Bonaldo Stringher, was a former treasury official accustomed to working closely with the government. And the new investment banks all had the same ominous weakness: they engaged in long-term industrial credit, however disguised, with depositors' money, which remained subject to immediate withdrawal. Thus the Bank of Italy and the treasury were an indispensable last resort against runs and panics, and no Italian investment banker could afford to ignore the wishes and dispositions of the cabinet at Rome. In their turn the investment bankers could perform certain political and financial services for Giolitti.

Giolitti's system worked well in the opening years of the new century. A modest but general prosperity enabled employers to meet some of the elementary demands of their workers, as the premier had foreseen. The state enjoyed a balanced budget, consolidated its public debt, and even improved some of its services. Between 1901 and 1908 the parliamentary system got a new lease on life, for which much of the credit must go to the premier. However, he was wafted by a favoring breeze.[12]

The years 1907–8 mark the great divide in Italian liberal politics. The world depression of 1907 hit the fragile Italian economy with special force, and in the following year the European state system moved into a new condition of chronic war crisis as a result of the shifts in Turkey and the Balkans. Europe's brink-of-war politics presented Italy with some new opportunities, but also with new dangers and higher military expenses.

Giolitti's response was characteristic of the man and of the system. He took periodic vacations from power, leaving the premiership to ephemeral opponents or lieutenants, all of whom had to govern with a parliamentary majority that owed its existence—and hopes of reelection—to Giolitti. Everyone knew that Giolitti would be back in time to manage the next general election, and the substitute premiers—Fortis, then Sonnino and Luzzatti—were often left to face ticklish problems without the prestige and authority of the master.

Eventually, during the most difficult crisis years, Giolitti came back for a long spell at the helm. He was called upon for decisions beyond the expediency and social umpiring that had made up his previous programs, and he responded with real statesmanship. It is easy to see Giolitti's "great ministry" of 1911–14 as a mere balancing act, with universal suffrage for the Left, war with Turkey for the Right, and state life insurance for the working masses. But this is an unfair belittling of the man. During the crucial final years of the Giolittian regime, there emerged the outline of a bold general plan, according to which industrial Italy would constitute the vital center of a new political order, with conservative Catholic agrarian voters balancing the "red" urban proletariat and the Socialist day laborers of the Po valley farms. The vital center would be reinforced by government protection and favors, but the industrial system's future was to lie in expansion abroad, peaceful or otherwise. In fact, Giolitti's eastward expansionist plans met a favorable reception in Milan, in contrast to that city's attitude toward Crispi's African follies fifteen years before. In 1913 Giolitti, using his Milanese prefect, actively sought for the first time to recruit an important Lombard industrialist (Ettore Conti) as a governmental parliamentary candidate, a sign of the new policies.[13]

The Giolitti program of 1911–13 really did represent something new: it would have ended, after a long time, to be sure, the regional character of Italian transformist politics. Universal suffrage, Giolitti's outstanding legislative innovation, would eventually do away with the rotten boroughs of the South. The extreme Left would have to be balanced in the future not by southern barons, but by Catholic votes in the center and North, votes coming from the more advanced regions of the country. For the sacrificed classes of the South, who had nothing to gain from the new industrially based political order, there remained the safety valve of overseas emigration—domestically, much of the South would become an unskilled labor pool for the North.

The universal-suffrage system that came into effect in 1913 kept the old single-member constituencies but widened the male suffrage to include most of the nation's proletariat and peasantry. It was a transitional compromise characteristic of Giolitti. By retaining the old constituency system, Giolitti had put a brake on the forces of radical change: a great many local notables could still stand for reelection, but they would be compelled to appeal to thousands of new voters. These provisions allowed a certain respite to the rotten boroughs of the South, which proportional representation would have swept away at once, but the implications of the new suffrage were clear. The old restricted political game, based on regional inequality, was coming to an end.

Giolitti's great design soon miscarried. Italy's new expansionism abroad was not matched by a broadening of the parliamentary consensus at home. Neither political nor economic conditions allowed the premier to carry out his audacious and far-reaching plan for a new transformist balancing act, and one can only wonder how so shrewd a man could have made such a miscalculation. The costs of colonial war outran all expectations and showed no signs of lessening with time; they put an immediate end to the expansions of the welfare program that formed an important part of Giolitti's new political operation. Even the wealthiest nations have been unable to combine empire building, parliamentary democracy, and social welfare; for Italy the reckoning came early. The intervention of 1915 marked the definite end of Giolitti's era, but in fact, by the end of 1913, after the first election held under the new broadened suffrage law, the premier's career was in decline.

The reasons for Giolitti's failure lay in Italy's precarious political balance and narrow economic margin. However, there were immediate reasons of a more personal sort. The premier's party was too small: it centered on his own figure instead of representing some idea or program.

The inner circle consisted of his Piedmontese friends and retainers, of whom the most influential were Urbano Rattazzi and Senator Frassati, editor of the great Turinese daily, *La Stampa*. His younger supporters included Luigi Facta, later to be his stand-in premier during the fatal crisis of 1922. A second circle, equally important in the workings of Giolitti's system, was made up of his prefects and police officials, a talented and dedicated body that provided the real backbone of the Italian government for more than a generation. All of these men were devoted to Italian public service, but many of them owed recognition and advancement to Giolitti.

The innermost circle, the Piedmontese group, provided Giolitti with behind-the-scenes backing, especially journalistic and financial, that few other politicians could match; but the second circle, the professional administrators, enabled him to keep a finger on the nation's daily pulse, on the doings of public figures and private conspirators. There is reason to believe that both circles served him even during his periodic retirements to the Piedmontese countryside. A third circle, outermost in every respect, consisted of the large body of deputies or ministers that owed their political survival and advancement to the premier and backed him primarily for that reason. These were Giolitti's southern parliamentary reserves, his colonial troops and mercenaries. In the old system of rotten boroughs, their not disinterested loyalty could be counted on; but the new universal suffrage of 1913 threatened their easy tenure, and they were ready to turn to new masters. Unlike the members of the inner circles, they did not enjoy Giolitti's confidence and respect.

Giolitti's party was deeply enmeshed with the peninsula's ruling and managing classes and had excellent connections in the Milanese banking world. However, it lacked intellectual prestige, mass appeal, and real moral force: Giolitti's unquestionable personal honesty failed to reconcile Italians to the built-in corruption of his system. Most ominous, the premier's person and program offered no prospects to the nation's youth. One of the most brilliant but representative young Italian intellectuals of the period, Giovanni Amendola, referred to his country's political system as "the temporary regime of Chevalier Giovanni Giolitti"; in Italian the title connoted not chivalry, but bureaucratic routine. The implication was that the existing regime was short-range and stop gap in character, while young Italians were expecting a far-reaching and organic solution to their country's problems. This was the lure and promise offered by the opposition: not a new man, but a new ruling class, a new political order, a new meaning to Italy's emergence as a nation-state among world powers.[14]

The Giolittian party, with all its range, by no means included or represented the whole Italian political establishment. There was another pattern of political evolution that brought together men as disparate as the Tuscan man of letters Ferdinando Martini, the Neapolitan journalist Edoardo Scarfoglio, and the Sicilian Marquis Di San Giuliano, as well as Giolitti's great adversary, Sidney Sonnino. The pattern was similar throughout, with all its individual variants. An early concern with social reform, a harking back to the ideals of the Risorgimento, faded with the harsh experiences of the 1880s and 1890s. Then disillusion gave rise to a conviction that only colonial expansion could provide a solution for the nation's domestic ills, a new chance for the working classes. It was expected that the Italian masses would thus become patriotic: loyalty to the nation would grow as Italy's participation in the common European mission in Africa proved her parity with the other great powers.

One especially disinterested career may serve as a model of this kind of politics. Leopoldo Franchetti worked with Sonnino in an investigation of the Sicilian peasantry's plight during the 1870s and became one of the chamber's leading experts on the southern question. In the 1890s, turning away in near despair from the homeland, Franchetti threw himself into an experimental study of the Eritrean colony's agrarian possibilities, hoping that on the highlands of East Africa the Italian peasant could find the social justice and homestead denied him by the traditions and necessities of Europe. In this initiative he ran into a wall of military-bureaucratic privilege and obstruction, but he did succeed in showing that East Africa offered prospects of agricultural development. In 1916–17 Franchetti was a leader in the campaign to get a guarantee of an Italian influence in Asia Minor acknowledged among Allied war aims, an endeavor in which he rejoined Sonnino, now foreign minister. A few months later, Franchetti chose not to survive the debacle of Caporetto.[15]

Franchetti was typical of the older Italian opponents of transformism: a well-educated man of independent means who moved from domestic reform to colonial expansionism only as a result of his bitter experience and his reformulation of cherished liberal ideals— a patriot rather than a nationalist. As a deputy, Franchetti took the lead in exposing the scandalous collusion between the naval ministry and the steel trust (Terni) in 1906, a move that no industry-bound Nationalist of the rising generation would have dreamed of making.

To many antitransformists, with all their austerity, bitterness, and disillusion, the Italian homeland remained the last ideal, to be clung to with a truly religious devotion. This patriotism motivated not only the idealists like Franchetti, but also many men who were outwardly only cynical or ambitious.

The most influential member of this group, though colder and more cynical than most, was the Marquis Di San Giuliano, who served as foreign minister from the spring of 1910 until his death in October 1914. A scion of one of Sicily's great noble houses, he had from childhood a keen awareness of being heir to a lost kingdom. The normal course for him would have been to pass his life among the clerical-minded provincial nobility of the island, repairing the declining fortunes of his family by careful management of his remaining properties. But the marquis felt himself born to greater things. Inevitably he was drawn to Rome and *alta politica*.

As he rose in the parliamentary political system, Di San Giuliano shrewdly stayed away from the embittered political moralists of the Right and took the stance of a "democrat," a liberal of the official parliamentary Left. His manner and oft-displayed literary culture marked him out as a Tory democrat with some overtones of public-square demagogy, a winning combination. The marquis was just as successful in the back rooms. He served his political apprenticeship as mayor and deputy on the seamy inside of public life: election fixing, bank favors, railroad financing, and franchising, all the logrolling and outright bribery that characterized Sicilian affairs. In supporting Giolitti's first cabinet in the early 1890s, he began his participation in transformist politics on a national level. His willingness to electioneer for the premier was to have important consequences for his later career. However, Di San Giuliano's political creed, "To conserve through progress and to progress by conserving," allowed him to support and take part in any governmental combination, under any premier. He was an available man.

In the decade of the 1890s, his career took a turn that eventually marked him as a potential statesman rather than a mere local political rainmaker. The change started with a setback. His home power base, eastern Sicily, was shaken by insurrection and the rise of a local Socialist party. The Socialist "saint" of Catania, De Felice-Giuffrida, threatened Di San Giuliano's control over local elections. Though the marquis continued to sit for his own urban constituency, he could not manage others; and his chances for advancement at Rome accordingly faded. Faced by the new politics of the 1890s, Di San Giuliano was intelligent and modern enough to know that repression alone would not suffice. On the basis of his experience, however, he doubted the efficacy of reform laws in the South.

What, then, was to be done? The marquis's social position and interests precluded any revolutionary programs. Moreover, he came to see that the South's basic problem was intrinsic, that it was caught in the chronic poverty of any area that depended exclusively on the price fluctuations of the world agricultural market. The South's backward, exploitive social system remained as an aggravating factor, recognized by all. But the fundamental way out that southern peas-

ants were spontaneously taking—emigration—was for Di San Giuliano, as for most upper-class southerners of his generation, a national
tragedy.

As early as 1891, Di San Giuliano began looking abroad for
solutions. Like many other Sicilians, he had been concerned about
Tunisia, which had offered a promising field to the island's emigrants
but had been lost to France in 1881. Thereafter, he had refused to
take any interest in the torrid Red Sea areas that were left to Italy as
a consolation prize. Only in 1891, when he took part in the parliamentary investigations at Massawa and Asmara, did he become an
Africanist.

Di San Giuliano came to the conviction that the highlands of
East Africa could eventually become a Magna Italia, a great white
colony under the Italian tricolor. As for the blacks, they would remain in the torrid coastal zones that were unsuited to European settlement. The marquis, a Darwinist, held that each race would eventually settle at its own appropriate natural level. However, he knew
very well that for Italy, in the financial straits of the 1890s, such ideas
were premature; and he thought that she should confine herself to
fomenting the internal divisions of Ethiopia until circumstances allowed for the imposition of direct colonial rule. He therefore re-
frained from compromising himself in Crispi's reckless lunges into
the Ethiopian backcountry. Nevertheless, in his public writing and
private thinking the marquis moved definitely, in the 1890s, from
domestic reform to foreign expansion as the answer to Italy's living
problems.

Beneath Di San Giuliano's veneer of enlightenment and mo-
dernity, there was an agrarian-conservative pattern of thought. He believed that Italian industrial tariffs advantaged the North at the
South's expense, but he had no idea at all of the general consequences
of industrialization. He believed that Britain's power and prosperity
were due to its victories over France in the preceding two centuries
and that Italian emigration was a drain on the nation, when in fact
it was probably a great economic benefit in the years 1890–1914. He
conceived of imperialism as a solution for agrarian demographic
problems, a way of providing outlets for peasant discontent, a safety
valve against rural revolution.

Di San Giuliano's new competence in foreign and colonial affairs gave him a fresh shot at Rome. After the Adowa disaster in 1896, the marquis favored the continuation of the Eritrean colonial effort and was willing to fight for it in the chamber. This was a difficult moment—the Italian colonial troops were hanging on to the rim of the East African highlands, while an outcry for withdrawal rose from the piazza and from many deputies. The Italians might have retreated to the coast and eventually steamed away had it not been for a discreet but decisive step taken by Humbert I behind the scenes. The House of Savoy was always concerned over colonial prestige, and several of its cadet princes went to Africa in search of the authority and exploits that Europe no longer offered to junior royalty. Hence the Africanists in the chamber earned in these years a certain tacit but real favor at court that was to further their careers in the future. They were the nearest thing to a king's party in the history of liberal Italy. Naturally the marquis found nothing out of order in this: he had always thought that the lines of foreign and military policy could not be subject to the vagaries of the chamber. Like most liberal politicians, he accepted the necessity of the royal prerogative in treaties and in high diplomatic and military appointments.

Domestically, Di San Giuliano was still available. A minister with Pelloux in 1899, he passed over to Giolitti's new combinations later, supporting child-labor legislation and similar reforms. In both domestic and foreign policy, the marquis remained a Tory democrat and knew very well how much public opinion and mass emotion would count for in twentieth-century international affairs, something that his more obtuse Triple Alliance counterparts in Vienna and Berlin never learned. Though he continued to champion the cause of Italian East Africa in the chamber, his interests began shifting toward the Balkans and Libya.

As a deputy, he had risen as high as he could go. Given his situation in Catania, it was all he could do to hold his own parliamentary seat, and even that was at great expense of time and money. After the general elections of 1904, he withdrew, receiving the customary reward for past political services—a royal-ministerial nomination as senator. That role was not retirement but the base of a new career as diplomat.

Di San Giuliano turned to diplomacy at a propitious moment. Almost continuously, from the end of 1903 to December 1909, the Italian foreign ministry was in the hands of a kindred spirit, Senator Tommaso Tittoni. Tittoni, too, had risen through transformist politics. Coming from a prominent family of *mercanti di campagna*— dealers and moneylenders of the Roman countryside—he had completed his legal education at Oxford before entering politics to sit on the right of the chamber. True to his family tradition, he combined Risorgimento patriotic principles with continuing Catholic loyalties and personal ties. Available and useful to successive ministries, he served for many years as prefect of Naples, the *cloaca maxima* of Italian politics. At the same time he took an active part in Roman real estate dealings. Some taint of scandal clung to him from both cities as he rose from the prefecture to ministerial office. At Rome he was briefly involved in a bankruptcy case in 1896, though the prosecution soon dropped charges, and the Neapolitan Socialists accused him of repeatedly using the city's organized underworld to insure the election of government-backed parliamentary candidates. The charges persisted, although documentary proof was never forthcoming. Tittoni, a fine speaker, was able to rebut his critics and even claim merit as an instigator of civic reform, though there is no doubt that the Neapolitan office of the state police often acted in collusion with gangsters, a fact that prefects and ministers knew.

In any case, Tittoni's achievements are more important than his possible misdeeds. As prefect of Naples, he established close, even confidential, relations with the heir to the throne, Prince Victor Emmanuel; and as a Roman businessman-politician intimate with Catholic banks and voter organizations, he had personal contacts with the "black" clerical world, ties of a sort that Liberal ministers from the North found very useful. After 1900 Tittoni was a man on the make. It was to Victor Emmanuel III that he evidently owed his elevation from prefect to foreign minister, which came as a surprise to parliament, but Tittoni's abiding importance as a minister was largely due to his role as a clandestine intermediary between the Giolitti government and the lay directors of Catholic Action. In the 1904 elections, the government needed the support of all the forces of order, including Catholics, to keep the Socialists from winning some key constituencies in Lombardy. Tittoni used some persuasive arguments with local Catholic spokesmen, urging them to intervene in spite of the Pope's electoral boycott. They in turn brought up the matter in a private audience with Pius X, who felt he had to give way, though on a "case-by-case" basis. This proof of papal pliability represented a notable success for Tittoni; he had shown his capacity to serve both king and premier. Only Di San Giuliano, among Italian politicians, had similar advantages, and between 1903 and 1914 these two, in effect, alternated in the office of foreign minister.[16]

In 1906 Di San Giuliano, as ambassador to Britain, negotiated the definitive arrangements between Italy and the Entente concerning Ethiopia's future. This achievement accredited him for even higher office, which soon came his way. Persuasive in public and amiable in private relations, Tittoni lacked real diplomatic talent and lost his footing during the prolonged Bosnian crisis of 1908–9. At the end of 1909, with a change of ministries, he left the cabinet, though not the foreign service; he was consoled the next year with the post of ambassador to Paris. The way was clear for Di San Giuliano, whose studies and experience in international affairs far outweighed Tittoni's.

In March 1910 Di San Giuliano became foreign minister under Luzzatti and continued under Giolitti and Salandra; he died in office in October 1914. As the marquis aged, his devotion to the cause of Italian expansion deepened, while the rest of his life atrophied. Bereaved, racked by gout, denied the consolation of religion because of his stubborn atheism, he had one ruling passion, one object of faith— the homeland. During those last years of his life, he won his place in history by sponsoring the Libyan War; planning penetration into Asia Minor; and, finally, sketching the conditions for Italian entry into the World War. He was true to his original aims. Di San Giuliano's designs formed the basis for Sonnino's 1915 war objectives.

This life pattern is important both in itself and for what it tells us about how Italy was governed during the Giolittian era. Though the Marquis Di San Giuliano served in Giolitti's ministries, his career ran counter to the trend of Giolittian politics. After 1886, Giolitti and Rattazzi had wanted to pull out of Africa but bowed to the royal will and said nothing about it in public. Later, when Giolitti returned to power, he made no effort to extend democratic principles into the sphere of foreign policy. On the contrary, the long service of Tittoni and Di San Giuliano under various premiers points up the fact that foreign policy was not set by the same parliamentary leaders whose views prevailed in domestic matters. To be sure, the king knew that public backing and parliamentary consent were sometimes vital, but much of Italy's diplomacy was carried on without it. Italy's martial ventures were presented as faits accomplis.

The Giolittian system was really a dyarchy, a tacit sharing of power mediated by a parliamentary manager. In liberal Italy power was apportioned not merely between the chamber and the crown, but between two diverging types of political leaders. The system worked in such a way as to keep the dyarchy intact but implicit: the political parties and divisions in the chamber and in the country did not reflect the fundamental political realities. Power was shared and exercised almost clandestinely. The reasons for this are clear at more than a half-century's distance: democrats like Giolitti and Nitti and conservatives like Salandra and Sonnino all had one presupposition in common. They all considered national politics to be the business of an educated oligarchy. None of them had any use for mass parties and charismatic leaders. Governments, wars, treaties, and suffrage legislation were best made and unmade far from the public gaze. This isolation was possible because the nation's press generally shared the establishment view. Those presuppositions worked until after the First World War, but none of the nation's political leaders were to survive the massive upheavals of 1919–22.

Italy's bankers and industrialists prospered by maneuvering between the parliamentary elites who shaped economic policies and the monarchic-military establishment that prevailed in foreign affairs and armaments.

Opposition to the Giolitti system was widespread after 1911 on both Right and Left. In the South it had a distinctly regional character, and in the North it took the form of a declared class hostility between capitalists who mistrusted the regime's softness toward strikes and cooperatives on the one side and on the other the labor spokesmen for syndicalism and revolutionary socialism who regarded the regime's war policies as proof of its murderous bourgeois nature.

But after ten futile years, much of the opposition had become a matter of routine or of pure principle. The significant post-Crispi element of opposition was the Nationalist movement, which took shape only after 1910.[17]

It has been the fashion to treat Italian Nationalism as an affair of literary men affected by delusions of grandeur, taking their ideas from the French far Right and their cult of energy from Rudyard Kipling, Theodore Roosevelt, and Cecil Rhodes. Only recently have the Italians begun to reevaluate Nationalism as an important element in both the intervention crisis of 1915 and the postwar emergencies that ushered Mussolini into power in 1922 and, finally, as the decisive force in bringing about Il Duce's abrupt dismissal in 1943. Such an enduring current in Italian public life cannot be disposed of with a few scornful commonplaces. The Nationalists had few original ideas, but their programs were more serious and consistent than their critics were willing to admit.

The Nationalists stood on common ground with many jurists and professional men in their deep distrust of twentieth-century mass democracy. As they saw it, a party system could represent the interests of categories or pressure groups but not the lasting interests of a whole nation. Indeed, a twentieth-century parliamentary system, dominated by mass parties, could at best provide a sort of market in which the spokesmen for various parties' interests compromised and bartered legal privileges. At worst, the system, with its lawful strikes and incitements to turmoil, could degenerate into a sort of perpetual, licensed civil war. Under any circumstance short-range special interests, adroitly coalesced, were the only elements of real power under parliamentary democracy, and the lasting aims of the nation went by the board.

The old liberal system gave mass organizations no direct power, but the new democracy used the freedoms of nineteenth-century liberalism to pervert or wipe out liberalism's essentially aristocratic values. Universal suffrage and parliamentary government together spelled eventual disintegration and ruin for the nation that adopted them. Against the shortsighted and turbulent masses, the Nationalists set their own ideal of a perennial national purpose, incarnated in the elite class of planners, producer-industrialists, and soldiers that owed their place in life to intrinsic competitive merit rather than to transient popularity. The Nationalist ideal fell somewhere between technocracy and outright militarism, with a strong dynastic tinge— the monarchy, too, was part of the nation's permanent nonelective establishment.

These ideas had an undeniable appeal to the professional middle classes as well as to students, especially those of the great metropolitan institutions like Milan's Politecnico. They implied no radical break with the elitist liberalism of Cavour, although Cavour's belief in the benefits of international free trade, with its corollaries of normal peace and cooperation among the great powers, meant nothing at all to the Nationalists, whose conception of the nation's enduring economic interest was jealously protectionist.

Though Italian Nationalism, in its political crystallization after 1910, presented itself as a new source of virility and self-assurance for the tired middle classes of the nation, who carried the real burdens of Italian society and were repaid for their pains by abuse and high taxes, Nationalist ideals turned out to have a distinct appeal to the restless syndicalist agitators of proletarian revolution. Between 1910 and 1914 there was born the idea of the proletarian nation, an idea-force, or myth, of great potency.

As seen by the Nationalists, Italy belonged to a whole class of producer nations—workshop states. On the world stage these states played the same role that the producer classes did within the individual nation. Instead of a world revolution carried out by the proletariat of the whole planet arrayed against the capitalists, the Nationalists began to propound the substitute of an international war of proletarian peoples, chiefly Italy and Germany, against Britain and France, the coupon-clipping *rentier* empires of the West, which now held colonial domains and amassed capital altogether disproportionate to their declining share in world production and their waning populations. If production and birth rates give title to expansion, then the time had arrived for the West to disgorge its territorial and financial hoards. Too long had Italy sold her manpower in the international labor market by raising young men to build other peoples' railroads and cities; too long had Italian industries struggled for life with insufficient capital and scanty outlets. Social justice and the redemption of the proletariat were the old ideals of the Left, but only the Nationalists could achieve them—by a redistribution of the world's wealth through a successful series of wars. Such was the myth of the proletarian nation as elaborated by Corradini, Rocco, and Dino Grandi in the years 1910–15: it later became the basis of Fascism, justifying that movement's claims to have risen above old divisions of Right and Left.

Behind these plausible formulas, all sorts of irrationality lurked. The Nationalists took the nation to be a natural fact, not the creation of men in history, and in their zeal for the interests of the nation they took no account of the interests of the human race as a whole. From this position to outright racism of the Teutonic sort, the step is short. Nationalist ideas concerning population growth, as expressed by the fashionable economist Corrado Gini, do in fact contain the germs of racial thinking: Gini explaincd to Italian audiences as early as 1912 that Italy's birth rate was evidence of biological youthfulness, of a sort of collective virility, in striking contrast to France's senescence, as shown in its stagnant population. Italy was at the beginning of a biological cycle, France—and other western nations—near the end. This was not racism of the thunderous sort common north of the Alps, but it was indigenous Italian racial thinking, in terms acceptable to Italian minds.

There were many other groups opposing Giolitti. His African war of 1911 marked the end of any possible understanding with the Socialists, and the subsequent curtailing of social welfare in the interests of rearmament marked the end of his system and his melioristic methods. However, it was the elite opposition of the Nationalists that really counted in the long run. The Nationalists' following in the nation's middle-class youth was far stronger than any electoral statistics could show. Most important, some industrialists of the North and many financiers found Nationalism more congenial than Giolitti's compromises and parliamentary moderation.

There is another reason why opposition from the far Right was more important than that from the Left. The Left was in continual disarray during the crisis years before Italy's plunge into international war. Between their conflicting goals—political democracy, republicanism, social equality, world peace, the completion of national unifi-

cation, the rescue of democracy threatened elsewhere in Europe
—few leftists could make a definite choice; and the War threw them
into utter confusion. In peace and in war the Left was unable to
establish any common program or agree on any common objectives,
and it ultimately left the decisions to the government, which had been
tending rightward since the spring of 1914.

In contrast, the far Right, the Nationalists, and the National
Liberals had a definite common objective—expansion abroad—and
a common program—a war of conquest. Their ideas were simpler,
their dilemmas fewer, and their access to influential sectors of the
public far easier than was the case with the democrats, radicals, republicans, socialists, and syndicalists that made up the many-colored
Left. Hence, this work will concentrate on the ideas and cultural
currents of the Right.

1

The Predicament
of Italian Industrialization:
The Steel Trust

Italy's passage from moderate, reforming democracy at the beginning of Giolitti's great ministry in the spring of 1911 to the imperialism of Salandra and Sonnino and their 1915 intervention—her four-year *via dolorosa* from the Libyan enterprise to the First World War—makes sense only in the light of the country's industrial pattern, underlying and largely motivating the train of political events. An unbalanced, top-heavy industrial system, backed by the four big credit and investment banks, acted as a perpetual spur to expansion abroad and repressive politics at home. The great centralized industrial groups, always dependent to a large degree on state protection, preference, and subsidy—geared as they were to growing national arms programs and to adventurous, often diplomatically sponsored foreign development schemes—constituted a political pressure group far more potent than Masonic lodges.

The way in which Italian heavy industry grew up in the narrow, inhospitable peninsula, so thin in resources and poor in home markets, set an early pattern of imbalance, of foreign ties and enmities, that by 1914–15 had become decisive: on one side, links with the French and Belgians, a few vital partnerships with British industry, and good development prospects in the Balkans and Asia Minor; on the other, continual rivalry with Germany on the Italian industrial market itself and unceasing competition with Austria-Hungary on

41

the high seas and in Italy's foreign markets. To Italy's unsteady industries the Entente offered financing and raw materials, while the Germans attempted financing and technical control. Italy's foreign policy from 1911 to 1915, however subject it may have been to considerations of military and diplomatic balance, admirably fitted the interests and alliances of her industries, especially the heavy industries most dependent on the state.

The dovetailing of political and industrial motives is just as apparent in the reactionary turn that home politics took; the narrow margin on which the industrial system operated made a policy of reform and compromise far harder to work out there than in more favored countries. Industrial-labor relations were tense, and union-management disputes often ended in lockouts and violence. The business press increasingly gave space and sympathy to an aggressive protofascistic doctrine of national social unity, self-sufficiency, and expansion that gradually suffused all the national press that was controlled or influenced by industrial interests. The deeply class-conscious and nationalistically colored conservatism of Giolitti's successors fitted industrial as well as agrarian concerns.

Politically, Italian heavy industry fell roughly into two categories: the industries dependent on continual, direct, and lavish state subsidizing and those that, however needful of political protection and preference, seemed economically viable in the long run. The steel trust (Ilva) and the shipbuilding industry are the prime examples of the first kind, and into the second category fall North Italian little steel, much of the merchant marine, and the machine, motor, and rail industries. By 1914 both types of enterprise were—with very few exceptions—geared to state railway contracts, arms production, and war needs as necessary supplements to their marginal operations. Any sharp division between the two types of heavy industry is bound to be artificial. Both were almost entirely in the same hands. Ownership and credit support were highly centralized: steel, shipping, rails, and motors were linked through an endlessly interlocking set of directorates.

The chronic marginality of the Italian economy goes far toward explaining the adventure-seeking of so much of Italian foreign policy and the willingness of Italian rulers to take the risks of war as part of a national speculative gamble on the grand scale.

One of the most experienced Italian economic administrators of our century, Felice Guarneri, has summarized the matter thus:

Italy has had an organically delicate economy from the time of national unification to the present. Her economy is dependent in the highest degree on the outside world and exposed, more than any other, to the ups and downs of the world situation and to the consequences of the actions taken by other states, and is hence easily subject to damage. It is an economy the distinguishing mark of which consists in a permanent unbalance between the labor forces available and the means that are needed for their profitable employment. Since this unbalance cannot be righted within the borders and with the sole forces of the Italian nation, it brings with it the elements of a genuine human and social tragedy.

Italian industrialization, paid for at high foreign prices, did not resolve Italy's imbalance, but rather, during the critical years before the War, accentuated it. Guarneri observes:

Foreign trade was indeed increasing sharply, but there was a proportionately greater increase in imports, so much so that the commercial deficit rises from a 165 million lire average for the years 1895–1900 to a 1210 million lire average for the two years 1912–1913, a more than sevenfold increase. The rise in the commercial deficit was above all caused by increasing imports of raw and semi-finished materials for industry, and of foodstuffs. A rise in imports which did indeed serve to show the progress achieved in the course of industrialization of the country, and in the standard of living of the population, but also left, at the same time, the clear impression that such imports could not, in case of need, be cut down without gravely compromising both the one and the other. In the two years 1912–1913 the average yearly ratio between imports and exports was most unfavorable for Italy, if compared with the same ratio of other countries. In Italy imports exceeded exports by 34%, compared to 22% for France, 19% for Britain, 9% for Germany, 9½% for Japan, while exports still exceeded imports by about 2% in the Argentine and 2.2% in the United States.

The balance of payments nevertheless closed with a credit, but that situation was primarily the result of that Italian phenomenon of emigration which had assumed such an exceptional size between 1910 and 1913, passing from 352,782 to the enormous figure of 873,000 departures, bringing to the country the equally exceptional benefit of a large flow of emigrant remittances in foreign credits: this was in addition to the flow created by foreign tourists and visitors, as well as, in lesser measure, the inflow of foreign capital seeking permanent investment in Italian industries which it was promoting. Already in 1911 Bonaldo Stringher [governor of the Bank of Italy] warned the country about the serious dangers inherent in a situation in which our balance of payments depended on sources of income as unreliable as emigration and tourist trade. These fluctuated with the internal situations of other countries, "even aside from political circumstances," and could diminish suddenly and severely, while Italy's need for imports could not easily be reduced.

Guarneri concludes by noting:

The hugeness of the Italian emigration between 1900 and 1913 showed that even in an exceptionally favorable period the Italian economy had not succeeded in providing full employment for its active population and in eliminating that state of permanent unbalance between available labor force and the means of employment which is one of its basic characteristics.[1]

Marginality and imbalance were not only characteristic of the Italian economy as a whole but were specific, though thinly disguised, features of the nation's industrial situation as well. But during the critical years before the Italian intervention in the War, the disguise could no longer be maintained convincingly, for the mainstay of heavy industry, the state budget, was itself in some difficulty.

The Italian state was going ever more deeply into deficit spending and debt. The deficit began with the 1909–10 budget and by 1912–13 had reached the notable sum of 257,492,000 lire. The government sought to dissemble by listing railway construction expenses as fruitful investment, in spite of the fact that the state railways made no profit. Huge war and naval expenditures were entered on provisional future budgets, although in fact the money was being spent immediately. Such artifices hid nothing of the truth, and one of the most noted Italian economists of the time put his finger on the real consequences of deficit spending:

The state has met its war and rail-building expenses by raising enormously the floating debt through the issuance of treasury obligations. Treasury notes—real promissory notes with fixed due dates—are an efficient way of dealing with state money needs, provided that their sum total does not rise above the point at which ordinary revenues suffice to pay them back. . . . At any rate, it is dangerous to throw on the market in a short lapse of time the enormous mass of almost 1300 million lire of treasury obligations, ordinary or five-year. . . . At present they make treasury operations inelastic and difficult, and they can make them even harder in the years 1917–19, when huge payments will be due.[2]

Although these expenses and debts acted as an immediate shot in the arm for Italian heavy industry, they had long-range consequences that were bad for the entire national economy, since they drained away fluid circulating capital needed for productive investment. In precisely the years 1912–14 the Italian economy suffered from high interest rates and a shortage of investment capital, a situation which, incidentally, accentuated the already serious dependence of heavy industry on its one great customer and financer, the state, and further unbalanced the nation's economy as a whole.

Though almost all basic state expenses rose, military expenses rose proportionally much more, thanks in large part to the naval program. Military entries took up 16.5 percent of the Italian state's expenditures in 1906–7, 19.5 percent in 1909–10, and 23 percent in 1910–11. But in 1911–12 they jumped to 30 percent and rose further to 34 percent in 1912–13; the end of the Libyan War did not bring notable relief, for in 1913–14 miliary expenses still took up 30 percent of the budget.

Italy simply could not afford to pay for war programs and social progress at the same time. Labor legislation in the years 1912–13 made no headway, the country's modest educational goal—completion of elementary school for every child in Italy—was set for 1922; state security-police expenses between 1906 and 1913 almost doubled, while the universities received only about half again as much in 1913 as they were given in 1906. The choice between reform and imperialism was for Italy far more sharply definable than it was for the more fortunate great powers of the Continent.

The Italian tax structure itself probably contributed much to the country's economic ills, since it weighed most heavily on those least able to pay and thus reduced the possibility of mass consumption, which would eventually have enabled the home market to absorb more of the country's industrial production. Out of total state revenues of 2,528,874,000 lire in 1912–13, no less than 683,049,000 came out of consumer taxes, including the internal customs, while the stamp tax on business circulation yielded 338,184,000 lire, and state monopolies (tobacco, salt, quinine, playing cards) earned 537,-618,000. Direct taxes gave only 519,401,000 lire. Of the indirect taxes, the internal customs were the most unpopular and outdated, since they impeded the free circulation of commodities within the country itself. The system operated to widen even further the growing gap between the advanced and backward regions of the country, for Italian direct taxes, as Luigi Einaudi acutely noted, fell far more heavily on agricultural property than on the easily concealed investments of northern bankers and industrialists. A prudent landowner was encouraged by such a system to invest in bearer bonds rather than in agricultural improvements, while the small peasant proprietor had no refuge at all.

Italian heavy industry was caught in an economic spiral. The very economic policies that had largely established and sustained it— the huge transfer of wealth from the agricultural sector that had made industrialization possible—had been directly or indirectly due to the action of the state since the 1880s. But the ruthless and improvident way in which this was done had lasting ill effects on the national market. Much of Italy looked like an impoverished agricultural and manpower colony, drained by an industrial oligarchy that put back into its colony far less than it took out. The 1914 crisis brought to light all the consequences of an uncharted, militarily motivated, and politically sponsored industrialization, and the social and economic errors of two generations returned to claim their penalties.

Clearly Italy was becoming an industrial power, and this fact had a determining weight in changes in Italian politics during the twentieth century. Italian industry was undergoing a crisis of growth in the prewar years: the Italians attempted to resolve that crisis by the conquest of "economic space," by pursuing an imperialist policy among the greater powers of the world, in spite of the peninsula's lasting weaknesses in resources and available energy.

True, the general census of 1911 showed 9,085,597 Italians engaged in agriculture, hunting, and fishing, while the total number of industrial workers was only 4,502,072—this figure out of a grand total of 26,580,048 Italians, of both sexes, that had an income of any sort whatever. Of the total number of industrial workers, only 388,-319 were employed in basic heavy industries. The manufacture of trains, automobiles, ships, and aircraft employed 137,687 workers, a total smaller than that for the building, textile, and food-processing industries; and the food industries had almost as many workers as the heavy industries. (Incidentally, the same census showed that almost 600,000 Italians lived on unearned income: this figure, which does not include pensioners, says much about Italian society.)

Trade figures also seem to show that Italy was still an agrarian nation in these years. In 1913 industrial products accounted for only 31.8 percent of the total value of what Italy exported, and this proportion marked a slight rise over industry's share in previous years since 1908. In the light of these facts, how can it be said that industry's interests and problems shaped the course of Italian political history?

The answer is threefold. First, the post-1876 Italian ruling class, from Depretis through Crispi to Giolitti, was committed to establishing Italy's rank as a great power. The reputation and future of the Italian parliamentary monarchy were felt to hinge on this prospect. The only route to international great-power standing started with military self-sufficiency at home and led to the eventual establishment of economic positions abroad to justify expansion. Original concern over Italian military prestige and firepower led Italy's rulers to force the tempo and direction of the peninsula's industrial growth. In this fashion the future of Italian heavy industry became tied to the future of the whole Italian political system.

Second, the nation's agrarian interests were diffuse and unorganized. In contrast a set of highly concentrated industrial firms, supported by North Italian investment banks, was in an excellent position to influence parliament, ministries, and the royal court itself.

Third, industry's privileged position was legislatively linked to similar privileges for certain landowning categories—notably wheat and sugar beet growers—in such a way as to forestall the formation of any regional or national agrarian movement of revolt. The sugar industry offers a particularly instructive example of how industrial and agrarian interests could in fact mesh. The sugar manufacturers were so heavily protected by tariffs that they enjoyed a virtual monopoly of the Italian market, although international agreements restrained them from exporting and undercutting other nations' sugar refiners. This group worked with other industrialists in negotiating with Giolitti over the financing of his newspaper in Rome and acted in every respect like the exponents of any other special-interest group enjoying state favor. The sugar industry's performance in August 1914 showed its real stripe: the War caused a speculative run on sugar, and the price started rising as excess stocks piled up. At this point the sugar manufacturers, evidently drowning in profits and in products, threatened to cut back and cancel the contracts they had made with beet growers throughout Italy. Their intention was clear: to keep prices as high as the new market conditions allowed and meanwhile to spend as little as possible in new refining. It took a threat from the government to alter matters. The ministers made it clear that they would raise the tax on sugar refining if prices rose, and at the same time they allowed the Italian sugar producers to export their surplus to Switzerland, where the War had evidently created a new market. The continuing crisis of Italian industry was due only in part to world economic conditions: basically, it stemmed from Italy's chronic structural imbalance. Even after the effects of the international depression of 1908 began to wear off in Italy, industrial investments never returned to their previous level, even in absolute figures. The yearly investment of new capital in Italian industry during the years 1911–13 was a mere fraction of the money put in during the pre-1908 peak-growth years. The situation of heavy industry was particularly dismal because its dividend yield, in relation to the capital invested in it, was so low. The money invested in banks, public works, construction, and utilities all yielded far higher return rates than investments in steel, machinery, and motor manufacturing. Investors got their highest return from sugar refineries, a fact which suggests that the Italian tariff system did more for landowners than for most industrialists.

Under these circumstances, it was natural that the Italian investing public showed slight interest in heavy-industry stocks, which languished in the exchanges of North Italy during the last prewar years. Automobile shares did especially badly, since banks had no wish to keep them, but rail and steel issues were also weak. Even firms with big munitions orders failed to attract Italian investors.

The figures that reflect Italy's international economic role during these years not only indicate Italian industry's precarious condition but also throw light on the country's inherent economic imbalance. They indicate that the South could not afford North Italy's machinery products, while the North could not absorb the masses that the South threw onto the labor market year after year. A further grim conclusion appears: Italy was still struggling to free herself from near-colonial subjection to the big European industrial powers, and the struggle was not going at all well in the prewar years.

Between 1909 and 1913 an average of 679,000 Italians emigrated every year—a yearly exit of almost 2 percent of the total population of Italy—of whom 405,542 crossed the Atlantic. In 1913 these figures touch an all-time high: 872,598 emigrated; 559,566—almost two-thirds—went overseas. Of course the bulk of these emigrants came from unindustrialized Italy: Sicily, the South, and the Veneto. What is significant, though, is that these masses left Italy during the years when the domestic production of steel, sulphuric acid, and chemical fertilizers was rising, when heavy industry was actually increasing its labor force. In spite of its modest growth, Italian industry could not come near to absorbing the excess manpower of the nation's countryside. Italy thus offered the odd and disheartening spectacle of a nation with two uncoordinated regional economies. A small northern industrial elite section grew up along with a huge, semicolonial southern labor pool. In the same years, and sometimes to the same countries, Italy sent from her ports automobiles, ball bearings, and rubber tires on the one hand and a mass of illiterate day laborers on the other.

Italy's industrial-trade situation was still fundamentally unfavorable, in spite of the country's evident progress. In the last normal prewar year, 1913, Italy imported 578,048,000 lire worth of ore, metal, and metal products, amounting to 15.9 percent of her total imports; but in the same year she exported 105,843,000 lire worth of the same commodities, which was 4.2 percent of her total exports. However, the absolute value of these imported heavy industrial goods was declining slightly from its 1908–12 average, and such goods were taking a slightly smaller share of Italy's total imports in lire. Just the reverse was happening in the export field, where heavy industrial products had averaged in the years 1908–12 only 3.7 percent of Italy's total exports in lire; the 1913 figure represents a notable gain in absolute worth as well as in its relation to Italy's total export trade. Nevertheless, Italy's industrial inferiority was still evident.

The same pattern holds true for other categories of industrial imports and exports in which Italy remained overshadowed and even threatened by stronger industrial powers. In 1913 Italy imported 48,-800,000 lire worth of vehicles and exported 43,353,000 lire worth; ominously, her imports were increasing a little faster than her exports, although both were rising notably. Concurrently, Italy's imports of rubber and rubber products were also rising, but here her export situation was brilliant. During the years 1908–13 Italy averaged yearly rubber exports of less than 30 million lire, but in 1913 she exported almost 52 million lire worth, or 2 percent of her total exports.

A breakdown of these industrial figures will show how hard Italy was struggling to win a place among the world's industrial powers and the uncertain extent to which she was succeeding.

In 1913 Italy imported 869,394 quintals of boilers and machinery, more than half from Germany, with Britain and America far behind. In the same year she exported 165,274 quintals of the same product, but her principal customers, according to the value of the machinery, were Argentina and Russia, with Germany coming in third. In the same year Italy imported 84,927,484 lire worth of electrical, optical, and calculating machinery (including gas gauges and electric light bulbs) and exported 16,296,364 lire worth of those products; Germany, however, provided almost two-thirds of Italy's imports in this line, while Italy's exports went primarily to Argentina,

France, and Brazil, with Germany taking less than 10 percent of them.

Italy's brilliant automobile industry found its best customers in Britain, France, Argentina, Brazil, and Russia; Italian rubber products went primarily to Belgium, Switzerland, and Britain. However, foreign giants were treading in these sectors, too. The American light car was beginning to win the Italian market, but Germany led all other nations in exporting vehicles to Italy. Largely because of this, Germany also became the principal exporter of finished rubber goods to Italy and thus cut into the new Italian rubber industry's domestic markets.

These statistics foreshadow a crucial development in Italy's foreign relationships. Before the First World War, Italy was struggling to get on her feet industrially and compete in world markets, especially in backward areas, but she was staggering under the weight of foreign rivalry, which dominated many of her own domestic markets, and her export market position was difficult and unsure. Unique among Italy's great rivals was Germany, which took less of Italy's manufactured products than did Austria, France, or Britain but sold Italy far more manufactured products than any two other countries combined. By 1914 these facts were becoming common knowledge and had their impact in determining Italy's eventual turn against Germany.

Thus precariously perched on the outer edge of the industrial world, the Italians made up for their economic deficiencies with political audacity. A restless and adventurous spirit entered their foreign policy from 1911 on, and by 1914 they had become objects of suspicion and alarm in the European diplomatic world, as the Isvolsky papers show. The Italians turned against every great power that might exert control over them—first Germany and then the Allies. Italy's mischievous antiwestern role in the decades after the First World War arose out of chronic Italian difficulties. Ministries and regimes changed, but not the fundamental lines of Italian expansionism.

Only economic precariousness and imbalance can explain the two essential features of twentieth-century Italian imperialism. First, it arose from a need to export industrial goods, systems, and skills, technical and even entrepreneurial. Italy was not an exporter of capital, like some other great powers, but her other export needs explain her drive for exclusive colonial space. The facts cited above indicate how hard it was for the Italians to make much of a dent in relatively free or open markets: their industrial exports kept lagging behind their imports in the crucial years 1911–15, when Italian imperialism really began to operate. Second, since Italy was exporting both manpower and industrial products, an ideal Italian imperialist policy would seek to reconcile those two clashing sectors of the nation by finding a colonial space that might absorb and sustain both. The future Italian empire would complement northern industries by providing new markets and raw materials, and at the same time it would serve as an outlet for the migrant masses of the South: Italian imperialism had more of a demographic, "proletarian" pathos than any other European great-power movement of national expansion. This, at any rate, was the double aim that imperialist Italy pursued until her final collapse and ruin during the Second World War.

All the worst features of Italian industrialization, militarism, speculation, and lack of serious economic planning, the errors and misdeeds that the Italian taxpayer eventually had to pay for, show most clearly in the iron and steel industry. The production of iron and steel in Italy was not in itself an absurdity. The country has a steady supply of high-quality, easily available iron ore from Elba, as well as even higher-grade but costly deposits in the Piedmontese and Lombard Alpine areas. But to be economically viable, such an industry must produce with great technical efficiency: the fuel for Italian blast furnaces, as well as certain alloy minerals, had to be imported, while the limitations of the domestic market were such that the costs of production had to be low enough to permit exportation at internationally competitive prices. Minimization of costs means complete-cycle production, in which the metal is never allowed to cool from blast furnace to rolling mill until it is in finished form, as well as efficient use of coal tar by-products and gases. It also requires long-term planning and rapid amortization and replacement of equipment that is continually going out of date—a sacrifice of immediate profit in order to put money back into the plants. But the Italian iron and steel industry arose as a highly speculative financial enterprise, projected by experienced public contractors who were assured of political support as well as military orders and were financed, insofar as there was solid capital in their first ventures, by bankers and stock promoters rather than by investors versed in industrial problems.[3]

The germ of the future steel industry was the Società Veneta per costruzioni ed imprese pubbliche, founded in 1872. The Società Veneta undertook all kinds of public works—government buildings, bridges, aqueducts—but its real base was railroad operation in the fertile plains of the Po Valley. Under the energetic presidency of Vincenzo Stefano Breda, the Società Veneta begin investing in various branches of the building industry and in banks, but the most fruitful initiative that the engineer-politician Breda took was toward setting up an autonomous steel and rail industry. Years of public contracting gave him a political inside track, further smoothed for him by his 1876 election to parliament. He seems to have realized immediately that there were opportunities for heavy-industry development in the peninsula, if only adequate government contracts, advances, and protection were forthcoming. His Società Veneta, which he was accused of running out of his vest pocket in almost total disregard of the wishes of most of the smaller stockholders, was the incubation bed of two enterprises fundamental in Italian industrial history: the Terni foundry and steel mill (1884) and the Breda locomotive and machine shops, founded in 1886 by his cousin Ernesto, one of the Società Veneta's chief railway engineers.[4] (The Società Veneta had already taken part-ownership in a Milanese railroad-car factory years before Ernesto Breda's establishment started with its more ambitious program, but with the founding of Terni we see the first example of the interlocking of the steel and mechanical industries so characteristic of Italian industrial development.)

Whatever purely economic and technical difficulties stood in the way of Breda's vaulting ambitions, his political backing could not have been better. The railway conventions of 1885, which entrusted the management of the state railways to various private groups for a period of twenty years, guaranteed to national producers the award of all rail-equipment contracts, provided their bid was not more than

5 percent above the lowest foreign offer; and this relatively modest measure was greatly reinforced by the high iron and steel tariffs of 1887, part of an omnibus protection bill. But the Breda group's real support was in the ministries, not in the texts of parliamentary acts. In 1887 the war ministry gave to Ernesto Breda an artillery-ammunition contract of such size that he built a special division for this branch of work. The naval ministry, under Admiral Benedetto Brin, one of the most important and influential of the government's supporters in parliament and in the nation, really put the new steel mill at Terni in business with big armor plate orders accompanied by generous advances without interest. When Terni failed to deliver the first lot on time, Brin, instead of applying the prescribed fines, gave new orders and advances, secured, it was later charged, by nothing more solid than a second mortgage, a mortgage on properties evaluated at no more than 10 percent of the sum advanced to Terni.

All criticisms were met by an argument, often used by V. S. Breda in speeches and pamphlets, that has never lost its efficacy: national security and self-sufficiency dictated the building of a great steel mill, whatever the risks and losses. Breda unblushingly praised his group's patriotic self-abnegation. The one accusation that he answered concretely concerned foreign interests: he denied that outsiders (the French Schneider interests were named) had more than 3,000 out of Terni's 35,000 shares. Indeed, 10,000 Terni shares were held by his own Società Veneta, which, to judge from some stockholder complaints, he was milking for the sake of his new steel ventures. (The Schneider interests are the first example of French collaboration in Italian steel-industry development. Schneider is generally believed to have installed the first equipment in the great plant at Terni.)

Breda's enemies were far from convinced by his patriotic self-justification. In 1899 they actually tried to bring him to trial in the senate with all kinds of sensational charges. They alleged that he had falsified company balance sheets for years, showing nonexistent profits to protect stock prices. Even worse, he was accused of having launched Terni with fictitious capital, funds that never actually materialized, and of having then made an enormous profit out of the speculative boom in the steel company's stock during the 1890s, a boom largely engineered by him and his associates. The senate found that the accusations of fraud, stock manipulation, and profiteering directed against Breda's management of the Società Veneta were all covered by the statute of limitations, since the Società Veneta had collapsed in 1893 and Breda had not been put under pretrial investigation until 1898. In fact, Breda appears to have been the victim of the 1893 crash, and the only charge to which he is definitely liable is that of having put off the day of reckoning as long as possible by methods that will not bear much scrutiny. As for the charges against his launching of Terni, the senate committee found that they were not proven and that the extraordinary fluctuations in Terni stock values were due to the market's giddiness rather than to any long-range manipulations on Breda's part. Therefore the old senator never had to stand trial, though a cloud afterwards rested over him and his enterprises. In any case, it is hard to believe that the engineer-admiral Benedetto Brin, a true pioneer in the technique of warship design and an old protégé of Cavour, would have done so much for Breda had he been nothing more than a speculator.

The relations between Brin and Breda must have been very close. Breda and his financial associates had set up a steel mill at Terni, an inland town in central Italy far from its sources of supply. The only real advantage Terni offered was its military security, and the prospects for nonmilitary production were slight. Undoubtedly Breda and his group thought that they could produce steel tracks at a profit, given the protected home market, but in fact it was their virtual monopoly of naval armor plate that put them in business. The navy did not go back on the commitments it must have made.

From 1890 to 1903 Terni was given big orders by Brin and his successors in the navy ministry at extraordinarily high prices. Only in 1903 did the navy begin to solicit foreign bids in order to force Terni to climb down. Critics made much of the comfortable executive positions that retired admirals and bureaucrats found in the Terni organization, and parliamentary investigators in 1904 wrote devastating reports on the connivance and secrecy that prevailed in relations between the navy and its industrial protégé. Terni, it was again charged, had been set up with largely fictitious capital: the real capital had been provided by the navy, without interest or guarantees, and Terni had furnished obsolescent material in repayment. Only then, after seven years of delay, was Terni compelled to buy the Krupp patents necessary to produce up-to-date armor. But by 1905, when the charges became public, Terni was no longer an isolated target for reformers' indignation. It was part of a great financial and industrial complex stretching over much of the peninsula, a citadel of special interests that no amount of radical muckraking could ever really threaten.

The first twenty years of Terni, as exposed by the special investigating committee of 1906, show just how appalling political industrialization can be.

Terni shares, originally valued at 500 lire, had by 1906 reached a price of 2,400. One experienced deputy figured that such shares had to be paying at least 20 percent dividends to account for such a price rise. Another deputy calculated that in 1897 Terni had been making about 200 percent profit in its dealings with the state, although most steelmakers would have been delighted with 30 percent. Nor were these earnings a reward for merit or achievement. Terni had not, in its first two decades, become the center of an industrial system that could emancipate Italy from foreign suppliers. Its only important customers were the Italian navy and the Armstrong cannon factory at Pozzuoli.

The great English munitions firm had set up a plant at Naples in 1885 by special arrangement with the navy, which wanted its own source of guns made by Italian labor. In line with these autarkic ideas, the navy required that Armstrong use Italian steel, and it had to look to Terni. But Terni, which was alone in the field, charged Armstrong the highest possible prices and provided steel that was often unsuitable or defective. Armstrong spent time and money, with repeated casting, to find steel fit for its cannons among Terni's lots.

The added cost eventually fell on the state: Armstrong's prices remained high and its deliveries often fell behind schedule. Finally, in 1903 Armstrong built its own steel plant.

Even more discreditable was the history of Terni's attempted rivalry with Krupp. The notion of such a rivalry seems absurd in view of Terni's poor record, but things began improving after September 1895, when an engineer named Sigismondi took over the running of Terni's steel plant. He was especially suited for the job: until only two months before, he had been head of the naval ministry's marine construction board and was thus familiar with the navy's requirements and what prices it would pay. He came at the right time, for Terni's special position was soon to be endangered by Krupp.

Since 1884 the navy had bought armor plate exclusively from Terni according to specifications that were becoming outmoded because of the tougher and more resistant armor that Krupp made with patented, constantly improving processes. By 1897 Krupp's superiority was internationally recognized: Great Britain, the United States, and Russia began using Krupp-process armor plate in some of their battleships. By contrast, Terni's progress was mediocre, even in its closed Italian market. Its 1898 armor plate was accepted by the navy in spite of the fact that it cracked under fire in subsequent tests. But such indulgence was at an end. Even before the tests the navy had decided to switch to Krupp.

During his last term as naval minister, Admiral Brin told Senator Breda that the state would thenceforth require that Terni meet international standards: the contracts with Terni gave the state that right, though, characteristically, they also provided that the state would have to compensate Terni for any costs of technical improvements and patent rights that meeting the new specifications entailed.

In the long run the arrangement would have been to Terni's advantage, although there would have been a drop in earnings during the changeover. But Breda, whose mind was evidently on the latter, strongly resisted. Brin died in May 1898, and shortly thereafter, Breda broke off the negotiations with Krupp that he had been obliged to start. He alleged that Krupp's armor, although it was in fact more resistant to cracking then Terni's, was not formally guaranteed against piercing. He also balked at the royalties Krupp demanded for use of its process—eleven pounds sterling per ton, which Brin, too, had thought exorbitant.

Between March and May 1899 Terni produced an unauthorized imitation of Krupp's armor plate, which did so well in its first navy tests that Admiral Bettolo, Brin's successor, told the Chamber of Deputies that the state's financial sacrifices had finally been justified: Terni was worth what the state had sunk in it.

Before long Bettolo had reason to regret those words. The next month Krupp wrote the ministry that its competitor's plates had been tested with outdated projectiles: the German firm said it would not dream of using ten-year-old shells in testing its own latest armor. The navy answered, in embarrassed and evasive terms, that the 1899 tests could not eclipse the reputation that Krupp products deservedly enjoyed. Nevertheless, Krupp eventually brought suit against its Italian imitators, and a settlement was reached out of court.

In reality, Krupp had little to worry about: its rivals were speculators and political operators, not industrialists. Terni, it turned out, could not produce its vaunted new armor plate in any quantity, and up to 1903 it continued making and selling to the navy the same type of plate that had proved so mediocre in previous years. The only excuses that Admiral Bettolo was able to furnish were that the German process was not yet in universal use elsewhere and that the relative quality of different projectiles and armor plates was constantly changing. The admiral's observations have a certain force; the Italians would have had to spend impossible sums to stay ahead of the obsolescence that pursued even the greatest fleets. Nevertheless, Terni did enjoy an unusual indulgence from the navy, which had carried its preference for homemade steel beyond all limits.

Bettolo's successor, Admiral Carlo Mirabello, soon put an end to that state of affairs. In the spring of 1904 the new minister, openly dissatisfied with Terni's product, sent an artillery expert to Essen, where Krupp and Terni armor underwent conclusive tests. The artilleryman determined that Krupp's plate was manifestly superior and so reported to the ministry in July 1904.

Terni had not waited for the official report. In March it had again offered the navy its "special" imitation of the Krupp plate, but the next month, finally yielding, declared that it was ready to use the authentic Krupp process, later adding that it would, of course, agree to meet international projectile and target test standards.

Although some Terni lots were still being rejected by 1906, the navy, Mirabello, and Premier Giolitti felt that they could face a searching parliamentary investigation and debate. Mirabello's administration came out reasonably well, but the discussions about Terni went far beyond navy contracts and entered the whole field of relations between the government and the new industrial complexes.

The chamber seemed to have few second thoughts about the navy's goal of industrial self-sufficiency, and no one ventured to suggest that Italy should depend on foreign arms makers. Apart from patriotic considerations, the deputies doubted that the international munitions trusts and coalitions would treat the Italian government any better than Terni and the Lombard steel and arms firms did, though the 1906 investigations had exposed these firms as extortionate in their demands, sometimes shoddy in their workmanship, and often conniving and intriguing in their dealings with government officials.

What most concerned the more knowledgeable deputies was the untouchable position of Terni. They knew perfectly well that nothing they said on the floor of the chamber would have any real effect on the growing Italian military-industrial complex, and no doubt they spoke largely for the record. But what they said throws an interesting light on the changing nature of the complex, which was then coming into the orbit of the Banca Commerciale of Milan.

F. S. Nitti noted that Terni seemed to be guaranteed against competition, since armor manufacturers abroad had failed to underbid the Italian firm, even at Mirabello's invitation. Behind this fact Nitti saw the workings of international high finance:

All of these big companies are, in general, tied to banking institutions, and these in turn are united among themselves. If anyone threatens even one of these interests, he either stops when faced with the difficulties to be overcome, or he is beaten. (The Chamber buzzed at these words.) Terni, the shipyards, steel companies, shipping lines, etc., let us recognize the fact, all follow the lead of one single bank, a bank which is German even though it has an Italian name, and which has not brought us productive capital, but rather an organization perfectly set up to extract big profits with limited funds.[5]

This indictment by an economist who had defended Breda's initial Terni ventures should not be taken as an appeal to revolution. What Nitti, an ambitious southerner, really wanted was the spreading of some state industrial benefits to the Naples area. However, the reference to the great Milanese bank and its directive role in industry was significant. In fact, Terni was no longer an isolated local enter-

prise, and the Breda group had become part of a much more powerful system of economic interests.

Another deputy enlarged on the same theme out of his personal
experience. Salvatore Orlando, of the Orlando shipyard at Leghorn,
a naval designer, took a position like Nitti's but blamed the state for
allowing the formation of a key industrial coalition under foreign
banking control.

*I quit the Leghorn shipyard and left my work with keen regret, solely in
order not to put up with the control of the steel companies, to keep my
independence. . . . The Italian government, by placing the note-issuing
banks under a glass bell, by preventing them from making discounts for
industry, reserving discounts only for the most important borrowers, and
for a term no longer than three months, with ministerial authorizations
being given month by month, preventing even advances against securities
—because it obliged the issue banks to devalue them by 20%, even in
the case of government bonds which all the banks accept at over 100%,
while the Bank of Italy receives them at 80%—in this way abandoned
all influence over the industrial development of the country, which was
taken over by banks whose funds and men from abroad feel no obligation toward the State. These are the faults of the state. . . .*[6]

In other words, the Italian state was not autarkic enough. The
issue raised by these two experts was to grow in importance as Italy,
developing industrial rivalries and strains with her Triple Alliance
partners, veered toward the opposing group of powers. As early as
1906, with the country still forming its industrial skeleton, the German economic presence in the peninsula was already arousing hostility among those who were in a good position to observe it. The
troubles and abuses of an autarkic military-industrial system lay deep,
and to a great extent the real sickness of the country's new industries was to be masked by concern over the problem of German
controls, a problem that lay closer to the surface and could serve to
divert the public's attention from the Italian economy's structural
faults.

Although the somewhat inaccurately named "steel trust" did
not take its final form till 1911, it was actually set up during the
great industrial development of 1899–1905. Like Terni, it had its
origins in the government situation of the mid-1880s, those crucial

years when Italy was set on the road to colonial empire, protectionism, and industrialization by a curious coalition of Left parliamentary politicians, military chiefs, and the court. Among the measures by which the Depretis government tried to create behind it a truly national property interest—measures that included protection for textiles, wheat, iron ore, and steel—was a law subsidizing shipbuilding and navigation.

After 1885 Italian shipbuilding interests—the Orlandos, the Oderos, and the heads of Navigazione Generale (Florio)—became extremely active in all industrial and maritime enterprises that might enjoy state backing. It was natural enough for them to take an interest in making steel: there was the remarkable prospect of being favored by the state to make steel that would then go into ships that would in turn be built with the aid of state subsidies. And all this could be achieved and defended in the name of national self-sufficiency, national security, and the welfare of national labor.[7]

Senator Luigi Orlando, developer of one of the largest shipbuilding enterprises, was a Sicilian, born heir to a humble little iron shop, who had risen with Garibaldi and Crispi. He was an authentic Risorgimento patriot, a high-level Mason who had joined Crispi in the eventual reconciliation with the Savoy monarchy. In 1865 the government let him take over the outdated yards at Leghorn, which he turned into a modern plant. The 1870s depression almost finished him, but he was saved by Naval Minister Brin, who ordered the big ironclad *Lepanto* from him.

By 1881 Orlando was back on his feet, foreseeing a great Italian maritime industry based on a national steel industry. Such a self-contained industry would, he thought, redeem Italy from her dependence on the great powers as well as resolve the social questions of the day by guaranteeing employment to the country's restless working masses. Orlando's sons followed him in politics and aspirations and were to become magnates of the steel industry soon after the turn of the century.

The Orlandos illustrate a familiar pattern in Italian politics and culture. The passage from Garibaldian democracy and republicanism to an aggressive nationalism is characteristic of a whole generation. Baratieri began as a Garibaldian legionnaire and ended as a colonial general at Adowa. In Italian literature Alfredo Oriani had a somewhat similar development, passing from Romagnole republicanism to a proto-Fascist philosophy that even envisaged genocide as an instrument of national policy. The reconciliation of Carducci with the monarchy followed the same general line. The compromise with the House of Savoy, the Triple Alliance, and the drive for great-power status were all steps on the road leading away from the Risorgimento and its internationally felt ideals.

The Florios were another Sicilian dynasty that combined steel and maritime enterprises. At first little more than grocers, the Florios had their beginnings in the nineteenth-century development of tuna fishing and fruit growing in Sicily. Tied politically to Crispi, they merged their lines with those of the Genoese shipping enterpriser Rubattino in 1881. This was a financial and political deal stimulated by French maritime competition and the constant mediation of Crispi and the Orlando brothers. It resulted in the creation of a large, state-subsidized shipping line with all kinds of industrial interests and investments—the Navigazione Generale Italiana.[8]

The Orlandos and Florios alike depended, directly or indirectly, on the state for their continued industrial existence, as did Odero, the Genoese shipbuilder associated with them.

Italian shipyards survived and grew, thanks to Admiral Brin, who had taken the initiative in setting up Terni and Armstrong in the mid-1880s. In 1885 Brin began to have the engines for Italian warships made in Italy instead of importing them from Britain. There was more economic sense in this move than in the rest of Brin's autarkic naval program. The construction of iron or steel hulls was bound to be more expensive in Italy than abroad, given the high domestic cost of metals; but engines, in which labor, not metal, was the principal item of expense, could be made cheaper in Italy, where labor was cheaper. Brin began with the two big naval workshops, Ansaldo of Genoa and Guppy of Naples, which at the naval ministry's prompting turned to the British for plans and technical aid, paying the British firms 5 percent royalties on the engines built.[9]

But the period of apprenticeship did not last long. Brin evidently resented paying tribute abroad for engines that did not perform perfectly. Hence he began to let Italian firms design their own engines, in spite of the atmosphere of self-distrust that surrounded every Italian enterprise at the time. The homemade engines performed well, and Italy took a long step toward naval self-sufficiency, with all its implications for domestic industries.

Brin's successors in the naval ministry carried on his work, and in an attempt to reduce the cost of the Italian-built engines, they invited other big shipyards to enter the field. In the competition of 1900 Orlando and Odero took first place, but Ansaldo and the Neapolitan yard appealed to the ministry to reconsider, alleging that their survival was at stake. Eventually each of the four yards was assigned one battleship apiece. Naval autarky had put another segment of the military-industrial complex into business.

Salvatore Orlando, in the 1906 parliamentary debates, gave Brin his historical due, and his words served as a sort of posthumous rehabilitation of the admiral:

We must go back to that period, when it was necessary to write to France or England whenever a plant needed a one-meter-square sheet of metal, when it was necessary to write abroad for machinery, armorplate and all other materials, and above all send hundreds of millions there. . . . we must go back to that period to understand that Brin's dream of giving machines, ships, armor and cannon to a country that had neither iron nor coal, seemed the dream of a madman, and if, in that dream, he committed some errors (for example, not guaranteeing reasonable prices to the Navy for its armorplate), we should not hold it against him, in view of the great goal achieved in the country's interest. If you want to put the dead on trial, it is necessary to go back to Camillo Cavour, before 1860, because Cavour planned to give the country not only political, but also industrial independence.[10]

Orlando's eulogy reflects a state of mind and a tradition that shaped much of the policies of liberal Italy. Considerations of national pride and power, present from the start of Italian unification, were ultimately to prove stronger than the universal democratic ideals of the Risorgimento. These considerations started to prevail in Italian politics precisely in Brin's years of power, and his unpublicized but far-reaching work laid the foundation for Italy's entry into twentieth-century competitions for empire and industrial space.

Italian shipyards worked almost exclusively on orders from the

Italian navy and a few foreign navies. Their nonmilitary work was largely commissioned by the subsidized sector of the Italian merchant marine, most notably the Navigazione Generale, which ran the new postal colonial routes essential to Crispi's 1890 African expansion policies. The independent and commercially viable Italian merchant marine preferred to get British vessels, some of them second-hand.

Senator Ignazio Florio began taking part in steel industry development as early as 1899, at the beginning of the industry's great leap forward. The Orlandos and Oderos came in a few years later, when it became clear that the exploitation of the Elba Island mines could provide the foundation for a truly self-contained "national" iron and steel industry.

The Elba iron mines, which were public domain, had been leased by the state to various concession holders, who sold the ore produced to foreign, usually Belgian, iron manufacturers. But in 1899 a new company, the Elba, acquired from the concession holder Ubaldo Tonietti the right to use the ore. In exchange Tonietti received a high price—5.5 million lire—as well as 1,000 of Elba's 60,000 shares.

The Elba was financed by a combination of French and Belgian bankers; by Schneider interests; and, most important, by Italian banking groups. The Credito Italiano of Genoa had the largest single block of shares (18,650), and many individual Genoese, Roman, and Neapolitan financiers figure among the founders. Florio had a 5 percent interest, and the Terni-affiliated Ferriere Italiane took a smaller share.

The new company proposed to set up a native iron industry in Italy. In carrying out this project after 1899, it committed two technical errors destined to weigh heavily on the industry. It built its blast furnaces at Portoferraio, on the island, where there was not enough space for complete-cycle steel production and milling. Then it installed some Bessemer converters, equipment that had become obsolete in the rest of the world. These mistakes did not come to light in the first years of the company's existence; on the contrary, the foreign steel-rail cartel became momentarily so alarmed by the growth of an Italian industry that it agreed to cease underselling native producers on the Italian market if only the Italians would refrain from exporting. Thus although in 1901 70 percent of Italian rail-track demand was supplied from abroad, in 1903 more than 70 percent was supplied domestically—almost the whole demand, since the remaining imports were of special categories not made in Italy.

With these lasting developmental flaws and momentary economic and political advantages, Elba became the nucleus of the Italian steel trust through a seven-year process of near fraud, financial manipulation, and sellout.

There was indeed something shady about the company's very beginnings. For tax purposes Tonietti had reported to the state a sale price to Elba of only 550,000 lire: the matter came out in 1912, when the finance ministry ordered Tonietti's heirs, together with the Credito Italiano, to pay 712,800 lire in fees and fines. The big northern investment bank was held to be an accomplice.

Then, the Elba company mined far beyond its legally authorized yearly quota of ore, a limit set to forestall the untimely mining-out of the whole island. Since the excess could not be used, thanks to close government surveillance, the company claimed to the government that its mining operation gave work to thousands who would otherwise be destitute and tried in this way to get around the limit, threatening that it would have to curtail its mining operations if it was not permitted to use the excess quantities already mined. At this point Ferriere Italiane intervened on behalf of Terni, evidently prompted by the coalition of shipping and banking interests centered in the Banca Commerciale of Milan, which proposed to enter the new industry and centralize it on a national scale.

The founding of Elba had threatened to break Terni's monopoly in Italian big steel, and it was suspected that Schneider-Creusot had put money into Elba with this purpose in mind. Meanwhile, at the death of V. S. Breda in 1902, the Orlando–Odero–Banca Commerciale group had acquired control of Terni. The same coalition immediately afterwards put double pressure on Elba.

When Ferriere Italiane got wind of the overmining of iron ore at Elba, it informed the Naples Chamber of Commerce, which started national agitation to get a state-sponsored steelworks set up in the Naples area. Nitti, who enjoyed excellent political connections, pointed out in 1903 that Naples was, after all, a better location than Terni, since it had access to the sea; at the same time, he was careful to praise Terni's initiative. These aspirations were, in fact, translated into law the next year in most generous terms: a portion of Elba iron ore was reserved for use in the South, all kinds of customs and tax exemptions were provided for new plants in the Naples area, and local waterpower rights were made available.

At the same time the banking-shipping coalition tried to get a majority of Elba shares, or at least working control. The Schneider group, seeing that there was no use in fighting it out, sold their Elba shares to the Genoese financier and deputy, Count Edilio Raggio, one of the initial investors in Elba, who also had steel interests in Liguria (Savona). He in turn sold everything to the trust organizers. The Elba parliamentary deputy, Pilade Del Buono, sold his 1,000 shares, claiming that the company had falsified its mining-production figures.

Thus the Elba and Ligurian iron and steel plants became part of a much larger complex. The marriage of interests was sealed by the creation of Ilva, set up to build a great complete-cycle plant at Bagnoli, near Naples. The new firm was endowed with a capital of $20 million lire, of which 12 million were actually paid out. The other 8 million were issued in the form of Ilva shares and exchanged for the same amount of newly issued Elba shares. This operation, declared lawful by the Genoa district court in 1906, put both Ilva and Elba in the hands of the same small group of corporate insiders, Orlandos, Oderos, and Banca Commerciale men. It completely eclipsed the small shareholder and allowed for the greatest arbitrariness and speculation in the future management of the linked firms. Iron-steel shares became, in fact, a great speculative attraction and hence suffered heavily in the 1907 crash.

The new industry's financial-speculative character proved to be its undoing. The new plant at Bagnoli was planned on thoroughly modern lines, and had the plan been carried through, Italy would have had complete-cycle steel production, perhaps at economically viable costs, even with the geographical absurdity of locating a plant at Naples. Unfortunately, after the 1907 crash the Ilva company could not command enough capital to finish a complete-cycle plant, and Bagnoli was left in the same partial and costly operating situation that prevailed elsewhere.

To further complicate and worsen the steel industry's situation, a competing steel plant was set up at Piombino by the Bondi group—again, it was generally held, with considerable French interests involved. Steel industry insiders suspected strongly that the industrial-financial group that started at Piombino intended, at the outset, to compel the existing firms to buy them out. Unfortunately for the industry, Elba refused, and the Bondi group went ahead with their big projects.

Thus, by 1910 the Tyrrhenian coast was lined with steel plants that operated in an uncoordinated and technically unsound fashion, trusting in tariffs and government contracts to save them from the workings of economic natural selection. Their production was rising but their situation was fast becoming desperate, for they could not withstand the price-cutting tactics used against them by the German-led international steel syndicate (Stahlverband).

Between 1903 and 1909 the Germans apparently sold *Formeisen* at cost in Italy. But the German coal-iron syndicates and railway systems were already (so Italian steelmen claimed) giving special premiums to Italy-bound exports, which represented barely 1 percent of German production. Under such circumstances, it is not surprising that Italian industrialists saw behind the operations the will to dominate the Italian market and ruin the Italian steel industry. But between 1910 and 1912—the years of near collapse for Italian steel—the Germans began selling below cost, passing from differential pricing to dumping, a tactic made possible by their superior, vertical industrial organization and made much easier by the technical and organizational difficulties of their Italian victims. Italian steelmen were forced to sell beams on the home market at a loss to meet German competition.

Italian industry reacted with nationalist indignation. One of its most articulate spokesmen, the engineer Lorenzo Allievi, noted that all this was nothing new:

Among the most vivid memories of my youth is my 1881 observation in Germany of the perfect organization of dumping in the field of railroad equipment. The ironic smile with which the manufacturers confirmed to

me the fact that, by mutual agreement, they sold to the Italian govern-
ment, f.o.b. Genoa, equipment at a figure in lire lower than the price in
marks paid on the spot by the German railroads, gave me the clearest
insight into the many-sidedly aggressive character of this procedure.[11]

And the economist Pasquale Iannacone pointed out that the nation
attacked by such methods of economic warfare could retaliate by
buying the steel offered at dumping prices, turning it into finished
products, and in turn underselling the aggressors on world markets.
A vertical organization of industry, he suggested, can support losses
in one sector (say, iron) to make greater profits in another (finished
machine products, for example).

Although this sort of vertical organization was becoming a goal
of Italian big business, it was too far away to solve the pressing problems of Italian steel in 1910–13. The big-steel plants along the west
coast of the peninsula were producing at a loss, disguised and wors-
ened by their payment of artificially high dividends to conceal the
disaster from the investing public. For example, Elba went to the
extent of paying 8 percent dividends while laying off part of its labor
force to avoid failure; and Piombino, in spite of its critical situation,
succeeded in selling new stock issues in 1906 and 1908 at above par
on Italian and French exchanges.

Italian steel was further burdened with marginal and destructive competition among Italian producers themselves; not only was
there a rivalry between Piombino and Elba-Savona, but big steel
was also being undersold by small, marginal plants that grew up in
the shadow of tariff walls and utilized low-grade scrap and outdated
methods.

Then, in 1910, an outsider, evidently the steel engineer and
dealer in steel products Oscar Sinigaglia, proposed a radical unification and renovation of the big-steel sector from the ground up—the
total merging of Ilva, Elba, Piombino, Savona, and Ferriere Italiane;
the closing of obsolete or unmodernizable plants; the centering of
production in a few big, new complete-cycle plants run according to
strictly industrial criteria, with less concern for stock quotations and
more for amortization and reinvestment needs. So clear was the urgency of unification in the industry that Italian big-steel executives,
after long negotiations, succeeded in overcoming their deep-seated

financial and personal differences and joining forces. But they did not go all the way because their legal counselors warned them that the taxes paid on transferring all properties to a new company would be prohibitively high. Hence they compromised by having each of the big five retain its separate juridical personality but entrusting the management of the whole group to Ilva. This arrangement eliminated harmful, uncoordinated overproduction and internecine pricewars but failed to get at the roots of the industry's ills. No old plants could be closed down and no new plants opened, nor could any radical modernizing be carried out, since one of the five would stand to lose or gain disproportionately thereby. Nor, in fact, was any system devised which would get around those obstacles and at the same time maintain the separate legal existence of the five member companies. The 1911 Ilva syndicate did not, indeed could not, get big steel on its feet.

Italian big steel was saved by the state when Ilva took over the management of the whole complex; indeed, the refinancing was formally concluded on August 7, 1911. The Bank of Italy, at the head of a syndicate including the four big investment banks—the Banca Commerciale, the Credito Italiano, the Società Bancaria and the Banco di Roma—and certain important private bankers and financiers, gave the Ilva group a total of 96 million lire in credits, largely in the form of extensions, consolidations, and reduction of interest or debts.

This salvage operation had some remarkable features. First of all, the marriage of public and private interest seemed questionable, particularly when private banks were remunerated at 5 percent and the Bank of Italy at only 4 percent. It was not the Socialists who took the lead in denouncing these pacts, but a wealthy and financially well-informed Republican deputy of the North, Eugenio Chiesa, and his denunciations hit home. He pointed out that some of the private financiers who had joined in the syndicate extending credit to Ilva were themselves, strange to say, Ilva executives, the most notable among them being Genoese lawyer, Senator Vittorio Rolandi-Ricci, who had been active in the financial-administrative side of the industry for quite a while. He turned up among the refinancers, to the tune of a million lire. It was he who had captained the operation that joined Terni to the shipbuilding interests in 1902, after which he had become a big holder in the new big-steel firms as well as a member of most key boards and, incidentally, an intransigent foe of organized labor. It was clear, argued Chiesa, that such financiers had, by virtue of their inside information and connections, enriched themselves while the steel industry went into crisis: they had bought and sold at the right times and now found themselves in a position to lend additional funds to the enterprises they had mismanaged, while the small stockholders had lost everything when the crisis finally broke. The means by which insiders like Rolandi-Ricci had managed to dominate the big companies were more than questionable: Chiesa argued that the exchange of stock between Ilva and Elba was a palpable fiction that enabled a small group to control both companies.

The deal had bad economic and technical effects on the industry itself, not to mention on the Italian credit system. The Bank of Italy, a privately owned, central note-issuing bank under state supervision, held a large number of short-term notes owned by the steel companies, which it had duly discounted. It now converted them into a long-term (five-year) loan, transferring the notes due from the general fund, intended to serve the business public, into an extraordinary reserve fund. The bank had the legal right to employ such funds, under state control, for long-term credits not allowed in the case of general funds; and Bonaldo Stringher, the bank's director general, assured the bank's shareholders at the 1912 yearly meeting that the short-term credits at the public's disposal had not been thus reduced. Indeed, the bank's position, the government claimed, was actually improved, because some uncollectable debts weighing on the general public fund had been taken out and transferred to the stockholders' reserve fund, where they were secured by the entire assets of the debtor steel companies under the terms of the 1911 refinancing. But in fact these assets, as Chiesa had shown, were heavily overvalued, consisting as they did of shaky securities and plants that were not at the peak of technical perfection.

The consequences to the industry, as the government inadvertently revealed, were harmful in the long run. Ilva could build no new plants until it was out of debt, and it could declare no dividends until it had first paid the yearly installments due on its new consolidated debts. That limitation put it completely in the hands of a few big institutions of credit, since private investors would henceforth steer clear of steel shares, and it also held back still further the radical renovation of the industry's plants, shown by the engineers to be essential.

The 1911 salvage operations, revealing how close and how manifold were the links between the steel industry and the state, kindled the indignation not only of social reformers and radicals, but also of respectable and conservative economists. There was an outcry against the enormous price that Italy was paying to the "barons" of iron and steel. The Italian taxpayer had to shoulder the burden of the markup the state paid for its domestically produced military and rail equipment—a burden that had become much heavier since the state assumed direct management of the nation's principal railways in 1905 and accorded a 5 percent advantage to home producers in bidding for large, new state contracts for rail equipment. (With state operation of the railroads in 1905 came a new 5 percent rule. Contracts were given out keeping 5 percent as a margin of preference for domestic over foreign bidders, as the 1885 conventions had provided; now, however, the percentage was no longer figured on the basis of the lowest foreign bid, but rather on the average of the lowest bids. At the same time the run-down rail system needed much new rolling stock. The result was that Italian industry was suddenly flooded with government orders and began to expand hectically.) The amount the state paid for preferring home to foreign military and rail equipment was estimated at not less than 224 million lire for the years 1905–12, in addition to the smaller sums paid to national shipyards in compensation for steel prices and tariffs. As a consumer the Italian citizen shouldered an additional burden—the artifically high prices of industrial products caused by protective tariffs.

In 1912 about 21 percent of Italian steel production went for military or transportation uses directly, that is, into state-managed or state-subsidized sectors; without the state it probably would not have been worthwhile setting up a steel industry in the peninsula at all.

Good arguments on the side of big steel were not lacking. Its defenders pointed out that laissez-faire and free-trade policies would have left Italy at the mercy of the German-organized international steel cartels, with no alleviation provided by selling at cost or dumping. Under these circumstances Italy would have had to remain a basically agrarian country, with national agricultural production and export conditions that would have put industrialization out of the question. They also fell back on well-worn arguments for military security, which gained new force in the crisis years after 1908. But even leaving aside the complex and perhaps irresolvable problem of total costs, it is hard to avoid the conclusion that the undoubtedly necessary industrialization of North Italy could have taken place with less economic loss and less political friction and damage to the parliamentary system.

From 1911 to 1914 big steel, though slowly convalescing, was still losing blood from the effects of foreign competition. True, the drain was held under control by the industry's new centralization, which led the Germans to seek a partial and unsatisfactory compromise. The Stahlverband in 1913 agreed to limit its exports of steel beams to Italy to 37,000 tons yearly, against an Italian production of some 140,000 tons, a figure close to the yearly average for German beams in 1910–12. The price was not to fall five marks per ton below the world market price for German exports. The agreement did not affect other categories of steel products, in which the Germans kept on with their usual practices, and the whole arrangement was described by one of the steel industry's spokesmen as an "honorable surrender" by Italian—not German—industry, after six years of price wars and losses. German dumping was now limited but recognized as a normal tribute paid by Italian steel producers; the participation of the Belgian *comptoir* and the Austrian Alpin Montangesellschaft in the German syndicate made it impossible for Italian steelmen to resist the pressure.

Italian big steel had one ally in Europe—the French-Mediterranean mining and prospecting companies operating in the Iberian Peninsula and North Africa. Both Elba and Piombino had close links with the French enterprisers: there were stock participations and the prospect of having big steel, located as it was on the shores of the Mediterranean, as a natural customer for French ores and minerals.

The direct connections of big steel to politics are hard to unearth, but there are some interesting personal links. The Marquis Camillo Garroni, the ambassador at Constantinople who was to put such insistent pressure on Djemal Bey for railway concessions in Anatolia in 1913–14, was the son of the Marquis Vittorio Garroni, on the board of the Elba company during the same period. The Marquis Luigi Medici was on the Elba board of administrators, and his brother Giacomo was on Ilva's board in 1913–14. In 1913 Giacomo was elected to the Chamber of Deputies as one of the first Nationalists.

By 1914 big steel was part of an industrial-financial chain of enterprises linking a large part of Italian heavy industry. The financial link was the Banca Commerciale; armor plate was the special production of the original plant at Terni; the Terni-Orlando-Odero shipyards handled naval construction; and a link, forged in 1909, connected this steel empire to the motor and machine industry. The new organization was Vickers-Terni, set up in 1909 at La Spezia by Guiseppe Orlando, director of Terni, with the support of the navy. The original purpose of the new company was to manufacture naval guns and turrets, joining the forces of Terni and the big English firm, Vickers, which held only a quarter interest but which seems to have wielded a disproportionate technical and executive power in the firm. Although Vickers-Terni was set up to insure Italian self-sufficiency in the building and fitting out of capital ships for the navy, by 1914 it had become all too clear that much of the material was being made in England by the parent firm. Terni and its affiliate had proved incapable of filling navy orders on time, and some had had to be entrusted to Carnegie in the United States.[13]

Though doing a mediocre job in its original specialty, Vickers-Terni found a new field of enterprise that in the end proved to be far more important, both militarily and economically: the making of field artillery.

The artillery question had been pending for years in the higher levels of the Italian army, subject to continual reappraisals and postponements. Italian industry, whose interests were well pleaded by *La Preparazione*, a military paper edited by ex-Colonel Enrico Barone, naturally wanted domestic production of this essential military line, with a steady, assured yearly quota of deliveries. Barone's campaign for the adoption of a domestically manufactured field gun went on through the spring of 1911, when the army was making its big decisions. *La Preparazione* came out strongly against the pressures and overcharging from Krupp and declared, "We could cite some very edifying figures of comparison between what certain materials cost when ordered from Krupp and what they came to cost later, when they were manufactured in Italy."

But the paper found that the French Deport model "marks a very notable improvement over Krupp's best materials; it could be made entirely by our national industry, and though better and more up-to-date than Krupp's, would cost much less. . . . the new Deport material . . . could all be manufactured in Italy by our national private industry . . . already . . . prepared and perfectly equipped for speedy mass production." [14]

On March 24, 1911, six days before *La Preparazione* came out with these assertions, army inspectors had decided that the Deport-75 was a real improvement over previously examined field pieces and recommended further tests. The following February the inspectors recommended the Deport model, and the Ministry of War adopted it.

Giuseppe Orlando of Vickers-Terni and the Piedmontese industrialist Dante Ferraris, who had a wide range of interests in motors, rails, and electrical enterprises in North Italy, joined forces to get the new field-artillery production under way. In May 1913 Vickers-Terni raised its capitalization from 10 to 15 million lire to meet the challenge, which must have been considerable to judge from Giuseppe Orlando's public account of December 1914:

When, two years ago, completing the work of a group of Piedmontese industrialists headed by Dante Ferraris, we took steps to have Vickers-Terni join in making possible the entire construction of the new field artillery in Italy, in competition with the famous foreign firms, Krupp and Schneider, up to then the exclusive suppliers for our army, we had to endure a powerful struggle put up by these firms against our initiative; and, in spite of the great superiority of the Deport artillery, we were able to win only by making the most serious sacrifices on our lot-prices, to meet those finally offered by the above-mentioned German firm.

Orlando and Ferraris carried the day, thanks to their financial mainstay, the Banca Commerciale, and Orlando brought this out strongly in his account defending the bank against charges of foreign —specifically, German—control:

> . . . *also on this occasion, the pressure, sometimes harsh and sometimes bland, that foreign competing firms used against us to make us give up our enterprise, never found the slightest help in our financial backers. On the contrary, it was the Banca Commerciale that, with praiseworthy enthusiasm, on the grounds of the confidence that our group inspired, furnished it generously with the means needed to complete the enterprise's working funds, a need that was made greater by the necessity of accepting the severe and new condition laid down by the state administration; that payment would be made after testing and delivery.*[15]

This was the greatest opportunity that had been presented to Italian industry since the rail nationalization of 1905. But the rail nationalization had come in at a moment of relative prosperity, while the artillery program was being offered to an industry in a state of depression. For years Breda had been eyeing the possibilities of an Italian-produced field gun and in the 1890s had twice exhibited models; now, between artillery and machine guns, there was work for the whole machine industry.

2

The Nontrust Industries: Entente versus Alliance Influences

The Banca Commerciale's steel, shipyard, and armaments chain—loosely called the trust—had only one great competitor in Italy: Ansaldo of Genoa. Under a succession of aggressive industrial promoters, Ansaldo was even more nationalistic, more export- and autarky-minded than its rivals, and it aimed far higher. Ansaldo's goal, clearly envisioned by 1914, was to create a genuinely vertical industrial combine that would start with ore and fuel and end only with delivery of a finished product to customers anywhere in the world. Although the farther reaches of such an empire came into sight for only a brief exciting moment at the end of the war, the foundations for it were well laid by 1914. Among its other assets, the leading daily of Genoa, *Il Secolo XIX*, and the influential *Il Messagero* of Rome were in the hands of the family that ran Ansaldo, the Perrones—such journalistic properties seem to have been as essential to a self-respecting industrial complex as the steelworks, electrical workshops, and locomotive plants that formed Ansaldo's patrimony when the war broke out. Ansaldo's emblem was two crossed cannons superimposed on a gear wheel and an anchor, representing its service to the nation and its competition with the trust.[1]

The original Ansaldo shipyards and machine shops, never profitable, were almost a relic by 1885, when the Italian navy after many investigations and committee reports gave them the prospect of enough orders to put them back into business; this was, indeed, the only way such an organization could survive in Italy then—the merchant marine clung to sailing vessels long after the rest of the world had switched to steam. In 1885 the railway conventions made locomotive production possible, at least economically, and the laws subsidizing shipbuilding and navigation gave rise to a limited amount of steamship construction in Italy.

The early fortunes of Ansaldo were linked to the Bombrinis, a dynasty of political capitalists from Liguria. The founder of the line, Carlo Bombrini, had started his career in the Genoese Banco Parodi, which became a part of the Banca di Genova in 1844. In 1849 it became the Banca Nazionale, a general credit institution for the whole kingdom and the chief financial instrument of Cavour's policies. Bombrini saw clearly the close connection between unification and ultimate economic modernization. The relationship between the bank and the government continued after unification. It became the principal bank of emission, lending to the state and benefiting from special legal tender. The bank's privileged position enabled Bombrini, by then a senator, to favor Ansaldo with extraordinary credits during its darkest years.

With the elder Bombrini's death, the family lost its tight control over the Nazionale but developed other enterprises. The two sons, Giovanni and Carlo Marcello, went on backing Ansaldo, fixing its tripartite division: ships, locomotives, and heavy machinery. They had the courage to sink millions into Ansaldo at the right moment. Giovanni was particularly outspoken in identifying industrial and national interests and ventured into many areas where the interests of the state and of private investors intermingled.

After the Libyan war in 1912, the government decided to favor setting up a chemical industry in central Italy which would be wholly Italian in financing and management. To carry out the plan, Senator Giovanni Bombrini joined forces with Leopoldo Parodi-Delfino, a chemical engineer, who furnished the capital. After the feverish wartime expansion, the Bombrini–Parodi-Delfino firm became one of the major industrial complexes of the peninsula, with large mining interests in Albania. Specialists in aqueducts, the Bombrinis financed Apulian land reclamation and after 1906 built and operated the rail system of the Salento. The manifold activities of the Bombrinis are perhaps the best example of political capitalism at work.

By 1889 Ansaldo was not only fitting out its own vessels but also making most of the heavy parts and machinery, especially engines, that went into ships launched by Orlando and by the Italian navy in state arsenals. Naval orders enabled Ansaldo to withstand the unfavorable effects of the 1887 tariffs, which raised the costs of machine manufacturing by putting a high duty on steel but failed to put proportionately high duties on imported machines. Thus Ansaldo paid 4,405.20 lire in duties for the metal needed to make a locomotive, while the duty on a foreign locomotive imported into Italy was only 4,155 lire. The tariff protected domestic steel, unfinished or semifinished, while it left machine industry at a disadvantage. Such a policy facilitated the rise of the trust in later decades.

The tariffs minimized Ansaldo's railroad work for many years, and the firm carried on almost exclusively with naval orders. But its troubles were not over. From 1903 on, Ansaldo found that competing trust shipyards got steel at cost, while Ansaldo received no such consideration. This pressure made itself felt much more after 1905. With the state's operation of the big rail lines, Ansaldo began getting volume orders for locomotives. But completion and delivery were repeatedly held up because of delays in steel deliveries. The state penalized Ansaldo, only to recognize that its failures to fulfill contract terms were due to *forza maggiore*, and Ansaldo in turn sued its steel suppliers. The firm was being squeezed between tariffs and trusts.

Instead of selling out to the trust, Ansaldo fought it. In just the two years during which the trust was taking shape (1902–3), Ferdinando Maria Perrone took over Ansaldo with the support of the Bombrinis and turned it from a private into a joint stock company of a peculiar sort. Perrone received unusual discretionary powers, and his chief aim was independence from the trust.

This captain of industry was a patriot who had fought in Garibaldi's militia during the Italo-Austrian war of 1866, and he had joined Garibaldi again in France in 1870. Like Orlando, he was a friend of Crispi's—in good times and bad. After 1883 Perrone came into close relations with Ansaldo through his brother-in-law, that company's chief engineer. Perrone handled the firm's foreign affairs, especially in Spain and Argentina, where he enjoyed excellent political connections.

Something of Perrone's importance and connections upstairs came to light during the 1897 bank scandal. Crispi, it turned out, had taken 600,000 lire from the Bank of Naples to help swing the 1895 elections, which were the old premier's last great political stroke. When Crispi suddenly fell after Adowa, his successors tried to discredit him once and for all: one of the bank's directors, Luigi Favilla, was put on trial and began to testify against Crispi. The receipts that Crispi thereupon put before the court did not prove that all of the money had been repaid; some documents were gone, and 200,000 lire were still to be accounted for. There was much talk in government circles of putting Crispi on trial, as if he were a common criminal instead of a patriot, a hero, and one of the ministers who had most often enjoyed the crown's confidence after 1876.

In the midst of this scandal, Humbert I consulted one of his most trusted political advisers, Domenico Farini, perennial president of the senate. Farini warned the king that Crispi's parliamentary immunity would be lifted in May if the minister of justice had his way. The king assured Farini that there was no longer any real danger of that and explained:

The missing documents are in Crispi's possession. A certain Perrone, who made a fortune in Argentina, was the intermediary for the purchases made by that state in our private shipyards. He made over a million in brokerage fees. It was he who gave Crispi the money to pay back Favilla. He says so to everyone, but now, called into court, he will always deny it.[2]

The king was not the only one in Rome who thought Perrone was the key to the case. Favilla's defense attorney, Alessandro Fortis, also knew Perrone, to whom he had given legal advice concerning the possible formation of a syndicate to build warships in Italy. When it became clear that Perrone might become involved in the sticky case, he, too, hired a lawyer, Pietro Rosano, a parliamentary friend of Giolitti, by then Crispi's worst enemy; and Crispi's surviving partisans were furious at the change of front. In fact, Perrone was acting on the advice of his most influential political patron, Senator Rattazzi, who had in turn, it was said, taken his cue from Fortis.

Perrone did not limit himself to ministers and deputies; he had other means of getting into public life. In these same months, April-May 1897, he joined forces with Bombrini and Piaggio to buy *Il Secolo XIX* for 200,000 lire. Perrone brought in his own editor, taken from a Roman paper generally held to be in the new government's service. This too, was Rattazzi's doing.

Eventually Perrone was let off the hook; the minister of justice died suddenly in the middle of August. With his death ended the prosecution of Crispi, which would have embarrassed the court and reflected discredit on the whole Italian political system. The episode, short but symptomatic, suggests something of the powerful connections that an industrialist could enjoy even before the great spurt forward in the early twentieth century.

Perrone sold warships to both Spain and Argentina, as well as to the Ottoman Empire; two of Ansaldo's cruisers, resold to the Japanese, fought in Togo's fleet at Tsushima. These international sales had some domestic political effects. During the parliamentary debates aroused by the naval investigations of 1906, the deputies repeatedly cited the fine performance of the Italian-built cruisers at the battle of Tsushima Straits. One orator even went back to the Spanish-American War: at the battle of Santiago Bay, the *Cristobal Colon* had proved resistant to American fire and was put out of action only because it ran aground. In these speeches economic profit and national prestige appear inseparable; in a country still mindful of the naval disasters of 1866 and perpetually concerned over its up-to-dateness, the existence of Ansaldo meant more than its balance sheets would indicate.

Perrone's biggest operation was in Constantinople. In 1902 Ansaldo got a contract to renovate the Golden Horn's naval arsenals with Italian men and machinery. Between 1904 and 1906 the company sold nine torpedo boats to Turkey, and there was even some talk in 1908 that Perrone was on the verge of concluding a contract for building the ports of Tripoli and Benghazi, in the future Libyan colony already clearly marked out for Italian penetration.

Meanwhile, at home Ansaldo tried to lessen its dependence on the trust by joining forces in 1903 with the English firm Armstrong, which since 1885, had been forging steel and manufacturing naval artillery at Pozzuoli, on the Bay of Naples, by special arrangement with the Italian armed forces. Armstrong, it was hoped, would supply steel to its new associates more reasonably and reliably than the trust did. Perrone did not intend to stop at these halfway measures but aimed at complete-cycle independence; Armstrong, however, did nothing to further that ambition.

The years after 1903 were good, in spite of continued difficulties over ordinary steel supplies. The firm started making naval turbines in 1907, the first Italian firm to do so, and it delivered its thousandth locomotive in 1912. In 1909 the company's stock was mostly owned by the Bombrinis and Perrones, though smaller lots were held by Admiral Albini—former director general of arms and torpedoes at the naval ministry—by the Rattazzi family, and by the Roman journalist Costanzo Chauvet. The only dark spot in the company's operations was the scarcity of merchant-ship orders, which left part of the shipyard running below capacity—a general trouble in Italian shipyards. Ansaldo's business in warships, turbines, naval machinery, and locomotives enabled it to weather the 1907 crash without ill effects.

As the Perrones moved toward industrial "autonomy" or "independence," as they variously phrased it, they broke off with Armstrong. Using a right of option that had been written into the Ansaldo-Armstrong agreements of incorporation in 1903, the Perrones bought out Armstrong's shares in 1912.[3]

Beginning in 1910, Ansaldo's real foreign ties were not with Britain but with France. Close working relations set up with Schneider and Nobel opened up new financial and industrial possibilities to the Perrones just when Italy was renewing her whole military establishment and Ansaldo was branching out into new operations connected with that renewal: armor plate, artillery, projectiles, and electrical equipment.

Ansaldo's yearly report for 1910, given to the stockholders on March 20, 1911, gave the first notice of the great leap forward:

We have been preparing to compete for artillery and armorplate contracts. The agreements we have made with the important French firm

Schneider, which owns the great shops of Creusot, allow us to make use of its long experience and great competence in the manufacture of cannons. This manufacture will begin very shortly with the construction of artillery and projectiles, which we will deliver to the Ministry of War in fulfillment of contracts which together with Messieurs Schneider, we have concluded with it. For the armorplate, we have secured the technical aid of an important firm that specializes in this sort of production, and we have at the same time secured the right to manufacture according to patented processes that have given results, in official tests, superior to any previously obtained.

Indeed, Ansaldo's yearly reports for this period read like the press releases of an advancing army. On March 2, 1913, the stockholders were reminded that they had been unanimously in favor of

our company's pushing forward every one of its activities along those lines that are an extension of our previous production and represent an indispensable necessity for our industry, which in order to guarantee its very existence needed to free itself from any kind of dependence, getting itself in condition to supply, with its own means, all the elements that make up, under today's requirements, the naval war unit. A program of this sort secured three basic benefits, to wit: guarantee of our continued existence as an industry, the possibility of entering competitions abroad, and the emancipation of the country from a dangerous enserfment to foreigners in the field of naval armaments. We have carried out this program with firmness, strengthened along the way we have undertaken by your unanimous votes in successive stockholders' meetings, and today we can proudly assure you that we have made our company independent from any other and put in condition to build, in its own plants, a vessel of war of any tonnage and type, complete and ready to get into action. We will go on dedicating our greatest efforts to the perfection and development of our artillery and armorplate plants, as well as of every other branch of our production. . . . In fact, we are in a position today to compete for the fitting out of two great warships and to produce about 8,000 tons of armorplate per year, in addition to our normal production.

These figures must have given the trust some cause for worry: the Terni plant, specializing in armor plate, had a total steel production of only 16,540 tons in 1913, and the whole country in that year produced 8,033 tons of armor plate. In 1912 10,088 tons of armor plate had been made. The meaning of Ansaldo's challenge could not be mistaken: the firm was driving toward leadership of the national market in this military product, undermining the trust's previous near monopoly, which it had enjoyed, with some grumbling from parliament and from the ministries themselves, since Terni was set up more than twenty years before. In fact, Terni's report of March 21, 1913, mentioned that the firm's recent expansion, necessitating enormous expenses, gave it a right to special consideration from the state—a steady and dependable flow of war orders—and Terni's administrators did not neglect to sound the familiar notes of "emancipation" from foreign suppliers.

The decision to go into artillery, ammunition, and armor plate finally brought to a head Ansaldo's rivalry with the trust and made vertical development a life-or-death necessity. The civilian production that Ansaldo engaged in was a secondary activity in 1913–14: although the firm was one of the leading locomotive makers in Italy, delivering forty-seven engines to the state rail system in 1913 and beginning thirty-two more as part of an order of fifty-four in the coming year, it never went into railway export or development projects abroad. At the end of 1913 Ansaldo contracted with Navigazione Generale, itself part of the trust that the Perrones resented so much, to build a 23,000-ton liner for the Rio Plata line. But all of this was little enough compared to the war production that Ansaldo was initiating during the same period.

Producing armor plate was an all-or-nothing venture, as the company explained in its 1914 report: an armor plate plant of even medium proportions would cost almost as much, initially, as a plant set up to meet the heaviest and most exacting foreseeable specifications, and Ansaldo set its sights for the latter.

These projects in turn required an independent steel plant; otherwise Ansaldo would remain at the mercy of what the Perrones stigmatized as foreign trusts practicing differential steel pricing. In fact, by 1914, Ansaldo was undertaking a great steel plant at Cornigliano Ligure, an essential part of the Perrone program of "industrial and political independence." Just what this program entailed the brothers spelled out during the postwar controversies:

We were perfectly aware of the means, of the methods, and of the strength of this bank monopoly. We were convinced that it would constitute a serious danger for the security of our country if it should be dragged into a great war. . . . And it is precisely in the struggle against the bank-industry coalition . . . that the origins, idea and prewar determining factors of the so-called Ansaldo vertical system must be looked for. . . . it was the essential condition for surviving and winning the struggle. . . . In order to keep Ansaldo industries immune from foreign infiltrations, we faced all difficulties, and rejected every insidious offer. Several times High Finance tried to outflank us or take us over by using fancy allurements. During the period of neutrality, when it had become certain what an important function Ansaldo would have in the framework of national defense, we were suddenly dazzled with the proposal to give up our whole industrial complex for a truly fabulous sum, to be paid in gold through foreign banks. We rejected this feeler without even discussing it.[4]

By that time the Perrones had every reason to aim high, for they, too, had the backing of important foreign interests.

First of all, the collaboration with Schneider eventually led to some army orders, though the first offers fell through. The Italian army had never found a 105 howitzer to fit its needs. The Krupp models were set aside in 1908, but the Ansaldo-Schneider–105 model could not be presented before the war because of the army's continual technical hesitations and reevaluation. But after August 1914 the need for heavy artillery became really pressing: in the case of the 260 mortar, Luigi Cadorna, the minister of war and the chief of the general staff, personally overrode the technicians' hesitations and doubts. Between September and November 1914, a decision to employ Schneider heavy mortars was, in effect, forced on the dubious artillerymen, while Pio Perrone, on behalf of Ansaldo, personally promised a complete remounting of the pieces to secure greater stability in mountainous or rough terrain, the problem so far in all medium and heavy artillery testing. Between January and April 1915, just before Italian intervention, Schneider and Ansaldo supplied four batteries to the army.

Schneider was not the most important French ally that the Perrones found in their competition with the trust. In September 1913, in the course of expansion, the Società Nobel-Avigliana, an affiliate of the Paris S.A. Dynamite Nobel, transferred its headquarters from

Switzerland to Italy, where it had a plant. Italian Nobel elected Pio Perrone as its new president, while the board continued to include the French industrialists Paul Clemenceau (brother of the statesman) and Charles Bardy. The new firm's capital consisted of 35,200 non-voting preferred shares (*azioni di godimento*) of a former Swiss affiliate. This fact alone was enough to arouse some suspicions, and the economic xenophobes of the Roman industrial paper *Rassegna dei lavori pubblici* noted as late as November 1914 that Nobel-Avigliana offered none of the capital and fiscal guarantees required by Italian corporation law. The paper went on to ask if a patriot like Perrone felt at ease about being head of a dummy corporation

which, masquerading as Italian, supplies important means of national defense. The officials of the war and navy ministries who do business with this company, and, it is said, advance it millions, as well as some Italian deputies who, it is said, promote the interests of this company with the state; have they thought of the situation that Italy would find herself in should there be a war with France?[5]

Ansaldo's need for vast capital after the outbreak of the war was met by an Italian banker of aggressively nationalistic policies and temperament, Angelo Pogliani. In 1912 Pogliani's Banca di Busto Arsizio had blossomed out as the Società di Credito Provinciale, the attractive new name a concession to the French financiers who had helped to raise the bank's capital to 25 million lire. (The mediator in the arrangements was Paul Doumer, then a senator but later to be elected president of the French Republic.)

In March 1914 the bank decided to open a branch at Trieste, the first Italian bank to attempt such a move, in response to pleas from the irredentists, who wanted to save Trieste from falling into the sphere of the big Slav banks. These were the crucial years when the petty ethnic and social rivalries between Italians and Slavs in Austria were becoming part of the larger emerging pattern of strife between Italian and Austrian economies and political systems. The irredenta question was coming to seem less a matter of national self-determination than of "hinterland" or "economic space," to use the current catchwords. Irredentism, shedding its old republican garb, was becoming a turbid, embittered doctrine of racial strife, of mastery of seas and markets. Pogliani's initiative was a challenge to Austria, and Vienna refused its authorization.

Pogliani's great chance came after the war broke out. In December 1914 he merged his bank with the important Società Bancaria Italiana to form the Banca Italiana di Sconto, the *banca italianissima*, as it liked to be called. Pogliani testified in 1926 that he had founded the Sconto in expectation of Italy's entry into the war and "with the enthusiastic approval" of Premier Salandra. He had in mind the eventual "emancipation" of Italy from "the international High Bank" that "for thirty years had directed at its pleasure the foreign and domestic policies of Italy." In fact, the new bank fitted well into Salandra's own plan to liquidate the whole Giolittian political system. A new government, with a new foreign and domestic policy, needed a new bank.

Pogliani's idea of emancipation from foreign control was peculiar: he himself was the *longa manus* of Parisian financiers. He said later that the Dreyfus Bank of Paris was his most faithful backer throughout. The fast-expanding Società Bancaria, heavily committed to the riskier sort of Italian industrial credit, was largely French. In 1914 its board boasted three Italian senators, one of them a Lombard hydroelectric-power magnate, but four of the remaining six were French: Laurence de Lalande, who had the rank of "minister plenipotentiary"; Louis Dreyfus and Leo Rappaport of the Dreyfus Bank; and Nathan Süss, a cavalier of the Legion of Honor.[6]

The nervous and suspicious premier may actually have been afraid of German influence in the Banca Commerciale, but French influence in the Sconto was obviously far weightier than the residual and intimidated German influence in its competitor.

In any case, the Sconto immediately went down the line in financing Ansaldo, which, it was later claimed, could get credit nowhere else in Italy.

The North Italian steel and steelworking industries relied on the French, not for financing, but for supplies and expertise. As they began replacing imported fuel with hydroelectric power, they grew in size and importance, and by 1914 the Lombard steelmakers had survived the worst effects of German dumping and were operating in the black. The principal concern, Falck, financed chiefly by the Banca Commerciale, was one of the originators of an industry-wide sales organization that had been effective in combating foreign dumping. The Falcks were allied by marriage and business to the Rubinis, a politically influential family tied to the Salandra-Sonnino forces; Giulio Rubini was minister of the treasury in Salandra's first cabinet. Another Lombard firm, Gregorini, achieved a genuine coup in 1914: in competition with firms throughout Europe, it sold the French railway system a lot of mounted axles, a specialty the firm had developed in the face of Krupp dumping. Gregorini, which had its own iron mines and blast furnaces, depended on its sale of railway axles and of ammunition for its continued existence; thus its most important customers were governments—Italian and foreign.[7]

The Banca Commerciale archives allow us a closer look at another Lombard steel firm, Franchi of Brescia,[8] the creation of one man, the ironmaster Attilio Franchi—an impulsive but persevering pioneer of the nineteenth-century type—aided by his brother, Camillo, an engineer. As early as 1890, the Franchis proposed to set up a modern rolling mill among the languishing, archaic iron mines and charcoal blast furnaces of Brescia. In 1896, oppressed by debts, the firm almost went under, but the Commerciale came to its rescue.

Until 1903 Franchi paid no dividends, but from then on things improved fast, as the Commerciale had foreseen. Between 1905 and 1908 dividends went up to nine lire per share. During those years there was a real market for the firm's products—pig iron, cylinders, rollers, wheels, and axles—because of the radical renovation of Italy's rail system and the increase in urban trolley lines. That momentary boom ended for Franchi, as for others, in 1908, and dividends for the following year went down to four lire per share. Thereafter recovery was slow, and in 1913 the firm was able to pay only six and one-half lire.

Franchi's modest recovery was due to a flood of munitions orders that began in 1910, directly from the war and naval ministries at Rome, others as subcontracts from Terni and Tempini. Franchi's ordinary peacetime sales of rail, trolley, milling, and mining equipment were not enough to keep him out of the red. As it was, even with growing munitions orders Franchi found himself in unceasing difficulties.

Franchi's operating costs were high. He needed coal for his modern blast furnace and mining operations; the only way of cutting fuel costs was to use oil as much as possible, which necessitated purchasing new French furnaces, a heavy expense in itself. There were other difficulties connected with military contracts. Italian navy specifications required special processes and equipment the lack of which forced Franchi to send pig iron to bigger outfits, Ansaldo or Ferriere Piemontesi, which returned it in a form suitable for projectiles. Franchi's big customers, the armed forces ministries at Rome, were sticky about specifications and slow in paying for what they accepted, while his suppliers demanded immediate cash.

During those tight years, Franchi lived on credit and short-term promissory notes, constantly renewed by the Commerciale, that amounted to almost as much as the firm's capital assets. Consequently, the Franchi family's stock all gradually passed to the bank as collateral. Both Franchi and the bank would probably have been glad if he could have found more credit elsewhere, but where could he turn? Given the tight Italian money situation, the Italian investing public was out. In 1912 Franchi tried to get a London banking firm to underwrite a bond issue, citing his export business and his satisfied customers abroad, but to no avail. Pointing to the unsettled political conditions and the uncertainties inherent in Franchi's business, the London bank asked for a rate of interest Franchi could not afford.

The Commerciale tried to limit Franchi's continual plant and equipment expansion to the needed minimum, but the industrialist, exhibiting new munitions orders, usually succeeded in breaking normal credit barriers. It seemed that the bank was again being towed along by a debtor, but there were signs that a limit was being reached. Touching on the besetting problem of Italian heavy industry, the Commerciale's industrial expert pointed out the irrationality of setting up expensive plants in Italy to do what could be done more cheaply abroad.

The war gave Franchi immediate relief. Not only did munitions orders rise, but German competition disappeared. After Italy's intervention the Commerciale, as part of its authorized wartime operations, acquired the Germans' controlling interest in the Mannesmann plant and saw to it that the property wound up in Franchi's hands without his even having to increase his capital. The history of the Franchi firm illustrates what rearmament and war meant to the hard-pressed Italian industrialist.

North Italian steel specialized in rare alloys, seamless tubes, and other high-quality lines. The production of seamless tubes, essential to naval construction, was begun by Mannesmann, which with partially Italian capital set up a plant in Lombardy using local hydro-electric power. But Falck took them up shortly thereafter, and by 1914 Italy was self-sufficient in the item.[9]

Rare steels were made by the Ferriere Piemontesi with the help of French technicians. Both this firm and the Ferriere di Voltri profited from the availability of cheap hydroelectric power and Alpine ore of good quality.[10] By 1912 they had recovered from the worst effects of German dumping and had begun to export some special alloys.

North Italian steel had an ambivalent relationship with Germany. The Germans pressed Italian steelmakers in their domestic markets, but German scrap metal supplied North Italian steel plants with a large part of their needs, and they were heavy importers of German pig iron.[11]

The outbreak of war in 1914 brought out the dangers of this situation. The Germans cut off their scrap exports right away and then began increasing their exports of finished-steel products to Italy. The Italian industry, in danger of folding up altogether, managed to get some degree of relief from the British.

Here, too, the pattern of German aggression and Allied accommodation worked itself out. Just when it was finally possible for Italian steel to make some profits, the Germans tightened the screws. It was clear, even at the outset of the war, that the trust, with its string of seaside steel plants, could not operate at all without Allied consent and supplies, but it was not so evident that the same would hold true for the steel industry of the northern valleys. These facts must be given their due in assessing the economic factors behind Italy's intervention in the war.

The technically advanced industries of the peninsula—rails, machines, and motors—had struggles much like those of the steel firms. In the development of those enterprises, there was the same early need to expand beyond the small home market, in spite of the shield of a tariff barrier. These industries, too, depended on government orders and export possibilities that were often as much political as economic, and they show the same general pattern of foreign relations. Here, too, the Entente powers were often customers or collaborators, while the Central Powers were rivals. To be sure, there were areas in which the Italians competed with the British and French as well as with the Germans, but the rivalry with the Central Empires runs through the whole early development of the peninsula's mechanical industries and was particularly in evidence at the moment the war broke out.

The Italian railway shops and the electromechanical plants that served them offer a perfect example of the imbalance and the peculiar problems that afflicted the peninsula's industrial economy during its decade of growth. Although the manufacture of rail equipment and locomotives was not new in Italy, mass production really began after the state took over direct management of the main lines in 1905. The previous twenty-year experiment in private management of the rail lines had not succeeded. Constant interference by the state administration, labor troubles, and uncertainties over the renewal of the 1885 conventions during the years just before 1905, had led the private companies to refrain from doing anything to modernize the country's rail equipment and rolling stock. When the government, in what amounted to a last-minute decision, took back the lines, they were all badly in need of renovation and heavy new investment.[12]

The state shouldered this burden well, thanks largely to the new director, Riccardo Bianchi. Bianchi was a tough, practical rails expert with a purely technical engineering background who had been inherited from the old management. He resisted extraordinary pressures of all kinds and laid down a long-term plan of national self-sufficiency, according to which the new expanded Italian rail system would be supplied exclusively by the steel and machine industries of the peninsula itself.

Defying all criticisms, Bianchi bought forty-seven old English-Midland locomotives to meet the immediate needs of the national rail system and at the same time provided that all long-term orders for new, modern equipment should be placed with Italian firms. This insistence, in the optimism and speculative climate of the Giolitti decade, was enough to lead the men of the Società Bancaria, the steel trust, the steel firms of the North, and industrialists like Dante Ferraris to pour money into the development of new plants. Bianchi's new system, using cars with an all-metal framework, gave a special incentive to the steel industry, and the domestic electrical industries benefited from the new requirements for electrical signaling and telephonic communication throughout the system.

Through 1915 government orders were divided among eleven to fifteen firms, with Ansaldo and Breda heading the list. In the heady years 1905–8, the nation's industry expanded far beyond what the Italian rail administration foresaw as its regular yearly needs. It is hard to attribute this overexpansion entirely to speculative optimism. If domestic industry was really to fill Italy's needs in this field, it was bound to develop a productive capacity far beyond those needs. In this growth there was a technical as well as a financial necessity, the result of which was that in 1914 Italian rail and machine shops needed export and war orders to maintain profits and full employment.

In the years 1912–14 Italian rail shops managed to get some export orders from Bulgaria and Rumania over German and Austrian competition and political opposition. (Reportedly the Germans got the Bulgarian government to cancel a locomotive contract awarded to Breda in 1912.) Out of more than eight hundred cars that Bulgaria ordered from abroad in 1914, an Italian plant at Pinerolo managed to get a contract for twenty; this amounted to getting a foot in the door, at the most. But in the years just before the war, North Italian industry did succeed in entering an area still predominantly under German and Austro-Hungarian control. Italy's other rail customer was France. The French ordered not only mounted axles but railroad cars as well.[13]

Italian concern with the much discussed Danube-Adriatic rail line becomes understandable if the interests of the country's rail industry are taken into consideration. It seems quite natural that Italy should fear the hegemony of the Central Powers in the Balkans, since her industrial prospects there ran so clearly athwart those of Germany and Austria. In these respects the Italian rail industry exemplifies the parallel between Italian economic interests abroad, however speculative, and the lines of Italian political influence and expansion.

The Italian rail system was not only nationalized and geared to Italian domestic industry; it was also electrified in the Alpine lines, a necessity for a mountainous and fuel-poor country. The "white coal" of Italy's northern rivers was her only source of cheap energy. The Italians could have adopted the prevalent system of overhead electric traction, based on a combination of German and American patents, but that would have made the Italian system dependent on the AEG and its local affiliates.

Instead, a group of engineers, largely Hungarian by origin but working for a North Italian firm, developed a triphase system of traction, peculiar to Italy, that enabled the state administration to electrify the country's northern rail lines with purely Italian-made equipment. This was accomplished in the face of all sorts of German financial and diplomatic pressure, which was reinforced by the widespread preference for German methods among German-trained Italian engineers. Of the various prewar efforts at economic independence from the Germans, this was perhaps the most successful.

Even though it extended to only a small part of the nation's total rail lines, the electrification of Italian rails between 1905 and 1915 had real importance. It showed what Italian industry was capable of doing with its own resources, and rail electrification itself powerfully stimulated the further growth of the peninsula's machine and electro-mechanical shops in new directions. There was a certain historical redressing of the balance in this development. The original spread of railways in Italy right after unification did not have the shot-in-the-arm effect on domestic industries that similar developments had had in other countries, most notably Russia. This was at least partly attributable to the western European interests originally involved in Italian rails. But the striking modernization of the rail system by the Italian state between 1905 and 1915 made up, in some respects, for that old handicap, though what was done by the workings of private enterprise in more favored lands had to be the work of the state in Italy.[14]

The first experiments in electric-rail traction were made between 1898 and 1902 by private rail companies, with the condition that the state would purchase the installations that proved successful. This set a pattern of far-reaching cooperation between the state and private industry that lasted long after the nationalization of the rails in 1905. Most of the plants and lines that fed the electrified rail system were built by private companies, sometimes, like the Edison company, already functioning and sometimes especially set up for the purpose. The electric system thus organized remained in private hands for thirty years, after which the government entered into possession of it as a result of the payment of fixed yearly fees in addition to regular charges.

Italian rail electrification had effects beyond the electric-power industry itself. It benefited and spurred on a whole range of subsidiary industries, some of which had, or were destined to have, great importance in the peninsula. The state rail system ordered locomotives and big machinery from the Tecnomasio italiano Brown-Boveri (an affiliate of an Anglo-German firm) and from the Società Italiana Westinghouse, which had developed the original "Italian" triphase-traction system. Mannesmann and Falck were called on for the steel girders and pylons that upheld the new power lines. The great Italian industrialist Pirelli provided the insulated cables and wires, while Olivetti, a firm that had pioneered in domestic typewriter manufacturing, supplied electric gauges and meters. Ansaldo and other metal-working concerns supplied copper conductors, and the Milanese firm of Marelli was called on for motors and small electrical apparatus.

But nothing showed the extent of prewar Italian industrialization better than the rise of the Italian motor industry, which by 1914 had international importance.[15] The rise in Italy between 1898 and 1914 of a whole range of related industries—motors, automobiles, motorboats, ball bearings, rubber tires, and insulated electric wire and cables—is indeed impressive. This was, finally, the qualitative leap that put Italy in a class by herself among the nations of southern Europe and the Mediterranean. Italy's early entry into the fields only a short time after they had opened up in the great industrial centers of western Europe and America is in brilliant contrast to her lag in the earlier steam-coal-iron phases of the Industrial Revolution. Undoubtedly there are many reasons for the sudden spurt: economists would certainly attribute much of it to the new investment-banking systems introduced into the peninsula during the 1890s, and historians of culture would point to the unbroken Italian tradition of research and experimentation in the physical sciences, especially in magnetism and electricity. But the fundamental causes seem to be sheer technical expertise, low labor costs, and the development of hydroelectric power, which all together gave Italy a chance to supplement her previous sources of national income by offering a variety of industrial products and skills to the rest of the world, qualitatively, if not always quantitatively, on a par with the other industrial exporting nations.

The effects of the industrial spurt were twofold. Not only did Italy take a place, however modest, among the world's great industrial powers and thus join actively in the twentieth century's cycle of wars for the partition and repartition of the world, but the fatal cleavage between North and South, already marked at the time of unification, grew deeper as a result of the industrial transformation of a few northern regions. The "triangle" Milan-Turin-Genoa had no counterpart in Palermo-Naples-Bari.

The Italian state was concerned over the problem but could do little. A special law for Naples, adopted in 1904, provided hydroelectric power as well as customs and tax exemptions for industries set up there before 1914. The state also reserved one-eighth of all future rolling-stock orders for plants to be set up in the Naples area as one of the provisions of rail nationalization in 1905.

These measures failed to have any deep effect. The big steel plant at Bagnoli, built after the special law, remained an isolated monument to governmental good intentions and subsidies. Some rail industrialists were indeed induced to set up shops in Naples after 1905, but they were soon beset by troubles with an untrained and unruly local labor force in an area with strong revolutionary-syndicalist influences. The industrialists tried to introduce piecework to raise output, but that led to outright labor violence in 1908. The motor industries, without such initial ties to the state, never went south at all. By 1914 the regional gap was wider than ever and was becoming an important theme in the arguments justifying Italian expansion abroad.

The history of the Italian automobile and motor industry between 1899 and 1914 was brilliant—to all outward appearances. Italian auto manufacturers had won international trophies and entered world markets in grand style with models of recognized quality. Furthermore, the country's progress in motor manufacture was achieved with exclusively "national" financing; the ubiquitous Banca Commerciale did not take as much interest in automobiles as it had taken in the electric-power industry.[16]

As in other industries, the boom of 1900–6 had been followed by a severe depression in 1907, worldwide in scope, which eliminated all but the strongest auto firms. But after the deficit years 1908 and 1909, the industry's profits began to pick up again. The largest Italian manufacturer, Fiat, which made about half of all the cars produced in Italy, was by 1914 expanding fast and along many lines.

Fiat's achievement of genuine self-sufficiency was due to the drive and foresight of its head, Giovanni Agnelli. He was a well-to-do young man with excellent business and social connections whose family had belonged for some time to the Piedmontese agrarian upper-middle class. In 1853 the Agnellis established themselves at Villar Perosa, probably to be near one of the local silk mills—they specialized in mulberry cultivation. The mill was owned by the Ratti family, one of whose sons, in Agnelli's own generation, became Pope Pius XI. Agnelli was in some ways rather like that pontiff: both men represented the sober and work-centered Catholic ideal of North Italy, far from the rhetorical and operatic stereotypes that the rest of the peninsula had fostered.[17] In his formative years Agnelli was a fashionable cavalry officer, but he had a passion for experimenting with newfangled internal-combustion motors. After leaving the army, he took up the life of a country gentleman for a while, but again with unusual energy and persistence. For many years thereafter he was remembered in the surrounding countryside as a shrewd trader in livestock. But his passion for motors eventually took him away from

rural routine; he spent much time in Turin watching the first automobiles in operation. In 1899 he joined with some other enthusiasts,
nobles, men of means, and engineers in founding the Fiat works.

Agnelli was not primarily interested in the automobile as a
technical stunt or as a new sporting thrill, although he understood
these aspects of the new invention. From the start he considered
automobiles an industrial product, and he was the one person among
Fiat's founders capable of persuading aristocrats, financiers, engineers, and shop and production men to work together with the aim
of setting up a big automobile plant in Turin, with profits rather than
prestige as its goal. Though Agnelli's political views were elastic, he
could not help reflecting part of his military and religious background,
and there was in him much of the technician's and businessman's
distaste for politics.

In 1906 Agnelli, entering a competition reserved to cars of exclusively Italian make, noted that the only parts that still had to be
imported were the antifriction bearings from France. He promptly
set up a bearing plant in his native valley in the Alps west of Turin.
This enterprise, called RIV, prospered to the point of developing an
export market of its own, besides supplying Italian industry. By 1914
Italy had even entered the American market, in modest competition
with Germany and Sweden.

Yet this most outstanding example of Italy's industrial skills
and enterprise also serves to show the troubles inherent in the peninsula's industrial system—troubles arising out of economic dualism.
The North Italian motor industry was grafted onto a national body
unable to support it. The future for any nation's automobile industry
lay in mass production of standardized models. But in Italy such
production was difficult because of the restricted and lopsided character of the domestic market. Some Italian automobile buyers wanted
luxury and custom-built models, which domestic industry could indeed supply; but the Italians who wanted middle- and lower-priced
cars were by 1913 turning to German and, above all, American
manufacturers, who, starting with a true mass market at home, could
flood foreign markets with their low-cost, mass-produced output. On
the mass level Italian manufacturers found it hard to compete. Fiat
built its first "utilitarian" car in 1912, five years after the first Model-

T Ford appeared. It had a more powerful motor than comparable American models and cost more.

In fact, the Italian auto industry's rate of recovery and expansion after 1908, while clearly marked in absolute statistical terms, was relatively slow. Italian automobile exports increased between 1909 and 1913 at a rate almost equal to the French but far behind the British, German, and American. What American mass production meant can be gauged from the fact that in 1913, the last normal year, Italy sold 116 cars (of $205,931 total value) in the United States, while America sold 241 in Italy. This indicated a trend—the number of foreign cars imported into Italy increased between 1912 and 1913, and exports declined. Not only in the United States, but in western Europe and Latin America as well, Italians were faced with German and American competition in both light and heavy models. In countering demands by their workers, Italian auto makers were able to make much of American competition and narrowing profit margins. In fact, even though Italy was still exporting far more cars than she imported, the whole industry was in crisis on the eve of the war.

The troubles of the automobile industry were symptomatic of a more general uneasiness. The nature of the 1913–14 industrial crisis deserves close scrutiny because of its political and military implications. The economist Riccardo Bachi, surveying the economic situation of Italy in 1913, was particularly struck by the plight of certain sectors of industry: "The various branches of the mechanical industries, particularly railroad equipment, present a decidedly critical picture; certain export contracts have been concluded, but on not very favorable terms." Bachi gives some particulars: "Especially significant is the dissolution of a big company, with machine shops in Naples, after a large part of its capital had been lost, which is also an indication of the difficulties of industries that have been created there artificially." Ominously, Bachi points out that in this field "almost the only profits came from munitions making"; some railroad equipment firms were turning to other branches of manufacturing, with military orders constantly increasing.[18]

Things were no better in the automotive industry. Bachi observed that the 1913 auto-export figures, though lower than those of 1912, were still artificially high because unsold stocks were included in the reported amount of cars exported. This was especially true for Argentina and Brazil. The same ominous possibility loomed for this industry as for rails: "The industry has been helped by large orders for automobiles, trucks, and bicycles for military use." The auto industry also got orders for marine engines; these, too, were mostly military.

The Credito Provinciale (not yet merged with the Società Bancaria to form the Sconto) came to similar conclusions in its report for 1913.[19] It found industrial activity sluggish, with automobile manufacturing, in particular, suffering from overproduction. There was an exception: "Those steel firms that dedicate themselves to war materials," which "have been able to count on a reasonable profit." That was, however, only gray relief against a darker background: the economist Gino Borgatta, in a survey of Italian corporations on the eve of the war, reported that profits in steel for 1913 were 6.3 percent compared to profits of only 5.52 percent for capital invested in mechanical industries. These were mediocre returns at best, and it was natural enough, Borgatta noted, that Italian investors shied from putting money into those branches of industry.[20]

A closer look at Italy's biggest automobile firm only gives substance to these general findings. Fiat branched out and diversified its production to meet pre-1914 crisis conditions. Even before 1909 the budding empire shared in developing the Stassano electrical steel furnace. Now it went into public transportation and war production. Agnelli joined with makers of steel, rail equipment, and armaments in the Fiat–San Giorgio combine to manufacture submarine and other diesel engines. His associates included Vittorio Diatto, head of one of the country's chief rail-equipment firms, and the arms maker Dante Ferraris. Thus the rail and automobile industrialists, facing the same problems, found a common solution—war production.[21]

At the beginning of April 1915, when Italy was already irrevocably committing herself to the Allies, Russia signed a contract with Fiat-San Giorgio providing for the Italian firm to give technical aid in designing warships of the Italian type, to be built in Russian yards, with the Italians to receive from 3.5 to 5 percent of the price of the completed vessels.

In 1916 a much bigger deal, in which Fiat was to provide Russia with an entire line of automobiles and trucks, was worked out. The necessary credits were arranged by consortia of Russian and Italian banks, and the deal would have amounted to a windfall for Italian motor industries if the Russian Revolution had not truncated matters. Since money had already changed hands, the Italians wound up as the losers; the Banca Commerciale alone lost over 3.3 million lire.

Italian heavy and medium industry presents a remarkable coalition of interests. The Agnelli-Ferraris-Diatto combination turns up on the board of Industrie Metallurgiche Torino, which in turn owned 45 percent of the Società Italiana per la fabbricazione dei proiettili, set up in 1911. Ferraris, a vice-president of Fiat, was also a director of Fiat-San Giorgio along with Agnelli. They were associated in that firm with Giuseppe Orlando of Terni and Attilio Odero, another participant in the steel trust who was also a top executive in various Genoese shipyards and automotive and rail-equipment plants. The Diatto brothers, together with Dante and Federico Ferraris, participated in owning and running two rail-machine shops, one at Turin and the other at Naples, with a total capital of 7 million lire. In 1914 Dante Ferraris also served on the board of another North Italian rail concern, the Officine Meccaniche of Reggio Emilia. During these years Ferraris was also president of the big northern manufacturing concern, Giovanni Gilardini, which had a varied production, including military supplies and shoes.[22]

Another striking example of interlocking ownership and management was the Società Metallurgica Italiana. The firm started with a sale of 2,652 tons of its products in 1893 and rose to 13,588 tons in 1911, a growth that was due mostly to the government's demand for cartridges. The firm's directorate reads like a roll-of-honor of Italian industry. Pirelli, Orlando, and Odero are the first names to strike the eye, but Commendatore Saverio Parisi is also there. The Parisis had big real estate holdings, ran a provincial railway system, and were linked by marriage to the Perrone brothers of Ansaldo.[23]

The web of relations joins the managers of the steel trust, so dependent on the Commerciale, to Pirelli, the rubber magnate, who was on the board of the Credito Italiano; to Agnelli of Fiat; and even to the fiercely independent Ansaldo group. In 1914 there was a nationwide, coalesced Italian industrial interest, identifiable both personally and institutionally.

Ominously, Fiat found that war paid much better than public transportation. In 1913 it actually lost money in that field, in spite of government subsidies for Italian bus lines and the brilliant showing of Fiat trucks in the 1912 St. Petersburg–Moscow route competitions. On the other hand, Fiat, together with its new associates in the rail and machine industries, made a profit by manufacturing submarine engines. Models were sold to the navies of Britain, Sweden, Denmark, Portugal, the United States, and Germany. The last, noted Fiat, was the only case on record in which the Germans ordered naval motors abroad. At the outbreak of the War, Fiat was finishing a submarine for the Russian navy. Its yards at La Spezia were even becoming an object of espionage and counterespionage, a sure sign of the firm's growing military importance.[24]

Naturally, Fiat found the best customer for its naval production in the Italian state, which also made extensive use of Fiat trucking on the sands of Libya during the Italo-Turkish war of 1911–12. Thus the Italian motor industry, which had arisen as an outstanding example of purely individual private enterprise and talent, was by 1914 becoming as closely dependent on the state as the other sectors of Italian heavy and medium industry were.

Indicative of this new state of affairs in the Italian mechanical industry were the reports appearing in *Il Sole* in October and November 1913. After announcing that the big motor and rail-equipment firm Officine Meccaniche of Milan had built two engines for Italian torpedo boats, an 8-million-lire contract, *Il Sole* went on to assure its readers that this would serve to dispel the pessimistic rumors that had been going around concerning that company's solvency. In fact, noted the Milanese paper, the Italian navy was ceasing to import marine motors from other countries and would in the future rely solely on domestic industry.

Another great North Italian engine-manufacturing firm, Franco Tosi of Legnano, shows the same pattern of development.

Tosi started in 1876 as a repair shop for cotton-mill machinery and went on to manufacture boilers and steam engines on its own account. By 1898 the company figured that its machines already in operation generated some 150,000 horsepower, of which 30,000 were outside Italy—in Spain, the Middle East, and Russia. These exports played an important part in the firm's development even before its big twentieth-century expansion.

Tosi's new lines of production—turbines, diesels, and generators—were developed between 1900 and 1916, mainly as a result of the Italian navy's torpedo-boat program. Like Fiat, Tosi found that war production could also bring in profits from abroad: the firm made four torpedo-boat engines for Rumania.

The final integration of Tosi into the emerging Italian state-industrial complex came in the spring of 1914, when the company decided to open a shipyard of its own at Taranto, far from the industrial North. The state made available much of the necessary waterfront land on exceptionally easy terms, as well as promising naval repair and construction orders large enough to make the otherwise uneconomic enterprise profitable. Tosi was acting in 1914 on the promptings of unidentified "political and industrial figures," although the assurances of the navy's general staff are mentioned as having been decisive.

In this way Tosi had in the first years of the century jumped from "semicraft" machine making into full-fledged industrial operations. But the workings of spontaneous economic forces, sometimes so favorable to Italian technical skill and enterprise, had been supplemented, and to some extent even overridden, by the "intervention" of the government. In this case, the intervention amounted to a partnership between the firm and the state military establishment.[25]

Tosi's dependence on exports or war orders set a pattern for the whole sector. The Società Anonima Bauchiero of Turin reported in its September 1911 balance: "If the construction of railroad material . . . has undergone a certain reduction . . . the war that Italy has undertaken in Libya has, on the other hand, offered the opportunity of putting the plant's industrial potential and perfected organization at the service of the country." The company was among the principal war contractors, proud of its promptness in deliveries and of its ability to manufacture on short notice "the most varied articles" for the Ministry of War. The almost equally important S.A. Meccanica

Lombarda of Milan reported in June 1911 that its production and profits were rising but that one-quarter of its yearly output went abroad. This induced the firm to spread out its foreign operations and seek new outlets in previously untapped countries.[26]

A few Italian industrialists were able to develop and expand their enterprises abroad through alliances with capitalists of other nations. Among these men Riccardo Gualino and G. B. Pirelli stand out as pioneers.

Gualino made part of his fortune by importing American soft larch into Italy. By 1911 he was president of the Unione Italiana Cementi and chief administrator of his own S.A. Riccardo Gualino. In his 1912 report Gualino said that his company was gradually "spreading its tentacles abroad" in an effort to become self-sufficient in construction materials and then to go into business in foreign markets. He started buying timberland throughout eastern Europe and in 1913 concluded an agreement with British lumber interests to create a new joint firm for that purpose. That enterprise was aided by a holding company, the Società delle Foreste Rumene, set up in Geneva in March 1914 with a capital of 22 million francs to sell shares of various eastern European lumber companies. Through the holding company Gualino entered into a complex of relations with foreign and domestic capital; on its board were representatives of three Viennese banks and one each of the Banca Commerciale, the Società Bancaria, and the Louis Dreyfus Bank of Paris.

But Gualino's real backing was British, and many of his interests lay in British and American enterprises and products. He seems to have had no relations whatever with Germany, but he saw Russia as the land of opportunity. Even before the war he contracted to build a residential section of St. Petersburg.[27]

Pirelli's operations were similar, though more solid and important. He had opened the first modest rubber-goods factory in Milan in 1872 and had developed specialties in insulated wires, cables, and eventually automobile tires. By 1914 he was much the biggest, though not the sole, Italian manufacturer in that field.[28] The capitalization and volume of business of the Società Pirelli put it in a class with Fiat as one of the peninsula's greatest industrial concerns.

Pirelli not only exported Italian-made rubber products and re-conditioned rubber but set up his own plants outside Italy, the first Italian industrialist to do so. Some of his foreign operations were financed by British capital—and for a good reason. Pirelli's great export trade in cables and electric wiring was with Argentina, and it was precisely there that German competition was keenest. In 1913 Italy sold about 2.68 million lire worth of wire and cables in Argentina and 2.8 million worth of other rubber articles. In May 1914 an Italian business journal noted, "The field for these industries can become more fruitful if we can in the future stand up against the ruthless competition of Germany. . . . In the last few years, the Germans have not only got a near monopoly on the production and distribution of electric light and power, but they have also expelled foreigners, especially Italians, from the management and labor force of existing plants that have come under their control." In fact, though notable in some cases, the Italian share of automotive, mechanical, and electrical imports to Argentina was always behind the German.[29]

These facts have a special bearing on the situation of Italian industry. In the South American market, the industrial powers were competing on purely economic terms. When big European powers jockeyed for industrial opportunities in the eastern Mediterranean, it was possible to view the contest as part of a military and political expansionism. But the rivalry between Germany and Italy in South America reveals something about the two countries' pressing need to export and suggests certain parallels in their industrial structures, in spite of their obvious differences in resources.

Pirelli met the situation by extending his operations elsewhere. He had a profitable branch already operating in Spain and in January 1914 joined with General Electric to form a London corporation, Pirelli-General Cable Works, Ltd., to serve the British Isles and the empire. Another Pirelli enterprise, the Società del Linoleum of Milan, made most of its profits through a branch in Switzerland, where it ran a hydroelectric plant as well as a factory and entered into sales agreements with its German and British competitors.

The prevalent pattern in Italian industry from 1911 to 1915 was, then, one of competition with Germany and cooperation with

Britain and France. Italian arms manufacturing, in particular, was geared to the Entente long before the government moved to change sides.

But there were other links as well. The growing production of phosphates and sulphuric acid in Italy in the years just before 1914 was made possible by French financing and French resources. The big Montecatini firm, run by the Donegani family, was backed domestically by the Banca Commerciale and the Credito Italiano, but it had support from four Parisian financial and industrial sources, which were represented on its board. And the Doneganis and the Orlandos joined Senator Leon Mougeot of the French Republic and the French engineer Charles Michel to set up further efforts in the fields of fertilizers and sulphuric acid. This network of interests embraced French companies in Tunisia, the French mining firm in Laurium, and the Società Maremanna, which supplied electricity to the Leghorn area. A vertical organization was in the making.[30] This branch of the chemical industry was just beginning to assume real importance before the war; thus the presence of French, rather than German, financial and technical interests in it is of special interest.

Statesmen and industrialists, patriots all, had worked together during the gray years of the old Left to make Italy self-sufficient in naval armaments, an indispensable prerequisite to her becoming a great power. The great developers—Brin, Bombrini, the Orlandos, Breda—had pursued that aim publicly and privately. In the process the country had paid heavily—directly through military contracts and higher transportation costs, indirectly through tariff-sustained prices —to have its own blast furnaces, steel mills, and shipyards. What return did the country get for these sacrifices? Had it achieved naval autarky?

An Italian nationalist, Giorgio Molli, tried to answer these questions in a little book that came out on the eve of the war. He concluded that Italy had acquired a substantial military-industrial complex without shaking off her dependence on the foreign arms makers. Even worse, the country was tied to Schneider of France through Ansaldo and to Vickers-Armstrong of Britain through Terni. Current experience was showing what those ties meant.

Recently Italy had projected forty-eight naval cannon of 305-mm for her new ships of the line, the heaviest type of gun Italian plants could make. Only three of the cannon were to be made abroad; Italian plants got orders for the other forty-five. But the Italians were unable to fill the orders, and subcontracted them to their "mother firms" in Britain. Eventually, only eighteen of the guns were made in Italy, much to the parliament's surprise.

In 1913 Italy, still a member of the Triple Alliance, was awaiting delivery of naval guns from England and artillery models from France, both her prospective foes.

How had this come about? Why had three decades of work and expense left Italy an industrial tributary? Molli's answer was simple and convincing: Italy had never been able to keep up with new developments; the goal of autarky kept receding. Continual innovations and the unprecedented size and number of new vessels needed to stay in the twentieth-century arms race had thwarted Italy's efforts. After 1908 her industries had been swamped and overwhelmed by new naval demands. Under the circumstances, Molli thought, it would have been better if Italy had admitted her inadequacies and ordered the largest available guns from abroad instead of maintaining the "made-in-Italy" fiction at the cost of underarming her battle fleet. It all amounted to yet another Terni scandal, only more appalling because of the imminence of war.[31]

Molli concluded that Italian war industries, which drew perforce on foreign sources, should gear themselves to Italy's prospective allies, not to her foes. This realignment would have reversed a trend that had prevailed since 1906.

3

The Shipping Industry

Of all sectors of Italian industry, shipping was most directly involved with the state and its expansion. In every respect, the maritime industry offers the clearest example of the economic and political patterns that also prevailed in steel, motors, and rails. Here, even more than elsewhere, there is a contrast between the modest but solid fruits of spontaneous economic enterprise and the swollen, artificial demand created by a government-military-industrial complex. Here, as elsewhere, directorates and ownerships interlocked, tying shipping lines to the big northern investment banks; to the steel trust; and, quite directly, to Nationalist political representatives. There are the same lines of foreign competition and foreign cooperation, but with this significant difference: the Italian lines' growing rivalry with Austro-Hungarian shipping interests directly paralleled Italy's most pressing foreign-policy concerns.

Italy's problems of maritime competition in the eastern Mediterranean became directly related to the questions of naval hegemony in the Adriatic and the imperiled Italian populations of Austria-Hungary's Adriatic ports. The irredentist movements reflect this development. What in 1880 was a purely local question of ethnic identity had by 1914 become another aspect of economic rivalries reaching from Trieste and Fiume to Asia Minor and beyond, even to India. The irredentist movements of the Adriatic provinces became the political reflection of the competition between two state-backed industrial-commercial complexes. A detailed look at Italian shipping interests will help to explain the reasons for postwar Italian insistence on what now seem secondary points—Fiume and Zara, with their small and isolated Italian populations—as well as the general Italian interest in the partition of Asiatic Turkey, an interest that was very much alive by 1914. The fact that Italian-speaking and Greek- or Turkish-speaking coastal areas alike fell within the range of Italian concern and penetration shows that economic and strategic considerations were uppermost in the formulation of Italian policy as a connected whole.

At first glance, one curious feature stands out in the maritime sector of Italy's economy: the subsidies and bounties that the Italian state paid to the merchant marine were always linked—both in legislative enactment and in the popular mind—to the exemptions and subsidies extended to the shipbuilders as equal parts of a national drive toward independence, self-sufficiency, and military preparedness on the high seas. It was understandable that prominent economists, notably Einaudi and Corbino, should be indignant over this fact. After all, ship operation and shipbuilding are, from a purely economic point of view, quite separate activities.[1]

In any case, the economists' objections had little effect. The interests that had every reason to complain—the big shipping lines—were by 1911 in large part controlled by the same banking and industrial groups that operated or backed the great shipyards of the North (exception being made, as usual, for Ansaldo), and it was natural enough for them to accept a system that assured benefits to the whole sector.

The reader will recall the importance that shipyards had in the strange and partly artificial rise of Italy's heavy industries. The Ansaldo, Orlando, and Odero yards survived the 1870–90 slump only by grace of some navy contracts. But they had gone on to develop their own special lines of boiler and machine construction. More important, Orlando and Odero had early entered into the management of Terni and the steel trust.

The connection between subsidized shipyards and protected steel was natural enough from a political and financial standpoint, however questionable its effect on the nation's economic health. Less apparent but equally important in bringing to light the network of interests that underlay prewar Italian expansion was the close financial connection between steel, shipbuilding, and the subsidized shipping lines operating in the Adriatic, the eastern Mediterranean, and the seas beyond Suez. That link appears in an examination of the actual situation of Italian shipbuilding between 1911 and 1914. Since the development of steamships, Italian shipyards had always existed by virtue of state subsidies and lavish naval contracts. This situation was formalized by a 1911 law that allowed builders of merchant ships to import, duty-free, one-quarter of the iron necessary for the hull. For the other three-quarters, the builder had a choice: he could import steel or iron from abroad, paying the necessary duty and receiving from the state a duty remission of about nine lire per quintal, or he could buy the metal in Italy, with government "compensation" of about ten lire per quintal. (The 1887 tariff on sheet metal varied from twelve to fifteen lire per quintal, in inverse proportion to the thickness of the sheet.) Thus, if the shipbuilders used Italian metal, they would be paid an amount greater than what they would have gained in duty remission had they used imported metal.

The shipbuilding aids fixed by law were not merely a disguised price support for the domestic steel industry. Out of the 5,047,480 lire that the state paid in shipbuilding subsidies in 1913, duty remissions amounted to 1,675,400 lire, while the bounties for Italian-built machinery and boilers amounted to 1,044,000 lire: thus the growing mechanical sector of Italian industry got its cut out of the public funds. Little wonder, then, that the machine builder Ernesto Breda should take his place along with the shipbuilder Orlando in managing new state-subsidized Italian shipping lines.[2]

What were Italian shipyards actually doing during the prewar subsidy years 1911–14? Not much, in comparison to the other big maritime powers; even Austria-Hungary had more tonnage under construction. In 1914 Italy had only 55,690 tons under construction, compared with her rival's 80,145.

Italian shipyards had essentially three kinds of customers: the Italian navy, the navies of a few nonindustrial minor powers, and Italian shipping lines operating with government subsidies. The free merchant marine, which consisted mostly of freighters and tramps in the hands of small and medium-sized operators, always preferred buying ships abroad—for the most part from Britain but occasionally from Germany. At the end of 1914 barely one-third of the Italian merchant marine's gross tonnage was of domestic make. Only in the largest and newest categories, most likely to be used by state-subsidized lines operating under special legal requirements, did Italian-made seacraft outnumber those purchased abroad. Even the two biggest subsidized lines, Navigazione Generale and the newly formed Servizi Marittimi, ordered only half of their new 1914 liners from Italian yards; the other half were to come from Britain and Germany.[3]

The important yards at Riva Trigoso were building seven vessels in June of 1913, all but one of them for state or state-subsidized customers. Five of them were motorships, fuel tankers for the Italian navy; one was a 3,985-ton steamer for Servizi Marittimi; and one, by far the largest, was for the transatlantic passenger-emigrant service of the Ligure-Brasiliana line. Of the navy tankers, three were fitted out with Tosi diesel engines, while the other two had identical Fiat motors, an excellent illustration of the tie between shipbuilding and the more recent branches of Italian industry.

The order from Servizi Marittimi is worth noting. The Riva Trigoso yards belonged to Cantieri Navali Riuniti, which were acquired by the Piaggio interests in 1913. But the Piaggios headed a management that included Giuseppe Toeplitz of the Banca Commerciale, as well as Ignazio Florio and Emilio Menada of Navigazione Generale. Exactly the same interests predominated in the newly formed Servizi Marittimi, headed by Ernesto Breda, whose machine manufacturing was heavily backed by the Commerciale. The link between subsidized navigation and state-favored shipbuilding could hardly have been more direct, although, as was often the case, it ran through a great investment bank. It was natural, therefore, for one part of the great complex to favor another. Indeed, in the spring of 1914 Servizi Marittimi ordered two ships for the state-subsidized express lines to Egypt. One order was placed in Hamburg, and the other, predictably, went to Riva Trigoso.[4]

The Odero shipyards were in a similar situation in 1913: their customers were—for civilian craft—the Mexican navy, Navigazione Generale, and the Italian subsidiary of Standard Oil, which had ordered two big tankers. It is likely that some understanding between Italian and American big business lay behind the last order, since

Standard Oil's Italian company was by far the biggest petroleum supplier in Italy. As for the Navigazione Generale's patronizing Odero, this is hardly surprising. The Oderos sat on most of the steel trust's boards. This tied them into the Banca Commerciale complex, since both the steel trust and the Navigazione Generale lines were backed by that institution. The connections between the great bank and Navigazione Generale were particularly close: two of the shipping line's directors, Ignazio Florio and Emilio Menada, were also directors of the Commerciale; and Federico Weil, one of the company's real managers, sat on the Navigazione Generale's board. The banker Cesare Balduino also belonged to both managements. And Balduino sat, together with the Oderos, on the board that managed Terni. His presence there shows the common bond (through the Banca Commerciale) that joined Odero the shipbuilder with Florio the shipping-line operator, and it was natural that the one should give his business to the other.[5]

The shipping lines themselves have a more varied history than the shipyards. They were more numerous and combined a wider range of interests, though they were not independent. Most of the country's steamship lines were tied into the larger banking-industrial complexes of the peninsula—and to an almost mathematically precise degree. All four of Italy's big investment banks had committed themselves heavily in this sector by 1913.

The Banca Commerciale took part in the financing of the Navigazione Generale, which was much the biggest of those enterprises, and joined forces with Credito Italiano to expand Servizi Marittimi, in which Navigazione Generale was heavily interested. Servizi Marittimi, reorganized just before the First World War, was to ply the new state-subsidized routes in the eastern Mediterranean. Other banks did what they could: for instance, the crisis of the clerical Banco di Roma was reflected in its maritime commitments. In 1912 Servizi Marittimi had Ernesto Breda as its president, with Commerciale backing, but Romolo Tittoni of the Banco di Roma was one of its two vice-presidents. When the company, still under Breda's leadership, was enlarged and reorganized in March 1913, Credito Italiano stepped in, and the Banco di Roma disappeared from the new company's directorate.[6]

But the Banca Commerciale of Milan always led. The Commerciale's Venetian associates, an influential group of aristocrats, senators, and bankers headed by Giuseppe Volpi, had a smaller shipping line of their own, the Società Veneziana di navigazione a vapore. This company served state-subsidized routes in the upper Adriatic and the run from Italian ports to Calcutta. Although its assets and profits were slight compared with those of the Volpi group's real industrial base, the electrical network of the Veneto, the steamship line nevertheless had a disproportionate political and financial importance as part of the Commerciale's far-flung oriental operations, which Volpi directed.[7]

Significantly, in 1913, the year when Italy stepped up her efforts to penetrate Albania, the Aegean, and Asia Minor, one of Volpi's companies, the Società Commerciale d'Oriente, essentially the foreign subsidiary of the Banca Commerciale, joined in refinancing and managing the Puglia line, which up to then had been a small, struggling enterprise. Puglia was based at Bari and served state-subsidized routes in the lower Adriatic between South Italy and the principal ports of Albania.[8]

In these various ways the Commerciale complex was involved in the shipping lines of Liguria, Venetia, and Apulia, a breadth of interests beyond the reach of the other Italian investment banks, which tended to concentrate in one area of enterprise.

The Banco di Roma had a one-third share in the capital of the new Sicilia line, which took over the bank's Libyan shipping line in 1913; two of the bank's representatives, Benucci and Tittoni, sat on the board of directors. One-sixth of the new line's capital was furnished by the Piaggio interests of Genoa; half of the line's ownership was in local hands. Among the Sicilian shareholders was a scion of the island's most ancient nobility, Giuseppe Lanza di Scalea, whose family had stooped to contract matrimonial alliance with the Florios of Navigazione Generale. Like the other lines mentioned above, the Sicilia was set up to serve state-subsidized lines.[9]

Two years before it joined with Pogliani to found the Sconto, the Società Bancaria had also gone into shipping. This Parisian-Italian bank had interests in common with the Genoese line Lloyd Sabaudo, which after some bad years in peacetime commerce had suddenly done well during the Italo-Turkish war. The Società Bancaria joined Lloyd Sabaudo in 1912 to found Marittima Italiana, which was to serve the upper-Tyrhennian lines that the state had authorized—including the route to Bombay.[10]

The financial underpinning provided between 1910 and 1914 by four big banks is strongly reminiscent of the refinancing of the steel trust in 1911. The ventures all had one feature in common: the guaranteed support and liability of the state, manifested by legislation or executive decisions, always in conformity with a tradition of national interest going back at least to 1876.

As for interlocking directorates, representatives of Milanese and Turinese finance sat side by side with Genoese shipowners, and the same names turn up on one board after another. In 1914 Lloyd Italiano's president was Senator Count Gerolamo Rossi-Martini, who was also associated with Walther Rathenau in Genoese electrical companies. Also on the Lloyd board were Domenico Brunelli and Dionigi Biancardi, directors of another Viennese line, La Veloce, where they sat on the same board with Federico Weil of the Banca Commerciale. Nor did Lloyd Italiano lack a director from the world of party politics—the Nationalist deputy Luigi Medici, who also figured prominently in the management of the steel trust. The subsidized shipping lines and the steel trust could not have been linked more directly than by such representatives.[11]

But in many ways the shipping lines were more important, more deeply rooted in the glories of the past, than the other sectors of the state-industrial complex. Nor were the practical possibilities of Italy's maritime resurgence so fantastic or farfetched. A nation without adequate fuel and ore might indeed find it hard to make a place for itself among the world's industrial powers, but Italian seamanship and enterprise could still place Italy among the great maritime nations.

The Italian steamship lines were in fact the oldest and best established part of the complex, antedating unification itself. The first of them was founded by Raffaele Rubattino of Genoa in 1838, in the same decade that Austria began its ventures in steam navigation at Trieste.

Rubattino was a pioneer of steam navigation in Italy; Italian shippers generally clung to sails until the opening of the Suez Canal made steam engines a necessity.[12] Politically he began as a Mazzini adherent and after 1850 became a supporter of the new liberal Piedmontese state, which rewarded him with postal subsidies. Rubattino also made his ships available to Pisacane and Garibaldi for their revolutionary expeditions, though without compromising himself directly: Cavour seems to have protected him against possible losses.

The most notable of Rubattino's supporters in parliament was Garibaldi's great lieutenant, Nino Bixio, mariner and soldier, who already envisioned Italy's future as a great sea power. Though the new state sponsored no industrial systems under the Right, Rubattino's line was voted subsidies in 1862 and again in 1868.

Rubattino's success was partly due to the digging of the Suez Canal, which spurred Italy to take a new look at her maritime prospects. Why should not Venice and Genoa, situated squarely athwart the new lines between East and West, regain their lost leadership on the seas? In 1868, on the eve of the canal's grand opening, the Italian naval ministry called on the nation's shippers to prepare to meet and eventually overcome foreign competition on the new sea routes. Rubattino promptly offered the government the draft of a contract for operating lines from Italy to the Indies, and he opened, on his own, a new service from Genoa to Alexandria, forestalling any possible domestic rivals.

The government was pleased with Rubattino's plan. He wanted to order five new steamers for the Indies line—of a sort that could easily be turned into transports for troops and horses—and all he asked from the state was an interest-free loan of 4 million, not much to pay for an auxiliary naval force. Parliament approved the convention forthwith, in a single stroke laying the foundations for a future colonial empire and for a lasting alliance between the state and private industry. The initial operation was modest enough, but the policy decision proved to be far-reaching and irreversible.

In March 1870 one of Rubatino's steamers paid a visit to Assab, on the Red Sea coast and bought the bay from the local "sultans." The purchase prepared for the birth of Italian East Africa.

During the previous decade, Bixio had seen the desirability of a fueling station on the Red Sea coast, since the Suez Canal was soon to open; and one especially energetic ex-missionary, Giuseppe Sapeto, succeeded in interesting Victor Emmanuel II in the Bay of Assab as the Italian base. Assab fell under no recognized sovereignty, and, Sapeto reported, the local tribes and potentates would sell the bay to Italy for a few thousand silver thalers.

The real obstacle was Italy's uncertain and isolated position among the powers of Europe on the eve of the Franco-Prussian War. The government preferred not to stake out an African colony officially, an act that might arouse international antagonisms and jealousies. The acquisition of Assab was not by the Italian navy but by Rubattino. The new colony, as yet unmanned, was the property of the Rubattino line, which had clearly acted at the behest of a timid and hesitant government.

The new colony lay fallow for the next decade, a subject of desultory diplomatic interchanges between Italy, Britain, and the khedive, who claimed sovereignty over the whole Red Sea coast of Africa. In fact, Egyptian troops had gone through Assab a few days after Rubattino's expedition and destroyed the markers he had left to indicate his proprietorship over the bay. This mattered little, since Rubattino's ship operations in the Red Sea were petty and served merely as formal support for his title to Assab.

Finally, in 1879, with Egypt in a state of collapse, the Italian government decided to appear under its own colors. During the next two years, the state bought out Rubattino's concession and started a genuine colonial policy. By then the Genoese shipowner was concerned with bigger African business operations, although at the end of ten years he had netted a profit of perhaps 300,000 lire as a result of buying and selling the Bay of Assab without having invested or risked anything himself. Colonial partnership with the state was not a losing proposition.

The last part of Rubattino's life was full of new ventures, stimulated by the accession to power of the parliamentary Left in 1876. The Left could not have arrived at a worse time, economically: even Suez had proved to be no boon to Italian commerce. On the contrary, the new lines in the Mediterranean showed how little Italy had to offer on the world's markets and how far she lagged technically as a maritime carrier. Rubattino himself had to switch some of his commercial shipping to Trieste or Marseilles to stay in business.

But Rubattino got a new role with the Left. He was elected to the Chamber of Deputies as a Depretis-Left deputy in 1876 and soon entered into a partnership with the Italian government in Tunisia. Rubattino had always run a subsidized service between Tunis and Italian ports; in 1879 he bought the country's only railway from a London firm. In this he risked very little; his financial returns were guaranteed by the state treasury. As the Left saw it, the time was ripe for establishing an Italian overlordship in Tunisia, where Italian settlers far outnumbered other European groups. Neither Rubattino nor his political sponsors foresaw the sudden showdown, the real test of strength in the summer of 1881 that turned Tunisia into a French protectorate and wiped out all chances for Italian penetration there.

The Tunisian disaster was part of a generally depressing picture, and Italy's prospects as a great sea power faded. The plight of the shipyards has been discussed earlier; the situation in steam navigation was not much better, thanks to an international slump in shipping rates. The French responded in 1880 with lavish subsidies for their merchant shipping, and the Italian government immediately followed suit. The French could perhaps afford that luxury, but the consequences to Italy were grave.

The Italian government's solution was to sponsor the formation of a single steamship line, representing most of the Italian capital investment in shipping, which would operate the state-subsidized lines in the Mediterranean and the East. Called the Navigazione Generale, the line was a merger of the only two subsidized steamship lines in Italy, Rubattino of Genoa and Florio of Palermo.

Florio was a multimillionaire who, like the Genoese, had come up from petty beginnings. The Florios had started as small dealers in spices and other imports in Palermo in the early nineteenth century. In the 1820s Vincenzo Florio, founder of the dynasty, entered the tuna fish business and became rich. His fishing fleet was the nucleus of the family's other shipping enterprises, which involved transporting sulphur, Sicily's principal natural resource. The family then got into credit banking to finance sulphur exports. By 1881 Senator

Ignazio Florio, Vincenzo's heir, owned forty-five steamships and an even larger number of sailing vessels. He was not only a power in Sicily but had excellent connections in Rome.

After unification, Bixio and Orlando had suggested a merger between the Palermitan and the Genoese steamer lines, and Rubattino and Florio did begin to share agencies and services, but matters dragged on until the French maritime subsidies of 1880. At that time Rubattino turned his line into a joint-stock company to make the merger with Florio possible. Parliament authorized the formation of the Navigazione Generale in 1881.

In the course of its many ministries, the Left made fundamental decisions that set much of the course of Italian development, both politically and economically, but that measure was among the most important, ranking with the naval program and the tariff law in its consequences. The Marxist-oriented historian G. Carocci notes that "while most of the industrial interests that met with the Left's favor were still of slight strength, the Florio and Rubattino lines represented dominating interests, and just in these years, thanks to the weakness of their competitors and to help from the government, they became, for all practical purposes, a monopolistic power with the creation of the Navigazione Generale, endowed with a capital of 100 millions."[13]

The ties between the Navigazione Generale and the state became stronger in the course of a colonial venture in which Italy's genuine economic interests were hardly involved at all.

The new line, which had eighty-nine steamships totaling 67,000 tons, became one of the chief beneficiaries of the Left's East African empire building. In both 1887 and 1896 the line transported the army's African expeditionary forces, while maintaining its own regular postal and commercial services.

By then, the Navigazione Generale had become the first part of the state-industrial complex; and without the initial nucleus of financial and industrial interests that the line represented, the other elements of heavy industry might not have come into being at all. As described in chapter 1, Ignazio Florio had an important part in founding the Elba steel industry only three years after the East African operations had reached their height. The financing, operating, and servicing of steamships seems to have been one of the principal starting points for the formation of broader industrial undertakings on the peninsula, and this holds true not only for the growth of financial resources but for the fostering of technical skills and a favorable political climate as well. In a sense the national shipping system supplied the industrial shot in the arm that foreign-dominated rail development had failed to provide, but it was not enough to make up for basic Italian losses in the 1880s and 1890s.

From the 1890s to the First World War, the ties binding the Navigazione Generale to the state proved unbreakable. In 1909 the great shipping line was able to thwart Giolitti himself when he tried to loosen the ties: in that episode, as we have seen, the components of Banca Commerciale group, of which Navigazione Generale was a part, acted together; and from then on the shipping line and its affiliates were as privileged as the steel trust.

In September 1913 the Navigazione Generale announced that it had acquired a large share of the reorganized Servizi Marittimi, which the big industrial banks had set up, together with Ernesto Breda, to serve the new state-subsidized lines in the Mediterranean. The Navigazione Generale's directors proudly explained that they had taken that step at the request of a highly placed source (*"anche in omaggio ad un alto desiderio manifestato"*), a reference either to the cabinet or, more likely, to the royal house itself.[14] A look at the company's directors suggests what sort of connection Navigazione Generale enjoyed in those circles.

The president of the line was the Sicilian blue blood Francesco Lanza Spinelli, prince of Scalea-Trabia. The family went back to Norman-Swabian times, but in the Third Italy it had found a new field of conquest in finance and industry. One member of the family was among the founders of the Sicilia line in 1913.

Francesco di Scalea was known in the Depretis-Crispi period as the financier of the Sicilian railroad system; he married Giulia Florio, daughter of Ignazio, and thus became a member of the board that directed Navigazione Generale. The offspring of this union, Prince Pietro di Scalea, became undersecretary of foreign affairs in Giolitti's great cabinet of 1911–14, one of the small group of Sicilians and South Italians that seconded the imperialist foreign policy of Di San Giuliano. In all this there is a curious Sicilian collusion: the foreign minister was a Sicilian, his lieutenant was a Sicilian, the Navigazione Generale was largely in Sicilian hands, and all of these islanders belonged to related families or, at least, to the same social class. The young prince of Scalea assisted in planning Italian expansion eastward, and his father, together with his mother's kin, shared in the direct benefits that the expansion conferred on the great shipping line that the families had joined in developing.

These facts do not seem to have aroused much notice in prewar Italy, but the other influences present in the Navigazione Generale's directorate proved to be more embarrassing. It was to be expected that the board would include two Florios, as well as the Sicilian prince of Paternò and the Banca Commerciale–Terni financier Cesare Balduino. But Federico Weil's name there gave rise to accusations of covert German control, and a German director was thought to be especially out of place in an industry so directly linked to the Italian state.

Moreover, that fact came to the public's attention in a singularly embarrassing way. The maritime labor union, under the audacious Captain Giulietti, had by 1914 succeeded in getting sailors, ship's officers and even ship's doctors into a single federation with the syndicalist philosophy of eventual management by producers; and the federation was strong enough to tie up the entire Italian merchant marine. Giulietti had an exceptional public relations sense and launched his campaign against Navigazione Generale by proclaiming that the big line was under German control; thus, he claimed, the forces of labor were not merely struggling to free the working class but were acting in the interests of the nation as a whole. For some time, murmuring against German economic penetration had been spreading in business circles, but this degree of publicity was unprecedented.

The Navigazione Generale's directors answered on January 23, 1914 with a public defense. The maritime union's recent attacks, they said,

repeat certain statements which form the basis of a campaign which some rivals, not disinterested, have been waging against us for a decade . . . a strange coincidence. . . . The Federation of Workers of the Sea defines us outright as German shippers. Now then: (1) The Navigazione Generale

Italiana . . . does not depend on any institution of credit. The ownership of the 200,000 shares that make up the company's capital proves irrefutably the completely Italian character of our enterprise. (2) The N. G. I. has, instead, helped to make truly Italian some shipping enterprises created by German capital under the shadow of the Italian flag, by purchasing them. (3) Thanks to the vigorous effort of our company, Italian transatlantic shipping has pursued a national policy. As a result, while before 1903 the Italian flag's share in transporting emigrants was limited to 31% for North America and 71% for South America, in 1913 this share rose to 55% for North America and 87% for South America.[15]

This was hardly an answer to the charges: in Italy German influence was a matter of executive personnel and of the policy followed in adopting lines of industrial equipment; it was rarely reflected in outright stock ownership. However, the Navigazione Generale's statement does reveal much about the drives and ambitions of the big Italian shipping lines, which were indeed "national."

In assessing the connections between Italian shipping interests and the course of Italian politics, we must start with the direct cash nexus. Italian maritime subsidies, like those that had helped Navigazione Generale enter the charmed circle of the nation's economic elite, had long been granted, but the Italian imperialism of the twentieth century vastly increased their scope. And every new act of Italian penetration in Albania and Asia Minor immediately added another subsidy to those already weighing on the naval budget.

The new subsidy system cost the state 19,909,124 lire for the year after it went into effect on July 1, 1913. Of this sum, 18,194,632 lire went to the Adriatic and Near Eastern lines, which cost about a third more than they had before. All subsidized shipping had cost less than 14 million lire in the previous highest year. Most of the new expenses went into stimulating Italian enterprise in ports of the Ottoman Empire, particularly Smyrna and Adalia in the future Italian "work zone."

The expenditure does not seem great at first sight; it was less than 1 percent of all state expenses for the year. But to this sector of industry it meant a great deal. Servizi Marittimi reported a net profit of 833,361 lire in 1911–12; and Navigazione Generale, more than 3 million. On such a scale the new state subsidies could make the difference between ending in the black or in the red.[16]

And the paltry 26 million spent on merchant shipping and ship-building, the 50 million yearly on new rail lines, the much larger sums spent on arms and public works—all together they spawned a variety of aggressive pressure groups with political funds and access to the press. The ratio of subsidy appropriations to the rest of the budget was not a measure of their political significance.

In any case, the expenditure failed to meet the demands of the shipowners. From 1901—when navigation bonuses were abandoned —to 1913, no law to help free shipping got through the chamber; only lines serving state-scheduled routes benefited from the naval budget. When relief finally came in the omnibus naval law of 1913, it went only to cargo vessels sailing nonsubsidized routes; passenger and emigrant ships were excluded, along with all transatlantic liners. Furthermore, the bonuses were limited to 2.3 million lire annually, with 5 percent withheld for a disabled benefit fund. Austria and France, the Italian shippers complained, had broader, more generous programs and were achieving far more.

Parliament got a dark general picture from the shippers' deputies. The free merchant marine not only drew less government bonus money than its principal competitors, but also suffered from higher costs for fuel, insurance rates, and interest charges. Consequently, about half of Italy's seagoing commerce went in foreign bottoms, taking away about 50 million lire of the nation's wealth every year: such, at least, was the logic of popular autarkic economics.

Fixed subsidized lines offered piddling relief; they accounted for only 3.7 percent of Italy's total sea traffic, 7.8 percent of cargo transport, and 11.7 percent of coastal traffic. Nor had the recent high tide of Italian emigration helped the nation's merchant marine as much as it should have—special agreements reserved some 40 percent of the North America–bound emigrant traffic for foreign shipping lines. Though the port of Genoa was growing, Marseilles was growing faster. Only in the shipyards was there a notable upturn: as of March 1, 1914, 67,725 tons of merchant vessels were under construction, thanks to new government aid.

Caught in this competitive vise, what did the shipowners ask?[17] Greater direct aid was not what they had in mind: marine subsidies, sailing bonuses, and shipbuilding awards all stuck out in the state budget, offering easy targets to critics. Hence the big ship operators of Genoa and Leghorn—the Orlandos, Menadas, and Parodis—asked for special considerations, favors that would not attract public or parliamentary attention. They wanted combined fares for rail passengers and freight destined to move on Italian vessels and they asked for the exclusive right to ship coal for the state—fat contracts indeed. And—most significant politically—they looked to the government for help in competing for foreign lines, concessions, and rights. Their patterns and models were Germany and Austria-Hungary; by Italian standards, the Central Powers' merchant marines showed phenomenal rates of growth. At the other side of the peninsula, the Società Veneziana complained that Far Eastern lines were completely closed to Italian initiative and called on the government to remedy the situation.

Before the war Italian shippers were locked in a struggle with the four shipping lines that operated out of Trieste and Fiume, the Dual Monarchy's "maritime lungs." The shippers did not stand alone—their struggle was part of a larger pattern of rivalries. The Italian-speaking middle classes of the Dual Monarchy's Adriatic ports sensed that the monarchy's consolidation and overseas expansion would end by denationalizing their cities. The Italian navy was engaged in a dreadnought-building race with the Hapsburg fleet; the Italian foreign ministry was jostling the Austrians in the "work zone" of Asiatic Turkey; the Commerciale's Balkan and Anatolian operations cut across Austrian lines of influence or control. The shippers' drives dovetailed into the complex of motives behind Italian expansionism.

The principal Triestine line was Austrian Lloyd, founded in 1836.[18] Even in its early days the company was binational; the early directors were as often German as Italian in spite of the fact that the Austrian ports were uniformly Italian ethnically. Austrian Lloyd was generously subsidized by the imperial government from the first, and as the line grew in importance, the Vienna authorities and Chamber of Commerce began to worry about questions of loyalty. There were grounds for suspicion: Italian was the official language of the port of Trieste, and the Germans or Slavs who worked on Austrian Lloyd vessels had to use it even in ship's logs and formal written reports.

Vienna did everything possible to remove the company from its Italian setting. After 1891 its president was named by imperial decree, and in 1906 the company's headquarters were transferred to Vienna. From then on, of Austrian Lloyd's seven directors, only two were Italian; but the day-to-day affairs of the line, carried on at Trieste, remained perforce under an administration staffed by Italians, and the Austrian effort to denationalize Trieste itself seems to have intensified irredentist feelings among the younger generation of Triestine mariners.

In 1906, when heated competition with the Italians had begun, Austrian Lloyd had no less than sixty-five vessels, more than any single Italian line. As late as 1914, no Italian line operated more than thirty-eight steamships, and the Società Veneziana, the principal Trieste competitor, had only eight.

Competition in the upper Adriatic started ten years before the War. The Società Veneziana began its subsidized line through Suez to Calcutta in 1904, with scheduled stops at Massawa, the principal port of Italy's Eritrean colony. Austrian Lloyd and other Austrian and German lines tried to strangle this competition in its infancy by offering cut rates and long-term contracts to firms that might be tempted to use the new Venetian line. The Austrians failed, for while they were preempting shipments elsewhere, the Italians acquired sizable cargoes of sugar in Austrian ports and shipped them to India. The Venetian shipowners also appealed to all patriotic Italian firms to send their freight on Italian bottoms.[19]

This was a note often sounded in the following years, when Austrian and Hungarian lines began cutting into Italy's Atlantic emigrant traffic, developing fast new services along the Adriatic coast, and running new lines between Adriatic ports and the Levant. German capital was behind some of these ventures and North German Lloyd itself ran a line between Venice and Alexandria. The Società Veneziana was among the Italian lines that suffered most from the Central Powers' Mediterranean ventures, but it managed to increase its volume of business. What disturbed the line most of all was the slenderness of the subsidy it got, while its Austrian rivals were reimbursed even for Suez Canal tolls. (No small matter; more than half the Venetian line's state subsidy was eaten up by these tolls in the fiscal year 1911–12.)

Italy's situation grew more complex as the war neared. Greece began to come up as a rival, but Italy's basic competitor remained the Dual Monarchy, whose flag began to appear in every sea.[20]

The general competition between Italy and the Dual Monarchy in the Near East was intense, but in the shipping trade, the two rivals went beyond the usual limits of commercial practice. Italy's new subsidized lines began operating in the Black Sea, the Aegean, Asia Minor, and the Levant in August 1913. They were still using old, substandard ships, but the law obliged them to renew their equipment completely within three years. The Austrians understood that the Italians meant business and did everything to forestall them.

Servizi Marittimi's agents began the game in Smyrna by offering to carry the local merchants' exports for half what Austrian Lloyd was charging. Then the Smyrna office was suddenly told to desist; the two lines had started negotiating at a higher level. In a direct agreement the Austrian line promised to charge five lire per ton more than the going Italian rate for cargo bound for Venice, and the Italians reciprocated on Trieste-bound freight. An innocent clause in the agreement provided that all existing contracts would remain in force. Immediately afterward it turned out that while Rome and Trieste had been working out the pact, Austrian Lloyd had been busy offering cut-rate contracts for freight from Smyrna to Venice on condition that the shipper commit himself to Austrian Lloyd for a year. The contracts were concluded before the pact went into effect, so the Italians' hands were tied. For the first year of operations, they could not undercut the Austrians at Trieste, but the Austrians had already preempted much of the traffic from Smyrna to Venice.[21]

It is impossible to separate political and economic forces in the history of a state or to assign priorities to one or the other. Sometimes governments cannot control their own economic satellites: the Navigazione Generale, which owed its very formation to the state, had become strong enough by 1909 to block a maritime-subsidy system that Giolitti himself favored. The steel trust depended on legislative and executive favor to stay in business, but Pirelli and Agnelli did not. They built up Italian industrial systems linked to foreign markets and collaborators without any Italian state favors at all. Only later did these systems come to have political weight as part of a set of national interests pulling Italy toward the Entente.

But Italy's economic interests in the Near East were real, and her commerce there was becoming ever more important. It was not entirely a matter of quantity: Turkey absorbed only 3.5 percent of the value of all Italian exports in 1913, the last normal year. But Turkey was one of the few countries in the world that bought more from the Italians than it sold them. The only other big country of which this was true was Argentina. It was unfortunate for the economic moorings of the Triple Alliance that Germany pressed Italy in Argentina and Austria rivaled Italy in the ports of the Levant.

Italian heavy-industrial undertakings in Turkey had to begin with political concessions, but even the old trade in consumer products had its political side: one of the biggest deals made by North Italian textile firms in 1913 was with the Ottoman war ministry for 1,500,000 meters of cotton cloth. The manufacturer beat heavy foreign competition but had to accept Turkish government bonds in payment, a dubious arrangement necessitated by the Empire's financial straits.[22]

In spite of such drawbacks, Austria coveted the Turkish market and resented Italy's miniature "drive to the East." There were constant pinpricks. During the Italo-Turkish War of 1911–12, the Austrians replaced the Italians as suppliers of matches to the Levant; in April 1914 the influential Catholic daily of Vienna, the *Reichspost*, warned that the Italians, with their cheap labor, their drive, and their energy, were becoming the ubiquitous Japanese of the Near East, a note gladly picked up by the Italian colonialist press.[23]

Most Italian business papers were enthusiastic when the Italian government began its political and economic penetration of Turkey in the spring of 1913, but the big shipping lines' Genoese information journal, *La Marina mercantile italiana*, struck an especially positive note:

We do not believe much in the possibility of European wars. . . . But we do believe . . . that it is necessary to be ready for a conflict arising from clashing interests and drives in that great process of expansion and partition that Europe has begun and will sooner or later complete on those lands of the East and of Africa which cannot and should not be left to regimes incapable of administering them and bringing them toward civilization. . . . Even if we grant that a little shred of independent Turkey might survive the ethnic and historic breakup of the Empire of the caliphs, it is nevertheless certain that a very great part of those vast and fertile Asiatic dominions will have to be absorbed in the future by Europe.[24]

The merchant-marine organ was concerned that Italy be prepared for future Mediterranean struggles, and it had the assurance of the Italian naval minister that the fleet would grow as fast as the treasury would allow.

It was natural that Italian ship operators should be the most outspoken partisans of Italy's new imperialism. But the nation's entire industrial establishment was in one way or another involved in imperialism. For Italy, the new imperialism meant colonial expansion in the East, alliance with the Entente, divorce from the Central Powers, and eventual war against them. These were the lines of a policy that matched the lines of Italian industrial "emancipation."

The new imperialism was not merely a device to plaster over the widening cracks in the Italian political system and confer new prestige on the lackluster monarchy of the Savoys, though these motives undoubtedly played their part. Given the lopsided, unbalanced structure of Italian industry, it, too, had to seek new colonial frontiers, areas of exclusive exploitation. The alternative of thoroughgoing, large-scale international economic cooperation did not exist in 1914.

4

Italian Industrial Financing and the Banca Commerciale

In the new industrial system that rose out of the wreckage of the early 1890s, the Banca Commerciale of Milan became the pacesetting institution in the basic branches of industrial credit, the guiding and mediating agent in the period of corporate expansion that lasted from 1896 to 1907.

The great bank, the most enduring fruit of the Triple Alliance, was founded in 1894 at Crispi's behest by a group in which Berlin and Vienna houses predominated: conspicuous among its foreign sponsors were the Bleichroeder Bank of Berlin, which was tied to Bismarck, and the Kreditanstalt (Rothschild) of Vienna. The Commerciale inherited the assets and liabilities of the Credito Mobiliare and the Banca Generale, the two big, ambitious North Italian institutions of industrial credit that had fallen the year before.

The Commerciale's new management group introduced into the peninsula the new methods of industrial financing, or "mixed banking," that prevailed in Germany. The managers themselves were all acclimatized foreigners: the three most important executives were Otto Joel and Federico Weil, who were in at the start, and Giuseppe Toeplitz, who joined them less than two years later. The first two were German Jews; Joel was of an old Danzig family. Toeplitz, a young cousin of Joel's, came from Russian Poland and had studied engineering in Belgium and Germany before an early and disapproved marriage compelled him to seek employment.

None of these men seems to have felt much attachment to the

past. Joel, general manager (*direttore*) of the Commerciale, had lived in Italy since 1878 and had risen to become a high officer of the old Banca Generale's Milan offices. The Joel family considered itself Italian by adoption even before Otto Joel was granted Italian citizenship in 1910, a move evidently sponsored by Giolitti and his adherents; Joel's son also chose Italian citizenship and was a reserve cavalry officer at the start of the war. Toeplitz, who had married a Netherlands noblewoman in spite of objections, had drifted farthest from his old moorings: he had adopted his wife's Catholic religion before coming to Italy in 1892, and he, too, raised his children as Italians. Toeplitz obtained Italian citizenship in 1912, leaving Weil, a bachelor, as the only remaining alien of the triumvirate.[1]

These three divided the principal functions of the bank among themselves. Joel, well-spoken and diplomatic, was the head and specialized in relations with the great steel and shipbuilding trusts; even more important, he was the principal agent of the bank in dealing with the government, the Bank of Italy, and the foreign financiers that continued to participate in the Banca Commerciale. Weil concerned himself with the financing of the big subsidized shipping lines. Toeplitz, a truly protean and omnicompetent figure, handled the bank's chemical-industry operations: he also developed personal contacts with the adventurous financial and industrial group of Venice represented by Volpi that played such a key role in Italy's overseas expansion. Though contacts with industrial and financial circles in Turin and Genoa were often in the hands of Italian managers or engineers, the one native Italian who seems to have really penetrated into this inside group was the electrical expert, Pietro Fenoglio, who had become a fourth wheel by 1912.

From its beginnings up to the war, the bank had to follow a double line of policy, cosmopolitan and nationalist at the same time. On the one hand the Banca Commerciale had to satisfy its international bankers—not only its original sponsors in Berlin and Vienna, but also the Paris group centered in the Banque de Paris et des Pays-Bas, the most cosmopolitan of the big French investment banks.[2] As late as 1907, the guiding organ of the Commerciale, the central committee, which was chosen yearly by the board of directors (Consiglio d'amministrazione), comprised four Italians, two Germans, two

Frenchmen, one Swiss, and one Austrian, in addition to the president, who was always a prominent Milanese. The directors (*amministratori*) remained largely foreign, even after the bank's capital had long since passed predominantly into Italian hands; when a foreign director died in 1912, Joel had to use all his tact and influence to get an Italian put in his place. The appointment established the principle that the places on the board traditionally allotted to the bank's foreign stockholder representatives were not "hereditary" but could change with the shift in stockholdings.[3] As a matter of fact, the Germans began selling their stock soon after the bank got on its feet, and by 1904 their holdings were small: by then the Triple Alliance had lost much of its intimacy, and German home enterprise needed all the capital it could find. In 1914 the Italians owned 195,554 shares; the Swiss, 64,097; the French, 42,922; and the Germans, a mere 7,411. Nevertheless the bank remained largely dependent on foreign financial interests for its operations abroad, for the funds so frequently needed to expand its equity capital, and for foreign investment openings that seemed prudent and profitable.

Until 1914 the Banca Commerciale was part of a delicately contrived international system, toward which it had definite responsibilities. Its foreign backers kept insisting on liquidity, on assets that could be turned into fast cash for emergencies, and on diversification of the bank's credit risks. These guidelines meant participation in the most varied international security issues, such as Mexican and Russian state bonds, American rail issues, and stock in the Baghdad railway, which interested the Germans. Even distant Katanga got a small cut of the Commerciale's investment capital in 1910—the bank had "friends" in the Brussels financial world. The bank's foreign associates and stockholder representatives objected vigorously to the Commerciale's tying up capital in long-term domestic industrial credit; warned perpetually against carrying a heavy portfolio of domestic industrial securities as margin against loans; and mindful of the pitfalls of Italian banking, tried to insure at least 75 percent liquidity of assets.

On the other hand the Commerciale had inherited the industrial customers of the older Milanese institutions, with their pressing demands for long-term development credit, continual new stock issues to underwrite, and bonds to market. In the rapid industrialization of 1890–1907, such requests became both more reasonable and more urgent, and no one proposing to do business in Italy could ignore them. Some of the bank's industrial customers, notably Terni, had passed over from the Credito Mobiliare. Besides these quasi-inherited rights to special consideration, a client like Terni could also claim patriotic merits of a sort that foreigners like Joel could overlook only at their peril. The Banca Commerciale, in short, had to steer a middle course between the demands of a cosmopolitan world credit system and the needs of a narrow national economy with autarkic pretensions and protectionist political connections. In its tacking compromise course, the Banca Commerciale reflected in microcosm the inherent perplexities and contrasts in the development of early twentieth-century capitalism, torn between the international and leveling effects of a new technology and the intensely local character of industrial development on a nation-state foundation.[4]

The bank's policy, then, was to reconcile these two fundamental opposites with expedients that proved markedly successful between 1896 and 1907. But after 1907 the expedients gave out, and the bank began treading the path of outright nationalism.

The bank's investment strategy was brilliant: it proposed to sink huge investment funds into the country's new public utilities, especially hydroelectric systems. These were, of course, long-term, irretrievable commitments of the kind that foreign friends might ordinarily discourage, but they were also secure income sources calculated to reassure the most timid investor. Electric-power and traction systems became the foundation of the bank's enormous success, a sort of financial snowball that kept growing up to the onset of the War. Another decision that proved sound concerned chemical industries: Toeplitz worked with the Donegani brothers, who had started pyrite mines in Tuscany, to develop and unify the whole fertilizer, sulphates, and industrial-chemical production of Italy, and they moved toward almost monopolistic positions in the domestic market. Montecatini remains the lasting monument to this shrewd policy. The conditions of technological change in the bank's first triumphant decade enabled hydroelectric power and mass production of industrial chemicals to develop jointly. However, its control of electrical networks gave the bank an advantageous position in many fields of industry that could grow only if they could get energy at favorable prices.

The Banca Commerciale's management, always with an eye to the sure fixed return on capital outlay, proved just as shrewd in assessing other fields. It moved heavily into fields that enjoyed special economic privileges: steel plants at Savona that made rails and conduits under heavy tariff protection; machine shops destined to great growth after 1900 by the imminent state appropriation and modernization of the peninsula's rail network; shipping lines, like the Navigazione Generale, that enjoyed postal subsidies and political pull at Rome; and flour milling, sugar beet refining, and papermaking.

On the other hand the bank, mindful of the frequent crises that beset the world's clothing markets, sedulously avoided all but the biggest and most diversified textile manufacturers. The textile firms that managed to get consideration were those headed by magnates like Senator Ponti or Silvio Crespi, people of such varied holdings and interests that no Milanese bank could afford to turn them down. The Commerciale wisely avoided the real estate ventures that had caused such woe to its predecessors. Only in the case of government-guaranteed public construction or the building of new industrial areas outside of central Milan did the bank make exceptions to this rule. However, this prudence had its negative side: the bank stayed as far away as possible from interesting new developments like automobile manufacturing that presented heavy risks and no guarantees. For example, Fiat found it hard to get credit from the bank; in spite of its excellent Turinese connections, Fiat never got a fraction of what Orlando or Terni regularly received.[5]

As an institution with foreign management feeling its way into the Italian economy, the Banca Commerciale was rarely ruthless or predatory. It tried, whenever possible, to coalesce with existing local institutions or enterprises. In Bergamo and Como it merged with existing banks. When it made heavy loans to local utilities or manufacturers, it would often put one of its managers on the board of directors to check, influence, or control the firm's future operations. In some cases, notably in the electrical field, this tactic worked to coordinate and standardize whole branches of industry, even from an engineering angle.

Typical of the Commerciale's strategy were the special credits and liquidations it undertook in connection with the house of Florio. The Florios, who had made their original fortune in tuna fishing, then branched into shipping and banking and married into one of the noblest Sicilian families, the Scalea. By 1900 the Florio-Scaleas had heavy interests in Italian rails and in the leading daily paper of Palermo; Ignazio Florio was also Sicily's leading banker. In 1902 Florio decided to get out of banking and sold out to the Commerciale, which gave him huge advances for his other operations. Florio's indebtedness to the bank kept rising, and his massive holdings in the Navigazione Generale eventually came under Commerciale control. That suited the bank very well; for years it had been trying to unify the postal-subsidy lines under the Navigazione Generale's control so that it could negotiate new subsidy arrangements with the government from a position of strength. At the same time the Commerciale was steadily buying up German holdings in other Italian shipping lines, and the credits extended to the Florios, their noble in-laws, and their daily paper in Palermo were a small price to pay for an eventual maritime monopoly. As a by-product the Commerciale management also achieved entry into the Italian power structure, of which the Florio-Scaleas were an integral part.[6]

More significant in the history of Italian expansion abroad were the relations the Commerciale set up with the aristocratic Venetian circles centering around the Papadopoli bank, Count Piero Foscari, the noble Revedin family of Padua and Ferraro, and the promoter Giuseppe Volpi.[7]

The honeymoon days of the Commerciale ended abruptly with the crash of 1907. The bank suffered relatively little from the immediate effects of the crisis; only two of its branches, those at Como and Udine, were involved in the wave of failures resulting from speculative mismanagement. The bank did have to dip into reserves to pay its usual dividends—a grave step that the president, Senator Mangili, justified on the grounds that since the bank had just expanded its capital, it had a special obligation to the investing public. Still, it emerged in far better shape than most other big Italian institutions.

The Commerciale's stability impressed others only too well. The bank was called on to join a consortium, backed by the Bank of

Italy, to save the tottering Società Bancaria, which had badly over-extended its credits to textile and shipping businesses. The rescue operation did not benefit the Commerciale greatly, but there was no way of refusing to join a group sponsored by the Bank of Italy. Much the same kind of pressure led the Commerciale to support two groups formed to maintain security prices on the Milan exchange. With its web of friendships and business connections, the Commerciale management could in turn call on the former rail companies, which after 1905 had been using their state-supplied compensations in various industrial-credit operations, often guided or guaranteed by the Commerciale. This was an extraordinary source of capital, much needed in the tight years after 1907.[8]

The depression deeply affected the whole future course of the Commerciale. The investing public was thereafter wary of putting new funds into securities, and the Commerciale had to take on the whole burden of financing in many sectors of the economy. It had to use depositors' money, make more by underwriting government bonds or treasury notes, and lower its standards of liquidity.

The Commerciale had little competition to fear in North Italy: it soon came to an agreement on credit rates with the Credito Italiano, the one big industrial-credit institution left. After the weakness and narrow margins of Italian industrial free enterprise had been made manifest by the 1907 disasters, the bank redoubled its efforts to arrive at monopolistic or oligopolistic positions wherever possible. It was precisely between 1907 and 1910 that Director Otto Joel began working out the details of a general agreement between the two rival heavy-industrial groups of the peninsula, Ansaldo and the trust, that would eliminate all competition in the central fields of arms manufacture, state-supported shipbuilding, turbine patents and manufacture, and foreign munitions and shipbuilding orders. Joel dealt patiently with Rolandi-Ricci, the vain, pompous, insistent representative of the trust, at the same time that he was negotiating with Urbano Rattazzi, Giolitti's old patron at court, who was heavily involved with the Ansaldo group. Both counted on Joel to use his influence with the stubborn executive of the trust, Giuseppe Orlando, the harshest and most authoritarian of the Orlando brothers.

In the end a general agreement between the rivals was unattainable, mainly because the Perrone brothers of Ansaldo harbored visions of fantastic projects involving future naval establishments in Turkey, ambitions that the Orlando-Odero group considered impolitic and imprudent, especially after the Young Turk revolution in 1908.[9]

Joel's aim throughout, as he told Rattazzi in 1909, was to secure the unity of Italy's industrial forces in order to conquer foreign markets without further cost to the government. The more ships, machines, and munitions Italy sold abroad, the lower the eventual cost to Italy of supporting her indispensable military-industrial complex. Joel had always maintained the Commerciale's special ties to the trust, but he thought in peninsular terms.

After 1908 the Commerciale's credit operations took an increasingly military turn, typified by its new relations with Fiat. The bank had always been grudging and indirect in granting credit to Fiat, but in 1909 its policy changed. Fiat began entering into combinations to manufacture artillery and naval engines with firms managed by Dante Ferraris and other enterprisers close to the trust. Fiat signed a submarine contract with the German navy in 1909 and another in 1914. In these operations Fiat got from the Commerciale the prompt and generous credit that had never been forthcoming for its civilian automobile business. The credit was always granted with Fiat's growing government contracts for munitions and rails in mind, and it often took the form of advances against future government disbursements.

Even more striking was the Commerciale's heavy involvement in the establishment of a Whitehead torpedo plant in Naples, an enterprise with no civilian prospects whatever. But by then, on the eve of the war, the Commerciale's credit was largely geared to military contracts. The bank was even financing Ansaldo, in spite of its alliance to Ansaldo's rivals. This move was in part a conciliatory tactic on Joel's part, but it also reflected the fact that war contracts were becoming the most profitable investments.[10]

In charting such a course Joel was following a national—indeed a European—trend beyond his control. But he was more than a mere creature of circumstance. He actively and personally abetted the particular nationalistic turn the Commerciale took in the decisive years before the war and tried to show in every way that he deserved the Italian citizenship conferred upon him.

Joel put his weight behind the plan to finance Ilva in March 1911 against strong opposition from his bank's stockholder representatives. At the central committee's decisive meeting, one foreign member, Wallich, abstained—for the first time in the bank's history —in a vote to approve the management's proposals. Wallich went so far as to argue that the steel industry had no reason to exist in Italy, a point of view that Joel felt no Italian business concern could accept. The matter went to the bank's board of directors as an urgent item; the other members of the refinancing group were awaiting the Commerciale's decision. Joel sent along a strong letter to Edgar Noetzlin of the Banque de Paris et des Pays-Bas pointing out how essential it was for the directors to uphold the Milan central management. He said the Commerciale was more involved in the steel business than any other bank—the Credito Italiano had been reducing its credits to steel for some time. Nevertheless, the Credito Italiano was putting up 17 million lire for the refinancing and in proportion to its means and previous commitments was offering to do far more than the Commerciale. Joel added a few other telling arguments: the state was throwing its influence behind the plan through the participation and supervision of the Bank of Italy. The total advance, the sum of 80 million lire, would be secured, except for 10 to 12 percent, by liquid assets or credits due the steel firms from their customers. Then Joel jabbed to the heart of the matter: the Commerciale, the most important credit institution in Italy, was often considered a foreign body. How could it stay out of a financial combination formed specifically in the national interest? Not a single Italian in the bank's executive group would vote against the plan.

Joel not only got his way but was also able to get another Italian director elected to replace a foreigner the next year. In fact, the events of 1911 proved just how responsive the bank was to the problems and political considerations of Italian heavy industry, to the detriment of its commercial credit facilities. Even the Italian members of the bank's central committee were worried by the charges that were being publicly aired against the steel trust. Ignoring the criticism, Joel actually extended further credit to Ilva just before the war, when the firm was getting ever-larger government orders. After lengthy critical discussion, the committee always wound up accepting Joel's proposals.

The other issue on which Joel took a strong stand was the Commerciale's operations abroad. He knew that much of Italian industry could survive and grow only by exporting more. Besides, the government was interested in expansion for the sake of prestige and power in the eastern Mediterranean. Joel was particularly vulnerable to appeals and insinuations from Rome and was willing to go further than some of his native-born colleagues in helping to finance Italian exports and enterprises abroad, especially in areas where the government had political objectives. Italian exports of rail equipment and munitions depended less on the workings of free international competition than on the interplay of political and military advantage. As early as 1901 the Commerciale raised its special credit to the Breda works from 2.5 to 4 million lire to finance the delivery of thirty-four locomotives to the Rumanian government. The Rumanians promised to repay the bank within a year at 7 percent interest. Such arrangements, usually with more uncertain prospects, kept turning up in connection with Montenegro and Asia Minor after 1908; and Joel went ahead, committing the bank to taking shares in enterprises that would pay off only after considerable time and under the most favorable political conditions.

When the central committee met in June 1914, the Commerciale's commitments abroad were among the main problems to be considered. Both the government and certain private firms were after the bank to advance funds for exports to the Balkans and Turkey; Gilardini of Turin was filling orders for both the Rumanian and the Ottoman armies with Commerciale credit. In this shaky area the governments paid their suppliers in bonds or notes, often long-term, which the suppliers, in turn, offered to the Commerciale as collateral for their immediate cash needs. The bank directors were deeply disturbed about entering this financial mine field but felt that their in-

stitution could not flatly refuse. Finally, at the suggestion of one of
the foreign directors, the committee decided to limit such operations
to 10 million lire. If they had guessed what was about to happen in
the East, they would have been even more cautious; the Commerciale
eventually lost almost all of what it had laid out there.

The bank was still following a double course. Its nationalistic,
autarkic tendencies increased after the crises of 1907–8, but it continued its cosmopolitan participation in world banking and industrial
affairs. Financial collaboration with Paris, technical alliances with
Berlin, investment capital from Brussels and Zurich, all these remained, up to 1914, indispensable to the building of modern industries in Italy; and the Commerciale served as the channel and
directing agency for them all.

French finance was essential to the Italian chemical industry at
a moment when Italy, previously merely an exporter of raw sulphur,
was beginning to process her own chemicals. Thanks to the collaboration between Toeplitz and the Donegani brothers, the Commerciale
had played a key part in unifying the sector by linking Montecatini,
Albano-Trezza, and the Unione Concimi by an intricate web of sales
agreements and stock participations. The key element was Montecatini, which had the entrepreneurial talent of the Doneganis and was
able to combine pyrite mining with the development of hydroelectric
power. However, the chemical resources of Tunisia, especially phosphates, were needed for the growth of this complex; and by 1911 the
Banque de Paris et des Pays-Bas (Paribas) and the Commerciale
were engaged in several joint ventures in the French protectorate,
ranging from phosphate mining to flour milling and commercial banking. Without both the colonial and the financial resources of the
French, this important Italian industrial venture, one of the outstanding successes of Commerciale, would have been out of the question.

Another conspicuous example of French collaboration was the
Commerciale's daughter bank in São Paulo, Brazil, set up to meet
the needs of the large Italian business community in South America.
Unlike the ventures in the eastern Mediterranean, this was strictly
business, a nonpolitical enterprise conducted by a Swiss general
manager, under whose cautious hand the bank managed to survive

1907 without great losses. Its need for capital turned out to be far greater than the Commerciale could meet, and Paribas financed its further expansion. This was a perfect case of Italian energy and enterprise combining with French resources.[11]

The German economic presence in Italy was entirely different. German banks could not pour capital into potentially competitive foreign economies, since they were concerned with the financing of big German operations abroad. Right up to 1914 the Commerciale kept receiving solicitations from Germany to increase its share in the Baghdad railway; and Carlo Esterle, an Italian electrical engineer and business friend of the bank, was a member of the board directors of the company that was building the Konia-Eregli-Bulgurlu section of the railway. (This appointment was made in 1904, when the Commerciale took some Baghdad rail bonds and a few stockholdings.) However, the Commerciale's slice of that pie never seems to have gone above a piddling 2 percent.[12]

In fact, Germany and Italy had much the same problem: an abundance of industrial energies and engineering talent along with a shortage of capital and solid international backing. Nevertheless, the differences were just as important. Italy was a relative late starter, and her industrial and engineering development was nowhere near comparable, at least in quantitative terms, to Germany's. Germany could launch its foreign operations from a powerful domestic base with willing, though insufficient, sources of domestic capital, while Italian talent and enterprise had to seek foreign outlets at the start because the peninsular market was so narrow and the Italian investor so cautious or anti-industrial in his attitude. Under such circumstances, German industry and industrial finance turned to Italy, especially after 1894, as a promising field for the exportation of products and of whole systems.

Those German-led operations in Italy that came within the purview of the Commerciale between 1900 and 1914 suggest that German banks and industries had a double aim in the peninsula. On the one hand German electrical enterprises tried to get in on the ground floor of Italian electrification by persuading Italian utilities to install German systems and equipment, and much the same happened in the fields of specialized steel products and machinery. On the other hand German specialist firms tried to get control of the key raw materials in Italy to forestall future competition or underselling.

The Commerciale, so the charge went, dominated many of the Italian electrical companies in one way or another and used its commanding position to impose a technical system that tied them to German electromechanical firms. There were also rumors that the Commerciale had financed many textile firms in North Italy on the condition that they use German machinery. By 1914–15 Italian industry wanted to stand on its own feet and resented any further effort to gear its activities to foreign specifications.

The engineer Pietro Lanino spelled out the case against Germany during the war:

In all of our past industrial development, every effort to create our own industry of dyestuffs was never encouraged, often resisted or even, when necessary, suffocated by the direct or indirect competition of German industry, and by the German bank . . . by means of him who, by its order, had set himself up, through his own strength, as supreme regulator of our burgeoning productive energies. This we state with certain knowledge, through our personal and direct experience. . . .

According to Lanino, the two titans of the German electrical industry dominated Italian industry in this field through the Banca Commerciale:

The AEG of Berlin soon set up in Italy its own affiliate. . . . regulated by the Banca Commerciale, it finally became the AEG-Thomson-Houston-Società Italiana di Elettricità, with a large amount of initial German capital, but also with genuine and considerable Italian capital supplied by the Banca Commerciale or by companies that it was backing. . . . The AEG-Thomson-Houston-Società Italiana di Elettricità, however, remained subject to Berlin in all of its internal management. . . . Its Milan plant in 1913 was working on only two million out of the ten million of lire of orders that the AEG received from Italy. . . .

The rest had evidently been passed to the mother firm in Germany.

In September 1915 Filippo Carli, writing in the most authoritative Italian business monthly, noted that there was organized

*as always, with the initiative of the Banca Commerciale, but also with
the direct participation of the big German industrial banks, the Società
par lo Sviluppo della Imprese Elettriche in Italia. This latter company is
part, directly, through affiliates, or through stockholding, of a very large
part of the electricity companies of Italy, which have thus become the
customers of the Italian AEG as a matter of course, and, through the
latter, of the AEG of Berlin, for the great mass of their necessary
supplies.*[13]

The extent to which Italian electrical industries were tied to
Germany was noted dryly by the Triestine nationalist writer on economics, Mario Alberti.[14] According to an article he published just
before the outbreak of war, the principal links were these: in 1894
a German bankers' group including Bleichroeder, the Dresdener and
Darmstaedter banks, and the Diskontogesellschaft joined in setting up
the Gesellschaft für Elektrische Unternehmungen, which in turn took
part in setting up the Società per lo Sviluppo delle Imprese Elettriche
in Italia of Milan, one of the most important companies in the Italian
electrical industry. By 1912 it was part owner of twelve electrical
companies operating from the Alps to Sicily in the utilities, transport,
and manufacturing fields. Its most significant tie was to the SADE,
the Adriatic electrical system that provided Giuseppe Volpi with his
base. The administration of the Società per lo Sviluppo delle Imprese
Elettriche was most distinguished, having at its head Otto Joel and
among its members the noted real estate financier Marco Besso and
the AEG's Dr. Walter Rathenau.

The Deutsche Bank, with Swiss collaborators, founded the Bank
für Elektrische Unternehmungen, also connected with AEG. This
bank took part in the Officine Elettriche Genovesi, a big firm that in
1912 had on its board both Emil and Walter Rathenau in addition
to the Genoese shipping financier Senator Count Gerolamo Rossi-
Martini. The same foreign concern had a substantial interest in the
Società Meridionale di Elettricità of Naples, one of the principal
utility companies of the South; its administration was composed of
southern nobility, Italian engineers, and German representatives.
Another affiliate of the same bank was "Dinamo," the Società Italiana per imprese Elettriche of Milan, which played an important part
in the electrification of North Italian rail lines. "Dinamo" had a half-

German board, which also included an outstanding Catholic conservative, the parliamentary deputy Marquis Carlo Ottavio Cornaggia, whose presence perhaps sufficed to give the concern authentic
Italian respectability.[15]

Siemens and Halske had the Schweizerische Gesellschaft für
Elektrische Industrie of Basel, which had a big Italian affiliate at
Turin, the S.A. di Elettricità Alta Italia. This firm, with a capital
amounting to 25 million lire, had a heavy preponderance of Germanic
names among both its administrators and its managers.

Lanino admitted that the adoption of uniform technical methods
and standards was unavoidable and that the uniformity had to be
German in view of the peninsula's inability to put out a complete line
of electrical equipment. Some 88 percent of the machinery in Italian
power stations was of German manufacture, and between 1904 and
1913 Germany exported to Italy more electrical machinery than
Austria-Hungary and France combined. Lanino concluded that Italy
had become a "German colony" in this field, thanks to the efficient
and coordinated work of German industry and finance.[16] But here the
campaign against the Commerciale appears in its true perspective: it
was a facet of Italy's aspirations to industrial great-power status.

However, the AEG and Siemens Schuckert were not the only
German industries that penetrated Italy. The Maschinen-Fabrik of
Esslingen and the Officine Meccaniche di Saronno, which specialized
in manufacturing locomotives and big machine parts for the state
railways and the navy, had set up branches there; and there was Mannesmann's steel-tube plant. The big German firms manufactured parts
and equipment in Italy for two reasons: Italian tariff protection made
it cheaper to make a product there than to ship it in; and manpower
was cheaper in Italy than in Germany. The German aims appear to
have been to keep Italy tied to German methods and machinery, to
keep their Italian subsidiaries dependent on the mother firms, to forestall the rise of an independent industrial system in Italy, and to
monopolize Italian industry as a customer.

The Germans always got financial and executive cooperation
from the Commerciale in their Italian operations. Once Italy entered the War, the bank's large share in the firms stood it in good
stead: it enabled Toeplitz to get control of them. The German stock-

holders, unable to collect dividends, were only too glad to sell out to Toeplitz, who was authorized by the Italian government to go to Zurich to buy the shares. If it could have been held before 1914 that the Commerciale was the agent of German penetration, it became evident thereafter that the relationship had been strictly economic and that, given the opportunity, a foreign-born banker could become as autarkic as any Italian.[17]

Considering world conditions, it is hard to see how Italy could have achieved what she did, especially in electrification and machinery manufacturing, without some dependence on Germany. In itself there was nothing sinister in this link, and the danger of German control was greatly exaggerated during the excited intervention period. The Germans could get a finger on a few technically specialized key points in Italian industry, but they could not have moved on to gain working control of the peninsula's economy. If anything, their joint operations with the Commerciale made it easier for Italian technicians and executives, profiting from the groundwork they had laid, to take over.

The German tendency toward preemption and market and sector control came out most clearly in the aluminum and mercury deals worked out with the Commerciale. These are industrially essential materials whose supply can be calculated and controlled on a world scale, and that was precisely the aim of the German banks. The question is whether they found in the Commerciale an agent or an independent partner.

The Italian aluminum-producing company was financed jointly by the Commerciale and the Dresdener Bank, with 20 percent of its capital guaranteed by the German specialist firm Beer Sondheimer and Company. The world aluminum market had been weak in the years after 1907, and the Italian company had kept going largely with credit from Beer Sondheimer, secured by the company's existing aluminum stocks. This arrangement suggests that the German firm must have had some large plan in mind; there were no short-term profits to be made in such a way. In March 1910 the Italian firm went to the Commerciale with a request: since Italian tariffs were especially high on finished aluminum products, the Italian aluminum company had decided to set up a rolling mill in Italy at a cost of a quarter-million lire. The Commerciale's local committee at Milan approved but set some conditions. It wanted an option on new stock issues; it wanted the majority shareholders to put their stocks at the bank's disposal to assure that its conditions would be ratified at the next stockholders' meeting; and—most extraordinarily—it wanted Beer Sondheimer and Company to agree to alter its agreements with the Italian aluminum-producing company and establish less restrictive terms for the marketing of Italian aluminum products. This episode reveals the long-range market-cornering nature of German operations in this field, but it also suggests that the Commerciale played its own hand, working with the Germans to get a share of the business rather than acting as a mere agent of German interests in Italy.[18]

Mercury, a product more easily monopolized than aluminum, provides another example of the same interplay of interests. Italian mercury ore is found in the Monte Amiata area of Tuscany. In 1912 Toeplitz gave the Commerciale's support to Merkur Gewerkschaft, a private firm with headquarters in Berlin. Bleichroeder of Berlin held twenty-five and a half carats of the enterprise, and the Commerciale another twenty-five and a half, a division that gave the two banks, which had ties going back to the Commerciale's beginnings in 1894, a controlling interest. The other forty-nine carats were held by the owners of potential mines in the Monte Amiata area—all foreigners, at least one of whom was evidently a German. The Merkur Gewerkschaft, which spent a lot of money between 1912 and 1914 in sinking shafts and digging tunnels, was strictly a prospecting firm, speculative in character and consequently an unusual enterprise for a leading bank to take a direct share in. Clearly Toeplitz attached some special importance to mercury mining, and his intentions became clearer in a few years.

The principal company mining mercury at Monte Amiata, already an established producer, was German-controlled before the war. Toeplitz got permission during the war to go to Zurich and acquire all German holdings. He bought in more shares than the government had foreseen and walked into the 1916 stockholders' meeting with a controlling interest. Before the war the Commerciale was the sole Italian stockholder, and after 1916 it was the owner, though the government impounded the stock that Toeplitz had acquired until the war ended. The Commerciale operated with its usual shrewdness by awarding the presidency of the Amiata company to Gino Luzzatti, son of the former premier.[19]

The import of these operations becomes clear if one recalls that Italy and Spain are the main sources of mercury in Europe and that the world price of mercury can easily be fixed by agreements between a small number of producers on two continents. The Commerciale at first worked with the Germans (as definitely junior partners) in their mercury operations, and then the bank struck out for itself when political conditions changed. In this sector, as elsewhere, the Commerciale's relations with Germany made it easy, during the war, to detect and eliminate German footholds in the Italian economy.

Germany's prewar predicament was neatly summed up by that intriguing figure, Wickham Steed, when he wrote (anonymously) in an English popular yearbook of 1912:

German discontent is as the discontent of a speculative businessman who, having built beyond his means and mortgaged his buildings, manufactured beyond the needs of his market without knowing where else to sell his produce, and speculated beyond his means and his friends' resources, is fearful lest every payday involve him in ruin. Such men and such countries are doomed to discontent until, through crisis or disaster, they are driven to place their enterprises on sounder bases. . . . At every business crisis in Germany—a crisis is menaced regularly at each quarterly settlement—the French banks advance to the German banks, without the knowledge and against the will of the French people, the millions required to square German accounts and to bolster up the great gamble for three months more. Thus, for many years, France has financed German industry and rendered possible the maintenance of the huge army and navy which could not have been kept up without the taxes levied on German industry. . . . The aim of German policy has not changed, will not change, cannot change until Germany puts her own affairs in order and lives, manufactures, trades and arms within her own means. . . .[20]

Steed, the leading foreign correspondent for the *Times* and himself a courier and coordinator for all the British and European enemies of the Triple Alliance, wrote these words in a spirit of malice, which should not keep us from seeing their kernel of truth. Both Germany and Italy were living beyond their means; but the remedy that Steed's hostility and journalistic perspective hid from his eyes can be seen only with a half-century's hindsight. The solution was not retrenchment, but integrative international arrangements. An industrial system, even in the modest dimensions of Italy's, cannot retrench or cut back after a certain point. Steel plants, auto factories, and machine shops are all-or-nothing propositions, and the decision to industrialize is irreversible. Once in operation, an industrial system like Italy's or Germany's can, given a minimum of goodwill, correct itself or adjust to international conditions. It can fit itself into a receptive world industrial-financial system if there are vast common-market arrangements and if military considerations do not prevail over all others. But it cannot renounce export sales, and it cannot fail to enlarge production and cut unit costs without committing suicide. Since goodwill and integrative economic arrangements were not to be found in Europe either before or after the First World War, Italy and Germany had perforce to tread the hard road of near autarky and expansionism through war. It is perfectly legitimate to blame them for letting military counsels prevail, in which respect, of course, Germany was far more at fault than Italy, but the West must take responsibility for never seeking the kind of international economic cooperation and integration that would have rendered autarky and a push for living space unnecessary for these recent arrivals in the world of industry. (Among the statesmen of 1914, only Wilson and House had a glimmer of this solution: their proposals pleased no one, least of all the Germans, who certainly would have had the most to gain from them.)

In the atmosphere of growing military tension that settled over Europe in the eight years before 1914, the big international banks of Germany and Austria tended to grow even closer to their governments. German bankers were noted in London for their patriotism and their willingness to carry out delicate political tasks. Similarly, the Commerciale's executive board put itself at the disposal of the Italian government repeatedly: business interests, long-range industrial development, and patriotic duty ran on converging lines.

Inevitably, the Commerciale became part of the Italian political system that Giolitti directed. An institution of its size could not refrain from playing a role in both domestic and foreign politics, though the evidence suggests that its role was essentially subordinate. Giolitti's correspondence, now published, gives some idea of the dealings between him and the bank—the only private bank that figures prominently in his 1900–1915 correspondence.[21] The Commerciale had close working relations with Giolitti dating back to 1902, when Otto Joel was first introduced to the premier to discuss some new Italian bonds with him. The relations continued when Giolitti took a convalescent leave from the premiership a little later.

Though Giolitti and the Commerciale had worked together at the time of the public-debt conversion, in succeeding years the maritime-subsidy question led to a serious breach. The Commerciale expected that before the existing contracts expired in 1909, the government would renegotiate them with the Navigazione Generale, Florio's (and hence the bank's) enterprise. Instead, Giolitti's minister, Schanzer, found their demands exorbitant and tried to conclude a new set of conventions with a group headed by Senator Erasmo Piaggio of Genoa; the Piaggio enterprises, which included both ship-building and ship operation, were similar in scope to those of Orlando and Odero but were less politically conditioned and better managed. However, Piaggio, too, was involved in the Commerciale's operations and even sat on the bank's central committee.

Piaggio's Lloyd Italiano was linked by a reciprocal shareholding arrangement with the Navigazione Generale, a fact that embarrassed and finally defeated the senator. Piaggio's agreement with the government was far-reaching and implied complete independence on his part. It provided for a profit- and loss-sharing partnership between the state and the new subsidized line, a five-year trial period to fix the amount of the government subsidy, broad ministerial controls, and the assembling or building of some eighty vessels to run the required routes. Piaggio needed to be released from his previous ties on favorable terms.

During successive negotiations, Florio's Navigazione Generale imposed onerous terms on Piaggio by asking too high a price for the necessary voting rights and vessels, while the Commerciale set afoot a campaign against Piaggio's proposed monopoly. *La Tribuna,* notoriously linked to the steel trust and hence, indirectly, to the Commerciale, led the chorus, much to the indignation of the government. In March 1909 Piaggio resigned from his position on the Commerciale's central committee, and the controversy, now a matter of general concern, went on through the summer.

Giolitti and his right hand, Bonaldo Stringher of the Bank of Italy, were understandably furious. They were particularly aroused over *La Tribuna,* since it seemed to them unthinkable that a paper backed by Rolandi-Ricci and the steel interests should turn against the government that had done so much for them. However, Giolitti was at the end of one of his long ministries and planned to take a vacation from power, as was his wont after every election year, rather than to fight the issue out. In December 1909 he suddenly quit over a question of tax revision, leaving the maritime-subsidy question unresolved. His opponent, Sonnino, governed till the end of March 1910; then Luigi Luzzatti, essentially a stand-in for Giolitti, took over for a year. The maritime issue, like most other matters, hung fire until Giolitti returned to head another long ministry at the end of March 1911.

This interim period was of great importance in the history of the relations between the Giolitti regime and the Banca Commerciale's financial-industrial system. In 1910 and 1911 the previous misunderstandings between these two power centers were smoothed over, and a far-reaching collaboration, amounting as time went on to mutual dependence, ensued.

After the uncertain and short-lived rule of Sonnino, which ended in parliamentary defeat after only a hundred days, it became clear that Giolitti would have to return to the helm before long; in the making was another great ministry, which would carry the nation through to the elections of 1913. However, at this point an awkward question came up: what journalistic backing would the new regime be able to command? Giolitti enjoyed a sure majority in the chamber but had to face a generally hostile national press in a country where newspapers constituted the principal reading fare and source of information for the voting public.

The greatest Italian daily, the *Corriere della Sera* of Milan, was directed by Luigi Albertini and his brother Alberto. Albertini was an uncompromising opponent of Giolitti in every respect. The journalist considered him dishonest in his electoral and parliamentary tactics and doubted that he had any long-range plans that would justify the corruption and favoritism of his transformist politics. Moreover, from the pages of the *Corriere* Luigi Einaudi consistently condemned the whole structure of Italian protective economics, a linchpin of the Giolittian transformist system. Other influential papers were not much better from the government's standpoint: either they reflected the resentments of Italian landowners and businessmen over Giolitti's permissiveness toward organized labor, or they carried on the old Right's polemic against a parliament without parties that alternated in power, or (in the case of the lively *Resto de Carlino* of Bologna) expressed the impatience of educated young Italians with the prosaic, uninspired succession of ministries without real change. The *Corriere*, like other opposition papers, was also cautiously and surreptitiously unfriendly to the Central Empires, with which the government had to work within the uncertain terms of the Triple Alliance. Among the major Italian dailies, only *La Stampa* of Turin supported Giolitti; and its backing was not enough: Turin was too regional. The new "long ministry" in the making needed a paper in the capital itself that would present the chief's point of view in convincing terms.

Nothing could be done as long as Sonnino presided. Prospective newspaper financiers had to watch their step carefully. As Rolandi-Ricci whimsically expressed it in a letter to Joel, his "sweet" clients, the sugar refiners of Liguria, were wary of offending a government that might upset their business by revising the tariffs or taxes on their product, while his "hard" clients—the men of the steel trust—were so much at the mercy of government orders that they felt they could not afford to put money into a paper that did not support the premier of the moment, whoever he might be. However, once Sonnino fell in a manner that showed unmistakably that Giolitti was "absolute master," to use Rolandi-Ricci's phrase, the sugar and steel interests of Genoa began to come around: after all, it was to their advantage to back Giolitti before he officially returned to office. *La Tribuna*, their traditional organ, had offended Giolitti during the shipping controversies of 1908, and it was up to them to atone.[22]

At that point, March–November 1910, the Banca Commerciale

got a chance to render Giolitti a secret favor of the kind that binds. *La Tribuna* was on the verge of bankruptcy after ten years of poor management. Its backers, Rolandi-Ricci's clients, hesitated. Giolitti's partisans wanted to take it over and make it into the editorial mouthpiece of the future "long government" rather than let it go down the drain. The editorship and policy of the paper were to be thoroughly "Giolittian." Without the bank's ready funds, without Joel's behind-the-scenes mediation, this project could not have gone through; and it is significant that Joel's citizenship was conferred in August, right in the middle of the tangled negotiations that led to the refinancing and total reorganization of the paper at the end of the year. (Giolitti had, interestingly enough, previously indicated to Joel, through Rolandi-Ricci, that he was concerned over the power that the bank wielded and the largely foreign makeup of its executive group. This confidence occurred in March 1910, at the moment that his majority in the chamber was bringing Sonnino down.)

The stumbling blocks, both political and financial, were many. Giolitti had to work through various intermediaries, lest the whole operation seem an act of personal revenge on his part. His three unofficial representatives, Rattazzi, Maraini, and Garroni, occasionally worked at cross-purposes and constantly fell into indiscretions. Rattazzi kept in touch with Joel, seeing to it that he and Giolitti were aware of each other's moves. Maraini, a sugar industry pioneer, financier, real estate owner, and parliamentary deputy close to the Commerciale, worked on the scene at Rome, preparing the terms of an emergency refinancing that would keep *La Tribuna* from folding. The marquis Camillo Garroni, who had been prefect of Genoa almost uninterruptedly since Crispi's regime, had the task of persuading the "Genoese group," made up of sugar, steel, and shipping magnates, to put more money into the paper: among these businessmen was Senator Piaggio, still resentful over what the Commerciale and its maritime satellite, the Navigazione Generale, had done to him two years before. Garroni, whose son sat on the board of Elba (a steel-trust constituent), was so perfectly attuned to the business world of his native Liguria that the local chambers of commerce protested strongly every time any possibility of his being transferred to another post arose. At the same time the marquis enjoyed the personal confidence of Giolitti, who had known him for eighteen years: this was an important particular, since Giolitti was especially choosy about his key prefects. Armed with such reputation and power, Garroni was the ideal intermediary. Nevertheless he found it necessary to use Giolitti's name directly and constantly when he dealt with the suspicious Genoese group and its legal adviser, Rolandi-Ricci, who held the paper's fate in his hands. All this maneuvering was not only indiscreet but also more than a little irregular, since, after all, the prefect was supposed to be at the service of Premier Luzzatti: Giolitti was officially a mere deputy. Moreover, *La Tribuna*'s relaunching involved the interests of important minority stockholders, like the Banco di Roma and the Bank of Italy itself, a quasi agent of the state.

Under such circumstances the question of future editorial direction and policy became a central political problem, almost an affair of state. Premier Luzzatti, himself tied to Albertini of the *Corriere della Sera* by old links of friendship as well as by certain common ideals of the old liberal order, wanted *La Tribuna* relaunched under Andrea Torre, a parliamentary deputy and the Rome correspondent of the great Milanese daily. This was a strong candidacy, but from Giolitti's point of view it could not have been more ill-advised. Torre was politically ambitious and wanted to use the paper as a personal platform, and he was also known to be against the Triple Alliance. As things turned out, neither Giolitti nor Joel had to move personally; Torre set such extraordinary conditions that his candidacy fell through of its own weight. This left Giolitti free to put forward his own candidate—Olindo Malagodi, a talented and unassuming writer who had been London correspondent for *La Tribuna* since 1895. He proved to be more than acceptable to the Banca Commerciale.

It was much harder to refinance the paper than to find a new editor. The dying paper's capital assets consisted solely of its machines, worth at most half a million lire. Its business supporters were organized in a separate company that had a paid-up capital of 675,000 lire—gone down the drain. Of that lost capital, the Commerciale and its friends had 300,000 lire; the Banco di Roma and an allied chemical firm, 100,000; and the Bank of Italy, 25,000. The reorganization plan provided for a new capital outlay of 1.5 million lire, with the Commerciale and its friends furnishing 650,000—a sizable increase, but still less than a majority. The Bank of Italy was to remain at its old level, and the Banco di Roma was to furnish a mere 50,000. The joker in the plan was visible to the sharp eye. Besides the Commerciale's large block of shares, several financiers known to be in the bank's orbit in one way or another were on the list of donors.

The "Genoese group" protested. Their share in the old firm was only 25,000 lire; under the new plan they were put down for 560,000, a block second only to the Commerciale's; thus they were going to pay heavily to remain a permanent minority in the new corporation.

They proposed two alternatives: either the Commerciale should persuade some of its friends to sell to them or there should be an explicit agreement that the paper's editorial board and policies would be subject to the Genoese group's approval. Joel agreed to put more shares in the hands of the Genoese and worked out the matter directly with Rolandi-Ricci. The whole affair ended to the Commerciale's ultimate advantage. Between 1910 and 1912 Malagodi got the paper back into good financial condition and began to use the profits to buy up most of the rest of the shares for the Commerciale. During the First World War, when the Commerciale was under continual public attack, *La Tribuna* was its principal defender.

Soon after these transactions, on March 30, 1911, Giolitti assumed the premiership with a ministry that was to last three years. The new government had to face urgent problems at home and abroad. The Italian public had before its eyes universal suffrage and the Libyan War, but the Genoese business world probably gave at least equal attention to the salvaging of the steel trust, officially concluded August 7, 1911. With Bonaldo Stringher of the Bank of Italy as supreme arbiter, the Ilva refinancing arrangements took on the character of an act of state.

Naturally Rolandi-Ricci was overjoyed. On August 8 he wrote to Joel:

Last evening the convention between the steelmen and their backers was signed, and I, mindful of the willing and effective personal cooperation given by you in order to conclude this difficult operation, offer heartfelt thanks to you, who in this as in other occasions, had confidence in the industry of our country, in the men who run it, and a little, as well, in him who put at the disposal of the industrialists and financiers his modest and straightforward counsel.

This tortuous utterance was typical enough. Rolandi-Ricci began by thanking Joel with good reason and ended by congratulating himself for even better cause, since the lawyer had discounted Ilva's notes, at 5 percent yearly interest, to the amount of a million lire, a profitable and guaranteed investment that was to run till 1916. Rolandi-Ricci's mixture of flattery and condescension, odd in a man who represented industries that depended on the Commerciale, is understandable if one keeps in mind the fact that Ilva was a "national" interest and Joel a foreign banking expert—Rolandi-Ricci would not have used this tone with a native-born Italian, nor would he have dared to offer advice on how to staff the bank.

Rolandi-Ricci, who soon became a senator, was not the only one to benefit from the new regime. In the final agreement the Elba corporation was represented by Vittorio Garroni, son of the prefect. Camillo Garroni had, in the course of the dealings over *La Tribuna*, let Giolitti know that he was tired of a prefect's life. When Giolitti officially returned to power, his faithful adjutant got an unusual plum: a royal decree named him ambassador to Constantinople. Transfer directly from a prefecture to an embassy was unheard of, but the appointment had its merits. Garroni's business interests and industrial connections fitted him for the post, where his principal task was to further Italian penetration of the crumbling Ottoman Empire.

The settlements of 1910 and 1911 ushered in a new period of close collaboration between the Giolitti government and the Banca Commerciale, but they also gave rise to new jealousies and suspicions, which took a superpatriotic turn. Italy's war in Libya was unpopular in much of Europe because it jarred a precarious balance in the East. In Italy there was an uncorking of chauvinism and accumulated resentments that fast slid into xenophobia. Joel and his bank were an easy target: their foreign connections and their coziness with Rome could be cited against them. When the Ansaldo representatives at Constantinople were evicted from the arsenal by the Young Turks, they complained to the Italian embassy that the real villains were certain Italian institutions associated with big foreign banks, a transparent reference to the Commerciale and its oriental subsidiary.[23]

Ernesto Pacelli, director of the Banco di Roma, was also a rival. Though the Church had numerous local banking institutions throughout northern and central Italy, the Commerciale had few dealings with them, and cases of collaboration with the one Catholic investment bank, the Banco di Roma, were also rare.[24]

The Banco di Roma, founded in 1880, differed from the Commerciale in almost every way. In origin it was a small institution, founded and directed by aristocrats of the old papal state. After the annexation of Rome in 1870, the "black" nobility, while shunning the new court, engaged itself heavily in the new real estate and financial world that grew up in the capital. Rome and its environs never took on any real industrial importance, and its local banking institutions remained small and limited in their operations until the end of the century. However, the growth of Rome as a capital city led to a lively, though unhealthy, stream of investment: the three bases of the *banca papalina* during the 1880s and 1890s were real estate, public utilities, and flour mills. The last group is especially important: tariff legislation gave flour mills a special protected market. The Banco di Roma could recoup in milling, gasworks and trolley lines what it lost in the unwise real estate ventures of the late 1880s, and these sources of sure-rising income constituted a base for the bank's later expansion.

The *banca papalina* did not take an important part in the country's life until 1905, when it set up a branch in Alexandria, where there was a large Italian commercial colony. In 1906 its capital rose to 40 million, and the bank took part in the founding of the Bank of Abyssinia. Thus began its imperial progress.

During the next six years of hectic expansion, one constant principle seems to have guided the bank: to concentrate on the two areas marked out in European diplomacy for eventual Italian control, Libya and (in part) Ethiopia. The coordination with the Italian foreign ministry was close and explicit and was perhaps helped to some degree by the presence in the Banco di Roma of the Roman real estate executive Romolo Tittoni, whose brother Tommaso was foreign minister until the end of 1909. Romolo Tittoni's presence on the board of a bank with such marked clerical ties is not surprising, since his brother Tommaso was one of the principal arrangers of the first Catholic intervention in parliamentary elections (in 1904) and had worked his way up to minister in the Giolitti era, partly by virtue of his contacts with the Catholic political world. Tommaso Tittoni was of impeccable Risorgimento-liberal background, but he was known to favor a reconciliation with the Church.

The president and moving spirit of the Banco di Roma was Ernesto Pacelli, of the best papal aristocracy, whose nephew, Eugenio, was already marked out for a brilliant career in the curia. His high position did not imply any conservatism on the bank's part. On the contrary, it was highly speculative and undiscriminating, combining routine banking with long-term industrial financing in a way that puzzled and dismayed foreign observers. The bank directly managed and controlled some enterprises: Pacelli was president of Cines, the only Italian film producer in a market dominated by America's Kodak and Germany's Agfa.[25]

The bank's real plunge was into the colonial world. At the outbreak of the Italo-Turkish War in 1911, the Banco di Roma was developing in Libya mills, ice plants, ostrich-plume and sponge agencies, agricultural projects, and a shipping line. The bank worked closely with Italian diplomatic authorities. In January it set up its first branch in Libya, and by the fall of that year it was already complaining of Turkish hostilities. It wanted to go on from industrial and commercial development to mining, but here the Ottoman government balked. The Turks had been forced to give Italy shipping and postal rights, but they intended to keep control of Libya, which was, after all, a Moslem country.

The Banco di Roma's speculation was double. On one side it saw possibilities of mineral wealth in the otherwise unpromising Libyan soil; on the other it was convinced that sooner or later Italy would have to annex the last remaining colonial space in North Africa. Hence its work was as much political as economic. It tried to involve local notables, especially the former ruling family, the Karamanlis, in credit and stock operations. It seems likely that the bank was partly responsible for the widespread impression in Italy that annexing Libya would be easy, that the Arabs were waiting anxiously for liberation from the Young Turk regime.

The government was well aware of the unsoundness of the bank's activities. Di San Giuliano would have preferred to have the penetration of the Ottoman Empire backed by a united Italo-Turkish bank. Volpi and his associates in the Società Commerciale rejected suggestions of a merger with the Banco di Roma, and the Bank of Italy did not feel itself in a position to back such an unpromising combination. Hence, despite its misgivings, the government had no choice but to work with the Banco di Roma in Libya.[26]

The Commerciale's operations in the East were directed by Giuseppe Volpi, a promoter of no ordinary ability. Before turning abroad, he had been the principal figure in the development of electrical power in the Veneto in projects financed by the Commerciale. He was behind the establishment of Italy in Montenegro, where the Commerciale and its industrial allies set up a railroad and seaport development company. The bank had managed to get a minority share in the French-controlled mines at Heraclea and was on the lookout for new opportunities in the Ottoman Empire.

But in the competition for favors at Rome, the Banco di Roma had one advantage: its chief officers, Pacelli, Jacomoni, and Romolo Tittoni, had connections in the ministries of the sort that only Roman "country businessmen" could enjoy. Its executives could take aim at Joel and his bank from the concealed positions that Rome gave them. They took off from a publicly known fact: the German press was largely hostile to Italy's war; and in Rome it was bruited about that the Banca Commerciale had had a hand in influencing the German journalists against the war. The premier took little stock in such talk and wired Di San Giuliano on October 8, 1911:

I do not believe that the Banca Commerciale is engaging in a hostile action. Director-General Joel even wrote me a letter to the effect that the German press unfriendly to us is the press opposed to the German government. At any rate, be on guard, but take care about the source of reports against the Banca Commerciale.[27]

It would have been difficult at that moment to persuade the foreign minister to oppose the Banca Commerciale; on October 3, 1911, the local committee of the Commerciale had approved a 10,-000-lire loan to him, a normal transaction guaranteed by one of his relatives at Catania. The marquis, a great gentleman, disliked administering his family estate in Sicily and occasionally needed ready cash for his life at Rome. For these needs it was reasonable that he should turn to the Milanese bank rather than to Pacelli, in view of the Banco di Roma's involvements in Libya, but it is unlikely that he would have indebted himself to a bank that he believed hostile to his policies.[28]

Joel's enemies made a greater impression at the Bank of Italy, as a carefully worded letter written by Stringher to Joel on October 11 implies.[29] Stringher warned Joel that "political and financial spheres at Rome" were disturbed over the unfriendly line taken by many German newspapers, the "economic-financial connections of which are well known. . . . Here it is being said, surely falsely, that [they do] not lack inspiration from Piazza della Scala," a direct reference to Joel's central office. Having given Joel this bad news, Stringher went on to suggest remedies. Addressing Joel "not as a banker but as an Italian," Stringher urged him to use his connections and influence in German high finance to get the German press to moderate its tone and give Italy fairer treatment. Stringher felt that the Commerciale's highly placed friends in Germany must see how important it was to keep good relations with a country that was both an ally and a customer. Stringher explained that he wanted his communication kept absolutely secret, that he was moved by a feeling of "regard for my country and for the eminent man who is governing it today." Stringher concluded by saying that he was convinced that his words would not be lost on Joel, "because I know that you have a deep sense of affection and gratitude toward your second fatherland, of which you are now a full citizen."

Stringher's bombshell reached Joel at Munich on October 15, and the harassed banker shot off no less than three telegrams of self-justification. He cited his thirty-three years of residence and work in Italy, always spent to the advantage of the country's economic development. Joel said that he had furthered Italian interests even when they clashed with those of his "first fatherland" and that he had explained frankly to prominent Germans that Italy "had and still has economic and historic necessities that she could never give up." He went on to point out that he had let his only son go off to perform military service, though Italian law allowed him exemption. In the light of this record, Joel felt that his patriotism should be above suspicion and, interpreting Stringher's remarks in the most favorable way, thanked him for "offering me the opportunity to destroy such a hateful legend." Joel assured Stringher that he was already at work along the lines that the latter had suggested and that the German press was beginning to come around. Passing to broader issues, he expressed the hope that the premier's admirable calm, firmness, and energy would see things through and that the war would mark the beginning of a "policy of expansion well planned and fitted to our means and resources."

These were not hackneyed patriotic phrases. Joel spelled out his meaning in a few tightly packed lines: the Ottoman Imperial Bank director Auboyneau had just died, and it was essential that his successor, who would be another representative of French, Belgian, and British high finance, take care of Italian interests in the quaking empire, in spite of the war in North Africa. From Joel's words it is clear that for him the trans-Balkan rail project was more important than ventures in the Arab provinces. This had always been the line taken by the Commerciale's Milan management, which had refused to get involved in schemes for Syrian railroads, although it supported Commerciale subsidiary enterprises in Montenegro and Anatolia. Even in the moment of patriotic tension occasioned by an African expedition, Joel did not fail to call Stringher's attention to what he considered Italy's main economic objectives in the East.

After 1911 the relations between the Commerciale and the Giolitti government became so close and confidential that the bank's foreign operations were really a part of the history of Italian foreign policy. The bank's principal foreign promoters became agents of the government, and its Venetian group became the vanguard of Italian penetration eastward—to the extent, at times, of towing the bank management with it and even tugging strongly at the ministry itself.

By 1911 the *banca papalina* had badly overextended itself in Libya, and the Libyan expedition did not rescue it; on the contrary, the Banco di Roma was really ruined by the Italian occupation. It soon became clear that the Arabs were not going to welcome the Italians with open arms. Indeed, they showed their preference for Ottoman over infidel rule by firing on the Italian troops when they could, often bringing down brutal retaliation on their own heads. All the bank's assurance on that score proved to be worthless after a few weeks of real war.

The bank also suffered heavily when its branches and agencies in Constantinople and Jerusalem were closed by the Turks, and it lacked the reserves to fall back on that sustained the Commerciale. Up to 1914 the Banco di Roma concealed its losses by distributing misleadingly high dividends in an attempt to keep the confidence of its small investors, who favored the bank for the small denominations and high returns of its shares, as well as for its religious and patriotic character.

The bank undoubtedly hoped to recoup its losses in Libya itself. It became, in 1911–13, the principal purveyor and supplier to the Italian armed forces there and would undoubtedly have profited heavily had it not been for a series of quarrels with the government, some of which, over provisioning, came out in public. The bank was accused of overcharging for its services and driving up the price of wheat so high that it provoked an Arab insurrection. There was also talk of military supplies that were rejected after tests and of other kinds of war profiteering.

The Banco di Roma's substantial holdings in Libya suffered from the war. First the Turks seized them; then the Italian army requisitioned them. Pacelli imperiously demanded that the Italian government recompense the bank for its losses. At the stockholders' meeting of March 1913 he declared:

Our position in this matter is not that of any ordinary citizen who undergoes the inconvenience of a war waged for the general political aims of the country, but rather that of a willing collaborator, who, though he should not make unwarranted profits from the enterprise, should not, on the other hand, lose what he has put into it. We have not neglected, at the right time, to present our reservations and our claims, and recently, after a careful study of the matter in its legal aspects, we have formulated precise demands which we firmly intend to uphold and follow up with the same awareness of being in the right that has always guided us in our operations. . . .[30]

At the 1914 stockholders' meeting Pacelli went over the same ground. He rejected the common charges of war profiteering and control of the Libyan wheat market. The Roman princes, senators, and deputies present were as zealous as their president. They held that the bank had gone into Libya and expanded its holdings there with the advice and encouragement of the government. Therefore, the Banco di Roma's war losses, contracted in the line of duty, should be made good by the state. It was only fair that the bank's losses should be "shared by all the citizens"!

In fact, the bank was not able to get the recompense it thought it deserved. Instead, in 1914 Pacelli was finally forced to admit a loss of over 53 million lire, which meant that the Banco di Roma was on the edge of total failure. This was the most sensational event in the Italian banking world since the scandals of the 1890s and soon put an end to Pacelli's leadership in the bank. Meanwhile, the bank tried to cut its losses by surrendering most of its exclusive position in Libya. Electrification there was taken in hand by a company in which the Banco di Roma had only a minority holding, while the Banca Commerciale and its allies supplied most of the capital and executive board. Thus Italian colonial electrical systems were incorporated into the national industry, which was in many ways a province of the great Milanese bank. In the same month, March 1914, the Banco di Roma gave up its shipping line to the Sicilia Company, in which it held a one-third interest.

The bank's disastrous position was also evident politically. The complicated and weighty political and financial negotiations with the Turks and the Balkan powers, which went on up to the eve of the First World War, were entrusted by the Italian government to Volpi and Nogara, the great international agents of the Banca Commerciale. The Giolitti government was well aware of the dangers of committing the nation's foreign policy to one group of financial insiders, but it could find no alternative. Hence the Banco di Roma and its vast network of supporters in the Italian Catholic world must be considered as among the most embittered national enemies of the Giolitti system and the Milanese bank that had become so closely tied to it.

The Salandra government could do little for the Banco di Roma immediately. The bank was in such straits that it could not form part of the new, truly "national" Banca Italiana di Sconto, since its previous losses would have weighed too heavily on the young institution. But Salandra did reopen relations with the Banco di Roma.

In June 1914 Di San Giuliano urged the new premier to settle the government's quarrel with the bank. He pointed out that it was unwise to rely entirely on one bank (the Commerciale) in planning Italian expansion and further observed that in Syria, Egypt, and— most important—Ethiopia, the Banco di Roma, because of its existing positions and its relations with the Church, was the only Italian bank that could give the foreign ministry the economic help it needed. The minister noted that Italian political claims in the East African area would lapse unless they were justified by economic penetration, and in a little aside that shows much of his positive attitude, he observed to Salandra that "today foreign policy is above all a policy of business."

There were other weighty reasons for the Italian government's continued regard for the Banco di Roma. The bank's agent in Cairo, an Arab, had close relations with the khedive, one of the wealthiest and most influential figures in the whole Ottoman system. In this respect the bank's agent made himself useful not only to the foreign ministry, which took an interest in the khedivial estates in Asia Minor, but also to the Ministry of Colonies. Through the intercession of the Banco di Roma's men in Cairo, the Italian government kept trying through all of 1913 and 1914 to persuade the khedive to convince the Senussite Arabs of Cyrenaica that they should submit to the Italian colonial administration. This was no mean service, since the Senussite order constituted a virtually independent state within the Libyan Arab world, and the khedive asked 40,000 pounds sterling from the Italian government for his help. These portentous matters were still pending in the first months of the Salandra government, and the Banco di Roma's contacts in Cairo were indispensable. Only the outbreak of war between Britain and the Turks in the fall of 1914 finally closed the chapter.

Salandra must have taken these ministerial recommendations to heart: on February 15, 1915, his government, ratifying a decision taken by the minister of war, agreed to negotiate the dispute with the Banco di Roma. By then the controversy had dragged on for more than two years, and the bank was in eclipse.

What is most instructive about the Banco di Roma episode is the view that it affords of another Italy. The world of Italian Catholics, so quiet and, at first, seemingly neutralist, finally gave Salandra strong support in his positions for intervention and against Giolitti and his system. Without Catholic help Salandra might have found it much harder to unseat Giolitti as arbiter of Italian politics.

Any discussion of the Commerciale should conclude with the extraordinary public campaign against the bank that began at the end of Giolitti's long ministry. The bank's foreign ties and its commanding position in the Italian economy were becoming matters for public discussion even before the War broke out. In the spring of 1913 an indignant professor in a Roman business school accused the bank of being a pump that sucked capital out of Italy into Germany. Most recently, he said, the bank had taken a central role in forming a new government-subsidized sector of the merchant marine after beating down a rival group with a carefully orchestrated "antimonopoly" campaign. Here the professor was merely echoing the charges made by Senator Piaggio, head of the defeated shipping group. At the Eleventh National Congress of Industrialists and Businessmen, held at Venice in June 1913, one of the reasons suggested for the failure of Italian exports to attract the market they deserved was that the big Italian banks were not "national" in leadership or policy. The discussion was hastily muffled—the Banca Commerciale was one of the sponsors of the congress—but the muttering probably went on. The Roman industrial paper *Rassegna dei lavori pubblici* accused the foreign financial groups of holding Italian industrial development back and betraying the state's credit abroad.[31]

On the far Left the mariners' federation denounced the Navigazione Generale as German because of the Banca Commerciale's share in the company. In January 1914 the Navigazione Generale retorted with a long statement of denial and self-justification. It said that the company's 200,000 shares were all in Italian hands; that the company had done much to buy out German interests in the Italian merchant marine; and that "with the vigorous initiative of our company, transatlantic shipping lines have followed a truly national policy, so that while before 1903 Italian ships carried only 31 percent of emigrants to North America and 71 percent to South America, in 1913 these percentages have risen to 55 percent for North America and 87 percent for South America."

After the war started, the campaign against the Commerciale intensified. Giolitti, strong in the parliament and in the higher state bureaucracy, had dominated Italian politics for ten years, and everyone knew that his stepping aside in March 1914 was only one of his periodic tactical retreats. He was still the political arbiter and ministry-maker, still the potential referee between capital and labor. The country was restless, and the Salandra government was fretful over his invisible control, but there was no way out until August 1914. The war offered many ways of getting around Giolitti's parliamentary majority and discrediting his system and his public image. The intervention policy of 1914–15, pursued by the government and the crown outside the chamber, united the Right and the Left behind Salandra and provided the levers to unseat Giolitti.

One of these levers was precisely the anti-Commerciale campaign: anti-Giolittianism on the financial front. It had two aims: to link in the public mind the neutralist Giolitti, the Banca Commerciale, and the worldwide political and economic interests of Germany; and to discredit Joel, Weil, and Toeplitz—the foreign financiers who ran the Commerciale behind an Italian façade.

Italian prewar resentment against foreign influences in banks was not a uniquely Italian phenomenon. A similar attitude prevailed in Paris, where finance and foreign-affairs officials told the czar's embassy how worried they were over "cosmopolitanism" in the French banking world. In the course of such discussions between French and Russian functionaries, the names that recurred were usually Jewish—Adler, Ullmann, Spitz—in short, Austrian or German citizens with special cosmopolitan connections. The Russians were concerned that the cooperation between Parisian and Viennese banks might result in a flow of French capital to Central Europe rather than to the Russian Empire, though in 1913 that seemed hardly likely in view of the current political alliances.[32]

From these reports we may form some notion of the possible origins of the interventionists' campaign against the Commerciale once the war broke out. The French may well have been behind much of it.[33]

How much fire was there behind this propaganda smoke? Very little, probably. The forces of high finance in the various capitals of prewar Europe served the great powers and could take few initiatives without the assent of the big foreign ministries. The connections between the major European banks look impressive, but many of their ambitious joint projects in the East were undertaken at the behest of the European diplomatic concert with all kinds of political guarantees. High finance was coming to depend on the European nation-states, and the cooperation of Europe's major investment banks was technical and without real political effects. Italy, in fact, is a good example of how financial institutions of clearly "cosmopolitan" origins soon acclimatized themselves to the nation-state: whatever international ties or sympathies the Commerciale or Credito Italiano may have had were clearly subordinated to the exigencies of domestic heavy industry. The debtor, not the creditor, seems to have called the tune, and nationalistic, not cosmopolitan, interests tipped the scale. The Rothschilds might have been able to foster peace and international cooperation in the previous century, but by 1914 international high finance wielded little power of its own. It could still render indispensable services to the diplomacy, treasury, and industry of many European states, services that would have been impossible without international understanding among financiers, but it is hard to see any invisible international power working behind the chancelleries of Europe.

The prominence of Jews in the world of high finance did not have the internationalizing effect that many xenophobes imagined. The Jewish bankers and enterprisers of the time did form a distinctive group, spread throughout Europe, with special economic functions. They brought new investment ideas and methods with them wherever they went. But they never served any collective, universal Jewish purpose. They often married outside; they rejected Zionism; and they did everything possible to dissociate themselves from anything but a distant philanthropic connection with the Jewish world.

The directors of the Commerciale, with their newfound Italian patriotism, were quite typical in this respect. The international Jew

did crave a national identity—German, French, British, Italian—
but never Jewish. Zionism never touched him before 1914.

In prewar capitalism no ubiquitous Jewish cabal was operating
to keep high finance at the service of the collective Jewish interest.
On the contrary, "court Jews" were still making their way up by providing needed services to rulers, especially in time of war. In the
early twentieth century they survived by putting their persons, resources, and skills at the service of nation-states, and they often did so
unreservedly. They worked to destroy the conditions that had made
their own emancipation possible, aiding and abetting a nationalism,
jealous and exclusive, which was to be turned against them.

At a distance of a half-century, the notion of a worldwide financial conspiracy seems bizarre. The plausibility it had in the Europe of
1914 was due to the seeming parallel between Second-International
Socialism and the cosmopolitanism of high finance. But what these
two "internationals" really had in common was their ineffectiveness
at the moment of crisis, their ultimate subservience to the nation-
state. In fact, the international of high finance proved even weaker
then the red international. The European state system, with its built-
in autarkies, proved far stronger than all the internationals combined.

THE POLITICS
OF ITALIAN
IMPERIALISM
ON THE EVE
OF THE WAR

5

Industrial Labor and Management Conflicts

The preceding chapters have tried to trace the deep-seated reasons for Italy's shift from liberal to imperialist—essentially pre-Fascist—politics between 1911 and 1915 and to show that those reasons lay in the pattern of Italy's industrialization. Domestic and foreign political contingencies helped to speed Italy toward autarky and imperialism in those years, but the direction Italian politics took was not merely the result of parliamentary regrouping and cabinet changing. Even the advent of mass-party democracy, foreshadowed by Socialist and Catholic voting strength in 1913, made little difference. Italy remained expansionist and aggressive in foreign policy and protectionist at home.

Many writers, not all of them Marxist, regard the imperialistic tendencies that culminated in European fascism as essentially counterrevolutionary, a reaction against mass-party democratic politics. Writers with a psychological turn of mind have spoken of fascism as an authoritarian anxiety-reaction caused by modern man's "transcendence," his crashing through traditional barriers in thought and society. Both intellectual aristocrats like Maurras and lower middle-class quasi-intellectuals like Hitler, uprooted and disoriented by the effects of "transcendence," which often look like unguided social change, find saving strength in a self-enclosed, authoritarian nationalism that protects them against the leveling influences of modern society, especially parliaments and socialism.

Such a thesis has much to recommend it; it goes far toward accounting for the prevalence of pre-Fascist modes of thought in prewar Italy. But it does not serve as a general explanation of the fascist phenomenon. In other countries democracy and egalitarian welfare socialism have prevailed without generating a serious fascist reaction or counterattack. There is something about the development of Germany, Italy, and Japan that sets them off from other modern nations, some common feature that found eventual expression in the Axis and Tripartite pacts of the 1930s and 1940s; and the reaction theory does not fully explain it. Fascism and socialism do indeed often arise in the same national society, but this duality does not mean that fascism always arises as a panicky reaction to socialism.

It appears, rather, that both movements arise almost at the same time as efforts to cope with a set of chronic national problems. The difficulties of industrialization and the imbalance it brings are likely to call forth both socialist and imperialist programs and movements; they are not primarily directed against each other but are opposed solutions to the same problems. Imperialistic tendencies do not emerge primarily as a reaction against parliaments and labor unions, although part of their middle-class appeal stems therefrom; imperialism appears rather as a positive, dynamic solution to the problems posed by national industrial development.

The foregoing generalities apply particularly to Italy. The structural imbalance and narrow margins of growing heavy industry in Italy created an especially painful and troubled labor situation that generated revolutionary-socialist tendencies in the proletariat on a national level. And Italy's imperialist aims were connected with the development and outlet problems of Italian industry. Finally, the same empirically discernible pressures that led to revolutionary discontent in the plants of Turin and Milan prompted naval displays and concession seeking in the eastern Mediterranean. Behind the political play of revolutionary Left and counterrevolutionary Right lay potentially tragic economic problems to which neither side could offer genuine solutions.

Even in the healthiest and most forward-looking sectors of Italian heavy industry, labor organizers were in a dark mood on the eve of the war. The motor workers of Turin, sober but militant Socialists, observed May Day of 1914 without cheer, and their union paper said:

This year the celebration of May First has an especial importance that we should note. Certain meaningful signs warn that we are headed toward threatening times. The brutality and haughtiness of the bosses [padroni] *are coming to the fore everywhere. The struggle between capital and labor becomes sharper every day, since the governments, with their brute power, take up positions against the moderate demands of the workers and give the bosses the strength to reject them. And while workers' conditions, even if they do not worsen, remain stationary, the fearful unchecked crisis that has been troubling Europe for about two years has caused a formidable price rise in all staples, especially foodstuffs. . . .*[1]

What is notable in the Turinese labor paper is not merely the tone of bitterness and pessimism, but a real maturity of mind. The Turinese leaders of the Italian Federation of Metal Workers (FIOM) gave an objective diagnosis of labor's lasting troubles. As they saw it, management's reactionary spirit was not due merely to class feeling or political prospects, but to real economic difficulties brought on by a dangerous imbalance between new mass-productive plants and possible outlets. Their summary of the crisis year 1913 (published June 15 of the following year) noted:

The automobile industry, which exports a large part of its production, has felt especially the effects of the international crisis situation, and also, though to a lesser degree, the competition of North America. Furthermore, it has been finding the markets of South America almost closed, as well as those of Rumania and Greece, the latter two because of customs duties. Hence there has been some significant overproduction, which has forced certain big plants to reduce the working week to forty-six hours. . . .[2]

These measured words reflect a long-troubled labor union experience. The big automobile strikes of 1913 were defensive in aim, protecting or regaining positions won previously, and behind the 1913 strike lay years of working-class frustration and disorganization. The Turin labor elite—even in the best years only about one-third of Turin's workers belonged to the union—had had an extraordinarily hard life since the 1907 crash. From 1907 to 1910, depression years, their union was moribund. In the two succeeding years of slow recovery, Turinese motor workers resorted to wildcat strikes instigated by revolutionary-syndicalists. The movements failed completely in the face of the employers' concerted lockout agreements. At the end of 1912 the Turin motor workers returned to their official Socialist union, which set about recovering lost ground: the very principle of collective bargaining had to be restored. At the same time the Socialists had gained new working-class credit as revolutionaries because of their stand against the Italo-Turkish War, while syndicalist spontaneity had lost its easy appeal.

Finally, in the spring of 1913 the FIOM was in a position to call a strike in an effort to rewin collective bargaining, recognition of the union, and a fifty-four-hour week, all ground lost since 1907. The Socialists pointed out that Fiat's production was rising from 3,000 cars in 1911 to an eventual 4,500 in 1913 and that Fiat, as well as Lancia and others, could afford higher wages. This sort of optimism, based on business prospects for the whole industry, was to disappear by 1914.

The Turin industrialists drew together and stood fast. A ninety-three-day strike resulted, with an industry-wide lockout that threw 17,000 workers into the street. The lockout strategy might easily have defeated the union, were it not for political intervention. With general elections coming in the fall, Giolitti warned the factory owners through his Turin prefect that the government would not guarantee protection if their lockout led to violence, and Giolitti's daily, *La Tribuna*, openly attacked the industrialists' spokesman, the French manufacturer Craponne, as a trouble-making foreigner. The industrialists then grudgingly gave way, and the FIOM got its minimum demands, together with union recognition.

But these events boded ill for the future. By May 1914 Giolitti was gone, the motor industry's troubles remained, and the union's cheerless view of the dragging crisis seemed more than justified. Future gains for labor were unlikely, and the auto workers anticipated a hard time in keeping under Salandra what they had painfully regained in Giolitti's last year of power.[3]

Such were labor conditions in the best-run part of Italian heavy industry; rails and steel presented a much gloomier picture. If the ceiling on labor was low at Turin, it was lower elsewhere, and the atmosphere was more stifling.

The FIOM included rail and engine workers' organizations; the union's report for the year 1913, after the darkening of the picture of the automotive industry, went on to discuss in equally measured and objective terms the situation in rail and engine enterprises:

Work has been scarce in the railroad-car industry . . . more plentiful . . . in shipbuilding, especially for war purposes . . . in arms plants of every sort, and in the manufacture of electrical devices. . . . It must not be forgotten that in Italy the dividend rate, even if it is high, is not yet a sure sign of the stability of the mechanical industries.

The report noted that those industries were "almost all young, and in continual renewal and development, or else set up in the hope of getting work from the state, without which there have been and will again be painful disappointments."

The FIOM concluded that workers' organizations were passing through one of their hardest periods. To be sure, in 1911 the FIOM had thirty sections with 8,000 members and had risen in 1913 to 10,600 members in thirty-nine sections, but this modest gain inspired no optimism.

Certainly the unceasing labor conflicts of Milan in 1913 gave little hope to the reformist union organizers.[4] At the start of the year, there were three different sectors of Milanese industry with labor disputes. The Edison electrical workers were engaged in a long-drawn-out strike for purely economic ends, which they were unable to win. The automobile workers, along with some of their fellows in the engine plants, wanted better hours and a pay scale equal to that prevailing in comparable firms at Turin, where wages were notably better. The railroad-car workers had a special grievance: thousands of them were unemployed because both the state and the local private industries were slow in allocating and filling new rolling-stock orders. The prefect of Milan attempted to answer the last complaint by announcing on June 30, 1913, that Breda had been given orders for some big locomotives and that out of the 40 million-lire rolling-stock orders just authorized at Rome, 22 million worth would go to Milanese firms. Nevertheless, railroad-car workers, too, were drawn into the general agitations of that difficult year.

Swayed by their sense of frustration at the gradual and legal tactics of the reform Socialists and carried along by the brilliant oratory of Filippo Corridoni, the one true leader that Italian syndicalism ever produced, the laborers of Milan, like those of Turin a little earlier, opted for revolutionary-syndicalist leadership. Twice, in June 1913 and again in August, Milan fell subject to the syndicalist tactic of turning partial economic strikes into general revolutionary strikes, a sort of rehearsal for the final violent confrontation between the proletariat and the bourgeoisie. The influential young Socialist editor, Benito Mussolini, cheered on the syndicalists' general strike, though it must be noted that he followed Corridoni at a certain prudent distance.

These general strikes were called off or petered out without achieving any definite goal. The Giolitti government, which had intervened so effectively shortly before to save the reformist labor leaders of Turin, refused to rescue the Milanese strikers from lockout and eventual defeat. The premier had never been lenient with revolutionary syndicalism; and at the height of the 1913 crisis, Corridoni actually went to jail for inciting to violence. Challenged, Giolitti explained the difference in his policies at Turin and at Milan by claiming, realistically, that the one was a political agitation, the other an essentially economic struggle.

Milanese labor paid high for stepping outside Giolitti's charmed circle. By the first months of 1914, all sectors of Milanese labor had surrendered to their employers, except for the automobile workers, who obtained some partial successes after months of arbitration. Strikers often found it hard to get reinstated, and as might be expected, the railroad-car workers fared worst of all. Their employers, in a position to dictate terms, retained scab labor that had been hired during the strikes. Union shop and collective bargaining were further off than ever on the eve of the war.

As elsewhere in 1913, the disputes engendered by these conflicts shed light on the real problems of Italian heavy industry. The knowledgeable Republican deputy Eugenio Chiesa, who had stood out in 1911 by denouncing the state-sponsored refinancing of the steel trust, continued the same line of attack this time. He attributed the Milanese machine industries' troubles to a 33 percent rise in the price of steel in Italy, an increase guaranteed by the recent agreements between Italian steel men and the Germans. Chiesa seems to have hit the mark: in 1913, following a consistent trend, steel's corporate profits were markedly higher than those of the mechanical industries. Corridoni inadvertently put his finger on a deeper ill when he reported that some automobile makers were paying dividends as high as 16 percent and concluded that they could therefore pay higher wages. Corridoni's figure was misleading—in 1913 Italy's fifteen chief automobile firms paid an average dividend of only 5.75 percent, with five paying no dividends at all. But all Italian industries had to offer investors a high rate of return to attract scarce and reluctant capital; hence, high dividends did not always reflect healthy business conditions. The reformist union leaders knew this, as their 1913 report showed.

Behind the arrogance and class spirit reflected in the lockouts and employers' fronts in North Italian industry, there were genuine economic pressures. And if labor had thin margins for possible action in the most progressive and internationally competitive sectors of Italian heavy industry, its lot was far worse in the steel trust's foundries and mills.[5]

In 1911, the year of the state-sponsored refinancing of Ilva, local Socialists noted that at Elba, the starting point of the whole steel-trust complex, management had set up a rigid class system in which technicians, white-collar employees, and overseers enjoyed all kinds of benefits and perquisites from which labor was rigorously excluded. At Piombino the trust had set up a blast furnace without a thought to housing, sanitation, or schooling for the labor force. As a result, the critics said, the town fast became unsanitary and overcrowded, with a surly, rebellious mass of workers. Supervisory jobs in the foundry and blast furnace, they said, were going to friends of shareholders.

The fatal strikes of Elba-Piombino broke out in June 1911 as a result, so the Socialists claimed, of long-standing irritation at the financiers and speculators who ran the companies that should have been run by industrialists. And the reform Socialists of the area are believable; they did not favor the strike and judged it ill timed and unplanned.

The immediate causes of the Elba-Piombino strikes were simple, but they reveal how the trust operated. At Elba two squads assigned to pour molten metal at the blast furnace at Portoferraio went on strike on June 29 when the management refused to reinforce the standing force of six workers with one or two men more than the number that had previously been added during the period of greatest heat and exhaustion. At Piombino the strike was set off by a minor dispute over paying for an accident, a matter of only twenty-two lire. The reformists, who knew that the steel companies were in serious financial difficulties and about to get government aid, warned the workers that it was no time to strike. They even suspected that the steel companies, with their overloaded inventories, welcomed a chance to shut down operations, reduce production expenses, and at the same time give prospective union laborers a stunning defeat. As the reform Socialists saw it, a set of industries that was so sick could not be brought to its knees by stopping work or shutting off ore supplies. The only thing that kept the trust alive was political pull, and against that influence the forces of organized labor counted for little indeed. Even the "intransigent" revolutionary Socialist Giovanni Lerda had come to think much the same thing by the end of 1911. He considered the Elba-Piombino strikes a trap set by the steel companies that wanted to reorganize and cut down the work force without taking upon themselves the onus of layoffs and shutdowns. With the 1911 refinancing and the plentiful summer market in international scrap metal, there was no chance that a strike at Elba or Piombino could starve out the steel trust, as the syndicalist strike leaders imagined; as at Turin and Milan, syndicalist spontaneity showed itself empty and irresponsible when put to the test.

The results were like those in the North. After four months of strike and lockout, the workers were allowed back by the trust on terms that amounted to unconditional surrender; organizers and independent-minded workers were not rehired.

The state's role in the strike was crucial. Even the reform Socialists thought the government played foul; riding roughshod over civil liberties, the police arrested about one hundred fifty persons in the Piombino area, in one ugly case opening fire on a crowd and killing a young boy. The local court backed the police with jail sentences, some of them for a year or more.

The events at Elba-Piombino cast a shadow over Giolitti's image. Eugenio Chiesa, that sharp and unsparing critic of Giolitti's policies, noted in parliament that the premier was far more partisan than Luzzatti had been in a previous dispute at Piombino.[6] Luzzatti, the deputy said, had not hesitated to force the Piombino management to end a lockout by threatening a reduction of the armed protection the state provided. Giolitti's contrasting behavior is not hard to explain. The 1911 steel refinancing, the *Tribuna* deal of the same year, and the onset of the colonial war were more than enough to account for the state's apparent partisanship on behalf of the trust. The Giolittian system made a sharp distinction between potential allies—the reform Socialists—and the fomenters of syndicalist revolution. Nevertheless these episodes form part of the seamy underside of the Italian liberal era.

Steelworkers, both because they were led by syndicalists and because they were in an artificial, politically maintained industry, never came close to achieving the benefits that were won at Turin. At Piombino, as a result of agreements in force since 1910, workers could strike only after giving forty-eight hours' notice. Otherwise they forfeited a deposit withheld from pay. The same was true at Terni. Unlike the Turinese unions, the central Italian steelworkers' unions had no voice whatever in determining factory conditions, and prospects for a successful strike were dim.[7]

At Terni, directed by Giuseppe Orlando of the wide-ranging industrial clan, there had been no union recognition or collective bargaining since the disastrous strike and lockout of 1907.[8]

During the next seven years, the local Socialists stood firm against calling another strike: they knew the local management could respond with a lockout and force the workers to come back on their knees. Though the Terni Socialists continued to organize and agitate, the only real hope they had was political: they wanted to take over Terni altogether. Since the state was already Terni's principal customer, a host of parasitic intermediaries would thus disappear.

There was no remedy in local action for labor's ills: Terni was in effect a company town. The only other substantial industry in the area was a calcium company under "clerical" Roman direction. The municipal government and the local parliamentary representation were patriotic and right-wing. In the general elections of 1913, an ex-Republican of nationalist leanings narrowly defeated his Socialist opponent, thanks to clerical votes from the countryside.

The scanty workers' pension and accident funds were wholly in company hands, even though they were largely accumulated through payroll deductions, and most workers were in debt to the company store. Even the watchmen and doorkeepers—privileged help—were told by Orlando in 1912 to sign a new contract forfeiting severance pay. When they protested, he told them, with a grim conceit, that he was a man of steel and tolerated no impositions from his employees. Within a few weeks, the rebels were discharged.

The Socialists of Terni knew that their situation was unpromising, but they had the courage to face it realistically and not to take refuge in the revolutionary strike illusions that were then Mussolini's stock-in-trade. During the 1913 general strikes at Milan, they pointed out to the young editor of *Avanti!* that at Terni the strike weapon would serve the company's interests better than it would serve the workers'. They had sound reasons for their pessimism.[9] They knew that Terni's steelworkers were kept alive by military favors, that Terni armor plate was so costly that the Italian state sometimes had to delay paying for it (as it did during the Libyan war), and that Terni was lagging behind its chief domestic competitor, Ansaldo, in filling naval gun and armor plate orders. They also knew that in 1913 the state, finally out of patience, had turned to Carnegie and Bethlehem for naval armor as the international naval race quickened. This was a savage commentary on Italy's previous decades of supposed military self-sufficiency.

Terni's association with the state did not spur it on to improved efficiency. The state arms factory at Terni, run by the Ministry of War with a general as director, was so mismanaged technically that the ministry at Rome finally sent out a special inspection team in early 1914. Because the inspection report was evidently not unfavorable, the factory workers, charging that there had been a whitewash, sent a three-man delegation to enlighten Rome. The Socialists reported that one arms worker who had given critical testimony to the inspectors was suspended for eight days as a penalty. In this atmosphere of vindictive inefficiency, the Socialists could do little but expose conditions—a work stoppage could force no real improvement.

What really discouraged the Socialists in the area was Terni's successful new political tack. The firm became the sponsor of Nationalist movements, coalescing moderate Republicans, monarchists, and Catholics, an arrangement that would have been inconceivable in the early periods of the nation-state. Patriotism and expansionism turned out to have real political drawing power with the public, as the 1913 elections showed. Italian conservatism was no longer presenting itself locally as a defense of private property rights and constituted order but had become aggressive, having found in imperialism an effective means of counterattacking Socialism on its own ground. If, as the Socialists claimed, Terni steel spent 50,000 a year on its lilliputian social services and 150,000 on politics and the press, it was beginning to get its money's worth.

Terni was the oldest and most antiquated component of Italy's big-steel complex, and its landlocked position, however comforting from the standpoint of military security, made little economic sense. Hence it would be unfair to take this backwater firm as typical of Italian heavy industry as a whole. Nevertheless the tense labor situation and the touchy, aggressive patrioteering of the management were symptomatic of the whole Italian climate.

In the big steel-trust plant at Bagnoli, in the Naples area, the management simply discharged any worker who showed signs of disaffection. A Socialist ex-worker from Bagnoli charged in 1911 that steel-trust employees were getting payoffs from firms that furnished material or machines to the Bagnoli plant, while management was loading the official payroll with useless personnel "recommended" to it by the police or other authorities. Nearby, at the Ferriere del Vesuvio, there was a nine-month strike in 1912–13 over the promotion of beginners to foremanships without regard to seniority.

In these years the Italian merchant marine had an entirely different labor history. Between 1909 and 1911, there appeared among Italian seafarers a labor union without precedent or parallel. The

Federazione Marinara was at the same time both syndicalist and superpatriotic. It denounced German economic penetration in Italy right from the start and called for war on Austria as early as August 1914.[10]

The Marine Federation was the personal creation of an imaginative and colorful ship's officer, Captain Giuseppe Giulietti, who gave up shipboard life when his new employer, the big Genoese ship operator Emanuele Parodi, wished to shift him from a passenger to a cargo vessel, a transfer that the captain took as an unwarranted demotion. From 1909 to the Libyan War, Giulietti devoted himself to setting up a new Italian mariners' union, filling a gap that had existed since the employers' successes of 1906.

Unlike other syndicalists, Giulietti took seriously the task of joining together all essential productive personnel: he federated cabin boys, seamen, engineers, deck officers, captains, ship's doctors, and clerks. A syndicalist ashore might imagine that the proletariat alone could seize and operate a factory or railroad, but a ship's captain had to be more realistic and bring in all necessary talents. Giulietti finally succeeded in joining all seafaring personnel into a single federation; and the shipowners of Genoa, Venice, and Naples found themselves faced not with journalists and improvisers, but with men of training and capacities comparable to their own. In spite of their best efforts, the shippers could never find any sizable group of officers or men willing to defy Giulietti's federation, which by 1911 had become the principal bargaining agent for Italian mariners of all categories and functioned as such until the Fascist period. This was a unique achievement; no other syndicalist union ever recruited engineers and technicians along with laborers or ever succeeded in dominating a whole sector of industry.

Giulietti differed from most syndicalists in another important respect: he had political sense. He knew that the shipowners of Liguria, in addition to their Milanese banking connections, had at their call a number of influential deputies. Some shipbuilding and shipowning dynasties actually had members sitting in parliament in 1913 and 1914—notably, a Parodi (a brother of Emanuele), Salvatore Orlando (a son of Luigi), and Senator Erasmo Piaggio. Against the retired admirals and North Italian business spokesmen in the chamber, Giulietti was able to muster a good number of moderate and reform Socialist deputies from the same regions to give political backing to his federation; this made a difference as long as the Italian premier cared about sympathy or passive support on the Left, as Giolitti did.

Giulietti's advantage over other syndicalists did not consist merely in his willingness to engage in parliamentary politics. As a patriot and an officer, the captain was able to deal with the naval ministry on personal terms unthinkable for any other union leader. On the other hand Giulietti's Socialist party friendships enabled the federation to count on the solidarity of longshoremen and dock-workers in case of trouble.

Giulietti's big chance came with the Italo-Turkish War and Italy's consequent expansion in the eastern Mediterranean, which brought in their wake new contracts for Italian shippers and generous new maritime subsidies. Italian shipowners, newly prosperous, stood to lose heavily in the event of any delay or stoppage. For those who operated subsidized lines, regular sailings became a matter of financial life or death. In case of labor trouble, they could not simply tie up their ships in port, as the owners of cargo vessels sometimes did. Transatlantic passenger lines were in much the same straits.

Giulietti took advantage of the situation while keeping generally within the limits of the law. As a captain himself, he understood and upheld the Italian sea code's provisions against mutiny, but he was able to employ the strike weapon anyway at the port of embarkation. The federation could keep any Italian ship from leaving its port by a simple and eminently legal device: having some essential crewman report sick on the day of departure and seeing to it that no replacement was found willing to sign on. This strike method, which required portwide solidarity among all seafaring personnel, worked very well and even benefited from one provision of Italian sea law which forbade shipowners to send out their vessels with crews that were less than two-thirds Italian, thus limiting the possibility of their making do with foreign scab labor.

The federation first showed its real strength in the spring of 1913, when it asked that a single nationwide mariners' pension be set up by law. All kinds of local interests stood in the way, and there was no chance that the chamber would come up with a bill that met the federation's demands. So the federation took the uncharacteristically rash step of closing Italy's ports for twelve days, while ministers and deputies debated and fumed. Finally Giolitti himself had to break the deadlock. The premier promised the mariners that they would get their fund, and he granted amnesty to those who had been arrested and tried for illegal acts in closing the ports.

The episode left conservatives convinced that both the chamber and the ministry had given in to union violence. In spite of the gain to Giolitti from the Left, much of the country's middle-class opinion, ably shaped or represented by Albertini's *Corriere della Sera*, came to see the premier as a shifty opportunist who systematically compromised the state's prestige for parliamentary expediency.

After this preliminary gain, the federation proceeded to unionize the whole Italian merchant marine step by step. Giulietti began with the subsidized lines, the most vulnerable part of the industry. As his first target he chose Sitmar, which ran many of the important lines from Venice to the East. For fifty-four days in the fall of 1913, Sitmar's ships were blocked in the port of Venice, and the oriental commerce of the Italian Adriatic was virtually paralyzed. Finally the government insisted that the lines operate, and Sitmar asked the naval ministry to represent it in negotiations with Giulietti. After only two days Giulietti and the navy reached an agreement satisfactory to the union. Then Sitmar backed out and got the navy to recall its negotiators. Giulietti rushed to Rome, alerted his Socialist allies in the chamber, and appealed to the naval minister, Admiral Millo. Millo, playing the part of the blunt, nonpolitical sailor, admitted to Giulietti that the shipowners were responsible for the impasse. The matter passed to the premier, who decided that Sitmar would have to accept the agreement worked out between the union and the navy. Within a few days all major subsidized lines accepted the federation's demands, and the big passenger lines soon followed suit.

Up to this point the federation had been having its own way. Its opponents, pressed by fixed schedules or government contract obligations, had had no margin for maneuver. Every marine-labor dispute had unavoidably become a political question, and Captain Giulietti had been able to carry the day, thanks to the premier's desire to have as little trouble as possible on the Left. In short, the federation's success was due only in part to its remarkably disciplined "vertical" organization. In 1913 the federation won because its foes depended on the state, and the state, under Giolitti's direction, looked sympathetically at labor unions that stayed within the law and followed the political lead of reform Socialist parliamentarians.

Things were quite different when Giulietti turned to unionizing cargo vessels at the start of the next year. Here the captain ran up against his former employer, Emanuele Parodi, and a group of independent ship operators who did not have to take their cues from Rome or Milan. To be sure, the Parodi and Menada interests were present in all three branches of Italian shipping: subsidy lines, transatlantic passenger lines, and freighters. In the first two they were tied to the government and the big investment banks, but when it came to freighters they were on their own ground, where they were used to setting their own terms of employment and fixing their own standards of shipboard discipline, often enforced, in the good old days, by officers armed with revolvers. The tough, independent operators of Genoa had no intention of putting their ships under the control of a captain who had once worked for them. They knew Giulietti, and to a certain extent liked and respected him, as he did them, but they had no doubt about his ultimate purpose. Giulietti was a syndicalist and aimed at organizing the whole peninsula's merchant marine in a great mariners' cooperative that would own and operate all Italian vessels. The necessary credits, unobtainable through ordinary channels, might easily be forthcoming from an obliging government. Under Giolitti the state had favored many enterprises owned cooperatively by labor groups tied to the Socialist party's reformist wing.

In order to undo the union, Italian ship operators did what other Italian industrial employers were doing. They formed an industry-wide front, with only one important firm abstaining, and chose Parodi as their representative. The shipowners hoped to frustrate Giulietti's piecemeal divide-and-conquer tactics and to expose him publicly as a labor tyrant. They began with a dramatic forestalling maneuver. Instead of letting the captain choose the time and place for his first attack, the shipowners, taking their cue from a minor dispute concerning the crews of freighters that had been requisitioned for subsidy-line service, declared a general lockout on March 20, 1914, and blamed the federation for the losses that the nation's economy would consequently suffer.

The move was well timed. Freight rates were unusually low, and the operators could lay up their ships without great loss: as the mariners' union pointed out, their earnings during the war with Turkey had evidently left them some reserve funds to fall back on. Moreover, Giolitti chose this moment to withdraw from the premiership, leaving the government in the hands of the conservative Antonio Salandra. This change at Rome deprived Captain Giulietti of political backing right at the start of his hardest fight, for Salandra's right-hand man and undersecretary in the Ministry of the Interior (a key position), Baron Celesia of Riviera Ligure, was closely linked to the Genoese business world of the Parodis and Menadas. To say the least, Salandra would not be as accessible to the mariners as Giolitti had been in 1912 and 1913. Admiral Millo left the naval ministry in August 1914, and the new minister was an admiral less friendly to Giulietti. There were to be no more easy, politically gained victories for the federation. This was to be a genuine battle of class organizations, without extraneous issues.

The federation decided to wait until shipping rates went up. Then, when the operators could again make a profit by sailing, the mariners would press home their demands. The shipowners used the three-and-one-half-month tie-up period to attempt to set up a separate ship's officers' organization but failed when Giulietti succeeded in taking over the organization himself. Then, in mid-May of 1914, a group of shipowners including the Parodi and Menada firms made it known to Giulietti that they would sell him their freighters for ready cash. Giulietti saw the offer as a maneuver to discredit him by exposing both his ultimate objectives and his lack of means to achieve them. He turned the tables on the operators by immediately making the offer public, though without mentioning the ready-cash requirement, which he could not have met. By publicizing the supposed offer, the captain got the jump on his opponents and was able to embarrass them with a simple question: if they were willing to deal with him, why would they not engage in collective bargaining with the federation that he founded and led? Giulietti brushed aside the shipowners' indignant rejoinder that he had violated the most elementary rules of "commercial delicacy" and announced publicly that he wanted no part of such a business. With more than a hundred ships now lying idle in Genoa, both sides began to lose their zest for what they had foreseen as a good, clean fight.

The scene of combat now shifted from the port of Genoa to the parliamentary lobbies and ministerial antechambers of Rome. During the first part of May, the shipowners' deputies in parliament began meeting together to discuss ways of resolving the deadlock. The Socialist deputy, Canepa, promptly informed the shipowners' chief parliamentary spokesman, Admiral Bettolo, that the federation was willing to talk and urged him to use his good offices with the shipping firms. The answer to this approach was a flat no: parliamentary mediation was not at all what the shipowners had in mind.

A labor problem of this size was bound to wind up on the premier's desk, and the shippers, though shying away from parliament, made a determined effort to bring the executive around to their way of thinking. On May 28 a delegation of shipowners was ushered into Salandra's chambers, escorted by the usual parliamentary figures from Liguria. As these conservatives saw it, Giulietti was building a private empire in defiance of the state, and his success was a concrete example of the social changes over which Italian jurists were agonizing in their perplexity over the status of labor unions. This sort of argument was bound to impress Salandra, himself a professor of public law. Giulietti had, they held, already ruined the subsidized lines financially by his exorbitant demands and had compelled them to withhold union dues from every crewman's wages, an unheard-of imposition. Even worse, they claimed, Giulietti was trying to extend the same system to Italy's cargo fleet, with the aim of ruining the owners and taking over the whole industry under the guise of cooperative management. As they saw it, the owners were fighting for shipboard discipline; for everyone's right to employ and work freely; and, above all, for sheer economic survival: the industry's conditions were fixed by fluctuating international freight rates, and Giulietti's pay scales would break the shipowners.

In view of the desperate situation, the freighter operators asked Salandra to authorize some departures from existing law and usage:

permission to engage crewmen on board ship rather than in the port captaincy, where union agents could interfere, and to sail with crews that were more than one-third foreign if the federation enforced a boycott among Italian mariners. They also wanted to impose a condition already in force elsewhere in Italian industry—a deposit withheld from crewmen's pay as a guarantee against nonfulfillment of contract.

It was impossible for a government that rested on Giolitti's parliamentary majority to yield publicly to such demands, but events were to show how susceptible Salandra was to their appeal. The premier was always concerned over labor organizations that usurped the authority of the "ethical" state.

The capitalists finally ended the tie-up on June 30 and released some 150 vessels to take advantage of rising international freight rates. The shipowners had failed to discredit Giulietti or break the federation's solid front. Now it was labor's turn to put the squeeze on. When individual shipowners refused the federation's terms, their ships were stopped in port by the "legal" method of sick report and boycott. The shipowners then resorted to hiring foreign "free" seamen, and there was much talk of using Chinese and Negro labor wholesale. As the conflict spread, state police began arresting seamen who refused to pull up anchor. The federation then invoked the solidarity of Socialist unions in the ports of Genoa and Leghorn, with the result that ships could be neither loaded nor unloaded. At the time of the war's outbreak, Italian shipping had been hindered or paralyzed for five months, with neither side disposed to climb down.

The war provided a way out. Marine freight rates soared, and the state began requisitioning cargo vessels, with lucrative contracts. Profit margins widened, and everyone saw a chance to make money. The federation adopted a patriotic interventionist attitude that was to prove very convenient to the Salandra government as it began moving toward war and needed allies on all sides. The federation suspended its agitation in the second week of August 1914.

At this juncture the government, urged on by the federation and by some Socialist deputies, might have imposed an industry-wide settlement, which would have been easy in a time of rising profits. But Salandra dragged his feet, leaving matters to Parodi and Giulietti.

Those two were able to arrive at an agreement in November, but the shipowners' coalition voted against it by a narrow edge. In February 1915 the shipowners declared that they would not recognize the federation as bargaining agent for ship's officers, though it might represent the seamen. The federation treated this as yet another effort at union breaking: the stoppages and boycotts recommenced on March 27 with port workers' and longshoremen's solidarity. This time things moved rapidly toward a general strike, with government troops and police protecting whatever scab labor could be found. At the same time the mariners' patriotic attitudes and well-presented case were beginning to get sympathetic treatment in some influential North Italian newspapers. Salandra, absorbed in steering Italy toward early intervention, had to give up his tacit backing of the shipowners.

The government finally acted, appointing an arbitration board with one member from the Genoa Chamber of Commerce, one representative of the port consortium, and one Socialist deputy to act on behalf of labor. The federation suspended hostilities on April 17 and accepted the arbiters' decision of May 1, which ceded the mariners many of their points. The shipowners had conspicuously failed to defeat the marine-labor organization after more than a year's violent struggle. However, the federation's success was due in large measure to a political contingency. Even a government as partisan and property-minded as Salandra's could not take time out to smash a big union on the eve of summoning the nation to war. The earlier events of 1914 had shown that Italian mariners shared the problems of other Italian industrial workers. They had to contend not only with the arrogance and stubbornness of Italian capitalists, but also with a hard fact: the narrow margins within which the peninsula's industries had to operate and grow in a world of richer and more powerful industrial states. The mariners had one advantage over other sectors of organized labor after mid-1914: profit margins in merchant shipping were artificially high and would stay so as long as the war lasted.

The exorbitant costs of Italian industrialization were borne mostly by the consumer; Italian taxes fell most heavily on consumption. But in the general category of "sacrificed classes," industrial workers were a special group. They felt the cost of heavy industry directly and personally. The disaffection of labor was one of the most dangerous and least understood consequences of Italy's modernization.

As Riccardo Bachi's economic yearbooks for the period 1912–15 continually observed, Italian labor unions simply could not achieve their minimum aims by calling strikes.[11] The prevailing business conditions were against them. Thus organized labor had to fall back on political solutions to its problems, solutions that fell into either the revolutionary or the reformist category, neither of which had very brilliant prospects of success. The syndicalist revolution was like a self-induced hallucination, a sectarian vision of the Last Judgment, sundering the producers from the parasites. And the reform Socialists ran head on into the ingrained tendencies of the whole European political system.

The reform Socialists kept asking the state to engage in public works on a large scale, with smaller programs to be carried out by municipalities, as both pump priming for the sluggish economy and a substitute for the arms races and competitive expansion abroad that were absorbing the country's resources and energies. The programs seem clear-sighted and sane enough from hindsight. In 1914 they were utopian. The ruling classes of Italy saw the national interest in imperialist terms, as did their equivalents in every other major state, and there were few Italians of political stature who were prepared to envisage Italy's unilateral withdrawal from great-power competition.

After the war of 1911–12 the state was operating at a deficit. Arms appropriations showed no signs of decreasing; naval expenses in particular were bounding ahead. The principal public works— railways and harbors—were in fact also military expenditures. In the mountainous peninsula the better the rail lines were, the greater would be Italy's chances of playing a decisive role in the event of a general war. But there was no chance for large-scale public works of a purely civilian nature, and there was no further legislation benefiting labor. The budgetary dispositions of these years reflect a set of long-range foreign policy decisions. By embarking on a program of armaments and foreign expansion, the Italian liberal state in its last years of vitality lost its final chance to win over the nation's working class—Italy could not afford imperialism and welfare at the same time.

One of the determining factors in the decline of the liberal political system was the attitude of the business class, particularly the part of it that organized pressure groups and subsidized newspapers. What was the line that Italian big business took during the tense and confusing months that preceded the outbreak of the War? Was there a genuine industrial interest group with definite political aspirations and long-term goals? And was there an identifiable political doctrine in the Italian party spectrum that became congenial to the peninsula's big-business interests?

The answers came, loud and clear, from the *Rivista della Società Commerciali*, official organ of the recently formed Associazione fra le società italiane per azioni. That organization, a sort of Italian National Association of Manufacturers, took a forthright, even aggressive political stance in 1914, testifying to the new energy of the Italian business class and its overt political concerns. Under fire from economists and reformers as "barons" or "bloodsuckers," profiteers of protectionism and war, the business interests retorted by identifying their own concerns with the lasting concerns of the Italian nation: what was good for the peninsula's industrial corporations was good for Italy. This flat assertion was not presented with the old-fashioned, patriotic rhetoric that had echoed in the 1880s or 1890s, but rather in a doctrinal, "scientific" form, as an answer to the free-trade economists, like Einaudi and Borgatta, who had written against the whole system of protection and privilege which sheltered Italian industry.

The Italian manufacturers maintained a lobbying group at Rome, the Comitato nazionale per le tariffe doganali e per i trattati di commercio, which was set up to work against the free-trade reformers, whose voice was beginning to reach the Italian public after years of apathy. The manufacturers argued that it was impossible, in dealing with a national economy, to pit the interests of the consuming public against those of the nation's producers; these interests were really identical. A nation that exported laborers and imported large quantities of manufactured goods was suffering from insufficient capital and lacked suitable "instruments of labor" of its own. Protectionism was one of the indispensable remedies for that plight. However weak that argument might have been from a strictly economic point of view, it struck home; few free-trade reformers were really willing to repudiate Italy's political ambitions. Einaudi, who was one of the ablest of the free traders, backed the Libyan War, unaware of, or unwilling to face, the inconsistency between his economic convictions and his political conservatism. A real free-trade position, as the manufacturers' exponents saw, requires that the nation-state spend and regulate as little as possible.

But the manufacturers' spokesmen took the national interest as an economic absolute, and their essentially autarkic reasoning led them to reject the whole international division of labor on which liberal economics rested. Since Italy's share in the world's producing and marketing system was subordinate and humiliating, they argued for a breakaway or go-it-alone economic policy, at least as far as Italy's evident scarcities would permit. As for the hardships that such a policy would impose, the national committee suggested vaguely that a more equitable system of internal distribution would alleviate them. In fact, this kind of argument carried with it the gravest consequences. The international division of economic functions was more than a theory; it was a central fact of economic life. To alter or abolish it meant establishing more than tariffs: it implied a new politics; new life values; new collective sacrifices; and, in the near future, new struggles between rival nation-states.

This was precisely the position that Alfredo Rocco took in an important featured article, "Economia liberale, economia socialista ed economia nazionale," that the manufacturers' organ printed April 30, 1914. Rocco pointed out that both liberals and socialists reject the nation as a primary value. Both proclaim the essentially cosmopolitan notion of a world economy, with a resulting international division of labor. Rocco traced the tendency to two Jewish theorists, Ricardo and Marx, and connected it with an individualistic and hedonistic view of human motives and behavior.

Rocco disposed of both liberal and socialist economics by showing that they lead, ideally, to the abolition of all national frontiers. For him and for much of his public, this seems to have been enough of a refutation. Against the two "pontiffs" of cosmopolitan political economy, Rocco extolled Friedrich List, "founder of German economic science," an economics that takes as its object of study the situation of a particular nation at a particular moment in history. Thanks to List, Germany had developed not only an economic science of its own, but also "that awareness of national necessities in the economic field that has made her, in fifty years, the feared and often victorious rival" of Britain in world industry and commerce.

Having thus cleared the field, Rocco launched into an exposition of his own national doctrine and its economic implications. As he saw them, individual men are parts of national organisms, from which they receive their language and culture. These organisms sicken and die when individual concerns and interests kill the "instinct of the species." Individualistic rot had spread in the ancient Greek democracies and was reappearing in the contemporary French Republic. Rocco denied that there is any common organism or society embracing the whole of mankind. On the contrary, the struggle to tame nature and build civilization is carried on by groups, often distinct national groups, that have no common goal; the specific aim for the sake of which societies live on for centuries is the armed struggle against other societies. Rocco facetiously remarked that only a struggle against outsiders, "Martians," would lead humanity to form a single, united society. At this point Rocco came close to the later formulations of Carl Schmitt, the constitutional theorist of the Third Reich.

In part Rocco justified the Italian tariff system with arguments taken from List's economics: tariffs are a means to arouse new economic energies and encourage new lines of production, and thus they pay off in the long run. But Rocco knew full well that this theory would not warrant the permanent high tariffs for which Italian manufacturers were pressing. His principal argument was therefore non-economic: a nation invests in certain branches of production for moral, political, and military reasons. Of course the public has to make sacrifices. These are not, as the reformers allege, a despoliation of the public for the sake of a small group of producers who have control of the state. On the contrary, they represent the subordination of short-term individual advantages to long-term national objectives. As for the profits that the industrialists reap, these are a just recompense for services rendered in the national interest. If the reverse should happen, if a mere numerical majority of consumers and voters should ever impose its short-term comfort or gain on the long-range interests of the nation, then not only the state, but civilization itself would speedily perish.

Even in the brief compass of his article, Rocco betrayed uneasiness over his divorce from traditional humanist modes of thought and even suggested, vaguely and half-heartedly, that the nation serves some sort of universal function in the total development of civilization. His economic prescriptions, for all their positive tone, showed equal uncertainty. He argued, cogently enough, that a poor country like Italy has to make special efforts if it is to achieve industrial parity with richer nations, but he had no idea of how or when industries can start paying for themselves by becoming internationally competitive. But if they are to remain a perpetual burden on the nation, what is their reason for being?

Rocco indicated three possible solutions. Italy might continue her industrial progress at a cost much greater than that for more favored nations. She might become a source of emigrant labor, a course that Rocco rejected as signaling the "ruin of the race." Or she might engage in a war of conquest, which would bring with it a "radical" solution. Rocco had started with a noneconomic concept of the nation-state, organically conceived, and he wound up with a noneconomic concept—war. He proposed to subordinate economics to those concepts and organize it around them.

Rocco could not have chosen a better time to propagate his views. What is important here is not that Rocco thought as he did, but that the Italian manufacturers' organ saw him as a spokesman and his ideas as a worthy answer to their liberal, democratic, and radical critics—men of the caliber of Luigi Einaudi. Above all, it is significant that their new ideologue had been the leading formulator of Italian Nationalist doctrine since the movement began to take definite shape in 1910. To be sure, Rocco was a distinguished jurist and an eminently respectable figure. But his presence at that moment in the manufacturers' journal raises some larger issues. Was this a sign of fusion, or at least convergence, between the Nationalists and the industrialists? The facts suggest that it was.

6

Italy's Drive to the East

Since her entry into the European concert, Italy had been an imperialistic power for much the same reasons that other European states had expanded. These reasons ranged from a vague sense of national honor and civilizing mission to a precise insistence on "compensations" and shares in the division of Mediterranean colonial areas to maintain status, prestige, and points of military advantage. Italy's ventures in East Africa and Libya had their roots in questions of prestige and in diplomatic mortgages: Libya "compensated," however poorly, for France's protectorates in Tunisia and Morocco, and the East African colonies represented Italy's share of disintegrating Zanzibar and overextended khedivial Egypt, Moslem states that had come apart in the late nineteenth century. It is impossible to argue that any of these colonies could serve as an adjunct to the Italian economy, and the history of Italian expansion in Africa therefore has little interest for us here. There were, to be sure, some ways in which nascent Italian industry could profit from the colonies. The Navigazione Generale found the transportation of Italian troops to Eritrea, under monopoly conditions, a lucrative traffic; and when Pirelli was just starting his insulated cable manufacture, he found Red Sea naval contracts to be a source of pride and profit for his firm. However, these bonuses were marginal, a part of the general shot-in-the-arm effect of military orders on heavy or specialized industries.

But there was another face to Italian imperialism, turned east rather than south. This was the main line of Italian expansion on the eve of the War. Italian imperialist programs in the Balkans and Asia Minor are interesting as examples of economically motivated expansion, however speculative or unsound they may seem from the hindsight of more than a half-century.

There are various ways in which a colonial area can serve as an adjunct to, or play a complementary role in, the economic system of a state. A colony can become an outlet for emigration under the national flag. Australia, New Zealand, and British Canada have all performed that function. A colonial area can become a source of cheap labor and foodstuffs, while serving as a captive market for the mother country's industrial output within an enclosed tariff system. Eighteenth-century Ireland might be a case in point. Neither brand of colonialism was available to Italy.

These forms of economic colonialism had become less common than others by the early part of our century. Plantation imperialism —that is, the use of a colonial or semicolonial area for the development of some specialized crop with industrial and commercial possibilities—dates back centuries but has assumed a new importance in our own time. Raw-material imperialism, often indirect, has taken on huge proportions with the development of new ores and fuels in the later phases of industrialization. There is another type of economic imperialism, harder to recognize but pervasive in our century, that may be called "infrastructure imperialism." A power that has already developed basic industrial skills, transportation lines, energy sources, and chemical processes may well, in the course of its growth, build productive facilities with an output in excess of its domestic needs. At that point the newly industrialized nation will become interested in exporting its skills and systems, in building infrastructures and productive facilities in undeveloped parts of the world.

These types of economic imperialism need not take the form of direct political control or annexation. Indeed, it is usually cheaper to avoid such overt domination and, in a more flexible form of economic imperialism, to extend and penetrate by finding local collaborators. Groups of industrial powers may combine to exploit the raw materials of an undeveloped area. Some undeveloped areas, notably in Latin America and China, have escaped becoming colonies by a sort of international open-door understanding. But in general, given the common European system of national tariff barriers, state subsidies, and domestic monopolies, the search for industrially exploitable or developable space abroad tends to become an exercise in colonial expansion or penetration, in which one power secures exclusive economic privileges in developing a given area. The railroads, harbors, and natural resources of the colonial area serve to integrate the economy of the industrial power that holds exclusive development rights. Usually, raw-material imperialism and infrastructure imperialism are two aspects of the same basic plan of penetration. The power that builds railroads and harbors obtains mining franchises as well: the Baghdad railway is a classic example. There is often a corollary to this kind of penetration: the local authorities remain semi-independent and obtain arms and military instructors from the industrial-colonial power that holds development rights. These military ties resolve themselves into yet another outlet for the colonizing power's industries and another form of dependence for the colonial area. Before the First World War this sort of imperialism prevailed in the Balkans and in the Ottoman Empire.

The Italians practiced plantation imperialism in Montenegro and attempted infrastructure and raw-material imperialism in European and Asiatic Turkey, and in both areas they acted with strong industrial motives. Italy, like Germany, had a "drive to the East." Though the Italians had nothing like Germany's power, they had many of the same needs for employment and outlets abroad.

Before discussing the concrete projects of Italian capitalists abroad, let us take a general survey of Italy's position at the start of 1908, when two crises coincided. In the Balkans and Middle East, this was the year of the Young Turk revolution, the last convulsive attempt of the Ottoman Empire to enter the modern world and survive. This was the year when Austria formally annexed Bosnia-Herzegovina, when Bulgaria declared its independence as an answer to the change of rulers in Constantinople. Finally, this was the year when, as another result of the Turkish revolution, the international police regime in Macedonia ended, leaving the future of the Ottoman Empire's European provinces in the gravest doubt.

In Italian economic history this was a dark period. After the boom years of industrial development, spurred on by Giolitti's policies in the fields of labor, transport subsidies, and railroad operation, came a period in which it was evident that Italy's new industries, particularly motors and rails, were overexpanded, with capacities far beyond what the domestic market required. The question of foreign outlets was becoming a question of survival.

An unprepared liberal ruling class was faced with challenges that would have daunted the greatest of statesmen. Italy's role as a great power, a full partner in the concert of Europe, was in question as a result of the 1908 crisis, in which Italy's real force had turned out to be negligible. The country had to walk a tightrope between her increasingly truculent "allies" in the Triple Alliance and her mistrustful "friends" in the Triple Entente. At the same time the makers of her foreign policy were all intent on securing a fair share of influence and spoils in the event of further partitions in the East. Rearmament and active—even aggressive—diplomacy, playing both sides of the street, were the only options open to the liberal regime.

In another area, too, Italian policymakers had to find a precarious balance. Italy's great-power policies required that she take part in any future division of new colonial spoils: Italian ships had taken part in demonstrations against Latin American republics that lacked respect for international law and contractual obligations, and the Italian armed forces had borne their share of the struggles in 1900 against the Boxer rebels at Tientsin and Peking, in return for which Italy had received a bit of Tientsin's harbor frontage. How much more, then, was Italy obliged to throw her sword onto the scales when the Ottoman domains were being partitioned and the balance of power in the Mediterranean was wavering. In relation to the Turks Italy had to be as tough and aggressive as any other great power.

On the other hand much of the Third World of the years 1908–14 was nominally independent or becoming so in the name of national self-determination. Countries like Serbia, Montenegro, Bulgaria, Rumania, Greece, and eventually Albania were rising to statehood or seeking new ways of becoming more independent economically and politically. In dealing with these new nations, the Italians had to take another tack altogether. The future of Italian commercial-industrial penetration in these lands depended entirely on the degree to which Italy could show that she was not a domineering or encroaching great power, but rather a sort of potential senior partner, a power that could offer economic benefits without political strings. Therefore, to ensure their share of future spoils in Moslem Asia and Africa, the Italians had to work with the Central Powers; but to win the confidence of the Balkan nations, they had to support the principles of national self-determination that France, Russia, and—occasionally—Britain were advancing in opposition to the hegemonic designs of Germany and Austria-Hungary. All this required the most delicate footwork.

The Ottoman Empire was a prisoner of the European concert of powers. Through the Ottoman Public Debt Council, in which British, French, German, Austro-Hungarian, and Italian bondholders were represented, the empire's customs and monopoly revenues were being held in receivership. The fixing of Turkish customs rates was a matter for international ratification, and the development of Turkish tobacco was an international enterprise. Under such circumstances real industrial development of the sort that was taking place in Italy or Russia was out of the question for Turkey.[1]

Naturally, there were other, related reasons for Ottoman stagnation. The empire's middle class was largely made up of minority groups—Greeks, Armenians, and Jews. Moslem enterprisers and professional people were few, and most of the opportunities for Turks to acquire Western professional skills came through the army, the one remaining area of Turkish self-rule. The Greek, Armenian, and Jewish bourgeoisies were often distrustful and disaffected. Many of the wealthier business elements among them acquired foreign citizenship to take advantage of capitulation privileges that exempted them from onerous Ottoman legislation and arbitrary Turkish administration. In Ottoman cities foreign consuls and postal services really acted as outposts of Europe in a hostile environment, and foreigners enjoyed various fiscal immunities. Domestic stagnation and foreign controls acted together, fed on each other, to drag the empire down.

There were stirrings of renewal among Turkish writers, young officer groups, and Masonic lodges, where Turks met minority radicals on a plane of equality, but the sultanate remained pan-Islamic and repressive. The old prerevolutionary state had one constant strategy, playing the great powers off against one another; and it had one prospect for the future, building up the army and the country's rail and telegraph lines in such a way as to inch toward real military independence. To achieve a minimum development of the empire's communications, transportation systems, and natural resources, the Ottoman rulers played a complex game of concessions and counter-concessions, favoring those capitalists and ambassadors who seemed to promise survival. The empire's constant concern was to avoid putting its future exclusively in the hands of one power group.

Therefore, the Ottoman Empire offered fabulous opportunities to foreign investors who were backed by a great power with capitulation rights and a voice in the Public Debt Council. But it was also a trap. Ministers and officials had to be won over with special attentions; Greek and Armenian dummy partners had to be set up in business; local commanders had to be mollified or intimidated. Foreign businessmen had to wait out months of ministerial delay, listen to well-founded protestations of pennilessness on the part of the Sublime Porte, and watch their competitors buzz around the same doors. Sometimes successful investment in Turkey meant loans to the impecunious empire as an initial *douceur*. Foreign business interests could force themselves into the country by relying on the privileges that Europe had wrung from previous generations of Ottoman rulers; but once there, they found that Ottoman delay, deviousness, and resentment could bog them down. In the competition and labyrinthine infighting of Constantinople, Italy was at a distinct disadvantage compared with France, Germany, and Austria. She had come too late.

In the whole Balkan-Ottoman area, from the Danube to the Euphrates, the lines of great-power penetration stretched and intertwined, leaving little room for the Italians. The Central Powers had been working for a generation on what appears, in hindsight, as something of a master plan. As it unfolded between 1908 and 1914, the plan required that Austria-Hungary dominate the Balkan rail lines, tying Vienna and Budapest with Salonika and Constantinople. A rail system of this sort would channel the commerce of the whole

developing Balkan area toward Central Europe, connecting Rumanians, South Slavs, and Bulgarians with the great economic centers
of the German world. From Constantinople eastward the Germans
took over, executing one of the great engineering projects of the age, a
central rail line tying Anatolia and Mesopotamia together. The Baghdad line involved much more than mere railroad building. There were
collateral projects of land reclamation, port construction, and, above
all, mineral and petroleum development. Germany and Austria would
eventually free themselves from the Anglo-American oil companies
by developing their own resources in Mesopotamia. This great design
meshed with other developments in Austro-German politics: the
Balkan rail program corresponded to pan-German notions of a Central Europe dominated by Germany, while the great Baghdad line
fitted well into other German aspirations, still vague, of using pan-
Islamic movements as an instrument to break up the British colonial empire from within. Accordingly, for two generations Germany
worked generously to modernize the Turkish army.

These designs held within them the real germs of the First
World War. The pattern of Austrian-German rail development coincided with the cleavages between German and Slav, between German
and Russian great-power aspirations, between British and German
exploitation of colonial resources. The rail projects alone, with their
political implications, would have sufficed to set the Central Powers
on a collision course against the Entente, even if Germany had not
also built a high-seas fleet, claimed colonial compensations in Africa,
and otherwise antagonized its great-power colleagues to the west. As
we have seen, the Austro-German schemes also implied new competition for Italy: the development of the Austro-Hungarian merchant marine, based at Trieste and Fiume, crossed and threatened
to cancel the lines of Italian maritime enterprise radiating from
Venice, since both aimed at the trade of the Adriatic and the Levant.
In this way Italo-Austrian rivalry paralleled the ethnic schism between Germans and Latins within the Dual Monarchy.

The Entente had positions of privilege in the Ottoman Empire
that dated back to the sixteenth century—in the case of the French,
positions that had been confirmed in the diplomatic-military arrange-

ments of the late nineteenth century. The British interest in the area was primarily naval and was well secured by Britain's protectorate over Egypt and Cyprus. The British were not interested in expanding their small existing interests in Anatolia, but they were developing a new concern over the Persian Gulf and the oil possibilities of Mesopotamia. Essentially, the Turks appeased them by letting British influence predominate in the navy, while the Germans worked in the army. However, the British were allied with French interests in the central financial institutions of the empire, the Public Debt Council and the Ottoman Imperial Bank.

The French had traditional privileges as well as new development rights in the Levant, but their real power center was at Constantinople. A compact group of French financiers controlled three key institutions: the Ottoman Imperial Bank, which was the state bank; the Jonction-Salonica, a rail company that had franchises and construction rights in much of the empire's European provinces; and the Régie des Chemins de Fer. This solid financial position was reinforced by other factors. The French group represented Belgian investors and worked closely with British finance. Availing themselves of the aggressive support of the French embassy, the French financiers essentially made the economic weather in the Ottoman capital. Any requests for rail or mining concessions were bound to pass through their hands before the Turks finally acted.

The French and their associates had one great advantage over all other European groups: a supply of ready funds and access to the Paris money markets. This was one respect in which the Germans could not oblige their Turkish friends. The Germans had spent millions to get their rail lines started, but their capital resources were limited. In 1909 the Germans were actually looking for foreign backers and approached the Banca Commerciale of Milan, offering to appoint an Italian director to the board if funds were forthcoming. However, the Germans made it clear that they would not give up the essentially German character of their enterprise, and the Milanese declined to go ahead: the Italian government would have encouraged them only if real internationalization of the Baghdad line was conceded. Under these circumstances the Ottoman regime knew that it could look only to the Paris bourse for future financial help, particularly in the event of war. Besides, French culture and schools, well subsidized by the Republic, were the most widespread agents of westernization in the whole empire, a fact that carried political implications and deeply affected the attitudes of the Ottoman ruling class.

The two big European power groups operating within the empire, the German-Austrian and the Anglo-French, had two basic aims in common. First, both wished the Ottoman system to go on. Should the Ottoman state falter or fall apart, the European powers would be faced with difficult decisions and dangerous rivalries. Moreover, few European statesmen could face with equanimity the prospects of administering Moslem territories. It was always better to work through local authorities, like the Ottoman sultan, the emperor of Morocco, or the khedive of Egypt; even the bey of Tunis had his uses. The old Moslem states had a continuing role in a world dominated by Europeans: to guarantee public order and acquiescence among Moslem populations.

There was another basic interest that the two rival blocks shared: the exclusion of interlopers. The French gave relatively little help to their allies, the Russians; and the Austro-Germans, almost none at all to their Italian junior partners in the Triple Alliance. Why should the entrenched powers wish to share the wealth with nations that had just begun the decisive phase of industrialization, neither of which inspired much military respect? The Italians had been routed by Menelik and the Russians by Japan; both countries were visibly in the grip of domestic disorders. The inside powers at Constantinople had a clear common interest. By the same token the two outsiders had much in common: they had the least interest in the survival of the Ottoman system and the most in the rise of independent nations capable of withstanding the Central Powers. Thus there were times between 1908 and 1914 when Italian and Russian diplomats were closer to each other than to their official allies.

The Ottoman rulers had a special reason to favor the Germans and the French over the Italians. By conditions imposed on the empire by Europe, foreigners theoretically had the same property rights as Ottoman subjects and hence could buy land and settle; the authorities wanted to avoid at all costs any agricultural settlements in Ottoman territory. In the last years of Abdul Hamid II, it became possible for foreigners to buy land without prior authorization from Constantinople, though the policy could not be admitted officially. It was also common knowledge that the great railway concessions in Anatolia and Mesopotamia had a secret clause providing that the concessionaires would refrain from attempts to set up agricultural colonies in the areas that their lines traversed. The French were not interested in such efforts, since their population was static. The Germans, concerned with maintaining Ottoman sovereignty, were willing to limit themselves to industrial expansion. But the Italians were specifically interested in land development and had special skills in that direction, and both the North African and the Albanian provinces offered fertile terrain for agricultural development and eventual colonization. Therefore, the Ottoman authorities treated the Italians in Libya and elsewhere with suspicion that amounted at times to open hostility. There was little that the Italian ambassador at Constantinople could do; only the joint pressure of the great powers could force the Turks to abandon their systematic obstruction and vexation.[2]

These handicaps, however, did not weigh decisively against the Italians in the critical years 1908–14, and the Italians did succeed in penetrating both the Ottoman Empire and the Balkans. What advantages did the Italians enjoy?

First, and perhaps most important, Italian labor, skilled and professional, was available everywhere. When King Alexander Obrenovic was murdered in a palace revolution at Belgrade on June 10, 1903, one of the witnesses was his Italian valet. When the Austrians, before the annexation of 1908, built a rail line in Bosnia connecting Sarajevo and Uvac, an especially difficult piece of engineering, they employed an Italian firm to build two diverging tunnels.[3] The Bulgarian government, intent on rail design and construction in the years before 1908, used as its principal consultant an Italian engineer, Ernesto Besanzanica.[4] However, the Italians were more prominent in the Ottoman Empire's remaining European provinces. Salonika and its hinterland were full of Italian businessmen, many of whom, particularly in mining enterprises, operated behind the screen of an ostensibly Ottoman corporation. The mines of Cassandra and Calcedica were developed largely by Italians at Salonika. The mills, the new customs buildings, the port breakwater, and the trolley lines of that city were all built or developed by Italians. Some seventy rail employees there were Italians, as were the manager of the local brick-yards and the doctor in charge of the state-monopoly health services.[5] Nor were the Italians to be found only in the European domains of the empire. Italians were indispensable in any railroad building, and Italian labor "colonies" were springing up all along the Baghdad line. Even the Greeks were alarmed as Italians invaded their old Levantine preserves. Italian labor was also to be found in the Black Sea coal ports.[6]

An advantage that the Italians shared with the other European powers was the weakness of the whole Ottoman system. The decaying empire had one real power base, Anatolia and its truly Turkish popu-lation, from which the sinews of the army were recruited. But Otto-man administration and diplomacy were in the hands of a multi-national class of officials whose loyalty and honesty were open to question. In negotiating with the Ottoman authorities, the Italians often knew the real intent of the Ottoman ministry and what the interests of the individual ministers were. The art of dealing with the Ottomans consisted largely in underhanded and private contacts. On March 18, 1911, the Turkish ambassador at Rome wired the Ministry of Foreign Affairs at Constantinople that the Banco di Roma and the Società Commerciale d'Oriente were merging in order to extend their joint projects in Tripolitania and Albania. The telegram wound up in the files of the Italian foreign ministry. A letter from Tittoni, then Italian ambassador at Paris, to the Italian foreign minister two months later suggests how these matters were arranged. He transmitted to Di San Giuliano a series of documents provided by a Turkish informer and asked whether he should pay the man from the embassy's special funds; the sum was 200 francs, 150 for documents and 50 for naval data. Di San Giuliano sent a courier with the bank notes, along with a personal letter.[7]

Perhaps as a result of such experiences, the Italian foreign min-istry became convinced that Turkey would soon fall apart and that Italy's opportunity lay in picking up some of the choice pieces. The revolution of 1908 aroused some hope in Imperiali, the Italian am-bassador at Constantinople, that the empire might pull itself together, but he soon despaired. In the summer of 1909, the influential Neapolitan journalist, Edoardo Scarfoglio, took a trip through Anatolia and afterwards wrote the foreign minister that the empire was dissolving into its national components. Prophetically he added that the Anatolian Turks would massacre the local Armenian populations. In fact, even in Asia Minor it was doubtful that the ethnic Turks formed a real majority, and few Italians seem to have foreseen the military and political birth of a modern Turkish state there. What they observed was the rottenness of the old system.

Besides the channels that corruption and betrayal afforded, the Italians had other means of working within the Ottoman system to get what they wanted. Though bonds held by Italians represented only a little over 1 percent of the total outstanding Ottoman debt, Italy had a representative on the Ottoman Public Debt Council in recognition of her great-power status. This meant that if any Turkish government wished to alter the country's finances by raising customs dues or introducing new fiscal measures, it had to get Italy's consent. The seat was not enough to give Italy a stake in the empire's survival equal to that of other European receiver-powers, but it did stimulate Italian interest in what the empire had to offer economically.

During the first years of the twentieth century, Italy's commerce with the empire was growing. In 1905 the Società Geografica Italiana sent a naval lieutenant, Lamberto Vannutelli, on a long "mission of commercial geography" through the Asiatic provinces of Turkey to investigate the prospects for Italian business and investment. The lieutenant found that Italian products were well suited in price and quality to the local market, with its small dealers and peasant consumers. At the same time he noted the disadvantages of doing business in Turkey. There was a general need for bribing officials, while concessions of any size could be obtained only through political pressure or through using Ottoman concession holders, who passed on their rights for a percentage. More interesting were his positive findings and his recommendations. Some primary-processing industries already existed in Turkey, especially in milling, spinning, and textiles, but large-scale, foreign-sponsored industry was hard to set up. Wholesale commerce was impeded in every port by the need to use intermediaries—Greeks and Armenians—whose services were costly and unreliable. Merchants in the Turkish interior were much better to deal with. Vannutelli recommended that the Italians penetrate these markets with a credit organization capable of furnishing ready cash to businessmen and a sales organization that could reach potential customers without intermediaries.[8]

The real economic question concerned the future of Italian heavy industry in a competitive international situation where opportunities were few. The Balkans and the Ottoman Empire offered an extraordinary field for electrification, transport lines, port and harbor construction, land reclamation, and agriculture, projects that could provide real outlets for Italy's expensive new machine shops, as well as employment for her growing corps of engineers and technicians. There was no similar unpreempted field elsewhere in the world.

During the Ottoman-Balkan crises of 1908, the Italian government joined France, Russia, and Serbia in sponsoring a trans-Balkan railroad and thus ran athwart Austrian rail projects. In 1911, after the settlements that sealed Morocco off for the French, Italy suddenly moved into Turkey's North African provinces. These were the last Moslem-governed strips of North African coast, and Italy had long held a diplomatic mortgage on them, recognized by both great-power blocs. Libya in itself was poor and offered limited possibilities, but its possession gave Italy a chance to claim a larger part in Ottoman affairs. These prospects soon became evident. When the Turks refused to accept Italy's coup and make peace, the Italians vaulted into the Aegean, seizing Rhodes and the Dodecanese Islands. The Ottoman Empire, faced in 1912 by a coalition of Balkan states that included Serbia and Montenegro (the South Slavs) as well as the Greeks and Bulgarians, patched up a last-minute peace with Italy but in the ensuing Balkan Wars lost both Albania and Macedonia; and the fate of the empire's Asiatic holdings came into question. The Italians, moving in on the exhausted empire, demanded concessions in Asia Minor, near their new bases in Rhodes. At the same time Italy joined Austria-Hungary as cosponsor of a new Albanian monarchy, over which the two powers envisaged a joint protectorate. This in turn gave Italy a chance to raise anew the question of the Balkan rail routes, in which her interests paralleled those of Serbia rather than Austria. All these matters, which concerned the whole concert of Europe, were still pending when the fatal shot rang out at Sarajevo on June 28, 1914.

In these maneuvers Italy's decisions were political, initiated by the foreign minister and the premier and ratified by the king himself. There is no reason to believe that Italian big business imposed them. They were consistent with Italy's traditional great-power policies, which aimed at securing military-diplomatic compensations every time another power scored colonial gains.

Nevertheless, the trends of Italian foreign policy after 1908 fitted neatly with the developing pattern of Italian industrial needs and expansion plans. This fact raises in turn certain central historical questions. Would Italy have pursued such an aggressive and risky great-power policy had there not been an industrial interest in the nation to support it? Would Giolitti, long known to be opposed to colonial ventures, have taken responsibility for such policies had he not been convinced that basic domestic interests were at stake? Ministries in the previous century, intent on Italy's attaining great-power status, had favored the growth of heavy industry. Now heavy industry had reached the point of being able to influence political developments.

There were three major capitalist groups operating in the East. The Venetian "friends" of the Banca Commerciale were the most important, spreading into all kinds of undertakings. The Ansaldo group worked only in Constantinople and relied heavily on its influence in diplomatic and government circles. It did not have a capillary network like that of the Venetians. The Banco di Roma was important in North Africa and the Holy Land; its real political advantage lay in its connections at the court of the khedive of Egypt. The Venetians were by far the most realistic, modern, and resourceful group.

At first Venice seems an odd place from which to launch imperialistic ventures. The Austrians had left Venice in picturesque obsolescence, judiciously preferring Trieste as their principal Adriatic outlet. Nineteenth-century Venice became a relic of past glory: Byron and Wagner were the century's famous Venetians.

Nevertheless, something was stirring in Venice. During Gabriele

D'Annunzio's long stays there between 1887 and 1901, the poet reacted not to the decadent cosmopolitan surface of the city's social life, but to the throb of vitality he sensed in its people.[9] It was natural enough that after the publication of his novel *Il Fuoco*, in which he celebrated the undying vitality of Venice, the poet became a friend of Count Piero Foscari, the moving spirit of the Venetian imperialist group. D'Annunzio first met Foscari through the Italian Navy League in 1901, and the fantastic images of his tragedy, *La Nave*, became the artistic counterpart of the Venetian group's vaulting projects.

The noble house of Foscari had come down in the world after the old republic fell. Sold soon after 1797, the family palace was still serving as an Austrian barracks when Piero Foscari was born nearby in 1865. He inherited little more than family tradition and discipline, to which he added a personal energy rare among down-at-the-heels patricians.[10]

At fourteen Piero enrolled at a technical school and from there advanced on merit to the naval academy at Leghorn. Upon graduation he passed in short order from technical to command functions and then to political militancy. Undoubtedly his African service brought out these qualities in him. At home the prestige of the armed services was always in question. Rank and command responsibilities came only after officers were too old to assume them with energy. But in Africa a junior officer might suddenly acquire absolute power over thousands and decide issues of life and death. The colonial environment turned young Foscari from a romantic patriot into a seasoned imperialist.

During his tours of duty on the East African coast in 1895–96, young Foscari had ample opportunity to observe and report to his ministry on the efficiency of German colonization, as well as on the growing rivalry between Britain and Germany in the colonies. In 1896 he was at Zanzibar with a force of Italian sailors disembarked to protect foreign consulates when the British bombarded that helpless Moslem capital and forced the young sultan to leave his throne. Foscari described the callous overkill methods of the British in pseudonymous articles written for Venice's leading daily.

The year after Foscari's African exploits, his life took a new turn. He married Elisabetta Widmann Rezzonico, a noble heiress with great estates in Carinthia, across the Austrian border, and was able to leave active service to devote himself to politics and business projects. In 1899 his wife gave him power of attorney (*procura*) over her estates. Foscari had become a man of some wealth.

As Foscari began to take a leading role in Venetian society, business, and politics, he met and soon entered into partnership with Giuseppe Volpi, a protean and enigmatic figure in the Italian financial world. The relationship was to prove fruitful for both.

Volpi was born at Bergamo in 1877, the son of a construction engineer. Because of his father's early death, he had to give up his studies and go to work. He started as a commercial traveler, soon became interested in Balkan trade, and began to sell Veneto farm produce there. On a visit to Naples early in his career, he met Giuseppe Toeplitz, the rising star in the Banca Commerciale management, and the two became fast friends. During the years that Toeplitz managed the Venice branch, 1900 to 1904, Volpi moved from farm produce into high-level industrial promotion, the basis of his future greatness.[11]

As a political figure, Volpi was to enjoy the personal favor of both Giolitti and, years later, Mussolini, no mean feat in itself. Volpi's financial and political skills made him the central connecting figure in the development of Italian imperialist enterprise during the years that led up to the War.

Volpi's surviving correspondence, much of which is to be found in the archives of the Banca Commerciale, the Bank of Italy, and the Italian Ministry of Foreign Affairs, gives some insight into his character, ambitions, and goals. In public he had the appearance and manner of a merchant prince; he tried to incarnate Foscari's ducal ideal. In his Venetian residence he kept a collection of antique armor, from which he occasionally gave items to appreciative friends. Everything he did bore a personal stamp. His letters altogether lack the megalomaniac tone of command characteristic of the Perrone brothers, nor did he take on the impersonal business style of the Commerciale staff. Instead he managed a personal, insinuating, and confidential tone, which was varied by occasional flashes of humor and raised to the level of rhetoric when he introduced Italy's national interests. In almost every letter that Volpi wrote to anyone of importance, he contrived to appear both discreet and revealing and thus left to posterity some hint of his unrecoverable personal charm and persuasiveness.

How did Volpi view his life work? The answer he himself gave in his 1927–29 correspondence with Toeplitz was that he had always been an industrial promoter and developer, abstaining from pure speculation and juggling. As he looked back on thirty years, Volpi felt that he could claim to Toeplitz, not a man likely to accept false coin, that he had always worked on a solid base of engineering information, technical prospects, and sound financing.[12]

To the list he might have added personal diplomacy. Volpi's first big ventures were the result of his friendships. Through Toeplitz and Foscari he was able to obtain bank credits and personal contacts among the wealthy landed aristocrats of Venetian society. The Commerciale was heavily involved in loans to the Papadopoli family, secured by estates and a big paper mill. It also extended credit to the Revedin family, of the Venetian and Ferrarese nobility, and eventually to Count Foscari himself, as manager of his wife's patrimony. These were the sources of Volpi's initial capital.

Volpi's first success came with his plans for the electrification of the Veneto. At the turn of the century the Veneto was served by a number of small firms within a limited radius. Envisioning early the possibilities of large-scale hydroelectric development, Volpi took the initiative in forming the SADE network, incorporated in 1905, which had the objective of supplying electricity to the whole Adriatic area. Significantly, he organized in these years the Cellina electrical company, part of the same overall hydroelectric scheme, with the intention of including Trieste, which was then far more industrialized than Venice, in his range of operations. Understandably, the Austrians balked; but the Cellina company, which was heavily backed by the Commerciale, offered an early indication of the direction that Volpi's plans were to take: Italy was too small.[13]

These hydroelectric enterprises formed the foundation of the Venetian group's power and provided a financial base from which it could launch its overseas operations. In the financing of SADE and its affiliates, the Venetian group began working not only with the great Milanese bank, which specialized in coordinating large-scale electrification, but also with the bank's industrial allies, the Breda plants, the Società Veneta, and the Trezza sulphur works. SADE received in addition some capital from the Commerciale's foreign friends. Volpi began branching out. He worked with the Orlandos in developing the Officine Galileo at Florence, and he and his Venetian associates looked overseas for new opportunities.

Volpi's Balkan operations also started with personal friendships. His early commercial traveling took him to the Balkan nations, Asia Minor, and European Turkey, and he got to know people in Belgrade and Constantinople. Through a Hungarian journalist, Joseph Strausz, with whom he became friendly during his first years in Venice, he met certain Serbs who often visited the city. Among them was Ivan Popovic, former minister of public instruction, and his daughter Mitza. Popovic in turn introduced Volpi to Dr. Milenko Vesnic, one of the heads of the young radical party that was to have such importance in Serbia's future. When Volpi first knew Vesnic, in 1900, the Serb jurist and diplomat was momentarily out of favor, but he was to rise to new heights after the fall of the Obrenovic dynasty. He and Volpi became fast friends. In 1901 Vesnic served briefly as Serb minister at Rome and secured for Volpi the position of Serbian honorary vice-consul at Venice. Vesnic was on close terms with the regime that came to power in Belgrade after the coup of 1903 and served as Serb envoy in Paris for most of the rest of his career, from 1904 to his death in 1921.

Among the other favors that Vesnic did for Volpi was bringing him into contact with prominent Montenegrins. Through Vesnic Volpi met Count Ivan Voinovic, a cabinet minister of the principality. In 1903 Voinovic, an aristocrat of Ragusa with a good Italian cultural background, invited Volpi and Count Ruggero Revedin to visit Montenegro as guests of Prince Danilo Negos, heir apparent to the princely throne. Count Foscari, a close friend of the Voinovic family, headed the party. By then there were other Montenegrin contacts. Prince Danilo had granted a number of concessions to a Dr. Boschic, who in 1902 had gone to Venice in search of the capital and personnel to develop them. Foscari had joined with Volpi to form an Italo-Montenegrin syndicate to look into the principality's industrial possibilities: hence the tour of Montenegro in 1903 under Prince Danilo's auspices.

Volpi's enemies later gave out another and more detailed version of what went on.[14] Professor Antonio Baldacci and his brother Giovanni sent confidential reports to the foreign ministry during Guicciardini's tenure there, 1909–10, an interim period: their reports were read and annotated by Count Carlo Sforza. As the Baldacci brothers told the tale, Volpi's friendship with Vesnic was due to certain favors of Volpi's at Venice that facilitated the Serb's "gallant conquests" there. For these services Volpi had become Serb consul in the city of the lagoons. They claimed that Volpi's Montenegrin contacts had a disreputable origin. Late in 1902, Antonio Baldacci reported, Prince Danilo, a notorious wastrel, came to Italy in search of a 300,000 lire loan. The Banca Commerciale had bad reports about the prince, and he was unable to make any headway at Milan, Genoa, or Rome. Vesnic, then Serb envoy at Rome, heard of the prince's needs, called Volpi to Rome, and proposed a deal. Volpi would use his influence to get the Montenegrin heir his loan. In return, Volpi would be awarded the management of a new Montenegrin state enterprise, which was to assume the production and marketing of the principality's tobacco.

The tobacco monopoly, regardless of whether it was the fruit of the machinations described by Volpi's enemies, was an historical fact that requires some explanation. It was the first major undertaking of the Venetian group bearing the stamp of Volpi and, in all probability, did owe its existence to Vesnic's intervention behind the scenes; that much we would know even without the Baldacci reports. It seems at first a little out of character for an Italian industrial pioneer—for such was Volpi's self-image—and a Serb statesman to sponsor a paltry scheme of this kind, but there were deeper reasons for their initiative. A few facts, however, may serve to explain the interest of the Veneto's landed aristocrats in these Balkan prospects: Danilo was brother-in-law to Victor Emmanuel III, and the aged Count Ruggero Revedin was close to the House of Savoy. The countess was a dame of Queen Elena's court, and it may be presumed that these facts were not without their efficacy in determining the count's prestigious participation and financial commitment. They may also serve to explain Foscari's willingness to serve as president of the Italo-Montenegrin syndicate that presided over Volpi's first initiatives in the principality.

Let us return to the course of events, as presented years later by Volpi's knowledgeable but embittered enemies. His affairs in the little principality went smoothly. The penniless Montenegrin government accepted Volpi's offer. The only efficient consumer tax possible in the picturesquely backward state was through a tobacco monopoly. The principality would certainly need outside help in setting up such an agency, and who could offer more skill and experience than the Italians? Volpi found himself in the patriotic role of building bridges across the Adriatic, in Italy's national interest and in Austria's despite.

The princely government contracted a loan, ostensibly for road building. Volpi, accompanied by Count Revedin, delivered the sum personally and signed a preliminary contract for the tobacco monopoly. According to Volpi's detractors, Prince Danilo spent the money on a pleasure trip abroad soon afterwards. However, they say, he tarried in Montenegro long enough to extract more favors from the obliging Volpi.

Volpi went back briefly to Venice to raise money. Given the penury of the Montenegrins, he needed to start with a substantial capital outlay. The Venetian group came through handsomely; that Foscari himself subscribed 250,000 gold francs, one-sixth of the total capital raised in Italy, is a matter of public record.[15]

According to Baldacci, when Volpi reappeared in Montenegro toward the middle of May 1903, his entourage included three investors in the undertaking—Count Revedin; a representative of the Papadopoli interests named Nicola Braida; and the parliamentary deputy, Roberto Paganini, who was a noted railroad builder of the Veneto. Volpi also brought with him Cavaliere Tani, an inspector of the Italian state tobacco monopoly. Finding the atmosphere a little chilly at Cetinje, the group broke up. The investors and technicians went to Podgoritza to choose a factory site, while Volpi went off alone to the little port of Antivari, where he had some unfinished business.

At Antivari he met with Prince Danilo and bought an old house from the prince for the exorbitant price of 30,000 francs. Danilo, so the story goes, put himself completely in Volpi's hands at this point, confessing that he was unable to look after his own affairs. Then, at Volpi's request, Danilo wrote to his father, the monarch, and begged him to conclude the tobacco-monopoly contract with the Italians.

The deal went through at Cetinje shortly thereafter, although there was strong opposition in the principality's council of state. On July 15, 1903, the Italian company was formally incorporated at Venice. Within a short time the Italians succeeded in setting up the joint enterprise, which proved profitable to both its initiators and the principality's treasury; but by doing business in this way, the Italians took on the onus of being identified with Montenegro's court party, a potential liability. Then, too, complaints were soon heard that the monopoly's finished products were uneven and often poor in quality.

There were other troubles. The Montenegrin people would not have welcomed a state tobacco monopoly under any circumstances, accustomed as they were to freedom in this as in other matters; but the particular deal of 1903, with its aura of corruption, with the flock of greedy South Italian employees and officials that soon lorded it over the local Montenegrin help, amounted to a recipe for instant unpopularity. However, it must be admitted that monopoly helped bring the little principality into the currents of modern Europe: it gave rise to the first strike in Montenegrin history.

The Baldacci report explains how Volpi smoothed over these difficulties, keeping them from ruffling his relations with the Italian government. Volpi had a contact man at Rome, Commendatore Carlo Scotti. A man of parts, Scotti was close to the Banca Commerciale; was the Rome representative of a great Milanese savings bank, the Cassa di Risparmio di Milano; and also served as Serbia's consul in the Italian capital. Scotti kept unfavorable echoes from reaching official circles at Rome and apparently used his influence to Volpi's advantage: as a result, the Banca Commerciale was willing to extend up to half a million lire in credit to the Italo-Montenegrin tobacco monopoly; Volpi was evidently more trustworthy than Prince Danilo.

On one point Volpi's admirers and detractors are agreed: the tobacco monopoly, though gratifyingly remunerative, was merely a foot in the door. Volpi, Foscari, and their associates aimed at taking over the total development of resources, communication, and transportation in the Balkan principality. Once the tobacco monopoly started operations, under the technical management of engineer Vittorio Paganini, Volpi and Foscari could turn to larger projects.

The original Italo-Montenegrin syndicate formed in 1903 to exploit available port and railroad concessions in the principality had Foscari as president. It proved inadequate to the task, and in 1905 a new company, with far greater capital resources, was incorporated in Italy to undertake the modernization of Antivari.

And Montenegro had really no choice but to welcome such projects. The Berlin Congress of 1878 had left its coastline demilitarized and hence subject to blockade by Austria. Austrian naval positions at Spizza dominated the little principality's shores. To cap matters, Austria had offered to build a rail line that would tie Montenegro's whole coastal section to Dalmatia: the project would have amounted to the economic incorporation of Montenegro into the Dual Monarchy. Naturally enough, the prince viewed his powerful neighbor with apprehension and turned toward the Italians as his nearest effective ally. He himself spoke Italian, his daughter was queen of Italy, and his army, fitted out with obsolete Italian artillery, was largely commanded by officers schooled at Turin. Even the Montenegrin ministers who detested Volpi and all his works admitted that the Italian presence was indispensable.

As for the Italians, their specific undertakings in Montenegro can be accounted for only as part of much larger long-range ambitions. The principality itself offered little, but the Adriatic coast as a whole held mineral wealth and hydroelectric potential that Volpi was quick in assessing. Montenegro was the one Balkan bridgehead that Italian enterprise could develop freely. The little monarchy offered not only advantages to Italian diplomats and admirals in their competition with Austria in the Adriatic, but prospects to Italian businessmen concerned about access to Balkan hinterlands as well. The seemingly trivial and unremunerative development of Montenegrin transportation systems was thus to be the start of much bigger schemes.[16]

The next step in the Venetian group's operations, founding the

Antivari Company, began a process of fusion between these local promoters, the Milanese banking establishment, and the central government at Rome; the history of the group's projects merges into the general stream of Italian expansionist politics. The process was tortuous and partly concealed. Its outlines become clear only years after the company's incorporation in 1905 at Milan.[17]

The Antivari Company proposed to set up and operate a harbor and free port at Antivari as Montenegro's window to the West, with wharves, modern loading equipment, and hostelries, and to build and operate rail and trolley lines. One rail line was to connect the new port with Lake Scutari, the principal link between the principality and north Albanian centers, and the company would set up a ferry service on the lake. These projects would, among other things, give the tobacco monopoly's plant at Podgoritza an efficient means of shipping its product to Antivari for export.

This program entailed direct competition with Austria-Hungary. Up to then the shipping lines of Trieste and Fiume had handled most of the commercial and passenger traffic of Scutari, with the inefficient Puglia line of Bari offering feeble competition. Scutari, located near the lake, had access to the Adriatic only through the Bojana River, which was becoming increasingly hard to use. It debouched at San Giovanni di Medua, an exposed landing place that hardly deserved to be called a harbor. The Antivari Company's projected system would eventually have diverted this traffic, via the lake, to Antivari, obviating the hazardous Bojana River transshipments.

The Antivari Company had behind it the Banca Commerciale and its whole retinue. Its original backers included not only the stalwarts of the original Venetian nucleus—Volpi, Foscari, Papadopoli, Paganini, and Count Amadeo Corinaldi of Padua—but also the shipbuilders Orlando, Odero, and Piaggio; Rolando-Ricci of the steel trust; Ernesto Breda, the locomotive and machine maker; and a number of other friends of the great bank. The Commerciale in its own name subscribed one-quarter of the original capital.

Between 1905 and 1909 the company carried out its program. Its great engineering feat was the rail line that linked Antivari to Vir-Pazar, designed by Paganini with the same narrow gauge that the Austro-Hungarians used at Bosnia-Herzegovina. A forty-three kilometer line, it passed through so many tunnels and over so many mountain slopes that the passage took two hours and fifty-five minutes. With the rail line completed, the company instituted a ferry service on Lake Scutari that used obsolete material and aroused no enthusiasm. Only the Hotel Marina, built at Antivari by the Italians, presented a light patch in the gloomy picture of the company's operations. Named after Volpi's daughter, it offered the amenities of a European gambling casino in backward Montenegro.

Baldacci's reports, sent to the foreign ministry only a year or so after the port's inauguration, indicate that the company's achievements offered little else to be cheerful about. It was widely held that Volpi's enterprises had succeeded only by corruption and favoritism. Baldacci claimed that Volpi, aside from giving local Italian diplomats gifts of horses, antique armor, and "perhaps other things," had presented an outright bribe of 180,000 crowns to the minister, Mijuskevic, who was Montenegro's representative on the board of the tobacco monopoly. These methods, Baldacci warned, would prove counterproductive in the long run. For the moment Volpi had secured the favor of Prince Danilo, the heir apparent; but in so doing he had earned the heartfelt enmity of the patriotic-constitutional party, which numbered Danilo's younger brother, Prince Mirko, among its adherents.

Even worse, the report alleged, the technical errors made by the Italians at Antivari had led to a lawsuit by a local engineering contractor, Segnic. Behind the suit stood a group of pan-Slav Croat bankers who wanted to make Antivari into the first Slavic free port on the Mediterranean. The Croat bankers controlled the important South Slav daily, *Nase Jedinstvo*, and it was conducting a violent campaign against the Italians in Montenegro. Baldacci said that the Austrians were backing Segnic to the point of promising him the contract for the rival Dalmatian port of Spizza. This was a truly ominous development, for behind the old diplomatic and military rivalry between Austria and Italy, there now appeared an ethnic cleavage between Yugoslavs and Italians that promised to be far deeper.

Baldacci's parting shot was a warning that the Montenegrins knew that the House of Savoy sent various subsidies and gifts to its in-laws in Montenegro and that an investigation could compromise the Italian crown. Baldacci doubted that he could offset Volpi's influence with the foreign ministry, where the promoter enjoyed an inside track.

By 1910, when these gloomy reports began reaching Rome, the Italian government was already committed heavily, though secretly, to supporting the Antivari Company, as well as Volpi's other ventures in the principality. Since early 1908, Joel had been recommending Volpi in high places. Tommaso Tittoni, then in the last period of his tenure at the foreign ministry, drew up in the spring of 1909 a set of agreements between the Antivari Company and the Italian state. These pacts seemed routine but carried a political charge not visible to the public eye. The company took over all postal and radio communications between Italy and Montenegro in exchange for a special subsidy. This had the appearance of a common arrangement, like those that the state had often made with private shipping lines, but the secret clauses that Tittoni wrote into the agreements went much farther. In exchange for government support, the Antivari Company guaranteed that its stock would remain in Italian hands and that it would allow none of its concessions in Montenegro to pass into foreign hands. One member of the company's board of directors was to be an official or semiofficial representative of the Italian state, and the company's principal official in Montenegro had to be approved by the Italian authorities. Most significant, the Antivari Company was to set aside in its new port a coaling depot for Italian naval vessels, to be used if the Berlin Treaty arrangements of 1878 were altered. All this should be seen as Tittoni's cautious and secret response to the Austro-Hungarian annexation of Bosnia-Herzegovina: it did not salvage his ministerial reputation, but it laid the groundwork for future Italian claims and operations in the Balkan peninsula.[18]

The Italian foreign ministry showed some awareness of the problems that Italian penetration was creating among the backward but touchy Montenegrins. The president of the Antivari Company, Paganini, who was also president of the tobacco monopoly, pledged himself specifically to appoint as many Montenegrins as possible to staff positions in both the company and the monopoly administration.

If Montenegro wanted to ransom the tobacco concession before its stipulated expiration date, the Italian group was to give its consent, with the sole proviso that the principality not pass the concession on to another foreign power. In return for undertaking these obligations, the tobacco monopoly was to receive favorable terms from its Italian state counterpart, which imported foreign tobaccos as part of its own operations. This point was quite important for the Venetian group: Italy and Dresden were the two principal outlets for Montenegrin tobacco, and the joint tobacco monopoly was the one truly profitable Italian venture in the principality.

The exclusively Italian character of the Venetian group's undertakings was never compromised. One of the original subscribers to the Antivari Company, an Austrian engineer named Deskovic, refused to pay the successive installments due on his original stock subscription and tried to transfer his holdings to a Slovene bank in Trieste, which Volpi regarded as Italy's worst enemy. Volpi and Foscari resolved the problem by having Foscari buy him out. For this purpose a loan of 20,000 lire was asked from the Banca Commerciale. The affair was dubious and went all the way up to Joel himself before it was cleared. Countess Foscari's Austrian estates served as security for the credits.[19]

By then, 1912, it was clear that Antivari was no gold mine. The company kept functioning with Italian government subsidies and a vital flow of bank credit, but its operations kept closing with yearly losses. By 1913 the Antivari Company owed the Commerciale 3.4 million lire and the Banco di Roma 1.8 million lire. (The participation of the Commerciale's Catholic rival can be explained only as part of the Italian government's fixed policy of encouraging all "national" investment banks to take a share in ventures abroad that seemed to have diplomatic or military importance.) It was not easy to fix on a remedy for the company's manifold ills. The company's trains, running on narrow gauge track over dangerous mountain terrain, led only to an unremunerative ferry line on the big lake, which in its turn led to an equally unprofitable small banking and commercial agency at Scutari. In this backwater all kinds of troubles came up. Though Antivari had been declared a free port in 1909, jurisdictional and administrative conflicts with the Montenegrin authorities never ceased. Then the Italian engineers and technicians took to squabbling among themselves. Especially serious were the divergences between Volpi and Paganini. Paganini insisted that the Banca Commerciale pay for his share of the Antivari's initial stock subscription—and this in an enterprise in which he officially figured as president. After Paganini's death in 1912, Volpi himself took over and tried to relaunch the whole affair. But precisely at that point the company suffered heavily from the requisitions that Montenegro imposed during the Balkan Wars. Finally, in the spring of 1914 it began to seem as if there might be hope for eventual success, but only because the trans-Balkan railroad schemes circulating then might have given Antivari some real importance as a terminal.

This brings us to the real reasons for Italian persistence at Antivari. The Montenegro projects made sense only as part of a larger program, the trans-Balkan or Danube-Adriatic railroad scheme. In an age of giant railway projects and achievements, this was Italy's supreme chance at something to match the Berlin-to-Baghdad, the Cape-to-Cairo, and the trans-Siberian lines. A rail line cutting across the Balkans, connecting southern Russia, Rumania, and Serbia with an outlet on the Adriatic coast, would find at Antivari one of its most likely terminals. Thus Venice and Bari would gain new traffic, and Italian machine shops and engineering firms would profit from contracts that the new international line would award. For Foscari and Volpi, that was the long-range goal that justified the Montenegro bridgehead.

Only on those grounds can Volpi's estimate of himself as industrial pioneer, not speculator, gain credence. They also explain the motives of Vesnic, Volpi's friend and sponsor in Balkan affairs, who appears as the real initiator of much of what went on. Through a secure connection between Scutari and Antivari, Montenegro might well give Serbia a convenient outlet for its foreign commerce, an outlet that would break Austria-Hungary's economic grip. Antivari might become the point where Serb and Italian interests converged, both politically and economically.

Any Italian moves in the Adriatic were bound to cut across Austria-Hungary's lines of penetration and control. But Italy needed the favor of local nationalities, which constituted her only political allies in the area, and the semicolonial nature of Italian operations in Montenegro not only jarred local sensibilities but also aroused the antagonism of Croat business elements. Croat interests, in turn, found links among the Slovenes of Istria, who were confronting Italian irredentism on Austrian soil. Both nationalities could find encouragement from other parts of the Slavic world. All this boded ill for the Italians: South Slav unity would close the Balkans to them. Italian expansionists reckoned with the Hapsburg monarchy, but they failed to apprehend the opposition they would find on a local level.[20]

The trans-Balkan rail project had something of a history by the time it became an official Italian foreign-policy objective in 1908.[21] There were two proposals in circulation. The southern route, connecting the Bulgarian Black Sea coast with the Albanian Adriatic ports, would have linked Bulgaria with Durazzo or Valona by a route that included Monastir and Berat. The northern route would link Southern Russia, Rumania, and Serbia with an Adriatic outlet near Scutari.

The southern route was by far the less interesting. It was extensively explored by the Deutsche Bank in the early 1890s and by an Italian syndicate in 1893. Both the Germans and the Italians had judged the costs to be prohibitive, and matters had lapsed.

The northern route was proposed as early as 1902 by the Serbs with the intention of achieving economic independence from Austria-Hungary. The Serbian plans presented technical problems, and it was unclear just where the northern route, the Danube-Adriatic line, would find a suitable Adriatic outlet. However, that very fact gave the Venetian group its real incentive to develop Antivari.

Both northern and southern routes had to pass through Ottoman territory. Thus the trans-Balkan railway question became a part of the general problem posed by the remaining Ottoman provinces in Europe, and the provinces were in crisis. Macedonia had become a zone of guerrilla warfare, and the decline of Ottoman control there was stimulating talk of Albanian statehood. However, the future borders between Slav, Albanian, and Hellene were all in doubt, and the great powers preferred not to run the risks of partition along lines of nationality. The Central Powers, in particular, played the part of the sultan's defenders against Slav encroachments, while France's capital investments gave it a vested interest in the empire's survival.

Each of the sultan's European champions asked for recompense from the aging Abdul Hamid II during the critical last years of his despotic rule. The Austro-Hungarians in particular wanted to extend their Bosnian rail line into the sanjak of Novibazar. The request looked modest enough, but the intent behind it was not. The Dual Monarchy aimed at linking Salonika with Vienna and Budapest in such a way as to direct the traffic of the whole Balkan peninsula. Significantly, the new line was to be built with normal-gauge rails rather than the narrow-gauge customary in mountainous provincial lines.

Austria had chosen its moment well, because the sultan badly needed support among the great powers if he was to maintain Ottoman sovereignty in Europe. The Austrians could point to a thirty-year record of pro-Ottoman stands; they also enjoyed German support at Constantinople. A committee of Austrian army officers, presided over by Archduke Francis Ferdinand himself, had studied the route, which had military importance. Secret negotiations at the Ottoman capital, begun as early as 1906, were apparently moving toward a favorable conclusion when in January 1908 the whole matter suddenly came to the attention of other great powers.[22]

Abdul Hamid, wary of committing himself unreservedly to one great-power group, leaked the news of Austria's requests to the Russian ambassador, Zinoviev. The Russians in turn informed the Italian ambassador, Imperiali, who had been kept completely in the dark by his Triple Alliance colleagues. The Italians moved right away, and to good effect. Imperiali's interpreter and private agent even managed to get a short look at the secret Austrian documents that had been transmitted to the Sublime Porte.

But there was little that the Italians could do to keep the sultan from granting the Austrians their rail extension. If they complained to him, he would have punctually informed the Austrian ambassador in the hope of keeping the two allies perpetually embroiled: Imperiali told Tittoni in February 1908 that remonstrating with the Turks would only prove counterproductive. The other powers had no pretext for complaining against Austria, but they could ask for compensating concessions. This was the tack that Italy had to take.

Deeply disturbed over Austria's moving behind his back, Tittoni decided to join with Russia, France, and Serbia in preparing a countermove. There was no formal repudiation of the existing alliance system: the rail project was officially nothing more than a business arrangement. Nonetheless, Tittoni's action was the first indication that Italy might reverse her alliances, and the reasons are worth noting. Tittoni's 1908 decisions were not the result of irredentist sentiment but arose from the nature of Italian imperialism. Austrian hegemony in the Balkans would have cut off Italian prospects there, both political and economic.

On March 12, 1908, less than a month after Tittoni first learned of the Austrian scheme, Serbia formally asked Turkey for permission to study a trans-Balkan rail project that would run over Ottoman soil. On March 17 France, Russia, and Italy transmitted identical notes to the Sublime Porte endorsing Serbia's request.

Italy's step at Constantinople was due to more than Tittoni's resentment over Austrian underhandedness. There were also positive arguments that the Serbs had been pressing for years, both to the Italian authorities and to private promoters like Volpi. The Danube-Adriatic line envisaged by the Serbs would lead to the modern industrial development of the kingdom's mines and forests, which had been the source of Serbia's medieval greatness. Moreover, at fifty kilometers per hour, an express train could go from the Rumanian frontier to the Adriatic in only eleven hours, speeding the export of Rumanian and Serb livestock. In this way Italy might well replace the Dual Monarchy as the principal outlet and shipper for Balkan products of all kinds. The Serbs argued in addition, that the line would also benefit the Ottomans because it would tie the Macedonian and Albanian centers more closely to the rest of the empire.

The Sublime Porte did not see matters in that light at all. When the Italian ambassador presented his note on March 17, the grand vizir, Mehmed Ferid Pasha, was visibly irritated. He observed that the empire had been asked to authorize all at once a total of almost one thousand kilometers of rail lines, at an average cost of some ten thousand pounds sterling per kilometer: how could the Ottoman treasury conceivably offer any financial guarantees, and where did the ambassador think the money was going to come from?

Touching specifically on the Serbs' proposed Danube-Adriatic line, the vizir passed from objections to veiled threats. He noted that the line would pass through Moslem provinces in Albania, where the local population was resentful and alarmed over European intervention in neighboring Macedonia. The Ottoman government would be hard put to maintain public order and protect rail workers' lives if the lines were laid down there. The grand vizir insisted that the Austrian request for a line from Bosnia to Novibazar would have to come first and the other lines later, when the empire could afford them. In any case, plans for a trans-Balkan rail line had been drawn up years ago and put on file with the Ottoman ministry of public works: why waste money with new projects?

The Italian ambassador answered point by point. The empire, he said, would not be asked to shoulder new financial burdens, at least for the moment; equity required that Serbia's requests get the same consideration as Austria-Hungary's; at any rate, the terms would be settled only after the formation of an international syndicate that would undertake planning and construction of the line. As for the problems of local Moslem militancy, Imperiali replied sharply that the Ottoman authorities could always enforce law and order if they wished: there was no reason for "depriving an entire region of the benefits of progress and civilization." In reporting the conversation to Tittoni, the ambassador put the grand vizir's objections down to preconceived hostility, but he held that they could be overborne by strong Russian pressure in support of Serbia.[23]

The Italian move and its sequels had far-reaching consequences. Italy was in effect claiming her share if the Ottoman domains in Europe were to be partitioned. The demand for rail-building concessions was a political act; both Tittoni and his successors, especially Di San Giuliano, viewed railway conventions as the instruments of political penetration, a staking out of future claims. In all this maneuvering Italy was merely following the lead of the other great powers: the novelty, unwelcome in the concert of Europe, consisted in Italy's late arrival and in her supporting her political claims with economic development schemes that would have been impossible in previous decades.

From the point of industrialization on, Italy's foreign policy acquired this new Levantine focus, which had more importance than the old African colonial programs. In 1908 Tittoni implicitly declared Italy's intent to obtain a sphere of influence in the Balkan provinces of the Ottoman Empire, in the concrete form of a port and railway project in which Italian capital would play a major role. In 1913 Di San Giuliano was to make the same declaration about the remaining portions of the empire in Asia. These new guidelines in Italian foreign policy required from diplomats and capitalists a unity of effort unprecedented in Italian history. Therein lay a fundamental difficulty.

The Italian foreign ministry had laid the political foundations for Italy's share in the future Danube-Adriatic railway syndicate by joining the Entente powers in their diplomatic moves at Constantinople. The French and Russian foreign ministries were naturally cooperative. In addition, the Russian embassy and consulates in the Ottoman Empire always maintained friendly and sometimes confidential relations with their Italian colleagues. The same could not be said of the French diplomats on the scene, and it was in them that the Italians, venturing for the first time into the uncharted territory of Ottoman rail building, found their greatest obstacle. Imperiali regarded his French colleague Constans as a tricky and inveterate enemy of Italy, even more dangerous than the reticent Austrian envoy. It turned out in the course of the negotiations in the spring of 1908 that Constans was far more responsive to the desires and interests of the French financial establishment at Constantinople than to the policy lines enjoined on him by his superior, the French foreign minister, Pichon. Imperiali suspected Constans of dragging his feet, or worse, when it came to supporting the Danube-Adriatic line. At any rate, after March 1908 it became plain that the Italians would have to clear matters with a powerful group of French financiers before any rail syndicate could be formed. This was a necessary preliminary, since active French diplomatic pressure would be needed at Constantinople if the Ottoman government was ever to authorize a new rail line across its European provinces.

There were two distinct issues to be settled with French high finance at Constantinople: the special privileges of the French establishment in the Empire and the claims that Giuseppe Volpi and his recently formed Società Commerciale d'Oriente had advanced against French competitors in the coal fields of Heraclea, on the Turkish Black Sea coast.

Volpi envisioned the development of the eastern Mediterranean with the same modern-industrial ambitions that motivated his empire building in the Veneto.[24] In 1902 he formed a mining company that acquired a sulphur and zinc concession in the border area between Turkey and Bulgaria. In the same year he and Paganini formed a private company with Count Amedeo Corinaldi of Padua and gained rights to a tract of the as yet undeveloped coal fields near Heraclea. Abdul Hamid II had parceled out the rights to this potentially valuable area among his various courtiers, who, unable themselves to make use of the concessions, sold them to foreign capitalists. Because of Ottoman legal requirements that foreigners could not have outright title to Ottoman land, these transactions had to take the form of fictitious partnerships or corporations. Foreign businessmen always found themselves in compulsory association with Turkish, Greek, or Armenian operators—Ottoman subjects who had some sort of influence at Constantinople. Hence the Italians started their operations at Heraclea with conventional but insecure legal disguises.

But Volpi and Paganini here showed shrewd judgment. Their initial operations in Asia Minor did not have the touch of petty farce that marked Antivari. At Antivari they were building either a prospective terminal for an international rail line that did not yet exist or an outlet for mining industries whose feasibility was yet to be determined, even on paper. At Heraclea, on the other hand, they had the possibility of supplying coal to the Anatolian rail lines, notably the Baghdad railway, that were actually under construction, indeed partly in operation.

Unfortunately for the Italians, their appraisal of Heraclea was shared by others. At Antivari they naturally found no well-financed outside competition, but on the Black Sea coast they had to face the complex of French financial and industrial forces that was already well entrenched in the Ottoman Empire. As the Italians began a rail line at Kouby, they ran into conflicting claims from a French concessionary company on the other side of the hills at Zonguldak. By buying out some of Volpi's Ottoman partners, the French were able to allege that the Italian concession was invalidated. Given the way business was transacted in the empire, they had a point, but the eventual resolution would depend on which side showed more financial and political muscle at Constantinople.

The French and Italians struggled over the matter between 1904 and 1907, with results that could have been foreseen. The Italian group formed a Swiss corporation, evidently with support from the Banca Commerciale at Milan. This was the Società Commerciale d'Oriente, which was incorporated in 1907 and took over the Volpi partnership's claims in Bulgaria and Asia Minor. The change did not hinder the French: in the same year, when the Ottoman treasury needed help, the French government authorized another loan on condition that the Ottoman authorities further French businessmen's plans for the consolidation of the Heraclea coal fields. Could the Italians possibly match this combination of political and financial power?

Under these unfavorable circumstances Volpi and Paganini turned to the Italian government for backing to salvage their claims at Kouby. Their chances were slim because the Italian navy lacked the kind of interest in Heraclea that it had in Antivari. On the other hand, the Italian government could hardly claim great-power status in the Levant without defending the business interests of its citizens. Thus the whole Heraclea dispute went on the agenda that the French and Italians worked on between April and June 1908 at Paris, and it formed part of the package deal that emerged the first week in June.[25]

In the high-level bankers' meeting at Paris that led to this result, the main difficulties came from the French financial interests involved in the Ottoman Imperial Bank and in the Jonction-Salonica, a rail company. The Ottoman Imperial Bank had serious claims. From the legal standpoint it was a recognized and legitimate Ottoman corporation, but financially it was international, drawing capital from British as well as French sources, a fact reflected in the makeup of its two directing boards. Any syndicate formed on an Italian initiative would be unmistakably the instrument of a foreign power, as the Ottoman Imperial Bank was not. Moreover, the Ottoman Imperial Bank and its associated interests had, as a result of decades of monopolistic operations in the Turkish capital, an advantageous position with the Ottoman authorities. They claimed to be the only foreigners that could get a firm concession for the future rail line from the Sublime Porte. The French financiers insisted, therefore, that they receive the lion's share of any future rail line in the Balkans as far as contracts, subsidies, and eventual profits were concerned. The one point open to compromise was the building of a terminal port, in which they were willing to grant parity.

The French position was stronger than the Italians at first knew. The French financiers, through their rail corporation, had stolen a march on everyone else by formally asking the Sublime Porte for a rail concession in the Balkan provinces. This request, dated, by no coincidence, March 17, 1908, amounted to French preemption.

Tittoni's remonstrances with Pichon had only a slight initial effect. Pichon tried to persuade the principal French financial negotiators, Auboyneau and Hottinguer, to adopt a more conciliatory line with the Italians for the sake of France's foreign relations. There was a link between the Quai d'Orsay and the Constantinople financial establishment: M. Henry, ex-director of commercial affairs at the French foreign ministry, was in 1908 an officer of the Ottoman Imperial Bank. However, from Henry himself the Italians learned that the bank felt it had fair claims that could not be disregarded for purely political reasons. At the most, the French bankers were willing to guarantee that Italy would have a share at least equal to that of any other nation participating in an eventual international syndicate.

The Società Commerciale d'Oriente, with its claims at Heraclea, fared no better. Pichon made it plain to the Italian ambassador at Paris on March 24 that French capitalists had some 30 million francs invested there and that any French government would have to uphold them. Less officially, Count Vitalis, the principal French financier involved at Heraclea and one of the major figures in Ottoman railroad finance, told a Banca Commerciale officer serving as representative of the Società Commerciale d'Oriente that the French concession holders would offer to buy out Italian claims in the area but would make no other terms.

The bargaining position of the Italians was generally poor. They could not mobilize anything like the capital necessary to compete with the French for favors at Constantinople and could only resort to diplomacy. At Constantinople the road was blocked: Constans, while formally backing the project to mollify his Russian colleague, in fact considered it a bad business for French investors. The Russians supported the project only as compensation for eventual Austrian gains in the Balkan peninsula. Imperiali thought the Russians would be content if the Ottoman government refused Balkan rail concessions to any side. Italy remained as the sole major power with an immediate interest in getting the railroad built. Negotiations went on through April without the slightest yielding from the French, in spite of the combined efforts of Tittoni and Stringher, who represented Italy at the Paris talks.

At the beginning of May Tittoni tried to cut the knot with another personal intervention. He told Barrère, the French ambassador at Rome, that Italy's political interests on the eastern shores of the Adriatic was far greater than those of France; hence it was only proper that France should show special consideration for Italian desires in connection with the Danube-Adriatic line. Tittoni further let Pichon know that if the French kept pitching their demands too high, Italy would opt out. Italy was willing to accept a minority shareholder position: given the paucity of available Italian capital, Tittoni could propose nothing else. But he held out for parity on the board of directors of the future international syndicate. His position amounted to admitting that Italy had ambition, and presumably the industrial executive talent to match, but could not put up the funds that shareholding parity with the French would have required.

The only advantage Tittoni held was diplomatic. If Italy should pull out, the consequences in Italian public opinion would be serious, incalculable. If the French wanted to face a united Triple Alliance in the future, let them persist in their unacceptable terms. Such was the unspoken but clearly implied message. Barrère could read it without straining.

The French, who had been working for years in the diplomatic sphere to keep Italy at a certain distance from her Triple Alliance connections, understood that now economic concessions would also be in order. Therefore the French bankers involved in the negotiations in the spring of 1908 were prevailed upon to make what looked at the time like substantial accommodations to the Italian point of view. Stringher was able to report from Paris that the contracting parties had reached an arrangement acceptable to all sides. To be sure, Stringher's words to Tittoni were restrained: he spoke of having safeguarded Italian interests as far as possible, but he did not exult over what the French had given.

The Paris negotiations ended in an international convention, concluded between a French financial group, the Bank of Italy, a Russian group representing five big banks, and the Serb government, whose spokesman was the minister to France, Milenko Vesnic. A syndicate was formed for the purpose of building a railroad across the Balkan peninsula, linking the Danube valley and the Adriatic coast. The French were to furnish 45 percent of the capital, while the Italians, who would form a group of investors under Stringher's sponsorship, would supply 35 percent; the Russians and Serbs would put up the remainder.

The French, as the heaviest investors, got the right to build the rail line, with the understanding that the Italians would get a fair share of eventual contracts and employment. For the building of a necessary terminal port on the Adriatic, a separate syndicate would be formed: there the Italians would have control, since they would supply 55 percent of the capital. The French, in turn, were to have a proportional share in the awarding of eventual contracts and jobs. These terms, taken all in all, left some opportunities open to Italian technology in spite of Italy's financial inferiority to France and therefore constituted a modest achievement.

The other arrangements made on June 5, 1908, at the end of

the Paris talks, were simply not to Italy's advantage at all, as soon became evident. The rail syndicate, in spite of its four-power membership, had to put its future into the hands of the French. The Ottoman Imperial Bank was to act as the syndicate's sole agent and intermediary at Constantinople. The bank's officials at Paris insisted that all matters pertaining to the international rail scheme be kept from the public eye to avoid eventual difficulties in dealing with the Turks. However, the secrecy also served to veil the monopolistic operations of the French financial establishment on the Bosphorus.

The Jonction, working with the Ottoman Imperial Bank, had so phrased its March 1908 request for a Balkan rail concession that it reserved the right to form a special company including interested third parties. The Jonction alone, however, was to hold the actual title to the concession that it would obtain from the Ottoman authorities. Once it secured the Danube-Adriatic concession, the Jonction was to receive from the international syndicate an indemnity of not less than 1 nor more than 1.5 million francs. This sum amounted to a broker's commission, and a steep one; but to sweeten the pill for the Italians, the Jonction agreed to pass along its future right to build a port at Medua or elsewhere on the Albanian coast without claiming further indemnities. There were further fees: the Jonction was to study rail routes and port locations, but all expenses incurred in the course of drawing up plans or obtaining final authorization from the Turks were to be borne by the international syndicate. In short, the international associates were to entrust their enterprise to the French financial insiders.

To clinch matters, the international representatives at Paris entrusted the Ottoman Imperial Bank with the supervision of the Jonction's negotiations at Constantinople. The Ottoman Imperial Bank would report to, and consult with, the international group on all important matters, such as rail routes, port location, and expenses. There was a gesture in Italy's favor: the French associates made a private agreement with Stringher reserving as large as possible a place for Italians among the higher staff positions in the future railroad company.

Yet another agreement, made between the international group

and the Jonction, provided that the Jonction would begin preliminary studies as soon as the Ottoman authorities permitted. The Jonction would add to its planning committee two Italian engineers, a Russian, and a Serb.

These arrangements all weighed against Italy. The Italians had reduced the French from majority control to a mere plurality only to find that the French had thus kept a commanding position while committing less capital of their own. What gave the French their lead over Italy was the total capital invested in the Ottoman Empire, not the relatively minor sums required for the particular railway project. French bankers did not intend to make room for the Italians, at least not as long as Italy invested so little abroad. The French officers of the Ottoman Imperial Bank offered some token concessions, to be sure. The Italian delegate on the Ottoman Public Debt Council was to follow the private negotiations at the Turkish capital. The bank was to ask the Jonction to give the first vacancy on its board of directors to an Italian representative. In short, the most the Italians could get, in exchange for their first major commitment in the Levant, was a recognition of their presence.

Little of these dealings leaked out to the press until the beginning of June. Then the London *Times* published a report from Paris that the Serbs, as well as the French groups interested in the trans-Balkan line, had wanted British capital to take a share but that the Italians had objected because of their alliance with Germany, a power that assuredly did not want British railways athwart the lines that connected Berlin to Baghdad. Everyone began disclaiming responsibility for this embarrassing report. Ambassador Di San Giuliano denied it to the British Foreign Office; Barrère told Tittoni he knew nothing of it; and the *Times* itself finally disavowed the story. The source, it turned out, was the Serbian minister at Paris, Dr. Vesnic.

On July 1 Tittoni fired off a furious note to the Italian minister at Belgrade, Guiccioli. After all Italy had been doing to uphold the Serb point of view during the recent railroad discussions at Paris, why should the Serb envoy there spread malicious reports tending to embroil Italy with another power? The Serb foreign minister promised to investigate. On July 9 Guiccioli wrote his chief that Vesnic's truly deplorable act was due to his congenitally hasty temperament, which often led him to speak without weighing the consequences. Moreover, he observed, much of the trouble arose from the influence Mme. Vesnic exerted over her husband. Guiccioli described Mme. Vesnic in detail. A sly, insinuating, and finely turned-out woman, she belonged by background and tastes to the world of "Germano-Semitic" high finance, where there were undoubtedly interests operating against the trans-Balkan rail scheme. (There may have been some truth to all this speculation, since Mme. Vesnic, who was much younger than her husband, had been born Blanche Blumenthal of New York.) But the Serb minister may have had other motives. Is it not likely that he chose this unfortunate means, leakage to the *Times*, to protest against the death grip that the French financial insiders of Constantinople held on a rail project that answered one of his country's most pressing needs?[26]

Serbia's interests in the railroad are clear enough, but what Italian interests were concerned? What was the real nature of Italy's involvement, political or economic? To what extent could the Italians coordinate political and economic forces, as the other powers had done in the Levant?

When Stringher returned to Rome, his first task was to organize an Italian financial syndicate in support of the Danube-Adriatic rail project.[27] There were three categories concerned: the peninsula's industrial credit banks, along with the private banks and industrial investors that often followed their lead; the railroad specialists, who had accumulated skills and excess plant capacity in the course of Italy's recent rapid infrastructure development; and, last and least, Volpi's Venetian group, in their new incarnation as the Società Commerciale d'Oriente, the only Italian business concern with Balkan and Ottoman experience and connections. Each of these groups, although overlapping in both financial resources and staff, had different reasons for wanting to invest in the affair.

The first organizational meeting took place at the Bank of Italy on June 16, 1908. The participants—the Banca Commerciale, with a private associate, the Ditta Zaccaria Pisa of Milan; the Credito

Italiano; the Banco di Roma; and the Società Bancaria—constituted the backbone of the nation's industrial credit system. Joel, already involved in the Antivari venture, became coordinator of the private financial participants.

There was also a representative of the industrialists. The Società Italiana per le Strade Ferrate del Mediterraneo, a railroad company that had turned into a holding corporation since the state took over railroad operation in 1905, sent the engineer Giuseppe Oliva, who also came as spokesman for North Italy's railroad workshops. The Milanese industrialist Silvestri was particularly interested in possible contracts.

Stringher regarded these concerns as premature, but Oliva made his corporation's entry into the syndicate conditional on Italian industry's receiving a share of future orders. The reasons for these demands were clear enough in the light of the Italian industrial situation. The state rail system, once renovated, would no longer suffice as sole customer for Italian industry's output of locomotives and railroad equipment. That branch of industry had expanded greatly during the boom that ended in 1907 and was now in search of export outlets. Penetration into the Balkans presented possibilities that other parts of the world, more subject to competitive conditions, obviously did not.

Volpi, too, soon knocked at the door with a case to present. In the last round of negotiations at Paris, the Italian government, in exchange for the concessions that the French government had secured for Italy, gave up its sponsorship of its citizens' claims at Heraclea. On May 16 Tittoni recommended that Volpi accept a compromise: the bankers, Stringher and Mangili of the Commerciale, got him to agree. The Società Commerciale d'Oriente gave up its rights at Kouby in exchange for 2.5 million francs worth of stock in the French Heraclea corporation, a minority interest.

Volpi's other foreign affairs did not make up for these defeats. The Società Commerciale d'Oriente still held title to the main lead-zinc mines of Bulgaria, engaged in various banking operations in the Levant, and handled much of the export trade for the Italo-Montenegrin tobacco monopoly. But Volpi was burdened by the

Antivari Company and could only hope that the venture in Montene-gro would finally pay off as an integral part of the new rail and port system. To this end he bent all his efforts.[28]

On May 17, the day after he got the bad news about Heraclea from the foreign minister, Volpi went to Senator Rattazzi. He in-sisted that his group, which had the Banca Commerciale behind it, could accept Tittoni's unfavorable settlement only if it got as com-pensation a leading position in the future Italian investors' group that was to participate in the trans-Balkan rail syndicate. Rattazzi's answer was a polite no. He pointed out that because the government was committing itself, Stringher would have to take charge of the Italian investors' group. Besides, the French would object, since in spite of all the senator's assurances, they still held that the Banca Commer-ciale was a German instrument.[29]

The next month Volpi wrote directly to Stringher to plead his case. He pointedly sent Stringher a list of the Antivari stockholders, who constituted an honor roll of the Banca Commerciale's financial and industrial allies. Volpi further asked the director of the Bank of Italy to give special consideration to the Società Commerciale in both the financial and the technical planning of the new group. He noted that his company was the only Italian bank operating in the Balkans, that it had set up an office at Constantinople against considerable foreign competition, and that it would therefore be a breach of justice if it were left out of the first governmentally sponsored Italian ven-ture in the eastern Mediterranean. He proclaimed his patriotism and that of his colleagues and appealed to the same feelings in Stringher. He concluded by recommending to Stringher an absolutely first-class technician for the project, the engineer Bernardino Nogara, who, Volpi said, had gained Ambassador Imperiali's highest praise and was well known to the foreign ministry.[30]

Stringher replied with the most frigid correctness and reserve that he could not subordinate the big affair—the opportunity to join in building an international rail line—to the little affairs of the Italo-Montenegrin companies. The international terminal port had to be on the Albanian coast, since the concession was coming from the Ot-toman authorities. But Stringher and the other Italians involved ex-pected the route to pass through or near Scutari. They could therefore expect that a spur from Scutari would tie Antivari to the main line, and Volpi's bank could join the other Italian banks that were to help finance the project. But Volpi could not handle matters at Constantinople—an international agreement had entrusted the necessary negotiations to the Ottoman Imperial Bank. As to Volpi's last point, the Italian engineers to collaborate in planning the line would be named by the Italian investors' group as a whole. Certainly Volpi's interests would be taken into account, Stringher said, insofar as they were compatible with the other interests involved.

Volpi was not deterred. On July 11 he made formal application for inclusion among the Italian investors and seized the opportunity to make a further appeal to Stringher. He called Count Georges Vitalis the Ottoman Imperial Bank's "deus ex machina" in the technical side of railway construction and said that Vitalis had the highest opinion of Nogara. One word from Stringher and the Ottoman bank would gladly accept Nogara as the special Italian representative, Volpi said, and thus give the Italians a means of checking on the negotiations at Constantinople.

Stringher answered with another formal explanation, the gist of which was that Nogara would have to wait until the various national groups appointed their engineering staffs.

The big Italian banks were lukewarm about the 1908 rail schemes, and with reason. The Banca Commerciale and the Credito Italiano had agreed to put up the capital, but on condition that the project offer some guarantees. As early as April 1908, Giuseppe Sahadun, director of the Società Commerciale, approached Enrico Ravà, head of the Credito Italiano, with the suggestion that the two institutions work together on the project. Ravà said that guarantees or subsidies would have to be clearly stipulated before he could move. He was connected with the Milanese industrialist Silvestri and must have been well aware of the opportunities the rail project might have offered to North Italian workshops, but he was not willing to commit his depositors' money without an assured return.

Joel, though committed to Volpi, could do no more than Ravà. Joel brought with him into the 1908 trans-Balkan project a group of the Banca Commerciale's friends, which naturally included many Antivari backers; the industrial financiers Luigi Medici, Carlo Raggio, and Senator Erasmo Piaggio participated individually. Joel had the same reasons as Ravà for being interested in the project, but he, too, was reluctant to lead his bank and its associates into committing large sums abroad without safeguards. The Commerciale had always turned down requests to invest in Levantine, Libyan, or East African development projects and made an exception for Libya only after Italy annexed it in 1911. In Montenegro, the one departure from that policy, the sums invested were relatively small, and the political interests of Italy were a sort of guarantee that the Antivari company would not fail. The Danube-Adriatic project, though it might make the small outlay in Montenegro really profitable, was on an altogether different scale.

The crucial question was, how much would the project really cost? In June 1908 the Ottoman railroad Régie, a French-controlled agency, had estimated some 50 million lire, and the Ottoman Imperial Bank had come up with a similar, surprisingly modest figure. However, when the Italian engineers began their independent study of routes and costs, they found that the French experts had underestimated costs by half.[31] The discrepancy did not come as a surprise; the Italian delegate on the Ottoman Public Debt Council thought 90 million was a more likely figure. As if this were not bad enough, it turned out that any port on the coast of northern Albania would require heavy additional expenses, since the area offered no ready natural harbors. The Italian experts advised close scrutiny of any further studies or estimates and concluded that the French must have arrived at their figures on the basis of the Serbian project of 1906, which provided for only a narrow-gauge line. The Italian experts advanced their own views; they thought that the line would cost 103 million lire, instead of the Régie's 50. As for the port, which the Régie had put at only 7 million lire, the Italian engineers estimated an expense of 18.5 million—more than double.

Where were these sums to be found? During the preliminary talks at Paris in May between Stringher and the French officers of the Ottoman Imperial Bank, a scheme had emerged. The population that would benefit by the line would help to pay for it—an ideal arrangement, at least on paper.

The Macedonian provinces of the Ottoman Empire were to

bear the basic costs. As matters stood at the start of 1908, Macedonia was under international control. Every year 250,000 Turkish pounds were set aside through the Ottoman Public Debt Council to cover eventual deficits in the budgets of the three Macedonian provinces. In view of the fact that these Macedonian accounts showed a net balance of between 90,000 and 100,000 pounds, the French bankers proposed to use the accumulated reserve as financial backing for the international rail project. There were additional sources to be tapped: 70,000 pounds out of the empire's ordinary budget and 75,000 pounds from the special funds allocated for public works in the Macedonian provinces, under the control of the International Commission for Macedonia.

The French proposed that the Jonction get the international commission to agree that these funds, available for public works, be used to guarantee the financing of the trans-Balkan rail line. These plans had simplicity and logic. As the French explained to Stringher, their formula required no new sacrifices from the Ottoman treasury, since the 250,000 Turkish pounds yearly were already allocated, and the control of the international commission would guarantee the marketability of future trans-Balkan rail bonds.

The plan had its undeniable attractions, but it put the whole financial future of the line in the hands of the same group of French corporate insiders at Constantinople that had taken control of the concessions and the planning. The Italians would have to remain on the outer edge, with the consolation that at least they would be called on for fewer financial sacrifices than would otherwise be the case; after all, they were unable to arrange for financial safeguards themselves. Stringher accepted the French proposals, with all their drawbacks, because Italy had no alternative.

Within a few weeks the scheme fell apart, much to Stringher's dismay. M. Deffès, director general of the Ottoman Imperial Bank at Constantinople, found that the financial guarantees outlined at Paris were impractical. The Macedonian budget was in far worse shape than the Paris conferees had thought, and the Ottoman authorities would allocate no money to cover European rail construction. Deffès thought that any guarantees would have to come from outside.

On that score the French bank manager offered some sobering suggestions. He pointed out that the Austrians proposed to build the rail line in the sanjak of Novibazar without asking for any financial guarantees from the Sublime Porte; instead they were going to draw on the revenues of Bosnia-Herzegovina, which was under their administration. The Serbs, who were after all the most directly concerned power, might well do the same. Deffès suggested that those governments that expected the greatest political and economic advantages from the trans-Balkan line should guarantee the capital to be invested in its construction. Indeed, they would find this kind of sacrifice necessary if they seriously wanted the undertaking to succeed.

Stringher, who passed these observations on to Tittoni, was scandalized at the notion that the Italian government might guarantee capital invested in a railroad to be built on foreign soil. That was a possibility he had always excluded during his talks at Paris with officials of the Ottoman Imperial Bank. Nevertheless, it was clear that some government had to protect the capital to be risked in the project. Otherwise no private investor would move.

The last chance of tapping any Ottoman funds vanished with the Young Turk revolution a few weeks later. At the end of July 1908, the officers of the Ottoman army stationed in the European provinces compelled the sultan, in a dramatic but bloodless coup, to sanction a constitutional parliamentary regime. The new order in Turkey was expected to institute rapid modernization and strike off the shackles of great-power tutelage. International control over Macedonia was finished; so was the old system of concessions, and with it the Danube-Adriatic rail project in the form that it had taken earlier in 1908.

The new regime, badly in need of financial aid, hesitated to break off with the financial-industrial insiders at Constantinople—the French and Germans already established there; they were indispensable if the empire was to be modernized. The Italians, on the other hand, had little to offer the new regime. Their projects simply served to weaken Ottoman authority and, in one fashion or another, to further deplete the imperial treasury. Italian plans in the Adriatic furthered no purpose of the Turks, and Italian penetration of the empire's North African provinces aroused active suspicion. Between 1908 and 1911 the Ottoman authorities showed a rising, stubborn ill will toward the Italians and galled them by treating them with less respect than they did the other official great powers. The only means, short of war, that Italy could use was the threat of a diplomatic veto against any change in Turkish custom and tax rates; this was her right as a creditor nation represented on the Ottoman Public Debt Council.

The Italian government and the Bank of Italy were well aware that the new regime meant trouble. One of the two Italian observers most qualified to keep Stringher informed was the Marquis Theodoli, the Italian delegate on the Ottoman Public Debt Council who also represented Italian interests on the board of the French-dominated Jonction, to which he had been appointed because of Italy's share in the trans-Balkan rail syndicate; the other was Volpi, who drew his information in large part from the Armenian ministers at Constantinople. Among Volpi's Armenian confidants was Gabriel Effendi Noradunghian, minister of public works in the first "constitutional" cabinet of 1908 and a distinguished jurist who had handled Italian legal affairs in connection with Heraclea. Yet another was Bedros Halagian, minister of public works and commerce in 1909, who had sold Volpi the original Kouby concession years ago.[32]

Volpi thought that the 1908 revolution would make the old style of business at Constantinople impossible but that Turkey would yet again become a great field for future investors. For the moment, however, he advised prudence and reserve. With regard to the trans-Balkan line, he thought that the Turks were in no position to refuse point-blank a request from the French bankers. From his reports it was clear that the affair would remain in French hands.

The developments of the next few years, from 1909 to 1912, showed how disastrous that arrangement was for Italian interests.

The Jonction, working with the Régie, did indeed go ahead with its surveys and plans and early in 1911 actually presented a preliminary project. Throughout this period the Italians had been kept at arm's length. The Jonction interpreted the 1908 agreements as giving the Italian engineers at most a role as "reporters" for their nation's investors. The Italians participated in no decisions, but the Jonction did not fail to bill them for the expenses incurred in the preliminary studies, expenses apparently padded by the presence of two French-controlled Ottoman corporations representing the same financial interests. Joel was much disheartened by such dealings, and Pacelli of the Banco di Roma lost interest altogether and wanted to pull out.

The route presented at the beginning of 1911 would have served only Ottoman civil and military interests; the proposal came as a blow to the Italians and Serbs. Instead of the 310 kilometers foreseen in 1908, the route finally approved by the Ottoman cabinet curved southward to link various Albanian towns and with branch lines ran over 430 kilometers. The proposed main line terminated at Medua, bypassing Scutari altogether. A separate branch would connect Scutari to Medua.

That project would have condemned Scutari to permanent stagnation and would have favored a flow of traffic away from the Adriatic and towards Salonika. Finally, in 1912, the engineers rejected Medua and decided to look over a clayey, swampy stretch of coast lying between the Drina and Bojana rivers. The proposed system of 1911–12 offered, instead of Adriatic ports, junctions with the main lines leading to Salonika. It was all very helpful to the Ottomans and indirectly to the Central Powers, but it completely defeated the purposes of the 1908 pacts and systematically thwarted the interests of Italy and Serbia.

Finally, the Italo-Turkish conflict of 1911–12 and the ensuing Balkan Wars put an end to the whole plan, although Joel, with Stringher's approval, kept up contacts with the Ottoman Imperial Bank even while Italy and the empire were officially at war.

The new Turkish rulers, their power consolidated after Abdul Hamid II's ouster in 1909, did everything they could to mortify Italian citizens, enterprises, and shipping, especially in Libya and in the Red Sea ports: by 1911 the Italian foreign ministry had a formidable dossier of insults and infringements to serve as a *casus belli*.[33] The trans-Balkan rail scheme, already denatured, was made part of a package with plans for new Anatolian lines, reclamation projects in the Albanian river basins, and other projects that furthered no

Italian interest. Was it not to Italy's eventual advantage that the Ottoman Empire disintegrate altogether? Would not the partition of
Turkey offer to Italian enterprise opportunities that the Franco-
Ottoman establishment in Constantinople now kept in its monopolistic grasp? Italy was among the states most eager to see the Turks
fall apart, and her war with Turkey in 1911–12 did in fact precipitate
the empire's fatal crisis.

Between 1909 and 1911, as matters built up to a showdown in
Libya, the general Italian position in the East was unpromising. In
Montenegro more than 8 million lire had sunk in a backwater. During the opening months of 1911, Volpi, Paganini, and Joel himself
complained to the Italian foreign ministry that the official trans-
Balkan rail route just approved by the Ottoman authorities completely bypassed Antivari. The Montenegrins, alarmed, had reportedly on their own initiative sounded out the Turks concerning a new
coastal railway line, and Paganini had thereupon reminded the foreign ministry at Cetinje that the Antivari Company had first option
on any future rail construction in the principality. Without a practical Danube-Adriatic rail line, the whole Italian initiative in Montenegro was becoming a financial burden and a possible liability
as well.

What was Italy's economic position in Constantinople itself?
The main Italian enterprise in the imperial capital was Ansaldo of
Genoa, which managed the naval arsenal. Ansaldo, holding a concession granted under the absolutist regime, soon found itself in
trouble with the new authorities. The men of the Union and Progress Committee, and especially their financial expert Djavid Bey of
Salonika, regarded the Italian presence as an undesired holdover.
Ansaldo owed its privileges, they held, to the corruption and favoritism of the old order. The new government, much under the
influence of the committee, kept Ansaldo at arm's length without
going so far as to expel it. The Italian firm got piddling orders for
bridges and drydocks but none for ship construction, its specialty.

The ambitious Perrone brothers then conceived an overall plan
in their Genoa headquarters, without any reference to the on-the-
spot conditions at Constantinople. They wanted to offer the new
Ottoman regime a complete line of naval services. A financial group,

at least 51 percent Italian and the rest Greek or British, would undertake to renovate the arsenal, operate the state shipping lines, and eventually manufacture munitions and artillery at Constantinople.[34]

The scheme had modest origins. Ansaldo's representative at Constantinople, the engineer A. O. Negri, had proposed to build a badly needed floating drydock at the Golden Horn. The funds would have been forthcoming largely from Salonika Jews holding Italian citizenship—the Allatini and Fernandez groups.

As matters developed, Negri's original plan was both too costly and too limited in scope. The question of cost depended largely on Italian bankers. Stringher doubted that Italian capital would take risks at Constantinople, but Primo Levi, the Italian foreign ministry's specialist on Balkan economics, thought it would be worth trying and volunteered his good offices with Joel and Pacelli.

At Constantinople, however, it seemed that it would take more than Levi's influence to secure Ansaldo's position in the Golden Horn. Certain members of the Union and Progress Committee were willing to back politically the formation of an Ottoman naval corporation that would undertake to modernize the empire's shipping, harbors and navy, and it seemed for a time that some of the leaders would favor a combination in which Italian interests predominated. Negri's modest original proposal would fit into this ambitious overall plan. But it was never clear that any Ottoman authority would actually support the plan, even if the Italians came up with the funds.

Without looking into the tangle of Turkish politics, the Perrones leaped at the chance to attain semimonopolistic power. They aimed at mobilizing Italian capital behind them as speedily as possible and thus outdistancing their rivals by entering into the proposed Ottoman corporation before the others knew what was afoot. Negri's floating drydock plan was held in abeyance while the Perrones, with Levi's help, promoted the more ambitious corporate plan. On Levi's recommendation, Pio Perrone got in to see Joel at Milan in January 1909.

The interview was instructive. Using all his firmness and tact, Joel explained the financial facts of life to his caller, who was proposing a *fascio*, or "syndicate," of Italian finance and industry. Joel said that any Ottoman maritime corporation would award contracts to the nation that provided the initial capital. What was needed for such an operation was not a single loan, but a large-scale, ongoing investment of funds, of the kind practiced in London, Paris, and, most recently, Berlin.

Such financing would require the sale of foreign bonds on the Italian market, something that no Italian government had ever permitted. Most recently Paris had tried diplomatic persuasion to get the Italian authorities to admit Russian state bonds on Italian exchanges. The Italian authorities had proved intransigent. Joel and his friends in Paris had been able to do nothing. Was it likely that Russia would be rebuffed and Turkey accepted? These discouraging remarks implied, of course, that Joel would not plunge in with his bank's own funds. He concluded by sending Peronne to see Attilio Odero, a competing shipbuilder; the referral was a polite brush-off.

In August 1909 it turned out that the Ottoman shipping line was no bargain after all. The Deutsche Orient Bank hatched a new plan to operate the line and invited the participation of Italian capital because of the tightness of the German money market. This fact alone was enough to stir doubts.

As Italian officials in Berlin reported the deal, it offered the advantage of using German influence to overcome Turkish suspicions of Italy. It might have proved a mishap economically. The line was to enjoy all kinds of privileges and monopolies, but it was obliged to carry troops and munitions and various officials and police at cut rates. All personnel except engineers had to be Ottoman subjects. And most ominous, in the event of war or emergency, the whole fleet was to be at the disposition of the Ottoman government.

Ansaldo's Constantinople establishment continued to get a few meager contracts until December 1910, when the Perrones decided to pull out. Then the Ottoman naval authorities asked Ansaldo to install two boilers that were still in its workshop in two of their state-line vessels. The Italian embassy suggested that Ansaldo accept and remain in Constantinople, but such moderation and patience were not in the Perrones' style. They sent a personal representative, Angelo Angeli. Spurred on by instructions and constant wires, Angeli broke off negotiations with the Ottoman authorities and demanded an indemnity. Shocked, the Italian embassy observed that the Perrones had no idea of how business was carried on in Turkey. They saw that the Turks would use the Angeli suit as a pretext to refuse to pay Ansaldo what they already owed. By March 1911 Ansaldo was gone, with only the most distant prospects of ever getting any satisfaction. Even in 1912, with Italy about to conclude a victor's peace with Turkey after the Libyan conquest, the Italian foreign ministry judged that Ansaldo's claims would have to be settled with heavy reductions.

The fiasco was really due to the high-handedness and poor judgment of Ansaldo executives. But in March 1911, Ansaldo's Constantinople staff claimed in tones audible to the Italian embassy that their eviction was the work of rival Italian interests tied to powerful foreign banks and companies that used their influence in Turkey. The reference to the Banca Commerciale and its network was unmistakable.

The Ansaldo episode did not damage the Commerciale or its relationship with the government, but the Italian foreign ministry was becoming aware that real industrial penetration in the eastern Mediterranean would be possible only when Italy could offer the required funding. To that end the ministry had proposed as early as 1909 the establishment of an Italo-Ottoman bank that would have the whole Italian banking system behind it. Tittoni tried to persuade Stringher to act as coordinator of the enterprise; only the Bank of Italy could get the big banks of Milan and Rome to work together. From 1909 to 1911 Stringher negotiated with the North Italian financial establishment without concrete results—the political sponsor, Tittoni, was at the Paris embassy and the government was in an interim, awaiting Giolitti's return. The moment was not propitious for such ambitious plans.

The elements for an eventual combination were nevertheless there. Volpi's Società Commerciale d'Oriente had a Constantinople office that had samples of Italian products. Pacelli's Banco di Roma had extensive holdings in Libya, as well as a position of confidence with the khedive of Egypt. It may be safely surmised that the two groups did not want to join forces, given the differences in their origins and methods. Pacelli was willing to venture only at Constantinople, but in return he wanted Stringher's support in raising the Catholic bank's capital from 80 to 100 million lire.

After 1911 the Banco di Roma and the Commerciale went different ways. If a joint action was being planned in the spring of 1911, it fell through as a result of the Libyan war, which began in the fall, and the ensuing general ban on Italian activity within the empire imposed by the Ottoman authorities.[35]

By 1908 Italian industry and technology had grown to a critical size without fitting into any adequate political or financial framework like those set up by other great powers. One possible outlet for Italian energies was business in the Ottoman Empire, but this required stable, long-range financing as well as immediate payoffs to the Ottoman authorities. Such funds would be forthcoming from Italian banks only if there were enforceable political guarantees. The Danube-Adriatic rail project of 1908 had shown how little Italian power counted on the larger scene.

Italy's political weakness impeded the mobilization of Italian capital for investment in the eastern Mediterranean, and this failure in turn balked and frustrated certain sectors of Italian heavy industry. After 1911, however, the Italians were able to make a bid for combined political and economic power in the East on a scale that disturbed and disquieted the greater powers of Europe.

7

Italian Imperialism on the Eve of the First World War

Up to the Libyan war of 1911, the Italian drive to the East consisted of a set of petty operations and projects on the flanks of the Central Powers' massive push toward Salonika and Baghdad. The Italo-Turkish conflict and the Balkan wars changed the picture completely. The South Slavs acquired a position that threatened the whole Austro-German program, and the Greeks took Salonika. Italy herself benefited from the disintegration of Ottoman rule: installed at Rhodes, she became an Aegean power and one of the principal claimants to a share in the eventual spoils of Asiatic Turkey, the last Ottoman redoubt.

When Giolitti authorized the Libyan expedition, he foresaw none of these consequences. For him, it was the routine foreclosure of a long-standing mortgage, a counterpart to the French moves in Morocco earlier in the same year. His foreign ministry, deliberately misled by the Banco di Roma, thought of the Libyan venture as a sure thing: the disembarking Italians would be applauded by an Arab population glad to see the last of the Ottomans.

Things turned out to be less simple. The Turks, cut off by the Italian navy, proved unable to hold the overseas provinces, but they were able to raise the Arabs in most areas against the Christian invaders. In this way they kept the Italian army pinned down in a brutal, bloody, and unexpectedly expensive colonial war with no foreseeable end. Then, too, much of the Arab population outside of Tripolitania itself took orders from the Senussi dynasty, heads of a powerful dervish order, rather than from the nominal overlords at Constantinople: local sovereignty presented as dangerous a problem as the sultan's officers. To end the war with Turkey, the Italians sent a fleet into the Aegean, seized Rhodes and the Dodecanese Islands, and threatened access to the Dardanelles.

The move had the desired effect of bringing the Ottoman government to the conference table, but it also changed the whole scope of the conflict. What had been a restricted African colonial campaign now became a complex operation that involved Italy in the whole Eastern question. The Italian armed forces were entrenched on islands that were juridically Ottoman and ethnically Greek; no great power wanted them there, but it was hard to see how to get them out. The Italians were now a stone's throw from the Asiatic coasts of Turkey. These were consequences that Giolitti had never reckoned with.

Even more dangerous for the transformist premier were the dramatic, polarizing effects on Italy's political parties. All hope for an eventual domestication of the far Left vanished: a new insurrectionary spirit was loosed in Italy.

Most serious were the ideas offered to the middle-class Italian public by the economist and staff strategist Enrico Barone. Lecturing at one of Rome's leading theaters in December 1911, Barone explained the relation between war and economic growth in terms exactly the reverse of orthodox liberal doctrine. The connective virtues—loyalty, hierarchical respect, social discipline—that made for victory in war also led to success in economic competition and new achievement in scientific thought. By fostering these psychological dispositions, war was a powerful coefficient of peacetime progress. Others had used Japan in 1905 as an example, but Barone applied the lesson to Italy.

There is a moment in the economic rise of the most progressive states, in which a war of expansion becomes an unavoidable necessity. This is the moment in which a country, after transforming itself from an agrarian into an industrial state, first tremblingly enters the great international competitions. Then the loss of wealth and human lives that might be caused by a war, serves to hasten the end of a crisis which cuts down far more lives and wealth.[1]

Libya was no promised land and offered no outlet sufficient to ease the crisis of Italian industry. In 1911–12 its potential for development was slight. At best it might have served as a minor outlet for southern peasant emigrants, once the basic transportation and communication networks were set up.

Even these modest prospects stirred Italian imaginations. Foreign Undersecretary Scalea was deluged with requests for employment in Italy's precarious new colony. Professional men, magistrates, civil servants, unemployed or migrant workers, musicians, and barbers all joined businessmen and agrarian developers in asking for a place on Italy's "fourth shore." North Italians pointed to their practical experience and success; Sicilians cited their geographical propinquity.

Italy's industrial establishment added its voice to the rising clamor. Vittorio Croizat of Turin, a specialist in oil-lamp illumination, offered to set up an emergency lighting system in the newly occupied towns of Libya. No stranger in the small world of Italian colonialism, Croizat had furnished lighthouses to the Italian navy in its Red Sea stations, and he gave Ferdinando Martini's name as a reference.[2]

There were bigger fish in the new pond. The industrial specialist of the Banca Commerciale, Pietro Fenoglio, joined with Dante Ferraris to get an all-inclusive contract for the first Libyan rail line. A year later, the Banca Commerciale, together with the electrical-industry executives it backed—Carlo Esterle and Ettore Conti—joined forces with the Banco di Roma to form the S.A. Elettrica Coloniale Italiana of Milan to begin the electrification of the new colony. Out of 2,000 shares, representing 1 million lire in capital, the Commerciale and its associates took 1,290 and the Banco di Roma only 710, accepting a decidedly second place in an area where it had done all of the pioneering work. Clearly, the Catholic bank had come on hard times.[3]

The Commerciale itself did not stand to gain much in the way of real development opportunities. In the years before 1911 the

Milanese bank had always refused Libyan investments, and even in 1913 it preferred to act through an affiliate, the Società Commerciale d'Oriente. Moreover, the paucity of the initial capital outlay shows how little Libya really offered to Italian industrial investors. The Commerciale had actually put more money into Montenegro than it put into any part of Africa.

The real importance of the Italian victory over the Ottoman Empire in 1912 lay not in the North African sector, but in the new chances it offered for Italian penetration into the heartland of the empire itself. And the Balkan wars of 1912–13 presented another opportunity: Italian influence and enterprise in the Balkans could serve as a counterweight to the oppressive presence of the Central Powers. Therefore the primary objectives of Italian foreign policy during the twenty months between the peace with Turkey and the beginning of the First World War lay in Anatolia and in the Balkans. Italian policies required a close coordination among diplomats, officers of the armed forces, and businessmen. The operations of Italian statecraft during these eventful, feverish months were generally secret, although an inquisitive press often inflated some of what was going on. What distinguished Italy's moves in 1912–14 from previous Italian foreign policy was that for the first time the Italians were engaged in combined operations. For the first time Italian business promoters and engineers were able to take initiatives and shape decisions on an international level.

The motivation was both political and economic. The diplomats, even the foreign minister, knew little about the precise conditions of their own country's industries. They sought to serve traditional foreign-policy goals. Their collaborators in the business world, on the other hand, practiced patriotism with an eye to real profits and industrial development possibilities. And the link between power politics and export contracts became clear in the affair of the Bulgarian railroad bids of 1912.

The Bulgarian government, engaged in building its own rail system, had opened an international competition for locomotive manufacturers. The bid offered by Ernesto Breda, whose firm led the Italian field, was judged most advantageous, and Breda was awarded the contract. But a German firm rushed in with a much lower bid, and the Italians were cut out at the last minute. This was not mere cutthroat competition, a case of faulty business ethics. Germany's political power undoubtedly had much to do with Bulgaria's final decision.

The whole Bulgarian affair deeply irked Joel, Breda's principal financial backer; and he hoped that Vico Mantegazza, with his experience and connections, might prevail on Sofia to return to correct business procedure. But he could not.[4]

The overlapping of domestic political and business concerns found its counterpart in the sphere of foreign affairs: the men of the Commerciale began in the summer of 1912 to take part in the day-to-day implementation of Italian foreign policy.

When the Turks, under international and domestic pressures, began to inch toward the conference table in July 1912, Giolitti named a negotiating team that included no professional diplomats. This fact must be understood in connection with the premier's direct intervention in the foreign ministry. He personally sent Salvatore Contarini, the Sicilian grey eminence of the ministry, to head the Italian legation at Lisbon. By the time Contarini arrived at that peripheral post, the course of foreign policy had been placed firmly in the hands of people who had had little contact with diplomacy: a new policy required new agents.[5]

The premier decided to entrust the Turkish negotiations to two "Giolittian" deputies, former ministers Pietro Bertolini and Guido Fusinato, a specialist in international law. At their side he sent one key business figure, Giuseppe Volpi, who represented the new orientation in Italian foreign-policy operations.

Volpi reached this new high point in his career at a time when he was beset by business troubles. His ventures in Montenegro had gone badly, with no international railroad terminal in sight to justify them. His dealings with the Italian government, in which he aimed at a greater and more direct subsidy for the Antivari Company, had run into several snags. And there was the government's insistence that the Banco di Roma participate in the financing and control of the Antivari Company. The Catholic bank took over the Società Commerciale d'Oriente's share at a time when the latter was in deep financial distress. Only in the course of the Libyan War did the links between the government and Pacelli's bank finally snap; and in July 1912, Joel, working closely with the authorities in Rome, was able to persuade Pacelli to sell out.

By August 1913 the Antivari Company's indebtedness to the Banca Commerciale amounted to almost 5 million lire, and there was no chance that the sum would be repaid in the near future unless the Italian government increased its aid considerably. The Antivari Company's indebtedness to the Banco di Roma, on the other hand, was secured by the debtor company's one sure source of corporate income, the Italian state subsidy, which in 1913 touched the new high of 605,000 lire yearly. Therefore the continued presence of the Catholic bank among the company's debtors was especially troublesome and threatened to become more so if Romolo Tittoni and Benucci, Banco di Roma officials, joined the Antivari Company's board, as had been planned. By 1913, with a Mediterranean naval-armament race in progress and great-power competition in the Balkans increasing, it was certain that the Italian government would raise its subsidies to keep Antivari operating as a "free port."

This prospect may explain Joel's persistence in edging Pacelli out of the Montenegrin enterprise altogether. There was always a chance that Antivari might turn out to pay its way or even yield a profit, and Joel was not inclined to share these eventual benefits with the Banco di Roma.

Collaboration between Joel and Volpi in refloating the Montenegrin venture was facilitated in 1912 by the death of the Antivari Company's president, Roberto Paganini. Paganini, useful only as a technician, had always disliked the Banca Commerciale. But Volpi, now in complete charge, found himself dependent on the salvage operations being arranged between Joel and Giolitti's ministers. Volpi's local patron, Prince Danilo, offered little comfort that year: he and all the other Montenegrin authorities were aiming at an early war against the Turks, a conflict that could only worsen the Antivari Company's immediate financial position.

The Società Commerciale d'Oriente suffered greatly from the general ban on Italian enterprises that the Ottoman government imposed during the Libyan War. By June 1912, when peace first appeared possible, the Società was ruined, and Volpi was reduced to asking Joel for help in that enterprise as well.

Volpi saw a way out. He proposed to sell his company's part interest in the Heraclea coal fields, which had a par value of 2.5 million francs. The shares might be unattractive to most investors, but in 1912, with the whole future of Turkey in doubt, Volpi found that he had a seller's market. The Parisian banking house Bardac had notified Volpi that German investors, operating through a Brussels bank, had been searching in vain for large blocks of Heraclea shares. Volpi was willing to sell his holdings at full par value plus interest for the three years that his company had owned them. This would save Volpi's hard-pressed Società Commerciale, but would anyone accept such a steep asking price, given the fact that the Heraclea coal fields had not been paying dividends up to that point? Volpi thought so. He was sure that if he had an offer from the Deutsche Bank, the Frenchmen directing the Ottoman Imperial Bank would meet his terms rather than let the Germans get an interest in the French-managed enterprise. Volpi passed the idea on to Joel with the implication that Joel might pull strings to get a German concern to make an offer. As he wrote to Joel from Belgrade on June 8, 1912, Volpi thought he could go to Paris shortly and arrange the sale. Instead, he got completely tied up in the secret Italo-Ottoman peace soundings, and the matter lapsed. Joel had other plans.[6]

A real believer in Italy's drive to the East, Joel preferred to plunge further. He liquidated the old Società Commerciale d'Oriente, officially a Swiss corporation, at a loss of 600,000 lire. The former stockholders agreed in November 1912 to form a new Italian company with headquarters at Milan. The new Società Commerciale inherited as assets the Heraclea shareholdings and Volpi's mining rights in Bulgaria. The former stockholders could either sell their shares at par value or trade them in for new shares at a one-fifth increase. The Banca Commerciale kept control, with Joel himself taking the presidency: Volpi, Sahadun, and Fenoglio made up the board of directors. The new company planned to set up branches in Venice, Constantinople, and Tripoli.[7]

By the end of 1912 it seemed as if these oriental undertakings might have some future after all. Peace had finally come, with Volpi as one of its principal architects. Joel's personal confidence in Volpi was thus amply vindicated, and the settlements of 1912 brought a new opportunity for Italian penetration into Asia Minor, with the Società Commerciale d'Oriente playing a key part.

Peace between the Ottoman Empire and Italy was no easy matter; the Turkish regime was unstable and disorganized to the last degree. The Young Turk groups that had taken over after the coup of 1908 were torn by personal rivalries and uncertain about how to save the state. One element among them, mostly from the Masonic lodges of Salonika, aimed at a European-style constitutional and multinational system. A pan-Islamic element proposed to exploit the theocratic-caliphate functions of the Ottoman state in the hope of finding a new bond between Turks, Arabs, and Moslem Albanians, the loyal nationalities of the empire. Yet a third element was Turkish nationalist, and only that element had any real future.

Between 1908 and 1914 Ottoman politics shifted toward that solution of the state's difficulties. The clashes between Turks and Armenians, the growth of pan-Hellenism, and the thinness of the Turkish bourgeoisie all militated against a liberal-constitutional outcome. By the time of the war with Italy, it was no longer a practical possibility, and power was falling into purely military hands. The pan-Islamic prospect also faded with the Albanian revolts of 1912 and the widespread disaffection among the Arabs. The ethnic Turks remained as the empire's last reserve. The European-Turkish army officers and civil servants began to see in Asia Minor their national home and their bastion.

The Ottoman disunity and confusion hindered peace with Italy until greater dangers impended. The cession of Moslem provinces to a Christian power, however swathed in saving formulas of continuing Ottoman religious primacy, was hard to swallow and threatened the survival of any government that agreed to it.

Italy's war seemed to have no happy ending, and any further Italian moves would certainly be counterproductive. An Italian operation against the straits or the port of Smyrna would stir up a hornet's nest of international claims and rivalries, after which the concert of Europe might well interpose between Italy and the Ottoman Empire, a step that would delay a decision indefinitely.

Even though the Italians had clearly won by cutting off Libya and threatening Asia Minor, under these delicate circumstances they had to try to get the Turks to accept defeat and end the war through bilateral negotiations. Naturally Italy had to offer the financial balm and religious guarantees that might make a settlement palatable, salvaging Ottoman prestige and the nominal authority of the caliph-sultan. It was essential to deal with the imperial authorities informally without involving other powers or giving the Sublime Porte a chance to invoke the concert of Europe in its defense.

The Italian government sent Volpi to appraise matters at Constantinople. The choice of a businessman made sense—conventional Italian diplomacy had never made much headway there. The Italian ambassador to Turkey under Tittoni, the Marquis Imperiali, had found the atmosphere stifling and the Italian colony there rent by feuds and intrigues.

The Italian embassy at Constantinople depended for information and influence on its relations with other European embassies, an unfortunate way to operate under the new Ottoman regime. Between 1908 and 1914 Constantinople became a center of international agents, influence peddlers, and journalists selling their pens, in addition to the customary concession-seekers and promoters who claimed foreign backing. From the varied quarters of this strange cosmopolis, Europe, Turkey, and the Levant looked out at each other, mingling hostility and calculation. The shaky new Turkish regime, open to corruption at every pore, offered encouragement to the subworld gathered in its capital.[8] Any foreigners having political and economic interests to further had to know how to move amid the underbrush, whom to pay and when, what friends to make, and what newspaper to favor. Adroitness and ready cash were more essential than a mastery of international law and precedent. Volpi proved to be the right man for the job.

Since its formal beginnings in 1907, the Società Commerciale d'Oriente had set up a regular apparatus in Constantinople that was able to get information out of the labyrinthine Ottoman ministries.

Volpi's local agent was Bernardino Nogara, a close-mouthed mining engineer with extensive experience in the intricacies of Levantine business and politics. During the preliminary phases of the 1912 negotiations, Volpi took his cues from Nogara, who managed to stay in the Turkish capital even during the war between Italy and Turkey.

Leaving from Belgrade, Volpi spent a week in Constantinople in mid-June 1912. Serbia furnished passports and diplomatic protection. Volpi saw a few highly placed Turks, noted that the Unity and Progress Committee really controlled the government, and sensed that the new nationalist leaders were in a desperate plight. These observations confirmed his former judgments that Turkey would go through a stormy period in which its institutions would finally break up. Volpi's evident, though cautiously implied, belief was that the riches of Asia Minor's subsoil would become available to foreign development only after the empire's fall. Then, he thought, there would be rare opportunities for Italy.

For the moment Volpi counted on bringing the Turks to heel by a mixture of corruption and pressure. Nogara paid certain newspapers on a day-to-day basis to further these aims. On his return from Turkey, Volpi reported to Giolitti that the Young Turk regime was incompetently led, trapped, and eventually doomed. In the subsequent peace negotiations, the Italians were able to deal with the Turks from a position of assured strength. Thanks to Volpi's network, the Italian government often knew what the Ottoman envoys were instructed to do, what informal steps were in the offing, and how the Turkish ministry would break seeming deadlocks. Thus Italy's greatest diplomatic success since the feats of Cavour—so it seemed at the time—owed far more to Volpi's skill in handling Turkish affairs than to traditional Italian diplomacy, which was absent in 1912.[9]

By then the understanding between the Giolitti government and the Banca Commerciale was closer than ever. Joel was in steady correspondence with the German financier Helfferich, arranging delicate matters in Berlin on Giolitti's behalf. Unfortunately the precise nature of that correspondence cannot be deduced from Joel's guarded expressions, but it is clear that Joel was close to becoming Giolitti's court banker, a traditional role. In his 1912 letters to

Volpi, Joel refers to Giolitti in admiring and almost familiar terms as "*il padrone.*"

All this indicated a community of interests between a political "regime" and a financial establishment, but it was far from leading to an institutional link between the state and the peninsula's greatest investment bank. On the contrary, the Bank of Italy's management maintained a certain distance. Stringher, the living symbol of financial probity, the guardian of the public interest, respected Joel, though he kept an eye on his foreign connections. However, toward Volpi Stringher nourished the abiding dislike of an established dowager face to face with a young social climber. In particular, Stringher resented Volpi's intrusions into the Balkan rail project in 1908 and the prominent part he took as the representative of Italian finance abroad after 1912. In 1913 Stringher even went so far as to suggest that when the Antivari Company was refinanced—an operation that concerned the Italian government deeply—Volpi should be removed from its presidency. In Stringher's eyes, the Commerciale group, however close to the premier personally and politically, had no claim to represent the national interest.[10]

Volpi believed that with the end of the Ottoman domain in Europe, the whole Danube-Adriatic rail project could be relaunched, and he counted on Joel to get the Italian government to take a more energetic stand. Volpi's ideas made sense. The government was renegotiating the Antivari Company's subsidy contracts, which had been the subject of direct discussions between Joel and the premier. The Banco di Roma was being eased out. Now that more Italian money was going to be put into Montenegro, why not press for the big rail line that would justify such commitments?

After the final conclusion of peace with the Ottoman Empire in October 1912, some new figures appeared among Italy's representatives abroad. The new ambassador to the Sublime Porte was not a professional diplomat, but a career prefect, the Marquis Camillo Garroni, who had arranged the financial salvage of *La Tribuna* in Giolitti's political interest. Garroni's appointment was more than a reward for services rendered: it was a recognition of the fact that Italy's objectives in the eastern Mediterranean required the coordination of political interests and business enterprises.

The other key representative of Italian interests at Constantinople was the Italian delegate on the Ottoman Public Debt Council. Since Italians held only a relatively small portion of the outstanding Ottoman bonds, Italy's place on the council was largely due to her status as a Mediterranean power. The Italian delegate, unlike his French, German, Austrian, and British colleagues, did not have to put the interests of the bondholders he represented ahead of other considerations. If so disposed or instructed, he could observe, maneuver, and angle for official concessions or favors in exchange for his vote on vital financial issues. Italy was the single power sitting on the council, officially an agency of the Ottoman government, that had no real stake in the survival of the Ottoman state: Russia was still outside.

Italy's position in the council was particularly anomalous during the Libyan War. Though other Italians were expelled from the empire during the hostilities, the Italian delegate on the council remained inviolate, a living symbol of Ottoman economic vassalage. But it appears that the Italian delegate, the Marquis Theodoli, did not realize how delicate his situation was. He indulged in some indiscreet language concerning the war, remarks that were relayed from the German embassy to the Turks. The Ottoman authorities, their patience at an end, expelled him and declared him persona non grata in 1912.

Thus, with the end of the war, Italy's seat on the council had to be filled. The appointment was vested in the Rome Chamber of Commerce, as representative of the Italian creditors. The president of that body was Romolo Tittoni, a high officer of the Banco di Roma, brother of Tommaso, and a part of the Roman real estate and commercial elite that included so much of the capital's old papal aristocracy. At the end of the war Romolo Tittoni nominated Bernardino Nogara to replace Theodoli, obviously with government approval, if not initiative. The appointment followed the new pattern: a businessman took the place of a diplomat. Like Volpi and Garroni, Nogara had long enjoyed close relations with the Banca Commerciale.[11]

There were special reasons for Tittoni's giving the nod to Nogara, in spite of the engineer's connections with a powerful competing bank. Nogara had come into the Banca Commerciale group through his participation in Volpi's earlier mining ventures. Like the other Italian executives of the Commerciale and its affiliates, he was a North Italian. Unlike the others, however, he was identifiably and publicly Catholic. One of his brothers was a high-ranking Vatican prelate, and Nogara himself seems to have enjoyed the confidence of the Holy See. Years later, after the 1929 settlements, he was chosen to reorganize Vatican finances. Undoubtedly his connections were useful in the Levant, where Catholic schools and missions often served European powers in their aims of political and cultural penetration. And his Catholicism may well have helped to dispel the widespread feeling that the Commerciale's organization was excessively Jewish in personnel and German in orientation.

Although businessmen had come to the fore as Italy's agents and envoys in the Ottoman Empire, eclipsing the professionals of the foreign ministry, Di San Giuliano himself kept control of high policy. The marquis had come into diplomacy after a parliamentary-ministerial career and was personally convinced that Italian penetration of the East had to be coordinated with business operations. With the partition of Africa now an accomplished fact, Di San Giuliano focused his attention on the Balkans and the Near East: there, too, disguised or overt partition among the European powers seemed to him unavoidable.

That was the presupposition of the new policy lines that Di San Giuliano proposed to the king and to Giolitti in a memorandum of January 22, 1913. Like many of his papers and statements, it is a model of lucidity and—within the limits of the diplomacy of his era —of foresight.[12] He held that Asiatic Turkey was in crisis now that European Turkey was lost. Italy's short-range interest was to maintain the status quo; the country would still be unable to get her fair share of the spoils in the event that the Ottoman Empire fell apart completely.

But Italy should, he thought, at the same time, move to stake out claims on Ottoman territory in preparation for the expected total collapse of the empire. Italian policy should aim at maintaining the balance of power in the eastern Mediterranean by securing for Italy her share of Asia Minor. The folly, corruption, and disorganization of the Ottoman ruling class, he surmised, gave little hope for the survival of the state. The final debacle would not be long in coming, he predicted.

Di San Giuliano realized that a policy of penetration in Asia Minor would be expensive and domestically unpopular, since it ran counter to the liberal traditions of the Risorgimento; but public opinion would have to be prepared to follow along, moved by a "cold calculation of our interests."

Naturally the foreign minister did not propose another military expedition with aims of direct domination. He thought it absolutely necessary to set up in Asiatic Turkey a network of economic interests and privileged positions. To better her bargaining position among the future partitioning powers, Italy had to be present not only in the areas that she was staking out as her future exclusive possessions, but also in other parts of Turkey. These considerations meant a policy of momentarily favoring the Ottoman state while moving to secure concessions.

Di San Giuliano advanced these proposals with a real sense of urgency. There could be none of the dawdling and hesitation that had marred earlier Italian initiatives. The Italian treasury and finance ministries, the banks and the business groups should be called in at once—to plan, finance, and coordinate a program of penetration and development in Asia Minor.

Di San Giuliano himself would, of course, handle the complex diplomacy needed to secure international recognition of Italy's claim. He intended initially to work within the Triple Alliance in the hope of arriving at a common plan. Only if that failed would he seek an overt understanding with the French and Russians. According to the foreign minister, Italy dealt most successfully with the Entente powers when her position within her own Triple Alliance was as solid as possible.

The foreign minister concluded this state paper with some carefully phrased reservations about the policy moves he was recommending. Italian aims in Asia Minor should not compromise Italy's other primary concerns: parity with Austria-Hungary in the Adriatic, especially in determining the political and economic future of Albania; the development of Montenegro; and the port and rail links that would tie the Danube areas with the Adriatic.

Di San Giuliano followed this memorandum the next day with a wire to Ambassador Garroni. He told the new envoy that in view of the likely breakup of the state to which he was accredited, Italy had to try to spread her culture and her economic enterprises as widely as possible and above all develop a tight-knit network of interests in the part of Turkey that Italy might hope to annex.

The foreign minister then asked Garroni to indicate a zone suitable for Italian penetration and not already preempted by another great power. If Asiatic Turkey should come up for partition, there was no doubt in Di San Giuliano's mind that Armenia would go to Russia, Syria to France, Arabia and lower Mesopotamia to Britain. Italy had to make her advance reservations. Di San Giuliano wanted a region along the Mediterranean coastline of Anatolia, where the new Italian team in Turkey could work out a "constant and organic program" of exclusive concessions, to include banking, shipping, and the local development of resources and communications. The foreign minister had already considered Adana and Alexandretta but had been forced to eliminate them because other, greater powers had interests there. His gaze shifted, consequently, to that yet unclaimed and undeveloped part of the Turkish Mediterranean coastline that lay near the new Italian naval positions at Rhodes.[13]

How is one to estimate Di San Giuliano's policy? Certainly he was an imperialist, differing little from other European policymakers of his era. He had no idea of the vitality of the new Turkish nationalism, but neither, evidently, did the Germans, who persisted in seeing Turkey as a pan-Islamic empire.

If Di San Giuliano was an imperialist, like the other foreign ministers of his time, he differed from some of them in that he was neither a bungler nor a gambler playing with his country's destiny. He compared well to the other statesmen of the Triple Alliance and equaled the French diplomats of the period. He understood perfectly that his country was on a diplomatic tightrope and tempered his policy aims accordingly.

The Italian dilemma was particularly evident in 1913–14. Italy, involved with Austria-Hungary in the Triple Alliance, pursued an Adriatic and Balkan policy that ran head on into the Dual Monarchy's ambitions. In the Balkans and, as it turned out, in Asia Minor, Italy's policies harmonized much better with Russia's.

Yet a switch to the Entente would have made little sense during those years. Germany, once antagonized, could block all Italian aspirations in Turkey and make life difficult for the Italians in many other ways. As for France, it was hardly a potential ally. The French showed resentment and jealousy over Italy's presence anywhere in the eastern Mediterranean. The French, like the Germans, really wanted the Ottoman state to survive. Italian spheres of influence in Asia Minor served no French interest, and the French establishment in Constantinople could be expected to continue the hostility to the Italians that had appeared so clearly in 1908–11.

Thus, neither the Triple Alliance nor the Entente really offered Italy any facilitations in 1913. Isolation or genuine neutrality would have made sense only if Italian statesmen were willing to give up all goals of expansion in the East and all concern with the balance of power in the Mediterranean. This would have meant the definite abandonment of great-power status and ambitions—an alternative acceptable to no Italian statesman of the time, democratic, liberal, or conservative.

Di San Giuliano aimed at a package deal, a global settlement between Italy and her allies covering both Asia Minor and the Balkans. He kept hoping that Germany would soften Austrian distrust of Italy and thus smooth the way for Austro-Italian understanding over the Balkan railway question. Neighborly cooperation with Austria needed German mediation. German goodwill would also be necessary in Asia Minor once the Italians had staked out their initial claims. Di San Giuliano's adherence to the Triple Alliance was limited and unemotional but perfectly sincere: he conceived of it as an instrument of peace and as a means of creating conditions in which Italy could engage in some colonial expansion without risking war.

The foreign minister was no warmonger. His policies required years of peace for their effects to ripen, and his diplomacy aimed at using both the alliance with the Central Powers and the possible friendship of Russia and the western powers to achieve a balance in the Mediterranean in which Italy might enjoy a position as fulcrum.

That conception, which is evident in both his communications with his collaborators in the foreign ministry and his dealings with the European powers, lay at the root of the errors he made between 1911 and 1914. He was willing to give the Ottoman system a push toward destruction without reckoning with the consequences. In short, Di San Giuliano suffered from the common handicaps of European statesmen in those years. He precipitated crises he could not foresee and set in motion forces he had no way of controlling.

Di San Giuliano attempted to explain his foreign policy to the Italian public in his parliamentary speeches of February 23 and December 16, 1913, declaring that Italy's position as a great power in the Mediterranean was growing ever-stronger and that the days of Italian subservience were gone forever. He thus encouraged jingoism and grandiose expectations that he himself was far from sharing. As a result of such efforts to create a domestic consensus, Di San Giuliano found it difficult to moderate the tone of the Italian press, which occasionally embarrassed him in the course of his complicated negotiations with the great powers and raised suspicion and barriers at Constantinople, for Italian reporting was indiscreet and often turned secret speculations into purported fact. On the positive side Di San Giuliano realistically recognized the importance of public opinion and the impossibility of committing Italian resources without its backing.

In embarking on his new policy lines in 1913, Di San Giuliano had an asset enjoyed by few other Italian liberal ministers—the unwavering confidence of Victor Emmanuel III. The king had induced him, against his own inclinations, to take the foreign portfolio in Luzzatti's ministry of March 1910. Victor Emmanuel's confidence was justified in at least one respect: Di San Giuliano faithfully sent the king all important dispatches and papers and conferred with him personally on important matters. In Italy the foreign minister was answerable not only to parliament, like the "civilian" ministers, but also to the crown, with which he had a direct personal relation.

The foreign minister had some distinct personal assets as well. He was gifted with a good memory and a capacity for hard, detailed work on prosaic foreign-policy matters, which he did not consider beneath his notice. He also had some acquaintance with the Adriatic coastline in the Balkans. Above all, Di San Giuliano had incentives of an especially private nature. He labored feverishly in 1913 and 1914 not only out of a sense of impending crisis in the East, but also because he knew that he did not have much longer to live.

Garroni and Nogara in Constantinople, responding to Di San Giuliano's queries, decided that the southeastern coast of Anatolia, especially the area around the seacoast town of Adalia, was the part of the empire best suited to eventual Italian penetration. As the Italians at Constantinople saw it, the whole area between Cos and Mersina was vacant, undeveloped, and full of possibilities. The navy confirmed their choice; it considered the harbors there of great strategic importance.

The Italian navy virtually ran its own show in the eastern Mediterranean. The fleet at Rhodes, commanded by a prince of the House of Savoy, the duke of the Abruzzi, kept close scrutiny on the nearby Turkish coast, cruising about and collecting information. The navy was especially interested in the port of Marmarice, which was best adapted for use as a naval base.[14]

In 1913 the duke was sending back glowing reports of southern Anatolia's mineral wealth, for which, he noted, German engineers were prospecting. The area's existing exports, lumber and agricultural produce, were in the hands of Greek, Armenian, and Jewish businessmen, who dealt mainly with Athens and Alexandria. Coastal shipping was mostly controlled by small Greek ship operators. The Turks showed no interest in developing the area along modern lines or even in using its abundant watercourses rationally. As the duke looked at these provinces in 1913, they were crying out for Italian enterprise.

The Italians moved fast in the spring of 1913, and for once their operations were well coordinated. A vice-consulate, with an energetic young diplomat in charge, sprouted in Adalia overnight. Hospital and school plans went forward—Italian penetration was to bring with it all the benefits of European civilization. The fleet based at Rhodes paid an official visit to Adalia. The state-subsidized lines of the Italian merchant marine began including southern Anatolia in their new schedules, with special attention to the hitherto neglected port.[15]

The Italian effort to cut into Anatolian coastal shipping had special significance. The state-subsidized lines, in exchange for their yearly subsidy of 26 million lire, ran the routes that the government specified. They also constituted an important link between the state and heavy industry: the subsidized lines were required to order new vessels from Italian shipyards to become competitive with modern foreign shipping lines in the Mediterranean.

Italy's principal competitor took these moves seriously. During 1913 and early 1914 the Austrian lines operating between the Levant and Trieste began to cut their prices and angle for long-term freight contracts in order to cut the Italians out of the market at the start. Smyrna became the scene of a price war. In 1914 the Austrians still had an edge, both in quality and management, but they would have been hard-pressed once the Italians began operating with modern equipment.

At Constantinople Nogara moved fast. In February 1913 he set up a dummy Ottoman corporation with Aram Halagian, an Ottoman citizen, as its head. The new Financial, Commercial, and Industrial Society, formed to obtain exclusive development rights in the Macri-Adalia coastal zone and to engage in business operations of a more general nature, had a nominal capital of 100,000 Turkish pounds, of which 10,000 were paid up. The directors were all to be Ottoman subjects who obligingly lent their names to the Società Commerciale d'Oriente to satisfy legal requirements. Needless to say, the Società was the sole stockholder.[16]

The new firm's incorporation papers were deposited with the Ottoman Ministry of Public Works with a request that official recognition be granted. This undoubtedly would have taken time, but Volpi and Nogara offered the Turks a more substantial argument in the form of an 8-million-franc loan. This was a mere stopgap to help tide the Ottoman government over a moment of absolute penniless-ness in the spring of 1913, but it was also a foretaste of what credits the Turks might hope to get if they proved cooperative. By the last week in April Nogara was ready to present the Ottoman authorities a contract that would award his new company exclusive rights to study and plan harbor works, ports, railroads, and hydroelectric networks in the coastal areas of southern Anatolia.

The contract had the form of a mere authorization to draw up projects, together with financial arrangements, to be submitted within a five-year period to the Ottoman authorities. However, it was stipulated that if the plans were passed on to another concession holder for actual execution, the Ottoman government would reimburse Nogara's company for the expenses it had incurred, plus 12 percent interest. The Turks could benefit, to be sure, from a political escape clause that would permit the Ottoman government to void the whole contract if it could be proved that the Italian-run corporation was engaging in activities extraneous to its ostensible aims. In addition to this trickily worded loophole, which in fact opened all kinds of chances for direct Italian intervention in the affairs of Turkey, there was another reservation in the Turks' favor: all nontechnical personnel had to be Ottoman subjects, and all foreign technical staff had to be reported by name to the Ottoman government.

This semicolonial pact may suggest that the Italians were finally getting a finger on the empire's jugular vein, but Nogara himself fostered no such illusions. The authorization that he had requested amounted to nothing more than a foot in the door, and Nogara sensed that getting a hard-and-fast concession would take a long time. Moreover, the southern Anatolian coastal strip, with its tangible economic possibilities, was separated from the central provinces of Asia Minor by a mountain chain that limited the extent of practical railroad building. Realistically, Nogara thought in terms of narrow-gauge local lines converging on a modern port at Adalia. Linkage with the empire's trunk line, the Baghdad railroad, was a prospect requiring concessions and expenses beyond Italy's foreseeable means; in any case, such an achievement would depend on international agreements and financial arrangements that were still far off. To make matters more complicated, the British-owned Smyrna-Aidin rail company had prior rights in southern Anatolia. It seemed doubtful that this small and not very profitable enterprise would ever want to do anything with its franchises, but they stood in Nogara's way. Once the Ottoman authorities were securely committed, an understanding would have to be reached with the British.

The corporate maneuvers of Nogara followed Volpi's earlier Montenegro model. The new Ottoman corporation was to be an emanation of the Banca Commerciale, and it was to receive substantial state aid from Rome under the guise of postal subsidies. Like the Antivari Company, the Adalia undertaking was to guarantee that control would remain in Italian hands by depositing its shares at the Bank of Italy.

Such Italian corporate activity abroad was facilitated by a court ruling made by the Milan tribunal on April 12, 1913, according to which all income earned abroad by an Italian corporation was exempt from taxes, even if it figured on a balance published in Italy. The ruling applied to any commercial or industrial activity carried on outside of Italy and finally cleared up a murky legal situation.[17]

Adalia, like Antivari, served for more than prestige or eventual profit. The Italian government acted with an eye to future naval bases. Both strategically placed ports could serve Italy in the event of a naval war in the Mediterranean. The Italian government had let Heraclea go to the French in 1908 only after the navy had advised it that the Black Sea port was not potentially useful from a strategic point of view. Adalia's ideal situation accounts for the zeal with which the government supported and spurred on private business initiative there.[18]

In their hot campaign of preemption between February and May 1913, the Italians clearly intended to create a fait accompli. There is a notable difference between Tittoni's operations in 1908 and Di San Giuliano's in 1913. Tittoni had commenced at the diplomatic level, attempting to work hand in hand with the other great powers, and he wound up with no tangible gains, frustrated by the collusion between foreign embassies, banks, and rail concessionaires at Constantinople. What he had seemingly gained at Paris turned out to be of little avail in Turkey itself. Di San Giuliano and Garroni planned differently. Italian business was to push ahead without preliminary diplomatic coverage and steal a march on the other great-power interests at work in Constantinople. Only after Italian business had obtained concrete privileges in the Adalia area would Italian diplomacy enter the picture. Italy notified neither her "allies" in the Triple Alliance, in spite of the foreign minister's personal belief in the value of that alliance, nor, naturally, her "friends" in the Entente.

But Constantinople was not the sort of place where foreigners could operate noiselessly. In spite of all their fast footwork and their aspirations to secrecy, the Italians did not get away with their coup. Their headquarters, respectably situated at Azarian Han in the Galata quarter of the capital, could not escape notice. And the Turks had the inveterate tactic of informing one European power of what the other was doing, however indirectly.

The German embassy, headed by Wangenheim, was especially well informed on all matters related to industry and railroading in Turkey. It had close, though unofficial, relations with the Deutsche Bank and the Bagdadbahn, and Wangenheim was able to send all kinds of notes about the Italians to Berlin, relaying rumors and reports that German business interests collected in the capital. They knew perfectly well that Halagian, a member of the Unity and Progress Committee, was acting as a financial front man for Nogara and suspected that the Italian government was using Nogara to get a sphere of interest in the Ottoman Empire.

Why were the Germans so jumpy about Italian projects in areas where no European interests had yet taken hold? The answer is to be found in the far-reaching, many-sided, and monopolistic ambitions of the Germans. The Bagdadbahn was more than a rail line. It was the backbone of a system that would tie in the mineral wealth of the Near East with the industries of Germany. Germany and Austria together would enjoy a monopoly of the means of transportation between Central Europe and the land masses of the Near East, thanks to the Bagdadbahn, the Austrian rail lines in the Balkans, and the Trieste-based Austrian shipping lines. The oil of Mesopotamia and the mines of Anatolia were not the only resources the system would develop; the Germans also planned large-scale land reclamation along the rail line and in the areas it would eventually serve. Turkey would become a reserve of agrarian wealth feeding into the German-Austrian system.

The Italians simply did not fit into those plans at all. The Germans, short of capital, would have preferred that the Banca Commerciale, with Italian government approval, take a larger share of the Baghdad line rather than strike out on its own. Besides, the Italians had economic interests and (by 1913) industrial complexes of their own, with capital and export requirements analogous to those of the Germans, though on a smaller scale. It was precisely this fact that rendered the Italians, in Ambassador Wangenheim's eyes, such active and discomforting neighbors in Turkey. Specifically, the Germans in Turkey wanted no Italian rail lines in Anatolia. Sooner or later they feared, Nogara would move toward Mersina with his provincial rail system and take business away from the main German line in those areas that the Germans themselves were busy developing. An Italian junction in the East would drain away the possible profits of the German Baghdad line, and an Italian port in southern Anatolia would eventually attract commercial traffic that would otherwise have been channeled into the German-Austrian transport systems.

On the diplomatic plane the Germans claimed the whole of Anatolia as their "work zone." They were able to base their claims on decades of development there, as well as on their particular diplomatic-military intimacy with the Turks: in 1913 they had more connections and influence at Constantinople than any other great power had.

That was the background against which Italy played out a miniature and inconclusive diplomatic drama during the year and a half preceding the outbreak of war. After the failure of the small coup in the spring of 1913, there was a direct confrontation between Italy and Germany, resulting in a compromise. It became clear that the Ottoman Empire was not going to break up as fast as the Italians had expected and that Constantinople still had a will of its own. Between August 1913 and March 1914, the Italians found themselves in an uncomfortable and undecided position. On the eastern side of the Adalia area, the Austrians, new competitors in the game, began interposing, while the Italians had to secure their position in the west through an understanding with the Smyrna-Aidin rail line.

A settlement with the Austrians on the eastern end was impossible so long as there was no clear delineation of rights in the west. Finally, after preliminary agreements were reached at London in March 1914, it appeared that the Italians could settle down in the Adalia area, though they were hemmed in by the Austrians on the one side and by the British on the other. Italy would join the other powers in a division of Anatolia into "work zones" and would eventually, it semed, build a network of provincial rail lines coordinating with Austrian and British undertakings, all of them tributary to the great German rail system. But there were still some questions hanging over the situation. The Ottoman authorities had not yet granted a firm concession to the Italians, and with the slight upturn in the fortunes of the empire, it seemed likely that the Italians would have to accommodate themselves to the needs and desires of Turkey instead of joining in the feast of partition that they had anticipated. A modest economic role in the development of the Near East would, in all probability, have been the most that the Italians could have obtained, given the unexpected survival of the Ottoman Empire and the diplomatic and military support the Turkish regime received from Germany. In any case, these lines of development were truncated by the First World War.

The diplomatic game began with a German move. In May 1913 the German government called Di San Giuliano sharply to account, showing him that Germany was perfectly aware of Italy's moves in Turkey. The interview between Flotow, German ambassador at Rome, and the Italian foreign minister took place May 23, and it was highly embarrassing to the Italians. Flotow warned Di San Giuliano that Nogara's angling for concessions in southern Anatolia infringed on Germany's rights, which covered the whole of central and southern Asia Minor.

Di San Giuliano, much put out, fended off the rebuke with a short, improvised answer that settled nothing. First he said, Nogara was acting on his own; and second, the Italians had had no idea that southern Anatolia fell within the German sphere. The first point was a transparent fiction, and the second was a feeble excuse. If the Triple Alliance had rested on any degree of mutual trust, Italy should have discussed her plans with the Central Powers instead of pushing ahead at Constantinople unilaterally and stealthily. The Germans had good reason to be annoyed and suspicious. In fact, Di San Giuliano had been caught out, and his chagrin was visible to the German ambassador, who took the Italian disclaimers as a mere feint. The Germans had made their point. Italy would have to get clearance from the German government before any concessions would be forthcoming at Constantinople.

A few days later the foreign minister gave the German ambassador a detailed official answer in order to open a new round of talks with the German government. Speaking as one diplomat to another, Di San Giuliano explained that the main aim of Italy's foreign policy was to maintain a balance of power in the Mediterranean. The area was unstable because Turkey was breaking up, and the recent Balkan wars had enlarged Greece's boundaries in both the Corfu Straits and the Aegean, to the detriment of Italy's interests. If the process of Ottoman disintegration should go on with the breakup of Asiatic Turkey, then France would take Syria. This acquisition would give France, already in possession of Corsica and most of the North African coast, a decisive edge over Italy. Therefore Italy had to arrange in advance for some sort of territorial compensation in the same area. But where?

The southern coast of Anatolia, between the bay of Cos and Mersina, with its "modest hinterland," as Di San Giuliano accurately put it, was the one part of Asia Minor that no other European power had preempted. In that region there were neither investments of the kind that gave Germany rights to other parts of Turkey nor the moral and historical heritage of the French presence in Syria-Lebanon. Since Germany had never shown any interest in those coasts, the Italian government felt justified in concentrating its efforts to develop economic interests there. These interests, declared the foreign minister, Italy had the right and duty to protect in all of Turkey, indeed in the whole world, following the example and principles of Germany itself. Italy agreed that everything must be done to preserve Turkey. Unfortunately, the information that the Italian foreign minister kept receiving from every part of the empire indicated that the final debacle was not far off.

The French and British, Di San Giuliano warned, were already making confidential overtures to Italy for a general Mediterranean agreement, but Italy had avoided such commitments: she preferred to arrive at an understanding with her allies first. Di San Giuliano made other appeals to Germany's self-interest: if Italy, alone among all civilized powers, should withdraw from the colonial scene, Germany would lose thereby. Other powers would fill the vacuum and hamper Germany's economic expansion. Italy would prove a co-operative neighbor in the Near East, whereas France was petty, jealous, and exclusionary.

Therefore, concluded the foreign minister, the Triple Alliance should formulate a common program. Just as Austria-Hungary had agreed to joint action with Italy in Albania, so Germany could recognize Italy's special interests in southern Anatolia.

This important communication certainly opened the way to further negotiations with Germany, but it also touched on some points on which Italo-German agreement would be hard to reach. Di San Giuliano's remarks about Turkey and Greece were indiscreet. Specifically, the Germans could not view the fall of the Ottoman Empire as anything other than a disaster, and Di San Giuliano's ideas on that eventuality ran directly contrary to their hopes. Moreover, Greece was a direct rival to Italy but not to Germany. Greek shipping on the Anatolian coast competed with Italian interests, but Germany was not concerned directly in such minor matters. On the contrary, there was some hope in Berlin that Greece might be drawn into the sphere of the Central Powers. Insofar as Italian aspirations in the Aegean and Asia Minor clashed with Greek ethnic and commercial drives, Italy was potentially acting against what might well prove to be German-Austrian interests. In short, Italy's declared ambitions could not be made to harmonize with German interests as easily as Di San Giuliano seemed to think.

Furthermore, the Italians were entering into negotiations with Germany just when the whole German master plan for the East was being endangered. On the political plane Germany's protégé, Bulgaria, was losing to the Balkan entente. Bulgaria's defeat left open the whole question of Balkan railroads, an essential part of the projected German-Austrian system. As mentioned before, in Bulgaria Italian industry had been excluded from an important rail contract in 1912 because of German pressure. Germany's Asiatic rail projects, like its related Mesopotamian oil enterprises, had run into trouble with both Russia and Britain. Germany's industrial projects and political commitments had outrun its capital resources, leaving it dependent on the financial goodwill of Paris and London.

To compound matters, the Italians, blocked in Bulgaria, had scored an industrial success in Rumania right under Germany's nose.[19] In April 1913 the Italians had secured a contract to build four torpedo boats for the Rumanian navy, a coup arranged behind the scenes without any international competitive bidding, thanks to King Carol's appreciation of Italian diplomatic support in the question of Silistria. Predictably, this victory aroused the resentment and alarm of the Deutsche Bank and Krupp; and the sentiments found an echo in the German foreign ministry, which saw all the more reason to stop, or at least limit, Italian intrusions.

However annoyed German business might be over Italian competition, the German government had to deal with Italy as an ally. This led in practice to a duplicity in Italo-German relations. While the two countries competed so underhandedly in the East, they were forced to rely on each other elsewhere: the Italians needed the tie with Germany to deal effectively with Austria, while the Germans still hoped for Italian military cooperation in the event of war with France. Germany had to deal with Italy in the double role of ally and competitor, and the Italians did the same when they could.

The negotiations of June–July 1913 culminated in a meeting between Di San Giuliano and the German foreign minister, Jagow, at Kiel. The two ministers concluded a secret verbal agreement, confirmed by the exchange of private letters and maps. The Kiel agreement recognized not spheres of influence, but "work zones." The Italians pledged themselves not to trespass on a German work zone that included the southern coast of Turkey up to Alaja, a little town on the coast between Adalia and Mersina. From Alaja on to the gulf of Cos, the coastline of Turkey was open to Italian economic activity. To be sure, the Italians had been kept at a healthy distance from the Baghdad rail line and its possible spurs or junctions, but in exchange Italy had a free hand in dealing with the British rail line at Smyrna and with the Ottoman authorities.

Italy's apparently limited success was crowned by a partial and preliminary capitulation of the Ottoman authorities. On August 19, 1913, Nogara's corporation obtained a *tezkere* ("permit" or "authorization") to execute railway studies and surveys in the coastal regions of southern Anatolia. It appears that the areas in question went far into territory in the Mersina area that the Kiel agreement had just recognized as outside Italy's zone, but the Italians were quick to assure the Germans that the Kiel agreement took priority, in their eyes, over any other accords. The *tezkere* raised other problems for Italian diplomats. The Turks, with calculated carelessness, had assigned rights in the Adalia zone that were in fact reserved to the British-owned Smyrna-Aidin line, an oversight that officially opened a diplomatic question between Italy and Great Britain; and Turkish authorities were happy to see the Italians embroiled with the English. Most ominous, the official Ottoman authorization did not mention port construction, without which all the Italian plans might prove impracticable. The Turks had given in to the Italians because they needed Italian diplomatic support in the question of the Aegean islands, Adrianople, and the financial matters being discussed at Paris and in the Public Debt Council, but they had done so in a way that hampered Italian initiatives as much as possible.

Right after the Kiel agreement was reached, a new competitor entered the scene in southern Anatolia. Austria-Hungary's foreign minister, Count Berchtold, had long had his eyes on the "Cilician-Pamphylian" coast, as classicizing European diplomats liked to call the southern coastal regions of Turkey, and had recently been sending engineers to reconnoiter those areas. Berchtold's objectives were largely political. He wanted to appear before the next meeting of the Austro-Hungarian parliamentary delegations with a diplomatic success, a resounding reaffirmation of solidarity with Germany, an achievement to match the accomplishments of his predecessor, Aehrenthal. The establishment of Dual Monarchy interests in the Near East, Austria-Hungary's formal entry into the ranks of European colonial powers, would constitute just the kind of political advance that would give prestige to the monarchy and also create new links of interest between the Austrian and Hungarian systems. Austria-Hungary's economic prospects in the area involved a real collaboration between Budapest, Viennese, and Fiume business groups. In short, the enterprise might give new concrete meaning to the union between Austria and Hungary.

Berchtold explained to the Germans, whose support he expected, that no other point on the Mediterranean coasts of the Ottoman Empire offered anything to his state. The hinterland of Haifa, the most likely prospect, fell under French influence. The same would be true of any other port on the Levantine coast. It was desirable, Berchtold thought, that any Austrian zone in the Near East adjoin an area staked out by Germany so that the two allies could work together. Eventual Austro-Hungarian railroad building could thus coordinate with the growth of the Baghdad line and its subsidiary systems. Where would this be possible but on the coasts of southern Anatolia?

The Germans at Constantinople were skeptical, and Ambassador Wangenheim said he did not think that the Dual Monarchy would act with speed or efficiency. However, Wangenheim's remarks were probably designed to allay Italian suspicions. His real views, expressed to Jagow, were to the effect that the Austrians would be much more comfortable neighbors than the "active Italians" in the areas that bordered on the Baghdad track.

Austria-Hungary opened a consulate in Adalia, where the Dual Monarchy could boast all of two resident subjects to look after, and increased its archeological and engineering probes nearby. In the fall of 1913 the Dual Monarchy presented a formal project to the Ottoman authorities: a railroad linking Alaja and Ak-Seki. This scheme in itself made no sense. As Di San Giuliano remarked, it seemed most unlikely that the Austro-Hungarians, with all their diplomacy mobilized, really had in mind a little rail line linking two "Oriental villages" with no economic assets and little future. The Italians feared that the Austro-Hungarians really intended securing the junction with the Baghdad rail system that Germany had refused Italy by the terms of the Kiel agreement. That would mean the draining off of southern Anatolia's commerce into the German-built ports of Mersina and Alexandretta, leaving the Italians with franchises and rights of no value at all.

Di San Giuliano had two lines of defense. He had kept a map, drawn up at Kiel in the summer, that clearly indicated that Alaja was within the Italian work zone and therefore closed to other powers. The Austrians had requested rights to develop Alaja from the Germans, and the Germans had encouraged them, since they held that the Kiel agreement, with its ambiguous wording *"bis Alaja"* had left that coastal town in the German work zone. By mid-November it was clear that Germany was standing behind Austria-Hungary and that the Kiel agreement was being interpreted in such a manner as to keep the Italians so far away from the German rail centers that Austria-Hungary could be wedged in as a buffer.

Di San Giuliano's second defense lay in the terms of the authorization issued by the Ottoman authorities in August, which left no room for the Austro-Hungarians in the southern Anatolian provinces. The Turks were perfectly ready to accommodate the Austrians but felt hindered by the terms of the grant already made. That, at least, was what they told the Germans. In November matters stood at an impasse at Constantinople. The Triple Alliance powers were working at cross-purposes, with only the Turks standing to gain: the Ottoman Empire survived because of the friction between its potential partitioners.

The Italians at Constantinople were inclined toward intransigence—toward holding the line against Austria at all costs. During much of the period between the Libyan conflict and the First World War, Italian diplomacy was actually carried on in Turkey by the chargé d'affaires, Count Nani-Mocenigo, an enterprising junior Machiavelli. During Garroni's frequent absences, Nani-Mocenigo handled the always delicate relations with the other big embassies in Turkey and sent back detailed and ambitious dispatches that went far beyond official Italian policy lines. As Nani-Mocenigo (the name was as nobly Venetian as Foscari's) saw the future, it was pregnant with good things for Italy. The Italian presence in southern Anatolia would draw into Italy's sphere the whole Armenian population of Cilicia (Little Armenia) and thus give Italy a basis for extended colonial gains when the Ottoman Empire finally broke up. Therefore, Nani-Mocenigo held, the Germans were doing everything to block the Italians before they could gain a foothold, and Austria was serving as a cat's-paw for the senior ally.

As for Austria, Nani-Mocenigo, like his superiors, wished that it could be redirected to seeking colonial spheres elsewhere. If Austria-Hungary had to be admitted as a neighbor in Cilicia-Pamphylia, then the Italian chargé consoled himself with the reflection that Austria's shipping industry was almost entirely Italian in language and ethnic background and that when Austria-Hungary finally broke up, Italy would reap the fruits of whatever maritime colonies the defunct Dual Monarchy might leave behind in the eastern Mediterranean. In any case, the whole Italian establishment in the Turkish capital agreed that Di San Giuliano should exclude the Austrians as long as possible, or at least until Italy and Great Britain had come to an agreement concerning railroad rights in the western part of Anatolia. Emerging from his usual place in the back room, Nogara took a particular position in November–December 1913: he held that if the Austrians really wanted to build a rail line at Alaja, there should be a discussion between his syndicate and the Austrian business group that actually proposed to do it.

From some indiscretions of Baron Friedrich Rosenberg, the German foreign ministry's Near Eastern expert, it emerged in November 1913 that the Germans were displeased with Italy's whole operation in Turkey. Particularly galling was Nogara's vote to admit Russia to a place in the Ottoman Public Debt Council, a purely political move made without reference to Triple Alliance interests. Russian capitalists held no Ottoman bonds, and Russia's presence on the council would work only to France's general advantage. Germany had no recriminations about this unfriendly act, but Germany did have a perfect right to back Austria without prior consultation with other powers. Rosenberg thought that the Austrian zone should extend as far as Eski Adalia. If Italy was going to get the whole coastline from Cos on down, why should a few miles more or less between Alaja and Adalia matter?[20]

The Italian establishment at Constantinople thought that it mattered a good deal. It was not certain that Italy could build a modern port at Adalia at a reasonable cost, and some other spot on the coast might turn out to be more suitable. If Austria-Hungary had to be wedged in between the German and the Italian zones in Asia Minor, then the limit, the absolute maximum, that Italy could allow would be the Manavgat River line. Thus Köprü-Su and Eski Adalia would remain in Italy's zone. If this concession should prove insufficient, let Germany make room for Austrian initiative on its side of Alaja. These considerations went to the foreign minister at Rome. Di San Giuliano knew that Italy could not stimultaneously oppose all the great powers concerned in the division of Asiatic Turkey and therefore yielded to demands for an Austro-Hungarian zone, but he also insisted on the Manavgat as a maximum limit. This amounted to little more than a token accommodation to Austria. Thus Italy, from December 1913 to June 1914, remained quietly but persistently at odds with her associates in the Triple Alliance over the whole question of work zones in Asia Minor.

What is one to make of this sorry story of Triple Alliance discord? There were various reasons for the failure of the alliance, but from the diplomatic aspects of the Asia Minor question of 1913–14, it is evident how poorly the Triple Alliance functioned, even on a diplomatic level. The Italians looked to Germany for coordination of the three allies' operations in the eastern Mediterranean and hoped that the Germans would be willing to mediate between Italy and Austria in that area. If the German government had wished to keep Italy as an ally, it should have kept up a constant and adroit work of persuasion to hold the two allies in line. When Austria began moving into the Adalia-Alaja area in direct competition with the Italians who had begun operations there a few months before, Germany, the Italians expected, would lay down guidelines for a joint enterprise by all three allies. But in reality German diplomacy altogether lacked that kind of talent and flexibility. It also lacked the minimum goodwill needed to make any alliance work. Once they had established that their own trunk lines and adjoining areas were inviolable, the Germans took no thought for their allies and let them become entangled over minor territorial questions. Officially Berlin held that the two allies should settle such questions by direct negotiation. In practice Germany was favoring Austria-Hungary behind the scenes. When Sarajevo intervened at the end of June 1914, Italy and Austria were almost as far from agreement as they had been when Austria first began moving into the southern Anatolian coastline.

The disputes over the borders between different work zones in

Asia Minor would not have disrupted the Triple Alliance had there been frankness and mutual confidence between the Central Empire and the Italians. That was precisely the missing element. In the difficult situation in the fall of 1913, Di San Giuliano suspected the Germans of dealing with France behind Italy's back over the partition of Asiatic Turkey. If so, why should not Italy deal with the Entente as well?

Italy wanted to get a consensus among the great powers that would enable her to stake out a sphere or zone in Asia Minor. The difficulty was that her starting point was unsure. Italy had to go out and deal with the Entente powers while leaving the unresolved question of the Austrian project at Alaja to disturb her relations with her supposed allies. The unsettledness of Italy's situation created other troubles that became especially clear in December 1913.

Before entering into detailed negotiations with Italy over the Adalia zone and the prior rights of the Smyrna-Aidin line, the British wanted to know what the prospective Italian concession would really amount to. The Italians at Constantinople, first Count Nani-Mocenigo, then Garroni himself, sounded out the Turks on an explicit and broad declaration of Italian concession rights, but they got evasive responses. The Ottoman authorities had obliged the Italians to the extent of holding up any firm concession to the Austrians in November, but in December they showed another face. The Turks clearly resented loose talk in the Italian press concerning spheres of influence, and they thought that the pressure from the Italian embassy suggested a lack of confidence in Turkish good faith. Italy would get her concession in due time, the Turks suggested, but bringing up the matter in the Ottoman cabinet would be premature. It appeared that Talaat Pasha and the grand vizir might incline toward Italy, while Osman Nizami, the minister of public works, was held by the Italians to be completely pro-German. Garroni, who was more prudent than his chargé d'affaires, saw that the Turks could not be budged farther at this point. Thus Italy had to face the Entente at the end of 1913 without having achieved a firm bargaining position.

Of the two western allies, Britain turned out to be much easier to deal with than France. Thanks to an indiscreet remark dropped by Fitzmaurice, the British chargeé d'affaires at Constantinople,

Count Nani-Mocenigo was able to let the Italian foreign ministry and the London embassy know that Britain did not actually attribute much political importance to the Smyrna-Aidin railroad company. This leak had effects in London, seriously embarrassing the British. Thereafter, the whole matter of Smyrna, Aidin, and Adalia passed quietly from the diplomatic to the business level. The British made one condition clear: there was to be no partition of Turkey. But there was no reason why British and Italian investors should not coordinate their interests in western Anatolia. These business negotiations, carried on between January and March 1914 in London, attracted little public attention. Joel and Nogara, the Italian negotiators, free of the indiscreet habits of junior diplomats, did their job without unnecessary dramatics. The preliminary agreement provided for the construction—to be shared by both groups—of a line that would eventually link Adalia and Burdur. It was understood that the eventual arrangements would be part of a larger picture. The British would link with the Italian system on one side and with the main Baghdad line on the other. This accord was in line with the arrangements that the British were making with the Germans in Mesopotamia and reflects the general tendency of European diplomacy to divide Asiatic Turkey into spheres of economic development, each reserved to a major European power.

France was another story. The French ambassador at Rome, Barrère, kept angling for a broadly based understanding between Italy and the Entente concerning Mediterranean questions. The Italian ambassador at Paris, Tommaso Tittoni, felt that such pacts would be a trap. The French would interpret them broadly while exacting strict compliance from Italy. Tittoni was generally disturbed over the chauvinistic tone of the French press and felt that the peaceful intentions of ministers like Aristide Briand meant little, given the frequent turnover in French ministries. The Italian ambassador at London, Imperiali, who had had much experience with the French in Turkey, agreed with Tittoni but warned that Italy had to come to terms with France over Asia Minor eventually. French enmity could make all kinds of trouble for Italy in the Ottoman Empire and could compromise her relations with Britain and Russia. Both diplomats agreed with Di San Giuliano that it was necessary to try to get France to come to concrete agreements concerning the questions that affected Italy directly. In fact, through 1913 and the first half of 1914, France was far from agreeing with Italy over either the Albanian border or the Aegean islands. Thus a great question mark hung over Italy's relations with France in the summer of 1914, when the outbreak of war suddenly transformed them.

By the end of March 1914, it looked as if the worst was over for Italian interests in Asia Minor. The British had come to an agreement that made room for Italian undertakings at Adalia, and Germany had given formal, though unenthusiastic, backing to the Italians in their dealings in London. Di San Giuliano was freed to turn to Austria-Hungary and suggest a compromise settlement of the two powers' conflicting claims. The Italian foreign ministry envisaged a definite renunciation of the rights at Alaja, which, so it claimed, were reserved to Italy by the Kiel agreement. Italy would yield her coastal zone up to the line of the Manavgat River. In exchange, Italy would expect the support of the Triple Alliance in defending the continued Italian occupation of Rhodes and the Dodecanese Islands. It is not known how this proposal would have struck the Austrians, who expected much more, or the Germans, who never officially admitted that the Italians had interpreted the Kiel agreement correctly. The Italians made overtures to Vienna and were still waiting for an answer in June: the last mention in Italian diplomatic memoranda of this question is dated June 28, 1914.

The Triple Alliance diplomats and their economic counselors did have a certain awareness of the problem of economic integration but failed to grapple with it in its concrete and most difficult forms. Characteristic is the example of the Baghdad rail line and its financing. The Banca Commerciale, because of its traditional ties with German banking groups, had acquired a 2.5 percent interest in the Bagdadbahn at an early date. In December 1913, with French shareholders withdrawing, the Germans wanted to "internationalize" the line by replacing the French with Austrian and Italian investors. To Di San Giuliano's annoyance, the Austrians got the first German approaches, but it turned out that the Germans were more than willing, in this instance, to give Italy parity. Had the Italians agreed, they would have received 5 percent of the line and some representation among the directors. That issue was still pending in the summer of 1914.

Then there was the collaboration between Vienna and Rome in projecting a bank for the new state of Albania. The arrangements all had one defect in common: they provided for a merging of economic interests on a purely financial plane, without regard to the industrial and engineering potential of the Italians. In 1913–14 the peninsula's workshops needed export orders—its steel plants had a need to export rails far more urgent than the need of any Italian bank to find outlets for its capital. In fact, Italy was even shorter of investment capital than Germany was. The Italians needed not a share in the financing and eventual profits of the Baghdad line, but a chance to participate in the industrial development that the line would provide.

In an optimistic article of September 1913, *Il Sole* referred to Nogara's railway plans as a "little Baghdad." But this was precisely what German business wanted to avoid. German enterprisers in the Ottoman Empire really did think in terms of exclusive rights and development areas, in which German industry and engineering skills would be the sole modernizing agents. In the long run it is entirely possible that financial collaboration might have led to some genuine industrial cooperation among the Triple Alliance associates, with Italian specialized skills receiving their due. In general, loans to Balkan or Near Eastern countries stipulated that the debtor would award major transport or utility contracts to the industries of the creditor power. If Italy had joined with Berlin and Viennese financial groups in such an operation, Italian industry might eventually have joined with the industries of Central Europe in the development of Balkan and eastern Mediterranean areas.

The smooth and efficient working of the Triple Alliance depended on all the associates' finding immediate and short-term common interests to pursue together. In the day-to-day unfolding of the international complications of 1913–14, long-term and speculative merging of economic interests did not make up for grinding, cutthroat rivalry like that between Austrian and Italian shipping lines at Smyrna or between German and Italian industrial interests in the ministries of Sofia and Bucharest. The diplomacy and high finance of the Triple Alliance failed to smooth over these short-term frictions or create a network of immediate common concerns that all three powers could work toward on both economic and political planes. The failure was primarily that of Jagow and Bethmann-Hollweg and of their counterparts at Vienna and Rome, but some of the responsibility must rest finally on German big business, which served its country's diplomacy poorly and never considered the possibility of integration in place of hegemony, especially when its own interests were at stake.

The motives of Italian expansion in the eastern Mediterranean often appear to have been primarily political and strategic. Even Nogara in the spring of 1913 recognized that the Adalia concessions had a political meaning that overshadowed any economic possibilities, although later on, when the Austrians raised difficulties and counterclaims, he argued vigorously for the autonomy of his business initiatives. Nevertheless, it might well be argued that Italian economic enterprises in the East were really instruments of naval strategy or symbols of great-power status and had little independent purpose. If this interpretation is correct, then there is little connection between imperialist politics and the industrial crisis explored in the first part of this study.

A closer look at the ambitious projects of the Italian foreign ministry and its unofficial collaborators in the Italian business world will dispel such impressions. The dynamic and hyperactive character of Italian foreign policy in the East was not merely the reflection at Rome of the European crises that culminated in the outbreak of war in 1914, however much those crises may have deepened Rome's sense of urgency. The correspondence between Di San Giuliano, Stringher, and Joel, which involved Volpi and Nogara as well from time to time, shows how deeply rooted was the connection between the needs of Italian heavy industry and the plans of the foreign ministry for an aggressive great-power policy in Turkey.

Up to 1913 large-scale Italian participation in Ottoman loans had been impossible. The Italian government had never allowed the floating of foreign bond issues on the peninsula's markets. Individual Italian banks having connections abroad had engaged in token subscriptions to international loans, but they had used their own capital. Thus the Italian investing public was not directly involved in any foreign transactions of that kind. When Di San Giuliano, near the end of his career and his life, reported to his new chief, Salandra, on these questions, he referred to private Italian bond subscriptions abroad as "clandestine" and of no political advantage to Italy.[21]

The Turkish loans projected in 1913–14 were therefore to figure as a departure in Italian financial practice and hence required special justification. This justification, as advanced by the foreign minister, was of course largely political. The Turkish loans were to give Italy a position of parity with the other great powers of Europe in dealing with the future of the Ottoman domains in Asia. But these projects had a financial and industrial meaning of the first importance.

At the beginning of 1913 the Ottoman Empire, broken by the wars in Libya and in the Balkans, was on the edge of financial ruin. Garroni urged Di San Giuliano to authorize and encourage Italian credits as an indispensable means of increasing Italian influence in the empire. However, as discussions began between Di San Giuliano, Giolitti, and Stringher, the choice of available means turned out to be a real problem. Matters could be arranged through the khedive of Egypt, or through the Italian bank that enjoyed his personal confidence—Pacelli's Banco di Roma—but Di San Giuliano was hesitant about any further dealings of that kind. The khedive, however indispensable he might be in mediating between the Italian authorities and the Moslem religious leaders of Libya, was clearly aiming too high in interposing himself between Rome and Constantinople. As for Pacelli and his bank, Di San Giuliano was wary of asking him to do anything further for the Italian government, since the government was still at odds with the Banco di Roma over claims resulting from the occupation of Libya. Any favors from Pacelli might give him new grounds to press his old claims against the government. Pacelli was ready to try operations at Constantinople, but before entering into any commitments with him, the foreign minister sounded out Giolitti.

The premier was against the whole idea. He was well aware of the political advantages that a fast loan might secure in Turkey, but he wanted to avoid even the appearance of having encouraged the Banco di Roma in such an operation. Then, the domestic market

was strapped for investment capital and the Italian government itself needed to borrow domestically. Giolitti was concerned over the
exchange rates, which were disadvantageous for Italy, and thought
that this was no time to export capital resources. Moreover, he observed, capital was tight all over Europe, except in France, and Italy
could not get easy credit abroad in the event of sudden need.

Giolitti's reply ended the possibility of an immediate deal involving the Banco di Roma in January 1913, but the question itself
remained on the agenda. At the same time that he turned to Giolitti,
Di San Giuliano also asked Stringher to look into the possibilities of
having other Italian banks make the loan to Turkey. Stringher had
the same commonsense observations as Giolitti, but he added a few
surprises. Some Italian bankers were willing to take under consideration a credit operation of this kind, with stipulations that they would
not have to put up too much capital at once, that the bonds in question would be easily transferable, and that there would be some international guarantees. These conditions were to be expected, but
the Italian financiers wanted something else. If the Turks were to
get funds from Italy, then they had to bind themselves to awarding
sizable contracts to Italian industrial firms. Steel and shipbuilding
were specifically mentioned.[22]

Di San Giuliano himself was surprised by the spontaneous reaction of the bankers. He had queried Stringher more out of duty
than out of any expectation of fast results, but he had received an
answer that was almost positive, an encouragement to go ahead.
Thereafter he fully expected to proceed, but a delay occurred. The
interruption was evidently due to the fact that any loan to Turkey
had to wait until the questions arising from the Balkan Wars had
been cleared up in the international conference that kept meeting at
Paris throughout the year. Italian credits to Turkey were part of a
larger pattern that had to include similar operations in Montenegro
and Albania, and they could not be considered in isolation. Instead
of the grand loan that Di San Giuliano had in mind, the Turks got
a much smaller stopgap loan from the Società Commerciale d'Oriente. It amounted to little more than a start, but it eased the way for
the Turkish authorizations to go ahead at Adalia.

As he argued his case with Giolitti in January, Di San Giuliano suggested that a loan of 30 million, with the ample benefits for Italian industries that it entailed, would not have adverse effects on the nation's economy. However, in questions of that nature, he admitted, he would have to defer to Giolitti and to the minister of the treasury, Tedesco. In any case, matters were suspended until the fall of 1913.

When he next turned to the question of Turkish credits, in mid-October, Di San Giuliano had evidently learned a lesson. He no longer operated through Stringher but instead dealt directly with the single Italian who combined domestic industrial interests, connections with international high finance, and a belief in Turkish and Balkan business prospects—Otto Joel of the Commerciale. Joel, unlike Stringher or Tedesco, was ready to sacrifice financial-budgetary orthodoxy to the long-range and speculative interests of the nation's heavy industries. The correspondence between the two men in 1913–14 shows an extraordinary affinity of personal tastes as well as a common risk-taking mentality in international affairs. Thus Joel, already a sort of court banker to Premier Giolitti, became in addition the trusted economic and political counselor of the foreign minister.

In the fall of 1913 the Turkish loan became a live issue again. Contrary to some of Di San Giuliano's predictions, the Ottoman Empire, far from collapsing altogether, had actually made a modest recovery. The international conference at Paris was moving toward a solution of the problems left by the Balkan Wars, which in relation to the eventual Turkish loan were twofold. On the one hand, it was necessary to succor Serbia, Montenegro, and Rumania, who were knocking at the doors of European high finance. On the other, there had to be a definite assessment of how much of the prewar Ottoman public debt would be assumed by each of the Balkan states that had annexed parts of former European Turkey. Only with these questions settled could the "high bank" of Paris and Berlin take up the international loan to the Turks.

The Commerciale's friends and associates abroad urged Joel to participate and to arrange for other Italian banks to take part. The Italian government's consent, of course, was a precondition, and it was on this point that Joel and Di San Giuliano began a regular and frequent exchange of letters in mid-October.

To encourage his banker friend, Di San Giuliano leaked a piece of inside information. At a meeting on October 16 chaired by Giolitti at Palazzo Braschi, the highest diplomatic and financial officials of the state had gone along with the premier and decided in principle that Italian banks would be allowed to take part in the next international loan to Turkey. Di San Giuliano and Garroni, called from Constantinople, were pressing for such a move, while Stringher and Tedesco were doubtful. Giolitti himself decided the issue and thus, in Di San Giuliano's estimation, rendered another great service to the country.

Joel thought that Italy could not decently take less than 10 percent of the international bond issue, which would probably total 700 million, making the Italian share 70 million at least. Di San Giuliano had to strain to justify such a financial bloodletting from the already anemic Italian domestic money market. On October 28 he sent to Giolitti, Tedesco, Stringher, and Joel a circular announcing that Russia, breaking precedent, would partake in the forthcoming Turkish loan: this announcement underlined the necessity for Italy's participation.

At the end of the month, Stringher wrote to the foreign minister for more precise information. He assured Di San Giuliano that he sincerely backed the operation—he was aware of its political importance—but needed to know how much Italy's share would amount to and when the bond issue would be floated. On October 16 he had heard mooted the figure of 100 million lire, a sum which posed serious difficulties at a time when the Italian government itself was preparing to borrow several hundred million from the domestic investing public.

At the beginning of November, Di San Giuliano answered Stringher with some reassuring remarks essentially culled from Joel's earlier communications. Matters at Paris were still undecided because of the French government's reluctance to allow new foreign bond issues, and there was no cause for immediate or extraordinary measures on Stringher's part.

After the Italian government's decision in October 1913, the future of the Turkish loan—and of Italy's share in it—depended on the negotiations between the Ottoman authorities and the Ottoman Imperial Bank, which acted as primary agent and intermediary.

It was agreed that the loan would be floated through the Ottoman Imperial Bank. Ten percent of the total bond issue would be assumed by Italian financial interests through the agency of the Società Commerciale d'Oriente, which would act as the intermediary between Constantinople and the Italian domestic security markets. The Italian embassy at Constantinople approved these arrangements with the understanding that Italian participation in the loan would be provided for in the contract between the Ottoman government and the Ottoman Imperial Bank. Nogara and Garroni together had worked out the details, and the Società Commerciale d'Oriente was to report the matter to Stringher. Under the aegis of the Bank of Italy, the peninsula's various investment banks would then form a syndicate to underwrite the Italian share of the loan. The Società Commerciale d'Oriente would continue to serve as the representative of the Italian underwriters in all matters that had to be dealt with at Constantinople.

The total amount of the loan would be about 500 million francs, of which the Italians would take 50. Interest was fixed at 5 percent, but the additional and equally important question of how much premium would be paid to the underwriters was still under discussion by the Ottoman government and the bankers in December 1913.

The loan was not going to help in the modernization of Turkey. Of the total 500 million, some 350 would go to pay war debts and other pressing obligations of the Ottoman government. The remainder, which would be doled out in monthly installments of 15 to 25 million, would not suffice to pay for any radical innovations in Turkey's economy.

In the latter part of March 1914, as the officials of the Italian foreign ministry reviewed the whole question (evidently for the new premier's benefit), it seemed as if the 500-million-franc loan would be floated in the late spring or summer. The foreign ministry's memoranda emphasized that the credit operations were already bringing prompt and direct benefit to the business affairs of Italian industrialists in Turkey. Even the Società Commerciale's modest loan in the spring of 1913 had brought preliminary rewards. Not only did Nogara's surveys in Adalia show how amenable the Turks could become, once in Italy's debt, but the Ottoman Ministry of War had been giving multimillion-lire contracts to Italian firms. Which firms were meant is unclear, but it appears that the Turinese arms company Gilardini and the Roman firm Società Metallurgica Italiana were the beneficiaries. These were both firms whose profit margin depended on exports precisely in the years 1913 and 1914. Both were part of larger industrial interest groups: the Turinese company was run by Dante Ferraris and the Roman firm numbered Pirelli, Silvestri, and Luigi Orlando among its directors. Everything possible was being done to protect the profits of heavy industry. The Turks were to pay for industrial orders in cash furnished them by the investing public of Europe. The arms, utilities, and transport industries of Italy—and of other European powers—would not bear the risk of carrying Ottoman state bonds. The assured profits would have gone to heavy industry, while the risks and possible losses would have fallen on the investing public or, perhaps, the banks that underwrote Turkish loans.

The foreign ministry itself was aware of how hard it was to set up viable Italian business activities in the area, but it tried to do so. One of the first steps was the mission of Primo Levi. Acting for the director general of commercial affairs in the ministry, Levi went on a tour of North Italian business centers in September 1913, accompanied by Dr. Adelchi Ricciardi, who had just written an analysis of Adalia's commerce published by the foreign ministry itself. His purpose was to survey the needs of Italian exporters and to try to interest them in doing business in southern Anatolia. He talked with Pellegrini of the Museo Commerciale at Venice, an expert in eastern Mediterranean business life, and also conferred with Volpi and Nogara. Through Joel he met Captain Emilio Menada, one of the leading executives in the shipping lines affiliated with the Commerciale, who promised to study the foreign ministry's reports from the Adalia vice-consulate and to come to Rome to confer with the foreign and naval ministries in October. In general, Levi found that the most interested businessmen were the cotton textile manufacturers.

Particularly significant were Levi's remarks about Breda, a firm he made contact with through Joel. Breda was just going into mass production of agricultural machinery and wanted very much to profit from export possibilities in eastern Europe and Asia Minor. But Breda reported that it met with unusual difficulties. Italian vessels that plied between Italian ports and the Levant generally belonged to the subsidized "postal" lines, which lacked either sufficient space in their holds or the equipment for loading and unloading heavy machinery. These ships habitually refused to transport such cargo on deck, and it would have been too risky anyway. Besides, loading and unloading such cargo in the ports of Genoa, Constantinople, and Salonika had to be done with barges or pontoons, which increased shipment costs. The cost increases, though trivial in themselves, put Italian manufacturers out of the running. Breda pointed out that not only was its agricultural machinery insufficiently protected in Italy but it had no help whatever abroad. Competing manufacturers in Britain and Germany could use port facilities, modern shipping, and favorable freight rates to export their machines at a cost that enabled them to undersell the Italians.[23]

Though neither Breda nor Levi said so, it was clear that nothing less than a thoroughgoing renovation of the Italian merchant marine and harbor facilities would put Italian industry on a competitive international footing. In fact, Italy was moving along these lines in 1912–14, though the possible fruits were still years away. For Italian heavy industry, at least in the competitive field of agricultural machinery, the future value of Italian zones in Asia Minor would depend on other factors.

The principal Italian "little Baghdad" project was to be a rail line linking Adalia with the inland agrarian center of Burdur: this was the main subject of the final agreement with the British in March 1914. The terrain was difficult; and the project, ambitious and costly. The zealous new Italian vice-consul in Adalia, the Marquis Ferrante, observed to Rome that such rail projects were premature. Any narrow-gauge lines would have to be abandoned, in large part, when Adalia was finally linked to the empire-wide rail system. Italy could establish herself faster and more inexpensively in Adalia and the surrounding regions by setting up motor lines, possibly with Ottoman postal subsidies and Italian state subventions. This was a type of operation with which Fiat had had much experience in Italy. The vice-consul even proposed an eventual trucking service.[24]

Garroni and Nogara did look into the matter. Their chief engineer made a survey of the area in the fall of 1913 and found that the roads connecting Adalia and Burdur were, at a certain inland point, absolutely impassable. Repair and maintenance costs would run into millions, even for a short time, and the Ottoman authorities, pointing to previous contracts with a French road firm, refused to discuss subsidies or kilometric guarantees. The idea died: as Nani-Mocenigo sourly observed, an Italian motor company, even subsidized, could not sacrifice its stock to Turkish road conditions. The one Italian operator consulted spoke of a subsidy of 1,000 lire per kilometer, which was 200 lire above the highest subsidy rate paid in Italy. The foreign ministry, on hearing these conditions, dropped the matter.

Fiat itself had begun to consider Adalia's possibilities in the same stretch of time. In 1914 the ambitious new mutessarif of Adalia planned to build a road connecting Adalia with Alaja. This Turkish official, a motoring enthusiast, took special pleasure in showing off his 12-horsepower Fiat car, offering rides to the Italian vice-consul. The mutessarif wanted a motor service on the Adalia-Alaja road furnished by an Italian firm with Ottoman postal subsidies. In November 1914 Sonnino queried the Constantinople embassy and received an unenthusiastic answer. By then Turkey had entered the War on the side of the Central Powers, and business there was more than problematic. The Constantinople embassy noted that the building of a road was not enough. Maintenance had to insure that a company operating on it would not ruin its equipment after a few trips, and business had to be remunerative. The embassy, while not rejecting the idea out of hand, noted that a representative of the Fiat company had in fact visited the Adalia region in 1913 and had been quite skeptical about business conditions there.

In the earlier months of 1914, Fiat was involved in another Turkish business proposition that further illustrates how hard it was to establish Italian industrial outlets in Asia Minor. This venture concerned an automobile line between Smyrna and Magnesia, covering a distance of less than fifty miles. A certain Soubhi Bey had acquired a concession to provide the service and, taking advantage of the fact that an authorized Fiat representative was then visiting in Turkey, proposed a special arrangement to the motor corporation. Soubhi Bey and his associates would attend to the eventual road work and run the concession, while Fiat would become a shareholder, not by putting up capital, but by furnishing the necessary motor equipment.

These—so Soubhi Bey was to claim—were the terms of an agreement he had reached with the Fiat representative. When the Turkish concessionaire came to Constantinople a little later to close the deal with Fiat's local representative, he was surprised to hear that Fiat no longer wanted to enter into the projected company but preferred to sell him the necessary equipment, though on especially easy terms. This new suggestion completely changed the situation, and much to the concessionaire's disadvantage.

Soubhi Bey, whose concession was due to expire before the summer of 1914, turned to the Italian embassy at Constantinople for help in making Fiat stick to its first offer. In a dispatch of March 21, 1914, Garroni referred the matter to Di San Giuliano, who certainly wanted Italian industry to take advantage of such rare opportunities.

Fiat thought otherwise. The prefect of Turin, who at government behest brought pressure to bear on the company's central office, reported that the Fiat management had gone over the correspondence between their representative and the promoters of the Smyrna-Magnesia line and had found no evidence that he had committed Fiat to such an undertaking.

Fiat's disclaimer rings true, and it certainly put an end to the affair. However, Fiat's pessimism about committing itself in Turkey to more than routine export sales, like those it engaged in on the Latin American market, suggests that Asia Minor was not open to easy development as a colonial area. The absence of a business class with European standards of efficiency and reliability was an incurable drawback. Roads and related services might eventually be provided, but business standards could not be readily improvised or inculcated in a country like Turkey.

The real question Italian authorities had to face in the Adalia region was plain. Given the absence of infrastructures, was it worthwhile for Italian business to invest in harbor works, port machinery, railroads, and utilities to extract profit thereafter from the area's eventual new commercial activities? Would an area that could not support an automobile service eventually pay for such massive infrastructures?

The answer to these questions could come in two forms. Either southern Anatolia might turn out to be as fertile as the countryside around Konia, in which case Italian investment was as justifiable as Germany's efforts there, or mines and forests might yield the profits lacking in local agriculture. These were the lines that Italian engineering probes and surveys moved along in their efforts to assess the potential of the work zone that Italian diplomacy was trying so hard to secure.

There was a certain difference of viewpoint between the foreign minister and the Italian ambassador at Constantinople. Di San Giuliano doubted that Italy had surplus economic energies that called for more colonial outlets and thought that Libya and East Africa were ample for Italy's needs. He saw that Italian banks, with the exception of the Commerciale, were opposed to colonial investments or ventures abroad. But Garroni knew the peninsula's industrial problems as Di San Giuliano did not. Di San Giuliano viewed Adalia and its hinterland as a "coefficient" of great-power balance in the Mediterranean, while Garroni hoped that the area might really offer opportunities to Italian industry. The differences between the two men came out clearly in their relations with business people.[25]

The Banca Commerciale's affiliates and technical consultants abroad lent themselves to expansionist schemes that originated in the Italian foreign ministry, but they did so with attention to eventual industrial development. With Garroni's evident comprehension and approval, Nogara and the other businessmen involved in the Italian penetration of Anatolia moved along lines quite different from what Di San Giuliano expected but in accord with the general policies of the Banca Commerciale and its tradition of industrial development.

The penetration of Asia Minor required Italian technical experts with varied qualifications and methods. The Italian engineers that figure most prominently were Coulant, Caprioglio, and Arrigoni. Coulant was a mining specialist who had studied at a school of mine engineering in Saxony before setting up residence in Turkey, where he married a wealthy Armenian woman. Employment was not lacking; Asia Minor was teeming with European engineers and prospectors. Coulant was retained by the Italian Ministry of Foreign Affairs as adviser to Ambassador Garroni. Nogara employed Caprioglio and Arrigoni to make preliminary surveys for provincial rail lines, harbor construction, and hydroelectric development. Nogara also employed a local prospector of Greek origin, whose activities were less likely to attract the suspicious scrutiny of Ottoman officials.[26]

Much Italian surveying was carried out by the Italian archaeologist and classical historian Roberto Paribeni, director of the Museo Nazionale Romano, who headed Italian archeological missions in the Adalia area. Paribeni's missions were a little unusual in that they included one member who studied contemporary economic conditions. Paribeni himself made many geographical and topographical observations that strict attention to archeology would not have required. In short, archeology provided an ideal cover for the foreign ministry's investigations in the area.

In March 1914, when it appeared that the Austrians were doing much the same, the foreign ministry wrote Paribeni, then back at his museum post in Rome, and inquired about the Austrian mission's chief, a Professor Wilhelm. Paribeni's answer was amusingly unprofessional. He told the foreign ministry that the news could not be worse, since Wilhelm was a man of outstanding scientific attainments. If the Austrians sent a man of his caliber, reasoned Paribeni, they must be serious. Paribeni hoped that "a little Adaliote fever" would send Wilhelm back to the academic chair that he graced so well. But both Italians and Austrians also used genuine engineers in their competing surveys of the southern Anatolian coastal zone, and the rival groups came to similar conclusions.

The Italian reported that Adalia was no promised land. The engineer Caprioglio figured that the streams near Adalia that fell from the inland plateau to the coastal plain could, if properly channeled, yield a maximum of 20,000 horsepower at a cost of something over 2 million francs. The port itself presented a worse problem. The principal export of the area was lumber, which was sent coastward on local rivers, picked up by ships anchored offshore, and transported to Egypt. This cumbersome route was necessary because all the ancient seaports had become choked with sand over the centuries. The best of the old seaports, Leara, was nine kilometers from the city of Adalia. It could be made into a good modern port, but at a cost that its distance from Adalia would not justify.

As for Adalia itself, the city's harbor was deep enough for modern steamships, but it was exposed in the fall and spring to violent southwesterly winds that often closed the port. Two piers, costing 7 million francs, would be needed to make the port usable year-round. To make direct transfer of freight between ships and trains possible, a special rail line would be needed to connect the piers with the city's projected railway station, which had to be located on a plateau behind the town at a height of 60 meters. This line, Caprioglio figured, would extend 2,500 meters, including a ramp and a tunnel. The total cost of all these harbor facilities would run up to 12 million francs.

Caprioglio's report, drawn up the first week of January 1914, suggests what the real problems were.[27] Undoubtedly the projects that he outlined would have provided orders and employment for Italian industry in search of outlets, but did the basic resources and business possibilities of southern Anatolia justify the enormous capital outlay required?

Two principal opportunities were offered to Italian land developers in the southern Anatolian provinces that fell within the Italian work zones: one was the estate held by Djemal Bey at the eastern end of the Italian zone, and the other was the vast landed domain of the khedive of Egypt at Dalaman.

The Djemal Bey estate consisted of three big farms lying between the Manavgat and Köprü-Su rivers, in an area eyed by both Austria-Hungary and Italy. The estate, insofar as it was accessible at all, could be reached equally well from Alaja or from Adalia and offered abundant seacoast frontage.[28]

Djemal Bey (not to be confused with the Turkish triumvir) belonged to the Toghai-Zade family, of the traditional Ottoman aristocracy, which had owned the estate for centuries. A landlord of the old school, he found himself in trouble and wanted help from the

Italians. He was at odds with the local mutessarif and in ill favor with the new regime at Constantinople. Besides, he was suffering from malaria and needed a change of climate—an ominous particular that was enough to put any prospective investor on his guard.

Djemal Bey was interested in renting his properties en bloc to an Italian management group, with a long-term lease that would give him security without the headaches of dealing with the Ottoman administration. He had some contacts that facilitated matters. His uncle worked for an Italian shipping line in Alaja, his doctor appears to have been in touch with the Italians, and he was able to keep dealing with the Italian vice-consulate at Adalia on an informal basis. The vice-consul put the Turkish landholder in communication with Alexander Telioudis, an Ottoman citizen of Greek background and the front man for Nogara in situations where Nogara could not act in his own name. Telioudis mentioned Djemal Bey's desires to Nogara but found Nogara cold to any real estate investment. However, the Italian government prevailed upon Djemal Bey to grant an option through Telioudis to any enterpriser willing to consider the proposition. The Italian foreign ministry was in a somewhat delicate position, since it could not operate or intervene in its own name but would have to find an Italian business firm that specialized in such undertakings. Di San Giuliano was personally much concerned, because Djemal Bey's properties, once under Italian management, would effectively block any Austrian encroachment on the areas that Italy was staking out between Adalia and the Manavgat River line, which was to be the eventual border between the Italian and the Austrian work zones. Paribeni, who knew the area, was favorably impressed.

These preliminary negotiations took place between the beginning of February and the end of April 1914. Djemal Bey was uneasy, fearing the hostility of the local Ottoman authorities, and he had to deal with the Italians furtively. Two facts worked against him. Not only was he dealing with a European power that the local officialdom disliked, he was also operating with fraudulent records and titles that rested on possession and custom rather than legal right.

This last difficulty typified much of what was wrong with Ottoman landholding and explains why no European businessman could contemplate agrarian rentals of this kind. Djemal Bey's holdings amounted to more than 150 square kilometers (about 40,000 acres), but the public records showed little more than 20 square kilometers —the result of fraudulent registration dating back to previous governments. All landholders in the Adalia area had registered their properties at a fraction of their real acreage and had then, through bribery, secured an official recording of their real boundaries, which often included more than five times as much as the area measurements registered; land registry was not based on, or checked against, any geometrical survey. If the Ottoman authorities ever wished to make trouble, all they would have to do was bring up these obvious frauds, a possibility that in itself should have been enough to deter even the most optimistic foreign lessor-manager.

What was the potential value of the estates that Djemal Bey was so anxious to lease? To the Italian vice-consul at Adalia they appeared alluring, a big stretch of gently rolling countryside bounded by mountains on one side and by the sea on the other, with a more suitable climate than Adalia's, but the eager young diplomat had no idea of how to assess their economic possibilities.

The foreign minister sent an expert to visit the estate during the month of April 1914. He was Cavaliere Pasquale Seccia, recommended by Senator Fabrizio Colonna. Seccia had much experience with modern methods of estate management and served as administrator of the House of Colonna. In his trip to Adalia he was accompanied by Professor Paribeni. In May 1914 Seccia submitted a written report to the foreign ministry in which he tried to put as favorable an evaluation as he could on the properties.

Like so many Europeans outside their own continent, Seccia could not refrain from amateur ethnology. He lauded the gentlemanly and dignified bearing of the Turks, their hospitality and truthfulness—so lacking in the local Greeks. But his praise of the noble savages was spiced with observations about their lethargy and need for contact with dynamic European civilization. The skilled agriculture of the Adalia area, mostly fruit growing, was all in the hands of Greek peasants and enterprisers, Seccia reported. Noting the chaotic nature of Ottoman administration, Seccia suggested that any Italian holding in the area take the form of an "autonomous community," like those that Jews and Germans had set up in Palestine, with its own police, courts, schools, health systems, and social services.

Getting down to the substance of the problem, Seccia noted that the whole area was potentially fertile and that most of it had profited by the centuries of *riposo* the Turks had left it in. The soil was alluvial, though, and needed phosphate and potash fertilizers to yield well, and the area's whole system of watercourses needed planning and systematization. For these purposes reforestation was essential. The Turks had stripped the hillsides for centuries—they built their houses entirely of wood and heated them in winter with charcoal fires.

The other essential in reclaiming the estates was irrigation—the area had a Mediterranean climate with a long, hot, and dry summer. Irrigation could well be accompanied by development of hydroelectric power: the watercourses descended from the mountain interior at a gradient that made such projects feasible.

Seccia concluded that with these improvements Djemal Bey's estates, now operating at one-fifth to one-tenth of their potential capacity, could yield excellent cereal, cotton, tobacco, and sugar beet crops and that the alluvial soil was especially adapted to Mediterranean conditions.

For the backward condition of such a promising area, Seccia blamed chiefly the scarce and lethargic local peasant labor, so different from what he was used to in Italy. Djemal Bey drew his labor force from local peasant villages. The peasants, who were all in perennial debt to him, worked on a sharecropping basis, with the landlord supplying seed and equipment. Contracts were by oral agreement. In many cases peasant families also had plots of their own as well as livestock. Peasant labor operated at a mere subsistence level, and land improvement was out of the question. Weeds and bushes grew apace, and workmen often steered their plows around the clumps rather than going to the trouble of uprooting them. Hence it was not surprising that much of the arable land on Djemal Bey's estate was in pasturage.

Seccia thought that the local labor difficulties could be overcome. He advised against settling the area with Italian peasants or laborers, since that would lower Italian dignity in Turkish eyes. He suggested bringing in a pilot group of a few highly skilled Italian farmers who would educate the Turkish peasants by example under Italian management.

There was another drawback in the proposed deal that Seccia mentioned only in passing. To reclaim the area and make it pay, there had to be suitable transportation. A carriage road made it possible to get from Adalia to the bounds of Djemal Bey's property, but from there on Seccia found only paths.

He recommended the proposed lease, admitting that he was swayed by the "eminently patriotic" idea of restoring Latin hegemony in Asia Minor. But he also thought the deal would be profitable. Even with primitive, inefficient cultivation methods, poor livestock, and inadequate manpower the estates had yielded an average yearly profit of almost three hundred thousand lire (a figure evidently furnished by the landholding family itself); with Italian equipment, animals, and working methods, that yield would soon multiply. The proposed rent, only 120,000 lire per year, seemed a bargain; the average rate by area in Italy would amount to about ten times as much.

The vice-consul at Adalia pressed on Rome the necessity of doing something as soon as Seccia submitted his report. Djemal Bey, it was feared, was receiving overtures from the Austro-Hungarians, who now had a consulate of their own in the town. And the Turkish landlord felt that he was being harassed by the local government officials. The foreign minister himself, with an eye to Austria, was personally concerned over the future of the estates, an example of his attention to details. In May 1914, when Seccia and Paribeni reported back to the ministry, it seemed as if Di San Giuliano had actually found an Italian businessman to undertake the management of the estates. Just at this point Telioudis's option expired, but the Italian vice-consulate secured a renewal of a month and a half, which gave Di San Giuliano a short breathing space in which to conclude matters with his prospective Italian lessor.

The enterpriser in question was Feliciano Bianchi, head of the engineering company Bianchi-Steiner. No novice in such matters, Bianchi had 3.5 million lire worth of construction projects under way in Sicily, Calabria, Libya, and Eritrea: clearly, backward areas did not bother him. He had evidently explored the possibilities of Albania as well. Bianchi observed with some interest that the ministry, by turning to him, had initiated a new policy. Up to then the ministry had preferred making use of bankers to dealing directly with individual industrialists. Bianchi was well aware of the pitfalls in his path: he thought the Banco di Roma, even if it had claimed too much compensation from the government, had suffered gross ingratitude from the country. He had no intention of incurring a like fate. The deal interested him, but he wanted to be safeguarded against mishaps. Bianchi made it clear that if he was to start with an initial expense of 600,000 lire, as the proposed deal required, he had a right to government protection and assurances for the future. He stuck fast at two points: he wanted eventually to buy all or part of the estates in question, a demand that seemed more reasonable when the Turkish landlord made it plain that he could not reimburse him for improvements; and he wanted the Italian government to guarantee against losses incurred through war, levies, confiscations, or raids by Ottoman authorities. He might as well have asked for annexation outright: these were terms that no Italian ministry could pledge itself to observe. Turkey was not yet ripe for colonial partition and Djemal Bey was neither willing to sell his properties nor even to commit himself to a lease for more than fifteen years.

Bianchi tried to get better terms from Di San Giuliano, suggesting that if he could get a clear guarantee against unforeseen dues or claims, he would close the deal.

Bianchi's firm finally sent an official with power of attorney to Turkey to go over conditions on the spot and check Seccia's facts and figures. Seccia himself accompanied Bianchi's agent, Arturo Seminati. By this time the Turks were thoroughly suspicious, and Di San Giuliano himself had to warn the vice-consul against an excess of zeal. In fact, Nogara had made it plain from the start that he wanted nothing to do with real estate, and Garroni had little interest in piddling provincial commerce and farming.

If the Italian team at Constantinople stalled, the foreign minister was truly eager. He held out real industrial possibilities to Bianchi. If Bianchi cooperated, the minister implied, he might well get rights to a quarry and go into the cement-manufacturing business in Turkey; and his name would be kept in mind for future electric utility concessions and other favors. Bianchi wrote Di San Giuliano that he was interested in electrical concessions but skeptical about quarries and cement, since he first would have to find some construction work. In any case, these interchanges left no doubt that the Milanese engineer would have to undertake the management of Djemal Bey's estates if he was to get anywhere in Asia Minor.

After Seccia and Seminati arrived at Alaja, there was a fortnight of silence. Then, on July 9, 1914, the Adalia vice-consulate transmitted a clipped telegram from Seminati to Bianchi, impeaching the accuracy of all of Seccia's figures, describing in unvarnished language the backwardness of the countryside and the primitiveness of all means of transport and production, and asking for instructions in such a way as to leave little doubt that he did not want to conclude any deal at all. The same wire carried a message from Seccia defending his original report and a warning from the vice-consulate that the Austrians were ready to move if the Italians did not close the matter at once. Seminati's and Seccia's wires both wound up at the prefecture of Milan, which delivered them at once to Bianchi.

Di San Giuliano was alarmed and suspicious. Conferring with the vice-consulate and Seccia, he suggested that Seminati and Bianchi, using a private code, were playing for time and more favorable conditions. Seccia answered that it was undoubtedly a "stratagem," as the minister had said, and the minister wired Bianchi at Milan, warning him to conclude fast or the deal might go to some other firm.

By that time, Bianchi was thoroughly on his guard. He answered that the discrepancies between the two reports were so glaring that he could make no decision without having first read the detailed written report that Seminati would deliver upon his return to Italy, and he told the minister to go ahead and negotiate with other parties.

The correspondence passed to the foreign minister's secretary, who got nothing but bad news from Milan. On July 22 Bianchi communicated the details of Seminati's findings. The estates yielded a gross income, according to his estimates, of less than half what Seccia had reported. As for the conditions he found, even the livestock would have to be imported from Italy, and capital investment would have to be massive and continuous. On July 28 the minister's secretary tried once more to get a definite answer from Bianchi, warning the engineer that his silence was creating a poor impression at the ministry. Bianchi answered the next day that his firm would indeed like to set up a branch at Adalia, as it had done in Calabria and Benghazi, but that the opportunity being offered was simply not worth taking.

This whole episode illustrates the limitations of Di San Giuliano in dealing with business people and engineers. He was apparently unable to see them in other than a Machiavellian light. Above all, it is strange that during the month that led from the Sarajevo murders to the outbreak of international war, Italy's foreign ministry was preoccupied, right at its summit, with the future disposition of Djemal Bey's thistle-ridden estates.

Far more complex than the Djemal Bey affair was the problem posed by the khedive of Egypt, who held vast properties in southern Anatolia that could not fail to interest the foreign ministry. Here Italian diplomacy had to deal with a semisovereign prince, not a timorous rural gentleman.[29]

The foreign ministry maintained a diplomatic agency at Cairo, which in 1913–14 was headed by Attilio Serra, who held the rank of counselor and was soon promoted to minister. Serra had what he considered a good relationship with the khedive, whom he regarded as a man of exceptional penetration and shrewdness. The Italian diplomat engaged in no petty tactics with the khedive, who was not to be taken in, but dealt with him directly and frankly.

In late 1913 the Italian government had two objectives in its dealings with the khedive: it wanted the Egyptians to cooperate with Italy in bringing the Senussi fraternity of Libya to accept Italian sovereignty; and it felt a special interest in the future development of the khedivial landholdings in southern Anatolia, which fell in the crucial area between the Italian work zone and the regions reserved to the Smyrna-Aidin line. One of the khedivial estates fronted on the Bay of Macri, which the Italian naval commander at Rhodes, the duke of the Abruzzi, considered one of the finest harbors in the whole Mediterranean. The foreign ministry aimed at persuading the khedive to put his Anatolian holdings under Italian management, an arrangement that would secure the western boundary of the Italian zone in Asia Minor. This was the task entrusted to Serra late in 1913, and the ministry authorized direct contact with Garroni and Nogara.

The possibility of an agreement between the Società Commerciale d'Oriente and the khedivial administration (*Daira Kassa*) was weakened by the fact that Serra was by no means the only channel open between the khedive and Italy. The khedive had a confidential agent named Abdul Hamid Shedid, who served as his representative in dealing with the Senussi chief. Shedid was particularly useful in negotiating the pacification of Cyrenaica, an accomplishment for which his master, the khedive, received 40,000 pounds sterling from the Italian Ministry of Colonies. Shedid had another position, however, as head of the Banco di Roma's Cairo agency, and he naturally told Pacelli all about the possibilities of the Società Commerciale's taking over the management of the khedivial estates. Pacelli, according to Shedid's reserved statements, did not wish to interfere with another Italian enterprise, even though it was natural enough that the Banco di Roma should wish to assume a "certain supremacy" in all business affairs in Ottoman territory. However, if Nogara failed to form a syndicate of investors, then the Banco di Roma might well have wanted to take over the project.

How did Shedid, whom the khedive employed for confidential assignments across the Libyan border, know so much about the khedivial estates in Turkey? His informant was Joseph Maurici, a specialist in the lumber business, whom the khedive seems to have retained for his expertise. Maurici, a big talker and schemer whom no one trusted, was anxious to take as large a share as possible in any syndicate that the Italians might form and therefore tried to involve the Banco di Roma in the affair with the hope of insinuating himself as the mediator between different groups and getting a fat reward. Serra distrusted him and frankly told the khedive so. The khedive said that he shared Serra's feelings but thought that Maurici could be useful because of his knowledge of the lumber market. As for Shedid himself, he would rise to the directorship of the Banco di

Roma's Constantinople agency in the event that the bank took over the management of the khedivial properties.

Those were the obstacles. Nogara took a three-month option for investigations starting January 1, 1914, with the uncomfortable proviso that Maurici would represent the khedivial administration in all surveys and plans relating to the estates.

One of the principal obstacles to any real agreement between an Italian business group and the khedive appears to have been the character and methods of the Egyptian prince. Abbas Hilmi Pasha, His Highness Abbas II, was a thwarted man entering his middle years when the Italians began dealing with him over Turkish real estate. Raised to the khedivial throne when he was barely eighteen, he had spent the years of his reign to no effect. Caught between the irksome, self-righteous tutelage of the British protectors and the potentially revolutionary Arab nationalism that was beginning to prevail in the Egyptian cities, Abbas II was out of his element. Insofar as he had any real loyalties or commitments, they were to the Ottoman Empire and its traditions. That was natural enough, in view of the Turkish-Albanian origins of the khedivial dynasty and the Ottoman-Turkish upbringing and environment that characterized the family. However, the Ottoman suzerain was far from Cairo and in no position to exert any effective power in Egyptian affairs. After a few abortive attempts to play an independent part, Abbas II turned to business as compensation for his political failures, which by the eve of the First World War were definite and irretrievable; indeed, there is every reason to believe that the British were waiting for a chance to get rid of him altogether.

That the khedive was invariably courteous and charming, even with the British, is evident from all accounts, but beneath the charm, he was sullen, vindictive, and devious. He dealt with the Italians only to find some way of escaping from British surveillance and tutelage. The Banco di Roma in particular was useful to him in his business ventures, a fact the British overlords resented.

The Italian foreign minister and the director general, De Martino, had the benefit of an insider's knowledge of Abbas II. Senator Enrico Lustig, one of the khedive's medical advisers, told them all he knew about his illustrious client. The Triestine pathologist appears to have been consulted by the khedive concerning health conditions on his great Dalaman estates, and he also seems to have treated some members of the khedive's entourage.

For some time it had been known in Constantinople that the khedive was planning to modernize his estates at Dalaman, and in 1913 the ever-active Count Nani-Mocenigo had been urging the khedive to use Italian labor. Senator Lustig discouraged this. First of all, the khedive's character stood in the way. According to Lustig's account, the khedive was an exploiter who imported cheap Arab labor from Egypt to work on his Turkish properties and consistently paid as little as possible. Moreover, he considered all Europeans basically inimical to his religion; he viewed Christians with distrust and was therefore unlikely to allow Italian farm workers to take up permanent residence on his Turkish properties. Then, too, the climate of Dalaman was murderous, and it would be inhumane to encourage Italian laborers to replace the khedive's poor Arabs.

Lustig had done everything possible, however, to get the khedive to use Italian personnel in technical and executive capacities. He noted that the khedive's entourage had some elements of exclusive Moslem fanaticism but that the khedive and his counselors tolerated the Europeans who offered real economic benefits. The senator owed his own close relations with the khedive entirely to the fact that he had rendered useful medical and economic services. He saw the khedive as a traditional Ottoman gentleman who concealed under his courtly, Europeanized exterior a profound dislike of the West. At the same time, Abbas II knew perfectly well that if his properties were to yield any great profit, they needed the kind of reclamation that only European technicians could carry out. Therein lay Italy's opportunity.

Whether because of Lustig's promptings or other reasons, Abbas II did employ Italian engineers from 1912 to the outbreak of the War. Even while the Libyan conflict was still officially continuing, in the summer of 1912, the khedive employed an official of the Italian State Civil Engineers to survey his Dalaman properties. Later, when actual reclamation operations began, an adjutant of the civil engineers, Sergio Pesso, was put on detached service by his government to supervise the Dalaman estates. Only the War, which brought

Turkey's intervention and Britain's decision to depose Abbas II, put an end to the collaboration between the Italian state and the khedive.

The khedive's properties had certain advantages over those of Djemal Bey. The Dalaman River gave easy access to the sea and was especially useful in transporting lumber. The khedive, a wealthy man, could and would put money into his properties. But what did such investments really offer?

The Italian engineers made two reports in 1912–13. Both documents, though drawn up for the khedive, found their way to the Italian foreign ministry at Rome. According to them, the khedivial properties, considered as farmland, presented serious problems of much the same kind that afflicted Djemal Bey's estate. The land needed the kind of intensive drainage and reclamation the Italians had carried out in Apulia and the Tuscan Maremma. Thereafter, with an efficient system of combined crops and pasturage and with a labor force willing and able to use European methods, the estates could yield well. Given the properties' alluvial soil and well-situated hills with plentiful watercourses, the land could become fertile, and the waters flowed at a gradient that made hydroelectric development possible. These advantages, combined with the area's easy access to the sea, promised an eventual "economic autonomy" to the Dalaman estates that could not fail to tempt the foreign ministry: autonomous development of this kind, immune to Ottoman official prying and meddling, was exactly what the Italians wanted in their zone of activity.

In 1912–13, in spite of attempted renovation during the preceding years, the khedivial properties were yielding little agricultural income. The traditional methods still in use were crude, makeshift, and wasteful. Plows were ancient and wooden; livestock was unsheltered; irrigation methods were antiquated. The new work on the estates was jerry-built by a listless and unskilled local labor force.

There was a good reason for this state of abandon and near ruin. The plain through which the principal watercourses ran was full of swamps and stagnant pools, forming a huge breeding center for anopheles mosquitoes, bearers of malaria. The insects were abetted by the local architecture, which allowed them constant access to their human victims. And every year fields were flooded unevenly, leaving the plains dotted with mosquito pools. The Italians decided that winter crops, which would not need irrigation since they grew during the rainy season, and an up-to-date system of irrigation ditches equipped with small locks would solve the problems. But if a modern irrigation system was set up, an industrious labor force would be needed to maintain it, and the local Turkish peasant was stubbornly set in his old ways. However, even before a new labor force could be trained, years of investment would be required. On alluvial irrigated land, agricultural work reached its peak during the height of the malaria season. Both efficiency and hygiene demanded that massive land reclamation precede any attempt at intensive crop cultivation. But with the necessary investment capital and modern methods, the Italian engineers and agronomists had no doubt that the khedivial estates could eventually yield a high revenue.

Abbas II knew this. He had been experimenting with cotton and had also begun importing agricultural machinery. The two French-made tractors the khedive had brought in were inadequate and unsuitable for weeding, but the Italians admired his boldness in attempting such an innovation at all. The land required heavy doses of phosphate fertilizer, but the Italians thought that the costs of fertilization would not be exorbitant once roads were completed. They even thought that the estates could yield some income during the years of necessary drainage and land reclamation if especially resistant crops of grain and oats were planted in alternation with forage and lucerne grass. The Italians concluded that an energetic, modern-minded executive should be put in charge of the whole area.

What conclusions can we draw from the facts of southern Anatolian land tenure and development possibilities? What relations do these facts bear to Italian imperialism?

Agrarian development in Turkey was not a chimerical proposition, as the German projects in Konia show. The Italian technician's experience with Mediterranean reclamation could stand him in good stead. On the basis of the surveys conducted both at the Dalaman and at the Manavgat–Köprü-Su alluvial areas, it appears that, (given a free hand,) the Italians would have been able to make something out of their zone in Asia Minor. But how free a hand could they have enjoyed under a social system that perpetuated the indolence of

Djemal Bey and the deviousness of Abbas Hilmi Pasha? What Italian investor or banker would have risked his money for the benefit of such landowners? If Italian capital had flowed into these projects, would not Italian business thereafter have demanded political guarantees and an eventual colonial administration?

But the confrontation between Ottoman society and Italian colonization never took place, although it was distinctly possible in early 1914. Of course, the Italian team in Constantinople never thought much of land development or rural credit in the southern Anatolian zone. It aimed to link Asia Minor to the world of Italian business by quite another kind of undertaking.

Nogara was mainly concerned about forests and mines. In the spring of 1914 he brought an Italian expert, Cavaliere Ottina, to look over the areas that the future Italian rail lines were to traverse and evaluate the prospects for exporting timber; the question was still pending when the war broke out.[30]

More serious were the mining possibilities. Iron and nonferrous metals are to be found in many parts of Asia Minor, and it was reasonable to expect that southern Anatolia might offer such resources. Unfortunately, the Adalia area itself turned out to be something of a problem in that respect. Nogara's agent, Telioudis, did a great deal of prospecting in the zone, but his methods were haphazard. He got local village headmen to collect ore samples, which were sent in to the company's central office at Adalia with a note of the exact site where they had been picked up. Nogara got all kinds of sketchy, vague statements from Telioudis about the possibilities of developing iron and manganese mines, but no quantitative estimates appeared.

Ambassador Garroni took a hand in the matter, sending Coulant to make a serious evaluation. Coulant found Telioudis's prospectives far too optimistic. However, Garroni was so intrigued by the idea of developing an extractive industry in the Italian work zone that he got in touch with Ilva (the steel trust) and persuaded the head of the trust, Commendatore Odero, to send a specialist to Constantinople to explore the region. At the end of May, Garroni was waiting for Ilva to send its agent.

Nogara, operating from his company's headquarters in Constantinople, was hatching another plan. His company, in its requests for railway concessions, had scrupulously respected the arrangements with the British Smyrna-Aidin rail line. However, the area that the Italians had left to the British included the Gulf of Mendelia. In that neighborhood there was a prospective iron mine that Nogara planned to get title to. Since the mine was thirty-five kilometers from the coast, he was also planning to get permission to build a narrow-gauge railroad to give the new mines an outlet to the sea.[31]

Nogara passed the idea on to Di San Giuliano in a letter from Constantinople dated July 17, 1914. He wanted to use the funds that the foreign ministry had made available to him for the Adalia rail surveys, and Di San Giuliano, referring the matter to Stringher for approval, saw no reason to oppose him. By the time the papers came to Stringher's attention, the War was imminent, and nothing further appears in the ministry's records. The episode reveals something of the close relations between Nogara's company and the Italian government, but, more unexpectedly, also something of the real possibilities the Italian engineer saw in Asia Minor.

The Austro-Hungarians, too, were considering the economic feasibility of establishing a sphere in southern Anatolia, and their explorations and surveys are of interest as a way of checking on the Italians' conclusions. It must be said that the two sides often came to the same result.

Toward the end of 1913 the Austro-Hungarians became increasingly active in developing their program in Turkey with sub-rosa German encouragement, but they did not move fast. Only in June 1914 did their new vice-consulate in Adalia acquire the same autonomy that the Italian office there had been enjoying for a year. They did send their own archeological expeditions, but these arrived after Paribeni had already surveyed the Adalia zone. Their shipping lines began calling at Adalia, but only at government behest, and no more signified genuine economic prospects than did the same activities by Italian-subsidied lines.[32]

There were, nevertheless, some real economic probings, which were closely followed by Italian consular offices at Fiume and Adalia. A group of lumber firms at Budapest with shipping connections at Fiume was seriously interested in the spring of 1914 in buying available forest land in southern Anatolia, including woodlands near

Adalia itself. The exploration work was undertaken in June 1914 by Joseph Jakobovics of the Royal Commercial Museum of Budapest, with a subsidy from the Hungarian Ministry of Agriculture, Industry, and Commerce.

The alarm of the Italian authorities can well be imagined when the Turkish paper *Tasviri-Efkiar* announced on July 11 the arrival of an Austro-Hungarian mission, made up of professors from Budapest, for the express purpose of studying local economic and agrarian conditions. The mission had a specific destination, Alaja and Adalia, and lost no time in arriving there. On July 18 three Austrian engineers reached Adalia from Constantinople, attracting the immediate attention of the Italian vice-consul. On July 30 Garroni reported that the engineers were operating in the Manavgat region, distributing money and fancy promises to the local population. Austrian enterprise, they were suggesting, would bring new employment and high wages to the southern Anatolian village.

The Italian foreign ministry inquired of the Italian consul at Budapest what information was available concerning the projects, which evidently involved lumber or land development of some sort. The Italian consul general reported that Baron Peter Herzog, a big tobacco dealer, had reputedly set up a Turkish company with investors from Salonika to exploit forests in Cilicia. The consul general thought that the Austro-Hungarian mission at Manavgat was probably connected with this scheme, especially in view of the fact that the engineers seemed mainly interested in wooded areas. By the time he reported, on August 16, some other facts had come to light.

Like the Italians, the Austro-Hungarians were discovering that southern Anatolia was no promised land, and their views became known at Rome in mid-August 1914. When the War broke out, the three Austrians hastily left Adalia, two of them on an Italian vessel. The Italian vice-consul was able to find out what conclusions they had reached before they left from a source of information that he had checked and found trustworthy. According to the vice-consul's report, one of the Austrian experts, Marcinkow, was a professor of forestry and the manager of the estates of Archduke Louis Salvator in Galicia. He and his colleagues had found that the area around Adalia was fertile and well-irrigated for fifteen kilometers eastward.

Then it turned bare and deforested, with paths that often compelled them to dismount from their horses and proceed on foot. The deforestation, they felt, was due to the habits of an ignorant pastoral-nomad population that burned pine cones and other detritus and thus often damaged or destroyed trees. The mission was supposed to report on the prospects of an eventual automobile line connecting Adalia, Alaja, and Konia, but there was little doubt in the Italian vice-consul's mind that the idea would perish after the mission's on-the-spot experiences. From what the Italians heard indirectly, the mission did a thorough exploration, going up the Köprü-Su almost to its mountain sources and then descending toward Alaja on a mule trail. Hence its impressions deserve special credence. The Austro-Hungarians, it seemed, were moving toward the same dark conclusions that Bianchi's engineering firm had reached after its own inspection of the area.

Like the Italians, the Austro-Hungarians thought about mining as a way of turning Asia Minor into a paying proposition. They had begun looking into that possibility before 1913, and the arrival of the Italians at Rhodes stirred them into actually acquiring some mining rights. The whole mining situation in southern Anatolia was confused by the patchwork manner in which small prospecting firms picked up options, surveyed, and then tried to sell their rights to some buyer with capital who could develop a genuine mining industry. In March 1914 the Austro-Hungarian government sent a section chief of the foreign ministry to look into the mining possibilities, and it is quite likely that the two allies might have become rivals for mining concessions in Asia Minor had not the War put an end to all such projects. In the spring of 1914, Di San Giuliano thought that the Austrian foreign ministry was going ahead with its probings in order to arrive at an eventual trade with Italy: the Italians would get a share of the new Balkan rail lines that were disputed between Austria and Serbia in exchange for some of Italy's concessions in southern Anatolia.

Certainly the mining rights themselves did not warrant much enthusiasm. There were iron mines in many parts of the stretch between the Gulf of Macri and Alaja, but they were not profitable. The costs of development and transportation were so high that no capitalist had yet been found to assume them.

In the spring of 1914 Garroni and Nogara finally had a program ready. They requested from the Ottoman government a set of concessions: two provincial railway systems, one radiating from Macri and covering the Dalaman area and another radiating from Adalia, without any junction between them; port development in both areas; and the right to develop hydroelectric systems. The program was certainly a boon for industrial North Italy, but its ultimate economic feasibility was uncertain.

Negotiations with the Ottoman authorities, represented by the financial expert Djavid Bey, were just getting under way in the summer of 1914 when the war began. One can only conjecture that the matter would not have passed easily at Constantinople. In February 1914, even before things had reached the stage of concrete talks, *Tasviri-Efkiar* had editorialized that it would be better to renounce the Dodecanese Islands and other Ottoman rights in the Aegean than to let the Italians get access to the heart of Anatolia. To the intense annoyance of the Turks and the grave embarrassment of the Italian foreign ministry, the whole European press was reporting Italian projects of penetration in the Adalia-Macri area, ranging from clinics and schools to railroads and harbors. It may be reasonably supposed that Turkish suspicions and resistance would have yielded only if Italy had subscribed to a substantial part of the international loan that the Ottoman regime needed for its survival. It might be further supposed that Italy would have had trouble in doing so, for Italian interests were more heavily involved in the Balkans.

8

The End Play in the Balkans, 1913-14

There is some question whether Italian holdings in Asia Minor could ever have fitted into the Italian national economic system; Italy's ambitions in the Balkans, however, had real economic grounds that cannot be dismissed as a cover for a military-diplomatic maneuver.

These grounds were clearly formulated in the pre–1915 writings of a young economist, Alberto Caroncini. Caroncini was not an autarky-minded protectionist and Nationalist of the Rocco stamp. Rather he was a "National Liberal" of the youthful group that saw no contradiction between national interest and genuine social reform. Caroncini believed in the necessity of Italian expansion abroad, but not as a demographic outlet. He also eschewed autarkically motivated raw-material imperialism. His concern was entirely with the peninsula's real productive energies and skills, which had to find outlets in a world where tariff barriers and political preemption often closed off legitimate business opportunities.[1]

Caroncini saw great possibilities for an Italian "economic hinterland" in three areas, the Balkans, the highlands of East Africa, and Asia Minor, but he gave definite preference to the Balkans. These areas would furnish cotton, wool, hides, lumber, and olives, the basic materials for a wide range of food and textile enterprises to operate under Italian control, and eventually they could take over the first stage of processing for the market. Italy would supply industrial planning, supervision, skilled labor, and certain basic means of production. Italy would build railroads; export agricultural machinery; and set up processing plants, canneries, mills, and tanneries of all sorts. Her political relation to this hinterland might range all the way from an energetic and paternal colonialism, which would apply in East Africa, to arrangements between independent states based on mutual advantage, which would, of course, prevail in the Balkans.

But what were Italy's concrete economic interests in the Balkan peninsula? Was this area really a prospective economic "hinterland" that could play a complementary role in the process of Italian industrial growth? And is it possible at this distance to distinguish the Italian government's strategic concerns in the area from the speculative interests of Italian business promoters and engineers?[2]

We can attempt an answer only by disentangling the various threads in Italy's Balkan involvements, by separating long-term plans from improvised policies, by distinguishing between strategic coastal areas and richer, potentially profitable hinterland centers.

Italy's long-term plan was to relaunch the 1908 Danube-Adriatic rail project, but this time with international control and guarantees that would secure a central part to Italian enterprise. However, that goal was distant, and Italy could reach it only by a complex policy of seeming to satisfy all the other great powers concerned. Hence Italy started a tortuous course of small local compromises and deals with Austria-Hungary, an apparent fixation on strictly Adriatic issues, all undertaken to maneuver the Dual Monarchy into a position from which it could no longer plausibly block the construction of the rail outlet.

This is the only way in which Di San Giuliano's moves can be understood. Italy worked to establish positions in barren Montenegro and primitive Albania to gain access to the truly profitable hinterland regions of Serbia and Rumania. The obstacles from the Franco-Ottoman group at Constantinople that had blocked the last project had been swept away by the Balkan Wars. Italy aimed at seeing to it that Germany and Austria would not put up new blocks. This goal meant that Italian diplomats and financiers had to play a double game—cooperation within the shaky framework of the Triple Alliance on the one hand and informal relations with France, Russia, and Serbia on the other.

It was hard for Italy to break through on the diplomatic plane. During the intricate and inconclusive discussions of 1913–14—it would be misleading to call them negotiations—the Austrians made every effort to get Italian diplomatic support for their own rail projects without offering in return a firm commitment on the Danube-Adriatic line. Austria's position was strong: in 1913 the Austrians gained control of the Chemins de Fer Orientaux, succeeding to the rights and options of the Deutsche Bank. These included, aside from extensive franchises in territories now part of Serbia, the option to build a line, the Valona-Monastir railroad, connecting the southern Albanian coast to the Macedonian interior. This option gave Austria two advantages. It could press its rights and build a railroad in Albania on its own, in spite of the general agreement that all local development there was to be by mutual consent of both Italy and Austria, or it could offer Italy a half-share in the southern Albania-Macedonia line in exchange for Italian support in its controversy with Serbia. The second alternative would leave Italy with nothing more to offer Austria in exchange for eventual Austrian approval of the Danube-Adriatic line, since Italy would already have received her half-share in the southern line in exchange for the one diplomatic commitment that Austria really wanted from her.

This kind of diplomacy, Di San Giuliano clearly recognized, was contrary to Italy's long-range interests, which required that Serbia become economically independent. The other Italian ministers appear to have been of the same mind, especially the outstanding economist of Giolitti's cabinet, F. S. Nitti, who held the portfolio of agriculture, industry, and commerce. Nitti pointed out that Austria's grudging proposals of March 1913 concerning an eventual trans-Balkan line provided for an international administration of the line with headquarters in Albania; only Albania and those states that financed the line were to enjoy preferential rail rates. Nitti objected that Italy had commercial prospects lying beyond the Adriatic littoral. In particular, any arrangement that excluded or penalized Rumania—and this was clearly the real purpose of Austria's schemes

—would work against Italian interests. Italy had only the prospective trans-Balkan line as a means of access to Rumania, while Austria had other routes. The Austrian proposals were designed to leave Rumania within the economic sphere of the Central Powers. In Nitti's observations we can discern how little economic sense remained in Italy's membership in the Triple Alliance. Even if Austria verbally gave ground to Italian desires, it hedged on questions of substance whenever Italian economic penetration in the Balkans was involved.[3]

In these years Italian interests in the Balkan hinterland were just beginning to develop. Latinate Rumania seemed particularly promising. In April 1913 Vico Mantegazza, visiting Bucharest, had a talk with King Carol I that lasted for an hour and a half. The Rumanian monarch was most interested in the renewed prospects of a Danube-Adriatic rail line that would transport passengers and goods from his country to Italy in less than a day and a half, and his ministers planned to extend the study of Italian in Rumanian higher education. These Latin affinities might well have provided favorable conditions for concrete economic relations in the future, once the rail line went into operation.[4]

Serbia, in contrast, was already entering into economic relations with Italy. After the Balkan Wars, Count Piero Foscari and his associates at Venice set up a Comitato Italo-Serbo, sponsored by the Commercial Museum of Venice and its affiliate, the Istituto italiano per l'espansione commerciale e coloniale. The Italo-Serb Committee acted as a liaison between the main Italian chambers of commerce, various business firms, and Italian diplomats. It concentrated on securing contracts for public works, especially provincial rail lines and military orders. By May 1914 Italian engineering firms had obtained subcontracts for eighty-six kilometers of narrow-gauge rail lines in Serbia, a modest but promising start, and ambitious plans for an Italian bank at Belgrade had become public knowledge. It appears that Volpi, not surprisingly, was the Italian financier most directly involved, and it is certain that the Serbs wanted to get regular credits from Italian banks to free themselves from Vienna.[5]

The future of Italian economic operations in the newly enlarged Serb monarchy depended on two preconditions, both dubious.

Serbia could award sizable orders to Italian industry only if the Italians could lend substantial sums to Serbia first. Moreover, future economic ties would be knit only if Serbia became free to plan its own rail system. Obviously, Italy's own capital shortages made the first condition problematical, and Austria's claims overshadowed the whole future of Serbia's economy. These were fighting questions. The deadlock between Belgrade and Vienna was more than a result of ethnic quarrels; Austria's economic hegemony in the Balkan peninsula—as well as Germany's clear road to Turkey—was at stake in these disputes over rail franchises.

As matters stood in the years 1913 and 1914, the Balkan hinterland tantalized Italy, but it was hardly within reach. Only in the coastal countries, Montenegro and Albania, did Italy have established economic interests. In themselves these areas offered questionable, at best mediocre, economic prospects. Their importance lay in the strategic potential of their ports and in the access they offered to the Balkan hinterland.

Still bantamweight in the Balkan league, Montenegro emerged from the 1912–13 wars enlarged in territory but with a depleted treasury and a doubtful political future. Had King Nicholas succeeded in holding on to Scutari, a last-minute conquest, he might have achieved a position as head of a South Slav federation, but the great powers had compelled him to withdraw. Thereafter, it seemed likely that Montenegro would become dependent on Serbia. The little kingdom worried both Austria and Italy, though for opposite reasons; their concerns momentarily balanced out and worked to the benefit of Volpi's economic enterprises there. If Austria insisted that Montenegro, once in the Serb sphere, would have to offer "compensations" to the Dual Monarchy, Italy could allege a vital interest in the integrity of Montenegro as long as Volpi was there.

With these considerations in mind, the Italian government realized by November 1913 that it would have to bail out the Antivari Company. The decision was pushed through by the foreign ministry, whose economic expert, Primo Levi, managed to clear the matter with the treasury and the Bank of Italy. The Antivari Company received 3 million lire and was thus enabled to pay some of its debt to the Banca Commerciale.

With this aid the company could regulate its affairs with the Montenegrin government, which had failed to meet its contractual obligations. In particular, Montenegro had not paid its port dues at Antivari and had not set up the free zone it had promised there. The Antivari Company made it clear to the Montenegrin prime minister that he would get no credits from Italian banks until he agreed to a fair settlement; and finally, in May 1914, Montenegro, which was expecting to qualify for a big international loan, paid the Antivari Company 360,000 francs and yielded to the company's demands for a free zone and special exemptions in the port area. The Antivari Company in turn planned an aqueduct and electric power plant for the city of Antivari. This burst of renewed confidence followed the relaunching of the trans-Balkan rail project.

The Antivari Company's prospects brightened in other ways. Between June and August 1914 a German engineer retained by Montenegro examined the company's port and rail constructions. He found that the Italians had not overcharged and that Montenegro had received fair value from the company. His assessments bettered the company's standing in Montenegro, and, given time, would have cleared the way for new developments.[6]

Albania presented a different problem. Of no less strategic and geographical importance than its neighbor to the north, Albania in 1913 had yet to prove that it could maintain itself as a sovereign national state. The least known and most primitive country of Europe, it had been the last to develop a national movement of its own. It had no historic capital or state tradition and was still a political crazy quilt in foreign eyes. The mountain regions had enjoyed virtual autonomy under Ottoman rule, which had little direct effect on the clans and tribes that constituted, in fact, a congeries of local governments, while the plains and valleys were owned by, or enfeoffed to, a few Ottomanized Albanian families that served the sultan until the end of Abdul Hamid's despotism. For centuries Albanians had risen to high place in both the military and civil services of the empire: the khedivial house of Egypt was only one instance of their success.[7]

Uniquely among all the peoples of Europe, more than two out of every three Albanians were Moslem. The heart of the little country was Moslem, while the Christians were numerous in the border regions at both ends. To the north the Catholics centered around Scutari and prevailed in the nearby mountains, which were dominated by the powerful Mirdite tribe. The Mirdites constituted a picturesque little realm with a Catholic hereditary chieftain, Prenk Bib Doda, and a mitred abbot, Monsignor Primo Doci. "Mirditia" was, in form and in fact, a minature of what Montenegro had been before the nineteenth century, and there is reason to believe that the Mirdite chiefs aspired to repeat Montenegro's rise to statehood. In the south much of the population was Orthodox Christian, officially Greek in culture. Fortunately, differences in religion mattered less in Albania than in other Balkan nations, since conversion to Islam had often occurred, over the centuries, as an accommodation to the Ottoman system and was recognized as such by the Albanians who remained Christian.

Relative religious tolerance was the country's sole asset. Beset by South Slavs on one side and Greeks on the other, much of Greater Albania had disappeared by 1913. The Albanian nationality had no allies, and the Ottoman overlord could neither develop Albania nor defend it. The Albanian notables, at first drawn to the constitutional Ottoman government of 1908, had soon seen that the new Ottoman rulers followed policies of centralization and Turkification that offered no hope to the Albanian people. After 1910 much of Albania was in a state of insurrection against Ottoman rule, which collapsed altogether in 1912 with foreign invasion. The Balkan allies of 1912 passed over a defenseless Albania, which would have been completely partitioned between the South Slav monarchies and Greece had not the concert of Europe interposed itself.

In 1913 the great powers agreed to sponsor the creation of an Albanian national state on the Adriatic coast, a rump of what Greater Albania might have been. The new frontiers were uncertain and subject to constant flare-ups. The Albanians lacked any central authority to face their new situation. Prenk Bib Doda exercised a sort of hegemony in the mountains facing Montenegro; Essad Bey Toptani, an Ottoman soldier and landowner, dominated much of the central mountain district; and Ismail Kemal Bey Vlora, an influential Moslem of westernized Ottoman cultural background, headed a makeshift "provisional government" at the southerly port of Valona.

Naturally enough, the two powers most concerned over the viability of the new Albanian state were Italy and Austria-Hungary. Italy aimed at securing a position in Albania similar to what she had acquired in Montenegro, thus increasing her potential naval bases in the Adriatic. Hence Italy showed particular concern over Greece's push into "Epirus" (North Greece or South Albania), which would eventually have brought Greece into the Adriatic at a time when that country was working closely with France. For Italy, an independent Albania at the entrance to the Adriatic was a far preferable solution. Austria, on the other hand, aimed at using Albania to fence in the South Slavs and to keep Serbia, in particular, from gaining an Adriatic outlet. Thus, for opposing reasons, both powers agreed on the need for an independent Albania including at least all the Adriatic coastal provinces, with enough hinterland to be viable. The two big powers agreed to work together in developing Albania on an equal basis: the Triple Alliance, for once, was going to function.

In spite of these good intentions, it is hard to see how the Italians and Austrians could have cooperated for long, since the future of Albania's economic development depended, to some extent, on railroad construction. It was on this point that the two powers entered Albania with clashing aims. For the Italians, Albania, like Montenegro, was the gateway to the Balkan economic hinterland, offering terminal ports to the future rail line linking Italy to Serbia and Rumania. For Austria, the new Albanian state would serve as a pawn to block such projects. Given these incompatibilities, it is surprising that the collaboration lasted as long as it did.

The Austrians, backed by Germany, made an initial political error. It was internationally agreed that the new state needed a monarch. The question was who, of what nationality and religion. For a moment, early in 1913, the way seemed open to chivalric enterprise. A Bourbon prince, the duke of Montpensier, appeared on a yacht to present his candidacy to the Albanian provisional regime at Valona. The Neapolitan noble house of Castriota, descended from the Albanian national hero Scanderbeg, had been helping the Albanian national cause with arms and money in evident hopes of enthronement. There was talk of crowning the duke of the Abruzzi, a heroic Savoyard prince, though surely Victor Emmanuel's jealousy would have blocked him. Even Theodore Roosevelt's name came up, though it is hard to see how the Bull Moose could have turned into the Double Eagle of Shkipetaria. In cold fact Europe's last available crown would go only to a candidate backed by the concert of the great powers.[8]

The Italians informally backed Prince Fuad of the Egyptian khedivial dynasty. The khedivial princes had always enjoyed warm relations with the House of Savoy, and Fuad had been reared in Italy. Fuad had the additional advantage of being, at least remotely, of Albanian lineage. Nevertheless, he ran into opposition from a number of Albanian nationalists who wanted a western prince who would symbolize their country's new European orientation and status. Finally and decisively, Fuad's candidacy was vetoed by Austria-Hungary, which wanted the usual Teutonic prince. In view of what was to happen, it would have been better to have tried Fuad.[9]

The Central Powers' candidate, Prince William of Wied, was a handsome German army officer of knightly bearing who knew nothing of Albania. The other great powers accepted him but without much enthusiasm, as the prince himself noted. He refused even to set foot in his new realm until he received an emergency loan, which was finally granted at the beginning of 1914. Arriving in March, William set up his capital at Durazzo, an isolated unhealthful, little harbor that offered as its only advantage the chance of a quick escape for the prince's wife and childen in the event of trouble. The new monarch offered little to Albania, since he proved unable to manage the local warlords, and nothing at all to the Italians, who had more of a stake in Albania than any other European power.

The Italians had an entrée into Albania that no other power had. Almost a hundred thousand Italians in the South were of Albanian descent and speech. Intercourse across the Strait of Otranto was easy. Italy thus had a ready source of informers and agents. In addition, both Italy and Austria maintained institutions at Scutari, the center of Albania's Catholics, and by 1913 were engaged in a heated scholastic and consular rivalry.

Thus, when Italian businessman began seeking outlets and resources abroad, it was natural that they should turn to Albania, in spite of the fact that the country was unmapped, primitive, and disorderly. The same general pattern we have observed elsewhere prevailed here. Italian engineering and speculative planning in Albania ran far ahead of disposable capital.

Italian penetration into Albania before the Ottoman collapse came in the form of private initiative, followed by massive operations sponsored by the Italian government.

As long as Albania was under Ottoman sovereignty, the Banca Commerciale and its Venetian associates stayed out of the area. The development of Albanian seaports and coastal areas ran contrary to their program, which envisaged building up Antivari as the main outlet for the trans-Balkan rail line. That route would have drawn Scutari into the South Slavic economic area, since any such line would have had to pass near that city. The independent development of northern Albania, with the construction of a new harbor at Medua, was desired by Constantinople not by Volpi and his friends.

Hence in the years between 1908 and 1911, the Commerciale looked with great disfavor on the operations of an upstart, the engineer Giacomo Vismara of Bologna.[10] Vismara entered into direct relations with an important Moslem family in the Valona area for the purpose of exploiting its vast forest lands in central Albania. The family, which bore the surname Vlora (Valona), had members strategically placed in the Ottoman imperial administration and foreign service, as well as in the dissident Young Turk parties. The Vloras were therefore particularly well insulated against the jolts and shocks of the empire's politics. The Vloras played the same double role in their relations with foreigners, cultivating both Austrian and Italian contacts. Their aim throughout was to establish a political and economic power base in the Valona area that would enable them to assume leadership in a future Albanian state. The Vloras were canny, industry-minded investors and hence well aware of the need for foreign technology and financing.

Vismara was the right man. He had started his engineering career with no capital, but he had accumulated a nest egg of a hundred to a hundred fifty thousand lire as a result of small real estate operations. During his early years Vismara had worked closely with an enterprising Milanese lawyer named San Pietro, known as a leading militant of Catholic Action. That fact alone would have put him out-side the Banca Commerciale's customary clientele.

Once he began dealing with the Vloras after 1908, Vismara emerged from his provincial cocoon to take off on some real specu-lative flights. He and Avvocato Cesare Goria-Gatti of Turin put to-gether an informal business syndicate, entered into close political and business ties with an Apulian parliamentary deputy named Sem-mola, and in early November 1909 appeared with the Honorable Semmola in Constantinople, to the astonishment of the Italian am-bassador there.

Though Vismara was unknown to the government, his plans aroused some concern. The Vloras were important people, and the Italian foreign ministry kept an eye on them. Vismara's projects, so the talk went at Constantinople, extended far beyond forestry. He talked of land reclamation, harbors, and railways. The Marquis Theodoli, then the Italian delegate on the Ottoman Public Debt Council, was perplexed and skeptical, and the ambassador, the Mar-quis Imperiali, was wary of offering any support. Imperiali did not even want to look at the draft agreement between Sureya Bey Vlora and Vismara.

Soon thereafter the government and the director of the Bank of Italy made inquiries concerning Vismara. From Cesare Mangili, president of the Banca Commerciale, they received negative reports, but Stringher also learned that behind Vismara's Milanese and Turi-nese forestry companies there stood a backer of real importance, the Milanese millionaire the Marquis Visconti di Modrone.

Just as interesting was the political side of Vismara's activities, which joined Turinese and Milanese capitalists with Bari business interests, represented by the Honorable Semmola of Monopoli. This connection was worth noting. While much Italian industrial enter-prise had in effect widened the gap between North and South, the Italian penetration of Albania, which had to use South Italian ports and personnel, worked to the advantage of both sections. Awareness of this fact became general in the years before the war. In January 1913 Antonio Salandra, the outstanding political spokesman of the South, referred publicly to the "historical fatality" that linked his region to the opposite shores of the Adriatic. Salandra envisioned

Italy's drive to the East (*inorientarsi*) as a kind of obligation that the whole nation owed to its southland. The idea was to prove to be more than rhetoric: Salandra acted in strict accord with these words when acting as wartime premier, he ordered Italian troops into Albania.[11]

Vismara's projects for public works in Albania were, of course, premature and questionable, but the forests offered an authentic chance to make a profit, and the engineer picked up support after his surprise debut at Constantinople.

Undoubtedly Di San Giuliano's rise to the post of foreign minister in 1910 helped Vismara. The new minister's concern over Albania's future was known to all. The Vismara group entered into negotiations with the Mirdite leaders, Prenk Bib Doda and Abbot Primo Doci, with an eye to foresting rights over vast private and communal lands in northern Albania. The group was backed by the foreign ministry and by 1911 was definitely ahead of its French and Austrian rivals in bidding for over a hundred million lire worth of timber. In September 1911 the Bank of Italy sponsored the formation of a syndicate that would bring together all interested parties. By then a number of new investors—Vimercati and Rusconi of northern Italy and Fernandez of Salonika, as well as various specialists and engineers—had joined Vismara's combinations, and the new syndicate seemed to enjoy excellent prospects. The last obstacle was the Ottoman government, which could be won over by posting bond money or advancing loans. Three million lire might have turned the trick, had not the Libyan war interrupted.[12]

Thus, in three years a purely private development plan turned into a combined operation involving diplomacy, high finance, and engineering groups. This was Di San Giuliano's new style, and the foreign minister aimed at bringing together all of the country's financial powers. It was not surprising, therefore, that when the curtain rose on an independent Albania in 1913, the Banca Commerciale and its subsidiaries should be in the center of the new stage, though Vismara was still very much there as well.

As the Albanian situation took shape in the course of the year, a provisional government committee at Valona under Ismail Kemal Bey Vlora exercised sovereignty under the supervision of an international control commission, although a rival committee at Durazzo under Essad Pasha claimed authority. Scutari and the Bojana River zone came under the separate supervision of an international admiralty, which had to keep especially close watch on Montenegro. The new nation's borders and administrative organization awaited international decision and the arrival of a monarch.

Amid these uncertainties Italy and Austria went ahead to fasten a political and economic condominium on Albania. The Banca Commerciale joined with the Wiener Bank Verein to project a Bank of Albania, which would serve two distinct functions: it would render Albania all the usual central banking services, and it would also extend substantial long-term credit to the Albanian state. In exchange the Bank of Albania would become arbiter and controller of public works contracts and business concessions. Thus the Bank of Albania would become the instrument by which Austrian and Italian industrialists would carry out a joint, monopolistic development of the new nation's resources.[13]

The provisional regime at Valona fell in with these plans readily. It awarded important contracts to newly formed Italo-Austrian groups: trolley lines, bridges, and modern hotels had first priority, with more ambitious plans to come. Volpi's Società Commerciale d'Oriente was particularly prominent, though Vismara had a head start. Of special importance was the projected coastal rail line from Scutari to Valona, which the Albanian provisional government awarded in September 1913 to the Italian firm Strade Ferrate del Mediterraneo. The Italian surveys would be undertaken in collaboration with the Austrian engineer Pogacnik to comply with the parity principles laid down by Rome and Vienna. These dealings seemed to portend a new era of good feeling, and the Italian government and business establishment did everything to publicize the new opportunities in this air of great-power harmony. In the fall of 1913 *Il Sole* blossomed out with a fulsome series of articles by Leonardo Azzarita, describing Albania as the Switzerland of the Balkans, though in fact Harlan County, Kentucky, would have provided a better analogy. It was all curiously like the exaggerated reports from Asia Minor.

This facade of optimism soon crumbled as the Italians began

to find out what really awaited them on the far shores of the Adriatic. In Anatolia the Italians had to act unofficially, almost furtively, and often did not know what they were getting into, but in Albania they were able to study the terrain methodically and thoroughly over a period of two years. The Società italiana per il progresso delle scienze, acting with Stringher, sent a mission of geologists, agronomists, and agricultural specialists across the Adriatic. The mission left in September 1913, and its final report did not come out until 1915. Italy's statesmen and business operators were thus able to assess the area's real resources without the illusions that had bedazzled them in Turkey.[14]

As they emerged from the findings of the Italian scientific mission, Albania's economic prospects were only fair, though they did represent a slight improvement over those offered by corresponding territories in Italy itself. Though Albania was on the same latitude as Apulia, it had a heavier rainfall. Hence the new nation's hydroelectric and agricultural potential was a little better than most of southern Italy's. In particular, the hills could yield excellent olives and fruit, while the plains, now given over almost entirely to maize, could grow wheat. A radical modernization would have to come first, however, and the Italian experts were quite clear about that: Albania needed roads instead of cow paths; the coastal and alluvial plains had to be drained, reclaimed, and properly fertilized; and, above all, the Albanian peasantry and landholders alike needed elementary instruction in the techniques of modern agriculture.

All this required political stability, a precondition for foreign investment and expert help. However, because of its geography, much of Albania was unsuitable for intensive, high-yield crops and would, even under optimum conditions, remain in a primitive pastoral economy, with migrant flocks and a regime of commons rights. In short, Albania's agriculture needed heavy initial investments and offered only limited long-term profits. The Italian geologists did not believe that Albania promised great amounts of petroleum or minerals, though they did not exclude surprises in this sphere. At best, Albania lent itself to a limited and indirect exploitation of a modern type.

These prospects, however modest, might have led somewhere

had Austria, Italy, and the greater powers been able to agree about the country's future. Instead, Albania became another source of contention between them.

First, the French objected to the financial monopoly that the Austrians and Italians planned to set up. Paris insisted that the future Bank of Albania be international. Since France alone could provide big credits for new nations, this requirement amounted to a veto and hastened the demise of the Valona government. By the end of 1913 Valona's authority, never very impressive, had faded away; and with it, the concessions and privileges that might have laid the foundation for an Italo-Austrian condominium. A strong man, the soldier-feudatory Essad Pasha Toptani, emerged as the main power at Durazzo, where Prince William's arrival was anxiously awaited. While the Austrians were strong in the Catholic north and the Italians made new connections in the coastal areas, thanks to their protégé Essad, much of the Moslem interior remained distrustful of all foreigners and in a state of incipient revolt. Ismail Kemal Bey Vlora, seeing that his power base at Valona was giving way, left Albania amid suspicions that he and his associates favored a Young Turk restoration. With him went the last vestiges of civilian leadership. When William of Wied finally landed at Durazzo on March 7, 1914, he was faced with tribal chieftains and minature warlords.[15]

He also lacked the consensus of the great powers. Had Italy and the Dual Monarchy agreed over the future Balkan rail system, they would also have been able to work together in Albania. But as their aims diverged ever more sharply, they began to work at cross-purposes on a day-to-day level at Durazzo; the plans of the previous year were abandoned. During William's short reign, Albania became the theater of their covert rivalry.

What finally sundered Italy and Austria was the question of the new monarch's army. William had disembarked without an army of his own, but the powers had provided him with a small corps of Dutch gendarme officers. The native Albanian troops awaiting the prince were divided. One faction, unofficially supported by the Italian military attaché at Durazzo, followed Essad, who served in the new monarchical government as minister of war. The other, calling itself

nationalist, was largely Catholic and openly anti-Italian. It constituted the unofficial pro-Austria party.

The new monarch was a thoroughgoing Europeanizer with no
patience or understanding of the personal and patriarchal ways that
were needed to lead Albania. He showed little trust in the local gen-
try and soldiery, preferring to appoint European officers and administrators to key positions in the new system. This raised a delicate
question: if the monarch engaged foreign army officers, would they
obey the Albanian minister, Essad?

These problems, put to the test in May and June 1914, led to
William's undoing.

The new Albanian army's basic equipment consisted of rifles
supplied by Italy and artillery from Austria. The Austrians obligingly
sent some officers with the guns. Essad wanted to appoint as artillery
commander an Italian reserve officer and African veteran, Captain
Moltedo, whose name was put forward by the Italian military attaché, Lieutenant Colonel Muricchio. The appointment went into
effect on May 18 and precipitated a crisis. The nationalists and the
Dutch gendarmerie, refusing to obey Essad, surrounded his house
and cannonaded it with William's approval. This novel form of dismissal proved effective, but it was a short-sighted move. Captain
Moltedo, in the uniform of an Albanian major, made his way to
Essad's house, revolver in hand, and escorted the fallen minister out.
Essad boarded a ship bound for Italy, pledging himself not to return
without his sovereign's approval. Moltedo never received an official
copy of his commission, nor was he employed in the forthcoming
operations, an overt blow to Italian prestige and authority.

The new military establishment at Durazzo soon underwent a
baptism of fire. The Moslem insurgents from the interior, determined
to sweep away the European monarchy and all its works, attacked
Durazzo on May 23. Because of the Austrian artillery and the shell-
ings of an Austrian naval vessel, the *Herzegovina*, the rebels could
not take the city, but they kept it surrounded.

Austria's intervention was clear to all. After protests, the *Herzegovina* discreetly raised the Albanian flag. At the last possible minute,
on May 22, the Austrians had turned over their cannon to William's

Dutch gendarme officers, just in time for the rebels. By then it was widely suspected that William, willingly or not, was serving the Central Powers, while his Dutch officers were known to favor Austria over Italy. Their role became plain when they actually arrested Colonel Muricchio on the evening of June 5 and held him for more than four hours. They found on him letters recommending Captain Moltedo, an annoying circumstance for both sides. Whatever the goodwill that Berchtold and Di San Giuliano found it necessary to profess on a high ministerial level, their Balkan agents were at sword's points, and the new Albanian state, symbol of their desire to cooperate, had miscarried irreparably.

By June 1914 the rift between Italy and the Dual Monarchy was widening. A year had passed fruitlessly. The Italian government had done everything it could to get Austria to agree on the Balkan international railway system. Vienna had remained by turns close-mouthed, evasive, and obstructive, leaving the Italians no choice but to appeal to the Entente powers, as Tittoni had done in 1908.

Although it is not easy to follow the course of events that led the two powers to this impasse, one point is clear. The Italians found diplomatic channels blocked and therefore tried to gain their ends through private financiers. Inevitably, Giuseppe Volpi, with the backing of Joel and the Banca Commerciale, took a central part in carrying out this kind of foreign policy.

In the spring of 1913 the great powers decided to hold an international conference at Paris to settle the economic questions stemming from the Ottoman Empire's defeat in the Balkans. There were three issues: the indemnities and liabilities arising out of the war between the Ottoman Empire and the Balkan allies; the reorganization of the Ottoman Public Debt Council, which had been shorn of its European revenues; and the future of concessions and public works projects in the territory wrested from the Turks. The last item embraced railroad rights, which posed a political, as well as an economic, problem. What were Italy's interests in this conference, and whom should Di San Giuliano send to further them?[16]

The foreign minister knew just what he wanted. In the settlement of the first two issues, it was against Italy's interests to take any strong stands, since she had to stay on the good side of both the Balkan allies and the Turks at the same time. However, the third issue involved the future Balkan railway system, in which Italy had vital concerns. Between 1908 and 1911 the diplomats had not done well in upholding Italy's interests in these spheres, so Di San Giuliano proposed using a businessman instead.

The Germans were sending Helferrich of the Deutsche Bank and Schwabach of the Bleichroeder Bank, along with Pritsch, the German delegate on the Ottoman Public Debt Council, so the Italian foreign minister proposed to send Volpi and Nogara as Italy's economic negotiators, with a diplomat as titular head of the group. But when he broached the matter to Giolitti, the premier objected to sending two men who both belonged to the same financial combinations; he thought the public reaction would be "disastrous." When Volpi learned of the objections, he pressed for his own nomination, even if Nogara had to be sacrificed. He explained that both he and Nogara were just "good friends" of the Commerciale, although perhaps Nogara should go to Paris as the representative of the Public Debt Council rather than that of the government. He also pointed out how useful Nogara was to the government at Constantinople. Di San Giuliano knew what Volpi was up to but felt that his services were indispensable.

Giolitti worried not only about the charges of partiality that would arise from appointing two of the Commerciale's operators (he needed Catholic votes), but he also had a real distrust of Volpi. He believed that Montenegro was doomed and suspected that in view of Volpi's "notorious" interests there, he would not hesitate at Paris to commit Italy to helping the principality. If Volpi was to go, Giolitti certainly wanted no business associates of his along. On April 15, 1913, he put the final conditions to Di San Giuliano: Volpi or Nogara, but not both. Di San Giuliano chose Volpi, since he held that Balkan railroad questions were decisive and that Volpi was the only Italian qualified to negotiate in such affairs. Nevertheless, the Giolitti government tried to hem him in as much as it could.

Whatever the effects of the subsequent conference, of which there seem to be no records, it did not serve to clear the atmosphere.

Later in June Stringher refused point-blank in strong language to have anything to do with Volpi. As far as the Bank of Italy was concerned, Di San Giuliano's confidential agent was an upstart.

In fact, diplomatic channels and financial orthodoxy could not help Italy in resolving the Balkan the railway question satisfactorily. In spite of all the agreements in principle and the projects on paper, Italy and Austria remained deadlocked during the year preceding Sarajevo.

At first the Austrians had shown some willingness to consider the possibilities of an internationally owned and managed Danube-Adriatic line. Italy and Austria, as Triple Alliance powers, would counterbalance the shares held by French and Russian banks, with Serbia and Albania figuring, in equal proportions, as minority shareholders. That was the scheme that aroused Nitti's concern over the exclusion of Rumania.

In the course of June and July 1913, however, it became apparent that the Austrians' agreement was purely verbal. Austrian interests had earlier in 1913 succeeded in acquiring the Balkan rail concessions and options held by the Deutsche Bank, which would henceforth confine its operations to Ottoman territory. This transaction fitted perfectly into the political alliance between Germany and the Dual Monarchy, amounting to a division of labor between the two. It affected Italy adversely, though, since the option to build a rail line from the Albanian coast (Durazzo or Valona) to Monastir (Bitolj) now fell into Austrian hands. Since it was essential for Italy to keep absolute parity with Austria in all matters relating to Albania, the Italians were forced to ask Austria for a half-share in any such rail line.

Austria was perfectly willing, at least in principle, to oblige its Italian ally. But Vienna wanted in exchange something that seemed reasonable enough to ask of an ally. Italy would be expected to give diplomatic support to Austria's claimed concessions and options on territory that had recently passed into Serbian control. This request, however reasonable, ran directly against Italy's real future interests in the Balkans and served to delay and impede any other railway plans in Serbia. In short, Austria first gave Italy a verbal consent to the trans-Balkan rail line and then emptied it of all positive meaning by advancing other demands for which it claimed priority.

There were two ways open to the Italians. One was to try to persuade Austria to compromise with the South Slav states and open the way for the construction of a Danube-Adriatic rail line, joining French, Austrian, Russian, and Italian financial interests. The prospects for this agreement faded once Austria had a real bargaining position of its own in the late spring of 1913. The other and more promising line of action was to try to go ahead without Austria-Hungary altogether, imperiling the Triple Alliance for the sake of Italy's enduring interests in the Balkans.

Volpi's real commission in the tense months between May 1913 and June 1914 was to act as the confidential and often unofficial agent of the Italian foreign ministry to explore both possible lines of solution. Given Austria's suspicion of South Slav motives, no one really imagined that Austria would consent to a rail linkage between these two countries. In such a case Austria might well have demanded "compensations" that would have annulled Montenegro's newly acquired sovereignty over its own coastal areas and cut into the rights of the Antivari Company. The most that Volpi could hope to accomplish at Vienna in the fall of 1913, as he told the banker d'Adler, was to try to moderate or delay any action that Austrian capitalists might press against Serbia, which still refused to recognize their rail franchises.

Serbia had become a pivotal area, the battleground for all the European powers concerned over the Balkan rail system. Di San Giuliano used Volpi at Belgrade to do what could not be done through diplomatic channels. Volpi was to work on the Serbs, encouraging them to hold firm against Austrian pressure. His action was to parallel that of French and Russian financiers at Belgrade. The Serbs, faced with the full power of the Dual Monarchy, could either conduct an overt resistance on the basis of their sovereign rights, or they could seemingly give in to Austria and then by some kind of direct action make it impossible for the Austrians to carry out their plans. In October 1913 Volpi reported with relief that the Serbian government, discarding this dangerous course of action, had chosen the high road of open resistance. Di San Giuliano hoped throughout these months that Volpi's special connections at Belgrade would be of some use in keeping Serbia firm and that France and Russia would accomplish the rest. Serbia's economic and political independence was hanging in the balance, along with the future of the Triple Alliance, and Italy had to move warily. Though Volpi was acting in concert with the foreign minister, he did not go through ordinary diplomatic channels. To be sure, at Vienna he coordinated his activities with the moves of the Italian embassy. Nevertheless, the Italian foreign ministry, which had after all promised its formal support to Austria in the Balkan questions, was free to repudiate Volpi if need be; about this loophole Di San Giuliano was explicit. Since in fact the Italian foreign minister was in the position of a businessman keeping two sets of books, he needed a prepared alibi against any charge of double-dealing.[17]

Fortunately for Di San Giuliano, in the fall of 1913 the Austrians were very slow in settling the question of the Monastir rail line. As long as they tarried, Italy could in turn delay taking an official stand on their side. Volpi was charged with taking advantage of this breathing space, during which there were many Italian concerns to be looked after. Besides working against Austria at Belgrade, Volpi had to ensure that the French and Austrians, Count Vitalis and Paul Doumer of Paris and d'Adler of Vienna, did not put together a Balkan rail syndicate that would include Russia and Germany, perhaps, but leave Italy out. Such a scheme might have allure for the Serbs as a way out of their impasse with Austria, but the very possibility alarmed the Italian foreign ministry. Volpi had to use his connections at Belgrade and Cetinje to secure for Italian enterprise a fair share in any trans-Balkan rail line. He could make up for his lack of real leverage at Paris and the other financial centers of Europe by calling on his local contacts in the Balkan states, and this was what he proceeded to do, with undeniable success, between October 1913 and March 1914.[18]

As might have been expected, Volpi started at the weakest link in the Balkan chain, Montenegro: that was where he was personally strongest. Using his new authority and ministerial backing, he was able to put the Antivari Company back on its feet in Montenegro.

Then he promoted a new railway plan at the same time that Italian diplomacy and finance was helping the little kingdom secure an international loan of 30 or 40 million francs. The loan seemed imminent in the spring of 1914; thanks partly to the Commerciale, Montenegro had already got some advances. On May 28, 1914, the Montenegrin government awarded important railway options to a consortium of the kind that Volpi had always wished for.

The consortium was formed by three partners: the Società Commerciale d'Oriente; the Régie générale of Paris, which was directed by Count Georges Vitalis; and the Banque Russe-Asiatique. It represented the fulfillment of one of Volpi's cherished ambitions— directing Italy's future railroad building in the Balkans. Back in 1908 Volpi and his companies had been assigned a back seat in the trans-Balkan syndicate that Stringher had formed at Rome. Stringher first had not consulted Volpi and then had barely tolerated his presence in the group. Now in 1914, quite without Stringher's control, Volpi was taking a one-third interest of the first link in a future Balkan rail line. As far as Italian railroad undertakings in the Balkans were concerned, Volpi, not Stringher, was in charge.

The consortium held two options. One was for a standard-gauge line between Antivari and Scutari; and the other, for a link between Podgoritza and Ipek in Montenegro's new territories. Since any eventual Danube-Adriatic railroad would have to pass near Scutari, the Antivari-Scutari line, once built, insured that Montenegro's port would become the main terminal of the whole line. That development was all the more likely because northern Albania offered no comparable harbor facilities. Moreover, the Podgoritza-Ipek line represented a first step toward the Serb border and an eventual rail linkage, with standard gauge, between the two South Slav states. It may be presumed that Volpi was pursuing a larger goal, that he was trying to confront Austrian bankers and industrialists with a set of accomplished facts.[19] He could thus eventually get them to compromise with Serbia and join in an expanded international rail syndicate that would undertake the Danube-Adriatic line as a whole. On the other hand, it is also possible that he was prepared to go ahead on a three-power basis, relying on Russia and on Count Vitalis's powerful French financial combination to remove any blocks that Austria might set up. Certainly the French had helped to unlock doors at Cetinje, once Joel and the Commerciale had enlisted the support of the Banque de Paris et des Pays-Bas for Volpi's operations, and the director of the Paris bank, Turrettini, had proved singularly helpful.

But the First World War caught Volpi unawares. He seems to have discounted the possibility of such a disaster just when matters were beginning to lok up for him and the Italian interests that he had so long promoted. The trans-Balkan rail line had no future, after all.

It may seem that undue attention has been given to railroads in this discussion of Italian foreign policy, but the study was not undertaken as a contribution to diplomatic history. Its purpose throughout has been to bring to light the relationship of Italian industrial development to the dynamic, expansionist direction that Italian foreign policy took after 1908. For such purposes, railroads are crucial. In the case of the trans-Balkan rail projects, we can see how rail development in prewar Europe was a nodal point where three separate motives joined: the needs of domestic industry, the possibilities of foreign carrying trade, and the great-power politics of the national state. Examining the rail projects enables us to glance beneath the surface of politics. The strained alliances and ethnic rivalries of 1914 provide material for a colorful and oft-told tale, but more was going on. In this study we have peered into a world of industrial financiers and businessmen that shunned publicity and oscillated between cooperation and competition, an essentially cosmopolitan world that was becoming dependent on nation-states in spite of itself. It was to be not the least of the casualties—and beneficiaries—of the Great War.

Conclusion:
The View from Trieste

Our account of the business imperialism of liberal Italy has taken us into the field of diplomatic history, and a few concluding observations concerning the basic shift in Italian foreign policy are in order. Between 1904, when Britain, France, and Italy reached agreement on East Africa, and 1915, when Italy entered the war on their side, the whole alignment of Italian foreign policy shifted from a Mediterranean-African axis to a Balkan axis. The African orientation of Italian foreign policy, which prevailed from 1878 to 1904, implied that Italy would turn away from the problem of Italian minorities in Austria-Hungary, and instead ally herself with the Central Powers and compete with France for space in Africa. The results, hardly brilliant, had little relation to Italy's industrialization and did not provide the demographic colonies that some liberals had imagined it would. However, the later orientation in Italy's foreign policy toward the Balkans and the Near East led to an ever more direct coordination between Italian industrial interests and the state's diplomatic efforts. Unavoidably, this new meshing of purpose also meant an ever more direct Italian competition with the corresponding economic and political systems of the Dual Monarchy—and, consequently, a sundering of the Triple Alliance.

Much of this process, which was not clear to most people at the time, appeared sharply outlined in the comments of Scipio Slataper between 1910 and 1914, and that is not surprising.[1] Slataper, the best political brain among the Italians of Trieste, was in an extraordinarily good position to gauge the real directions that the two states were taking and to foresee that the focal point of the rivalry between Italy and Austria-Hungary was going to be Trieste and Fiume, the "maritime lung" of the Dual Monarchy.

In fact, Trieste and Fiume and their environs became the central problem of Italian foreign policy from 1915 to 1924, overshadowing Italian aspirations in Africa and Asia Minor. The problem often appears to be ethnic, a question of unredeemed provinces and threatened Latin populations. That is, of course, how the Italians themselves presented the matter—misleadingly. After all, Canton Ticino is equally Italian, but it has not aroused such fanaticism. In origin the question of the ports was indeed a matter of nationality, but nationality in itself does not come close to explaining the part that Trieste and Fiume played in Italian politics during those violent years. Their particular importance in Italian eyes resulted from Italy's drive to the East and her consequent rivalries with Austria-Hungary. The two cities, with their Italian populations and their Slav hinterlands, became enmeshed in a web of imperialist competition. Once imperialist great-power rivalries were superimposed on a situation of local ethnic diversities, the "unredeemed" minorities themselves became radicalized and potentially violent. The chances for compromise and urban autonomy that had often saved the fate of these areas were now ignored. Even worse, through the channel of Trieste and Fiume, something of the tenseness and extremism of Central European ethnic strife entered into the mainstream of Italian politics, envenoming all discussions of foreign policy and giving new energy and issues to the far Right. Eventually, the passions and tactics of Adriatic irredentism were to provide not the least important of the preconditions for the emergence of the Fascist regime.

The situation of the Adriatic Italians within the Hapsburg monarchy was something of an anomaly. Unlike the Slovenes who were pressing into their cities from the backcountry, the Italians of the coast were a "historic nationality" comparable to the Germans or the Poles and had many reasons to consider themselves well off in the empire, at least until the closing years of the nineteenth century. The Adriatic Italians had, to be sure, played some part in the Risorgimento and, excluded definitively from the new kingdom of Italy, continued to regard themselves as Italians by nationality, if not by citizenship. Their "irredentist" tradition was tied up with the cult of Mazzini and Garibaldi and took the concrete, continuing form of Italian Masonic lodges, which constituted the real backbone of the dominant Italian liberal party in Trieste. Their local and municipal autonomies, together with Austrian electoral systems, guaranteed them a secure control over their own city administrations and schools, and the Austrian protective tariff system helped the development of their ports and commerce. Often German and Jewish Austrians, after a few years of residence in Trieste or Fiume, became Italian in speech and culture, and much the same had happened to Croat or Slovene settlers on the coast. There was little reason in the 1890s for the Adriatic Italians to look toward the Italy of Crispi and Humbert I as a utopia. As long as the Triple Alliance functioned, Rome would not encourage such aspirations even if they occasionally cropped up among young Triestines.

Matters changed radically in the new century. The Austrian state began confusedly moving toward universal suffrage and trialism. Simultaneously the industrial development of the coastline brought large numbers of Slavs into the port cities. The older patterns that had insured Italian domination and the Italianization of new arrivals began to break down. The Italians of Trieste and Fiume still dominated the inner cities in numbers as well as in economic and social power, but elsewhere, farther down the Dalmatian coast, the Italian urban bourgeoisie began losing its grip. Nervous Italian professional people and students in Trieste could see the handwriting on the wall.[2] As the Austrian state moved to take the Slavs into a fuller partnership in the Hapsburg system, it bore down hard on the Italians. With the rising influence of the Archduke Francis Ferdinand and Field Marshal Conrad von Hoetzendorf, the Austrian authorities began discriminating against Italian civil servants and encouraging the spread of Slovene and Croat militancy. This was more than a mere divide-and-conquer tactic. By the early years of the century, as we have seen in earlier parts of this work, the commercial and maritime rivalry between Austrian and Italian business had started to sunder the two allies on a practical level; now, with the rise of an Austrian battle fleet, with Austrian aspirations toward a new dominion over the

Balkans, and with Italy's evident unreliability as an ally, it became essential for the Dual Monarchy to turn Trieste and Fiume from Italian cities into Austro-Hungarian cities, with a citizenry that would reflect the ethnic makeup of the empire rather than that of Italy. "Slavization" was at hand.

With some reason Italian businessmen at Trieste began to feel that their Italian identity was under attack. The city began sprouting Slavic banks with important backing from the centers of Austro-Slav capitalism, Zagreb, Lubiana, and, above all, Prague. Italian students who went to Austrian universities at Innsbruck or Vienna ran into an ever more virulent pan-German enmity among their own peers, and the Austrian authorities refused to open an Italian university anywhere in the Italian-speaking areas of the empire. This refusal to recognize the elementary cultural rights of an ancient and "historic" nationality not only deepened the alienation of young middle-class Italians within the empire but also worked to undermine the Triple Alliance. Nothing could have offended the Italian public more effectively.

How did the Italian middle class of Trieste react to the slow squeeze that Austria was putting on it? The older liberals relied on their ties with the Masonic lodges and ministries of Rome, while the young activists, abandoning liberal beliefs and methods, attempted new roads. Attilio Tamaro worked with big Italian newspapers, persuading them to feature stories and reportage on the plight of the Triestine outposts of "Italianità." Ruggiero Fauro (Timeus) began to define the rivalries between Italians and Slavs as a racial war; and in fact, the Italian Nationalists of Trieste were friendly to the local Germans, sharing their racial contempt for the "uncivilized" Slavs in blatant disregard of what the Austro-Germans were doing elsewhere in the empire to uproot Italian language and culture.

Most significant, a young Triestine economist, Mario Alberti, took on himself the task of explaining to the Italian business establishment why Trieste was vital to Italy's future. Alberti first came into the public eye in a series of economics articles published by the Rome business paper *L'Economista d'Italia* in 1913 and by the *Rivista delle Società Commerciali*, a Milanese periodical, in August 1914. Alberti interpreted the economic life of his own age as a struggle among monopolies based on national states or races. Because of its location and racial makeup, Trieste was bound to be either the ruin or the salvation of Italy's economic prospects in the eastern Mediterranean, depending upon whether it ended in Italian or Austro-Slav hands. This kind of thinking put Alberti and his friends into immediate and fruitful fellowship with Foscari of Venice and the Nationalist group centering around *L'Idea Nazionale* of Rome. The young Nationalists of Trieste brought into the Italian establishment something of the narrowness and fanaticism that had marked the pan-German and pan-Slav youth of the Hapsburg monarchy, to everyone's detriment.[3]

Naturally, there were many Italians who did not see the traps and ultimate disappointments of an Adriatic war. Among them must be numbered Count Piero Foscari, whose agitation on behalf of the unredeemed Italians led to his permanent expulsion from the monarchy in 1909. The measure was a serious one: Foscari in that year had become a parliamentary deputy. But all the best efforts of the Italian foreign ministry availed nothing against the Austrian police. For Foscari, this was a real sacrifice; as manager of his wife's estates in Carinthia, he urgently desired safe conduct to see them. To the hard-pressed foreign minister, the affair was a first-class nuisance. Di San Giuliano finally learned that the Austrians considered Foscari an Italian intelligence agent, an assumption that offended the marquis. Did the Austrians, he asked, imagine that the Italian government would pick the Honorable Foscari, a marked man, for delicate secret work? In reality, the days of Di San Giuliano's life and his policy were numbered, while Foscari's moments of influence were just approaching. Younger men like Alberti and Volpi were to assume increasing importance in Italy's future as the Adriatic question came to dominate Italian affairs.[4]

Autarky and imperialism, the foundations of Fascist policy, ran like scarlet threads through the thinking of political and economic elites in liberal Italy, even during the period of Giolittian reform and democratization. Few were immune, except the intellectual and political outsiders of the radical-reformist Left, like Salvemini and Giretti. Even a broad-minded National Liberal like Caroncini thought "living space" a necessity. And all during these years, there was a steady stream of converts to imperialism coming in from the far Left, the revolutionary syndicalists, and the Socialists. In their minds international revolution easily turned into a worldwide war between proletarian and capitalist states; Mussolini was merely the most conspicuous, though not the most original, of the latecomers who shared this vision.

Likewise, all major Italian business groups were expansionist, often beyond their means. Even those cosmopolitan capitalists of the Banca Commerciale seem never to have thought of integration or common-market arrangements as alternative solutions to the chronic imbalance of the peninsula's economy. Imperialist presuppositions reigned, and Italian heavy industry never came close to shedding its character as part of a "military-industrial complex."

The new antiliberal political doctrines of Nationalism came from many pens, but the synthesizer of Nationalist thought, Alfredo Rocco, was close to business circles in his thinking and associations. It is a mistake to treat the movement as a cultural fad born of poor education. Not only was Rocco a jurist of some reputation, but his followers were largely professional men and university students, not lumpen elements. This fact has decisive importance in any consideration of the origins and class roots of the Fascist regime.

Much has been made of the petty-bourgeois origins of Fascism. That vast element of the middle class below the professional and commercial elites—school teachers, postmen, white-collar workers, middle bureaucrats, and military officers who were "bourgeois" without ever having shared the ideals and battles of 1789 and 1848— easily slipped from a pro forma, superficial liberalism into a totalitarian pseudoidentity that remedied its own rootlessness and lack of commitment to higher values. So goes the argument, and it has some merit. No doubt many Fascists came from precisely that background. Those who had been revolutionary Socialists or syndicalists were typical, semieducated petty bourgeois with a culture that followed journalistic patterns: the Duce is the perfect example.

However, the Italian Fascist regime cannot be reduced to such lines. The regime's general staff came from the Nationalist movement, and the "totalitarian" state was shaped by men like Rocco— not coffeehouse semi-intellectuals, but serious professional men.

Sometimes—like Giovanni Giuriati—they had eminent liberal antecedents. Totalitarianism of the Right, at least in Italy, was the work of educated men, and one must ask what drove them to such doctrinal and practical extremism.

I think the answer lies in the predicaments brought to light in previous chapters. Professional people, particularly engineers, were in surplus, offering their services all over the world. Hence the totalitarian solutions of the Right were arising precisely among the professional and business elites: they were already implicitly present in the life patterns of men as diverse as Dante Ferraris and Giuseppe Volpi.

This does not mean that we should not look downward to see what was brewing among the various strata of the petty bourgeoisie. The structural crisis of which the elites were so aware was also having profound effects on military personnel; minor civil servants and teachers were stirring in their genteel misery; most of the agitators who tried to bring Italy to a grinding halt in June 1914 were petty bourgeois, not genuinely proletarian. But this restlessness, lack of viable life goals or ideals, and disposition to impulsive violence ran through the whole nation and cannot be imputed to any one social class. Even in the royal house, the duke of Aosta was a potential rival to the lackluster king. Italy was in ferment.

The totalitarian solutions then aborning on the far Right were responses to the chronic ills and problems of the nation-state in an inhospitable modern world, and they transcended class and sectional interests. They were foreshadowed everywhere in Italy, but to pinpoint their appearance in a concrete, programmatic form, we must look to the industrial elite and its political allies. In the coming Fascist movement the operatic panoply and noise would come from the impoverished culture of the petty bourgeoisie, but the programs and the legal framework were to be the work of an elite that had consciously turned against the parliamentary heritage of the Risorgimento. In Italy totalitarianism arose out of a situation that bedeviled rulers and ruled alike. It was not class-bound.

Notes

Prologue

1. Italy lost her pristine liberal virtue when she joined, though late, in the colonial race between 1878 and 1885. This story appears clearly enough, from a radical point of view, in Roberto Battaglia, *La prima guerra d'Africa* (Turin, 1958), which gives special attention to the change in Italian "liberal" establishment opinion concerning the white man's burden. The question that concerns us here is different: when and why did Italy pass from colonialism to imperialism? The paltry East African undertakings of 1885–96 did not touch upon the vital interests of any great power. It is hard to imagine Somalia or the mountains of Ethiopia as the starting point of an international war. On the other hand in the years just before 1914, Italy was angling for control in precisely those areas upon which the great powers' interests all focused; matching such policies, Italian representatives were aggressive and underhanded. See in particular the references to Tommaso Tittoni, the Italian ambassador at Paris (a specialist in the art of cultivating the Parisian press), and to the bankers Volpi and Nogara in René Marchand, ed., *Un livre noir, diplomatie d'avant-guerre d'après les documents des archives russes*, 3 vols. (Paris, 1922–31). The first two volumes, dealing with the years before the outbreak of the war, show that the Russians took a considerable interest in the designs of Italy.

Although this study attaches great importance to the formation of industrial interest groups, the liberal ruling class in Italy was concerned over the country's rating as a great power during years in which modern heavy industry was still on the drawing boards. A generic expansionism, intended to demonstrate Italy's presence and status as a great power, characterized Italian foreign policy from the early 1880s on, and it should not be confused with the precisely definable industrial imperialism that this work deals with.

2. See particularly Giuseppe Are, *Il problema dello sviluppo industriale nell'età' della Destra* (Pisa, 1965). More generally, I have used Epicarmo Corbino, *Annali dell'economia italiana*, 5 vols. (Città di Castello, 1931–38), covering the years 1861 to 1914, and Gino Luzzatto, *L'economia italiana dal 1861 al 1914* (Milan, 1963), of which only one volume has appeared, covering the period up to 1896. I have also consulted contemporary essays by Pareto on protectionism and by Maffeo Pantaleoni on banking problems; these works are cited in the above-mentioned volume of Luzzatto.

3. The personal history of the House of Savoy is not without importance in Italian political history. The royal line—Victor Emmanuel II, Humbert I, and Victor Emmanuel III—somehow never captured the public imagination or the esteem of the Italian establishment, especially in the gray years after 1876. In the 1890s

there was real concern about the future of the monarchy. The heir, Victor Emmanuel III, was dwarfish, introverted, and something of a misogynist. The scion of the cadet line, the duke of Savoy, cut a contrastingly dashing figure. He married Princess Helene of Orléans, a sister of the pretender to the French crown. Soon blessed with male progeny, the Savoy-Aosta line promised, in the fullness of time, a clerico-legitimist succession to the Italian throne. The only way to forestall such a disaster was to arrange a marriage for Victor Emmanuel that would bring new life to the senior line. That was not easy. The rift between the papacy and the monarchy ruled out a union with one of the legitimist Catholic dynasties. A Protestant marriage was unacceptable to the queen. It appears that the solution was suggested by Crispi. Given his Albanian background and concerns, it was natural that he should look at an indigenous Balkan dynasty for a future queen. Such a marriage fitted both his vaguely expansionist ideas and his plans to tie Humbert I to his ministerial chariot. The chosen vessel was Elena, daughter of the reigning prince of Montenegro. The marriage, concluded in 1896, put an end to the nightmare of an Aosta succession.

My chief hypothesis—that the opportunistic liberalism of the senior Savoys stems from their involvement in the network of economic investment and political influence that linked Rattazzi, Giolitti, and the world of Italian big business—is not susceptible to proof, but evidence in Giolitti's correspondence of the 1890s and in D. Farini, *Diario di fine secolo* (Rome, 1961) of the same period suggests the conclusion very strongly.

The Savoys were typical, in a purely negative way, of a certain Latin middle-class mentality. They were far more aware of their eight centuries of dynastic interest-politics than of any identification with the Italian nation. Victor Emmanuel's philistine convictions—that political skill consisted in slyly exploiting international rivalries to increase the area under Italian rule, that government really came down to running an honest and efficient administration, that ideals were verbal screens behind which the power game went on—all gave him something in common with much of the respectable citizenry of Italy. His personal peculiarities—a pedantic mania for counting, a zest in noting down small inaccuracies in what others said or did—seem to have turned in time into a perpetual effort to disparage and run down those who towered above him in mind or, more commonly, in stature. In other respects he was an ordinary man with a taste for regular-army soldiering; like most ordinary men, he was the victim of forces beyond his understanding.

See Silvio Scaroni, *Con Vittorio Emmanuele III* (Milan-Verona, 1954); Alberto Consiglio, *Vita di Vittorio Emmanuele III* (Milan, 1950); Giovanni Artieri, *Il tempo della regina* (Rome, 1950); and an interesting reference in Ettore Conti, *Dal taccuino di un borghese* (Milan, 1946), 464; as well as Amedeo Tosti, *Emmanuele Filiberto di Savoia* (Milan-Verona, 1941); and idem, *Vita eroica di Amedeo Duca d'Aosta* (Milan-Verona, 1952). See also Tommaso Sillani, *Luigi di Savoia* (Rome, 1929). On the monarchy's African ambitions, see Riccardo Truffi, *Precursori dell'impero africano* (Rome, 1936), 9–17; Arturo Codignola, *Rubattino* (Bologna, 1938), 323, 447–448; and Elena di Francia (Savoia-Aosta), *Viaggi in Africa* (Milan, 1913), an authorized translation from the original French adorned by 800 photographs made by the duchess herself. On the naval influence exerted by the dynasty, see L. Vannutelli, *Sguardo retrospettivo sulla mia vita nella Marina* (Rome, 1959). More generally, see Domenico Bartoli, *La fine della monarchia* (Milan-Verona, 1966). Much can be gathered, of course, from the Farini diaries, which contain a running commentary on the dynasty during the 1890s. Antonino Repaci, *La marcia su Roma*, 2 vols. (Rome, 1963) has many important observations on, and reconstructions of, the part played by the king during the crisis of October

1922, as well as comments on the danger of an Aosta usurpation. The matrimonial alliance with the Negos dynasty of Montenegro created some possible troubles for the king, as we shall see later on in this work. On the reckless character of Victor Emmanuel's Balkan in-laws, see V. N. Kokovtsov, *Out of My Past* (Stanford, 1935), 357–359; and Francesco Tommasini, *L'Italia alla vigilia della guerra*, 3 vols. (Bologna, 1934–37), I, 99.

4. On the makeup of the Italian bourgeoisie, see Nello Quilici, *Origine sviluppo e insufficienza della borghesia italiana* (Ferrara, 1932), a most lively and penetrating essay. Quilici was a newspaper writer who had started in 1912 on the *Resto del Carlino* of Bologna, a well-written daily with a strongly "National-Liberal" or neo-bourgeois orientation. During the Fascist era he was part of Italo Balbo's entourage, which constituted an intellectual *fronde* within the regime; his work in the field of Italian history is worth noting, in spite of the conformist notes here and there. Much of what he has to say parallels or supplements the observations of Marxists like Gramsci or Emilio Sereni or those of southern writers, notably Salvemini, S. F. Romano and Rosario Romeo, all of whom sense deeply the uneven regional formation of Italy's bourgeoisie. Quilici's observations on the insecurity and uneasiness of the Italian liberal bourgeois are more than borne out by the profound researches and judgments of Federico Chabod. But what were their own "self-images" or order of values? What political ideas and connections did they have? To these questions there are no easy answers; few of the captains of industry talked much in public or committed their thoughts to print. There is one interesting exception, Ettore Conti. (See Conti, *Dal taccuino.*) Conti was a pioneer engineer and promoter of the electrical industry and a senior member of the Milanese economic elite; he often reflected the views of his associates or peers in his diary notes and retrospective judgments.

5. Unlike the technological efforts of Third World countries, the Politecnico did not come as a foreign innovation but grew out of the Italian indigenous tradition. The engineering profession, with its own schools and official corporate organizations, had existed in Lombardy since the Middle Ages. Even in eras of trouble or stagnation, the profession carried on much as it always had, since the Po Valley's economy depended on irrigation and reclamation. In the Italy of the old regime, the profession was a closed corporation. To be recognized by the official *collegio*, a prospective engineer had to show that his family had practiced no "vile or mechanical art." Though this class barrier vanished with the old regime, very few Milanese engineers or industrialists had proletarian origins. When Italy achieved unification, the Milanese business elite, anxious to achieve parity with western Europe, founded the Politecnico in 1863. Among its sponsors were the influential Società di Incoraggiamento d'arti e mestieri (founded 1838), the Museo Civico, the municipality of Milan, the great Milanese Casse di risparmio (Italy's most important savings bank), and many private industrialists, including, eventually, successful alumni. See Ferdinando Lori, *Storia del R. Politecnico di Milano* (Milan, 1941).

For a long time the Politecnico was more exacting than other universities, and students could not pass from one year to another without finishing all their examinations. There was no goliardic spirit, and any political dissent withered. Yet the Politecnico in the early twentieth century was as political as other Italian universities, in a rightward direction. In 1915 the student body was militantly interventionist, and in 1919 it sided with the fascist squads during the attack on the Socialist daily *Avanti!*

6. Terms like "liberalism" and "bourgeoisie" have a special Italian coloring and do not mean exactly what they do in other historical situations and places.

In Italy liberalism meant the rule of a parliamentary bourgeoisie, a class that accepted the political-constitutional outcome of the Risorgimento. To put it in Mosca's terms, liberalism was the "formula" of legitimation covering the rule of a particular ruling group. It could indeed have become something more if the Italian parliamentary leaders had really been willing to face liberalism as the "method of freedom," with all the new possibilities and risks that liberalism in that higher sense opens up. In fact, Italian parliamentary groupings *within* the liberal camp all rested on a common presupposition of bourgeois class rule, a fact that can be shown if we define liberal parliamentary alignments by reference to concrete situations and choices. The question of labor offers one real touchstone. The conservatives of the Italian political world conceived of a working class without any militant organizations of its own: Italian workers would go on entrusting their future interests to outstanding figures in the parliamentary establishment. This was Crispi's view in the 1890s. On Crispi's jealously paternalistic attitude toward the masses of his own Sicilian constituency, see S. F. Romano, *Storia dei fasci siciliani* (Bari, 1959), especially 519–521; and Farini, *Diario*, I, 323. Instead, the democrats or Giolittians envisaged the rise of labor unions, the corporate interests of which would find representation through the election of Socialist deputies to the chamber. But in this fashion much of the nation's working class would obtain *influence* without really exercising *power*. Power, of course, would remain in the hands of the parliamentary bourgeoisie, with the working classes getting their rightful share of the benefits of economic modernization. Bourgeois political leaders would guide the country's economic policies, but with the understanding that labor would have to get some material rewards for its acquiescence in bourgeois parliamentary rule. Both reactionaries and progressives, then, tacitly understood liberalism to imply perpetual rule by a particular enlightened bourgeoisie. This consensus was to weigh heavily on Italy's political future, and it is not hard to see why both lower middle classes and the organized proletariat often had such distaste for parliamentary-liberal rules of the game.

7. Transformism, the "scandal" of Italian liberalism, was the manifestation of a political fact: after it had become clear that the old distinction between a monarchic-constitutional right and a republican-democratic left was outworn, both sides having accepted the compromise settlements of 1861 and 1870, no alternative parties, one of order and one of progress, emerged out of the marshy center of the Chamber of Deputies. This seeming failure of Italian liberalism became the central problem of the varied literature of disenchantment that tried to explain Italian transformism in the late nineteenth century. One is left with the strong impression that the principal virtue of Italian parliamentary liberalism, like that of other liberal systems, lay in the freedom to criticize, investigate, and denounce. See in particular Mario Delle Piane, *Gaetano Mosca, classe politica e liberalismo* (Naples, 1952) for analysis and bibliographical references; and Giampiero Carocci, *Agostino Depretis e la politica interna italiana dal 1876 al 1887* (Turin, 1956). Concerning the Italian property owner's obsessive fears of rioting, see d'Annunzio's "La morte del duca d'Ofena" in *Le novelle della Pescara* (1884–86), an outstanding work; and E. De Michelis, *D'Annunzio a contraggenio* (Rome, 1963), 15–31.

8. The relations between Italian science and the nation's productive systems were at best uneven. Much of Italy's most brilliant scientific work was done in academic isolation—with the good and not-so-good effects that such isolation has—and the state-university system tended to segregate pure and applied science from each other. Most marked was Italy's failure to apply scientific methods in agriculture beyond a certain point. Of course there were some bright spots, such as the restocking of the Lombard lakes by Italian ichthyologists and the first legal

efforts to check ruinous deforestation; significantly, they benefited the northern regions. Little was done to transform southern agriculture, where scientific replanning was most needed. The absentee southern landlord, abetted by the intensely privatistic southern peasant, stuck to the time-honored and often antieconomic cultivation of wheat, perpetuated by tariffs even in the hills. The southern regions remained in large part an inefficient and expensive granary instead of becoming a profitable orchard or vineyard. The fault was not so much in the quality of Italian applied science, which could have risen to the challenge, but in the character of southern bourgeois property owners, as well as the government's tacit lack of interest in modernizing the southern countryside. See Adriano Carugo-Felice Mondella, "Lo sviluppo delle scienze e delle techniche in Italia dalla metà del XIX secolo alla prima guerra mondiale" in *Nuove questioni di storia del risorgimento e dell 'unità d'Italia* (Milano: Marzorati editore, 1961), II, 429–509.

9. See Nello Quilici, *Banca Romana* (Milan, 1935), an antiliberal treatment of the theme that seeks to indict the whole pre-Fascist political world; it is, however, based on good source materials. Quilici is especially valuable on the interventions in the financial world by politicians like the Marquis Di San Giuliano, as well as on the subsidies that financiers like the Medici del Vascello family and Ignazio Florio accorded to like-minded parliamentary politicians.

10. Before 1912 Giolitti's relations with organized Catholic social and electoral groups seem to have been in Tittoni's hands. However, with the new universal-suffrage law, it became necessary for the premier and his party to establish direct contact with Catholic leaders in the Unione Elettorale, since Catholic votes were now needed in many constituencies that could have been considered safe even as late as 1904 or 1909. From Giolitti's inquiries to various prefectures, it became clear to him that most Unione Elettorale leaders were local notables or professional people who had long since watered down their opposition to the Italian government at Rome; and such people were perfectly willing to support government candidates in many local constituencies in the elections of 1913. They also elected a few of their own leaders in those areas where they had important credit or labor organizations or could profit by personal prestige. Giolitti's party felt perfectly at ease in dealing with this sort of restricted Catholic leadership, which was formed by co-optation and Vatican selection. After the First World War, when Catholics formed a genuine parliamentary mass party based on Christian-Democratic principles, Giolitti and his remaining friends reacted with extreme hostility, preferring Mussolini. In this whole history of relations with organized Catholicism, Giolitti's essential characteristics as a politician emerge with special clarity. He felt most at home in a political situation managed by small groupings, provincial and upper middle-class, which could easily come to private agreements with ministers or prefects. At this kind of political game Giolitti was a master, and he was convinced that his maneuvers furthered the nation's real interests.

11. In Italy the main rail lines were state property, privately operated between 1885 and 1905 under the terms of a twenty-year contract. The private operators, uncertain about the renewal of their conventions, let service and equipment deteriorate. Only the state could invest heavily in new locomotives and rolling stock. Hence the assumption of rail transport by the state was not a "socialistic" measure but an effort to further the development of a modern capitalist economy. Direct state operation of the rail system meant more orders for Italian mechanical industries and better service for Italian exporters. This was not "nationalization" of the sort that would alarm private enterprise.

12. Giustino Fortunato asked whether the solid financial state of Italy in 1901–8 was due to the flow of emigrants from southern Italy overseas, with its

resulting rise in emigrants' remittances to Italian banks: was this not as important a factor in the new Italian prosperity as the industrial spurt of the North? See Gioacchino Volpe, *Italia moderna* (Florence, 1949) II, 269, as well as Gaetano Cingari, *Giustino Fortunato* (Florence, 1954). Volpe's work shows the immense impact of Italy's emigration on the whole course of the nation's history. On the economic side it was of course a boon, an indispensable part of Italy's moderniza- tion. Politically it also had good effects, since without the outlet of emigration, the South might have collapsed into endemic anarchy. On the other hand the psy- chological effects of Italy's being represented abroad by unskilled laborers cannot be underrated: much of the Nationalistic uneasiness and defensive pride that the Italian upper classes developed toward the end of the Giolittian era stemmed from an inferiority complex.

13. In 1926, as the Fascist regime was taking shape, Communist observers (notably Angelo Tasca) recognized that the old policy lines of Giolitti (protectionism, predominance of big investment banks) still prevailed, and that Italy's indus- trialists, faced with a chronic problem of overproduction and underconsumption, were turning again toward the conquest of overseas outlets as their output kept rising. In fact, the regime tried to meet this crisis of imbalance in the late 1920s with a policy of deflation and concentration—with a consequent stagnation in industrial development—and only in the 1930s, with the world depression, did the Italian state finally stake the country's future on a new imperialist policy. At any rate, it is not fanciful to see the underlying continuities between liberal and Fascist policies, both of them responses to an objective and perennial structural imbalance. See Paolo Spriano, *Storia del P.C.I.* (Turin, 1969) II, 31.

14. The really devastating criticisms of Giolitti as a political manager came from men who understood and accepted parliamentary rule. In their respective spheres Gaetano Salvemini, Luigi Albertini, and Luigi Einaudi brought in not merely a general indictment, but a bill of particulars that has proved historically unanswerable: they saw what was really happening and what Giolitti's system was doing to the country.

The central point of all these criticisms is the same: Italy's liberalism was skin-deep. Parliament did not really legislate in the national interest; it failed to check the ministers' or the government's operations; and it kept sinking in public esteem from one election to another. Giolitti's perpetual majority in the center of the chamber was a ragbag of deputies without programs or commitments, with survival as their only goal. (In fact, Giolitti's administrators, prefects or specialists, have a far larger and more interesting part in the premier's correspondence than do his supporters on the floor of the chamber.)

The results of Giolitti's rule, the critics insisted, were disastrous for the political education of the Italian people. Italy was moving into an age of mass democracy, following France, Britain, and Belgium, a trend that Giolitti himself understood and even anticipated. But Italy lacked the solid foundation of more or less correct liberal parliamentary practice that the Atlantic states had laid in the late nineteenth and early twentieth century. Much of the responsibility for this rests on Giolitti himself, the man who (to use his own image) cut a crooked suit of clothes to fit a political hunchback. It is possible to see in the premier a corrupter, a trimmer, and even, at times, a cynic; "I did not invent the South" was his favorite excuse, and it covered a multitude of sharp practices.

Salvemini, in particular, insists, and with good reason, that in the May 1915 crisis, in which the crown and the Salandra ministry overrode the chamber and led Italy into the War, Giolitti reaped what he had sown, for his "majority" of more than three hundred deputies proved eclectic and spineless. Worse yet, the crisis showed how seriously the chamber had fallen in the nation's eyes after more than a decade of Giolitti's management: in 1915 Italy's parliamentary institutions stood lower in public esteem than they had in 1900 and proved far less capable of defending themselves.

The central issue between Giolitti and Salvemini remains more than a simple question of morality. None of Giolitti's legislative measures or central policy decisions brought great benefits or relief to the country's backward areas, which continued to suffer from an unfair tax system that Giolitti never set his hand to reforming. Giolitti (and his southern colleague, Nitti) saw industrialization in its most advanced form as the central concern of Italian public life, taking priority over questions of regional equity. Salvemini saw the South as Italy's gravest general problem and aimed at reforms that would give the backward regions a chance to develop through their own local energies: Giolitti was a short-range modernizer, while Salvemini (a critic with no political deadlines to meet) was a long-term modernizer. On the whole it seems most likely that Giolitti shared the tempered pessimism of a specialist in the southern question, Senator Giustino Fortunato, that emigration would eventually improve matters for the South and offered the only real hope for that section. History has arbitrated between Giolitti and his critics, justifying both sides: Golitti presided over a great and irreversible process of industrialization, but he lost the cause of Italian liberalism and for the reasons that Salvemini discerned so clearly. See Nino Valeri, "Giovanni Giolitti nella storiografia del secondo dopoguerra" in *Question di Storia del Risorgimento*, ed. Ettore Rota (Milano, 1951) for general orientation and bibliography; also Riccardo Bacchelli, *Nel fiume della storia* (Milan, 1955), 183–219, an early attempt at reevaluation. More recently Giampiero Carocci, *Giolitti e l'età giolittiana* (Turin, 1961) uses new archival material; *Dalle Carte di Giovanni Giolitti: Quarant'anni di politica italiana 1885– 1928*, ed. D'Angiolini, Carroci, Pavone, 3 vols. (Milan, 1962) is an important source which should be supplemented by consulting the Fondo Giolitti in the Archivio Centrale dello Stato (hereafter cited as ACS). Much about Giolitti's personality appears in Olindo Malagodi, *Conversazioni della guerra*, ed. B. Vigezzi, 2 vols. (Naples, 1960).

For Giolitti's chief critics see, first of all, Luigi Einaudi, *Cronache economiche e politiche di un trentennio (1893–1925)* 8 vols. (Turin, 1959–65).

Salvemini's basic writings on Giolittian liberalism are collected in Salvemini, *Opere IV* 2 vols. (Milan 1962–63).

For Albertini's views see his multivolume, posthumously published work, *Venti anni di vita politica italiana* (Bologna, 1950–53).

15. See Umberto Zanotti-Bianco, *Saggio storico sulla vita e attivita' politica di Leopoldo Franchetti* (Rome, 1950). On Ferdinando Martini, see his *Lettere* (Milan-Verona, 1934), which show something of his real political temper; his African diaries, which were published by the Italian government after the war in an extraordinarily slipshod fashion; and his autobiographical essays, which are models of felicitous Italian prose.

The literature by and about the Marquis Di San Giuliano is peculiar. He served as the model for Consalvo in Giuseppe De Roberto's famous novel *I vicere*—hardly the kind of fame that Italian statesmen aim at. Some idea of the Marquis' talent and articulateness can be got from his book, *Le condizioni presenti della Sicilia* (Milan, 1894), while his political realism and ambition come out very strongly in his correspondence with Giolitti (to be found in the first volume of *Dalle Carte di Giolitti*); in what Quilici has to say about him in the Banca Romana scandal (see his *Origine della borghesia*); and in Farini's acid remarks in *Diario*, II, 1476. See also Giacomo Paulucci di Calboli, "Discorso tenuto a Catania il 5 ottobre 1939," in

Confederazione fascista dei professionisti e degli artisti, Celebrazioni siciliane, Parte I (Urbino, 1940), 517–542. Some of Di San Giuliano's speeches and lectures of the 1880s and early 1890s, published in pamphlet form, are to be found here and there in Italian libraries. Of some biographical value are Francesco Cataluccio, "Lotte e ambizioni di Antonino Di San Giuliano," in *Studi in onore di Niccolo' Rodolico* (Florence: Faculty of Political Science of the University of Florence, 1944), 41–62; and Rino Longhitano, *Antonino Di San Giuliano* (Rome-Milan, 1954). Concerning the Marquis' unorthodox business and banking interests, see the *Giornale di Sicilia* (a Palermo daily) for its running comments of August 1893; it seems that Sicilian contractors who backed Di San Giuliano could count on his help in getting favored treatment when they needed extended bank credit and that Giolitti himself was not above interfering in such matters, though undoubtedly with disdain, in order to help out the marquis.

Di San Giuliano's manipulative skills stood him in good stead during the Libyan War, when he had to orchestrate the Italian press; then he worked closely with Scalea and Contarini, the Sicilian clique in the foreign ministry. See Luigi Lodi, *Venticinque anni* (Florence, 1923), 149–150. Concerning the Sicilian circle at the Consulta and its extraordinary influence both before and after Di San Giuliano's tenure of office, see R. Cantalupo, *Ritratto di Pietro Lanza di Scalea* (Rome, 1939) and idem, under the pseudonym "Legatus," *Vita diplomatica di Salvatore Contarini* (Rome, 1947). Concerning Contarini, see also Alberto Pirelli, *Dopoguerra 1919–1932* (Milan, 1961). Di San Giuliano's parliamentary speeches during his ministry bear out the impression made by his reports and notes kept in the archives: an acuteness of mind and sharpness of expression which lasted to the end.

16. The most notable work about Tittoni is Tommasini, *L'Italia alla vigilia*, a historical rehabilitation written with access to both Tittoni's papers and the archives of the Italian foreign ministry, the latter by Mussolini's favor.

On the early political career of Tittoni, see Cilibrizzi, *Storia parlamentare* (Rome, 1923–1952) III (1929), 245–251, and Alberto Caracciolo, *Roma capitale dal risorgimento alla crisi dello stato liberale* (Rome-Florence, 1956). The latter work also offers some notes on his brother Romolo, of the Banco di Roma and the Rome Chamber of Commerce. For Tittoni's relations with the Catholics and the special services he rendered to Giolittti in that connection, see Giovanni Spadolini, *Giolitti e i cattolici*, 2nd ed., (Florence, 1960).

The case against Tittoni, as it was repeatedly made between 1906 and 1914, was not the sort that would lead to conviction in a court of law, but it is worth some serious historical consideration. Prominent Neapolitan Socialists and radicals, notably the deputy Ettore Ciccotti and the crusading journalist Roberto Marvasi, accused Tittoni of having worked with the organized underworld of their city.

17. Nationalism was a movement in its own right and should not be reduced to a "forerunner" of Fascism, of which it became, rather, an essential component during Mussolini's dictatorship. Nor should it be confused with the style, fashions, and ideas of Gabriele d'Annunzio. Though the poet had many personal links with the "Adriatic" Nationalists, he was in fact a pan-Latin, for whom Italy and France together constituted an island of culture amid the commercialism, barbarity, and decadence of the rest of the world. This sets him apart, for the true Nationalist never loves any other country.

The Nationalists were a dissident force within the Italian liberal establishment. This distinguishes them from the syndicalists and the Futurists and from Mussolini himself, all elements destined to converge in the making of the Fascist regime years later but at that time outsiders in liberal Italy. Before 1915 the Nationalists were at home in the universities, the big urban newspapers, and the corridors of official Rome. To some extent they represented a generation gap within the Italian liberal bourgeoisie.

Their real origins are to be sought in that wing of the "classical" liberal bourgeoisie that refused to come to terms with twentieth-century democracy. Salandra is a good example of such tendencies: far-Right, but of liberal extraction and culture. Nationalism should not be identified wiith populistic, rabble-rousing, or clerical right-wing movements, with which it shared enemies, but not programs or ideals. The Italian Nationalist movement drew its support from the younger generation of this particular elitist bourgeoisie. To the end the Nationalists remained a breakaway group, in permanent secession from parental liberalism. Consequently, they were later able to endow the Fascist regime with a constitution, a doctrine of state, and a small inside group of officials, all things quite beyond the Duce's scope or intent. These Nationalist contributions were to prove their worth, for without them Mussolini could not have been constitutionally ousted by the king: they also show how true the Nationalists were, though in an utterly reactionary way, to their bourgeois-constitutional origins.

The Nationalists did not spring from the business classes of northern Italy, but from a subsoil of middle- and lower-class students, lawyers, journalists, and would-be writers. The convergence between Nationalists and industrial enterprisers was not a simple brute fact resulting from a single, undifferentiated class interest.

Why should the industrial bourgeoisie look to the far Right? Industry is not, in itself, always imperialistic in a nationalist sense. When international trade allows, it may develop marked cosmopolitan-liberal preferences. The chauvinistic man of letters, committed to a particular language and culture, does not have the same class interests as, say, the exporter of machines or chemicals or industrial methods; and the schoolteacher or government clerk may well have worries about maintaining middle-class standards that an investment banker would not even understand. Modern political nationalism is not an emanation of manufacturers. The special close relationship between Italian Nationalists and Italian industrialists needs explanation in terms of a particular set of crisis conditions. Franco Gaeta points out that the years 1908–15, in which the Nationalist movement takes its definite political shape, mark the end of Italy's first industrial boom and the start of a long series of crises and hard times in the nation's new industrial sectors. F. Gaeta, *Nazionalismo italiano* (Naples, 1965) surveys all that has been written about the subject, as well as the historiographical evaluations of it.

In addition to the political writings of Alfredo Rocco, there are some youthful articles by Dino Grandi, dated Dec. 1914, that express perfectly the practical views of young Italy in its Nationalist incarnation. Grandi held that the First World War broke out in such a way that two issues were intertwined and confused. The issue of national self-determination and unity—which had to put Italy on the side of Britain and France against Austria—was an unsolved problem of the nineteenth century carried over into the twentieth because the Hapsburgs had survived. The real war, that of producer nations against nations that hoarded capital, would eventually put Italy on the side of Germany and Russia against the West: the real war was to be a social revolution, pitting nation against nation on a class basis. (See the reprinted selection in Dino Grandi, *Giovani* [Bologna, 1941].) Grandi's political formation has special interest, of course, because of the leading part he played in the Fascist party and regime: together with other Nationalist-oriented members of the Fascist Grand Council, he was instrumental in precipitating the ouster of Mussolini in 1943. See Giulio De Frenzi [Federzoni], *Il lucignolo dell ideale* (Naples, 1909); and idem, *Un eroe Alfredo Oriani* (Rome, 1910); as well as N. Matteini, *Alfredo Oriani* (Rimini, 1952). The Nationalist elite leadership could not bring forth a charismatic political chief., someone who could really command this petty-bourgeois public, and Mussolini eventually stepped into the breach. Oriani's books inspired the Duce in the prewar years: see R. De Felice, *Mussolini il rivoluzionario* (Turin, 1965), 67, 187.

1. The Predicament
of Italian Industrialization

1. See Felice Guarneri, *Battaglie economiche* (Milan, 1953) II, 500–503.

2. See R. Bachi, *L'Italia economica 1913* (Città di Castello, 1914), 271–272. This invaluable series of yearly studies of the Italian economy came out as supplements to Einaudi's *Riforma Sociale* but were also published separately. Together with the government's *Annuario Statistico* and Luigi Einaudi's running comments in vols. 2 and 3 of his *Cronache*, already cited, they constitute the basis for my remarks here. Einaudi's critique of the Italian tax structure—a constant theme in the first three volumes of the *Cronache*—is especially useful. The reader is referred to Bachi's *L'Italia economica* for the years 1910 through 1914 for most of the facts presented in this chapter. See also Gino Borgatta, *Quadro delle società azionarie italiane alla vigilia della crisi europea* (Rome, 1916).

3. For some general ideas about Italian steel and its problems, see A. E. Rossi, *Oscar Sinigaglia* (Rome, 1955); Oscar Sinigaglia, *Alcune note sulla siderurgia italiana* (Rome, 1946); Pietro Lanino, *La nuova Italia industriale* (Rome, 1916), I, 20–22 (this last book is by a professional railroad engineer and was published by the *tipografia Idea Nazionale*, a Nationalist publishing outlet); U. Ricci, *Protezionisti e liberisti* (Bari, 1920), 192; G. Scagnetti, *La siderurgia in Italia* (Rome, 1923); Corbino, *Annali dell'economica italiana*, V, 119–128.

4. On Breda, Brin, and the origins of the steel industry, see Edoardo Giretti's indictment, "La Società di Terni," in *Giornale degli economisti*, Oct. 1903, 309–364 and Nov. 1903, 422–459; the *atto costitutivo* of Elba, with a complete list of initial investors, registered by the court on 3 August 1899 and printed in Ministero d'Agricoltura, Industria e Commercio (hereafter cited as Ministero AIC) *Bollettino ufficiale delle Società per Azioni*, Anno XVII, Fascicolo XXXI (8 Aug. 1899), published at Rome; Pilade Del Buono, *Il trepido grido dell'anima elbana* (San Marino, 1916), concerning alleged fraud on the part of Italian industrialists; and an interesting item in *Il Sole* (Milan), 18 Jan. 1914, 3 on the same score; *Le ordinanze del Senato (alta corte di giustizia) sul procedimento a carico del Sen. Breda, Estratto dal giornale "La Legge" Anno XXXIX (1899)*, Vol. I, no. 8, Vol. II, no. 9 (Rome, 1899); F. S. Nitti, *Napoli e la questione meridionale* (Naples, 1903), 151–152. Parliamentary deputies, in particular Eugenio Chiesa and Salvatore Orlando (whose family were shipping and steel magnates), often took up the merits and demerits of state-sponsored industry; see particularly E. Chiesa, *Discorsi parlamentari* (Milan, 1960), 193–255, a detailed indictment of the Ilva trust and its political-journalistic connections, and the exchanges in the Chamber of Deputies on 28 June–3 July 1906, *Atti parlamentari, Camera dei Deputati, Legislatura XXII, discussioni*, 9249, 9261, 9270–9271, 9290, 9353, 9380–9385, 9395, 9416, 9612, 9644, from which, among other things, it appears that the Italian naval ministry did not distinguish at times between self-sufficiency in steel production and self-sufficiency in motors and shipbuilding, two propositions which, whatever their close

military relation, were economically contradictory. Concerning Elba's links to the Orlando, Florio, and Garroni clans, see in particular *La Metallurgia italiana*, 31 Mar. 1911, 144–145, which reports the stockholders' meeting held in Genoa earlier that month; there are also some interesting notes on Elba's holdings and prospects in Tunisian mines. Concerning the administrative irregularities and fictitious capital of the steel trust Ilva, see *Giurisprudenza italiana*, 1906, I, 2, 816, commenting on a decision of the Genoa court of appeals; Ilva "increased" its capital by exchanging shares with the parent corporation, Elba. The economist Einaudi had an interesting debate with the steel industrialists in *La Metallurgia italiana*, 31 July 1912, 439–453 and 28 Feb. 1913, 117–123, in which the steelmakers argued that free trade would not benefit Italy, since the international market in iron and steel was tightly controlled by German-French-Belgian marketing agreements. *La Metallurgia italiana* also offers, for the years 1913–15, a wealth of facts and figures concerning the Italian steel industry's dependence on defense contracts, German penetration into Italian markets, and the new technical developments in Italian mechanical industries.

The background of Terni is mysterious and full of controversy. For some details see Carocci, *Depretis*, 408–409. On Breda, in addition to the senate indictment, see the laudatory company history, *La Società Veneta per imprese e costruzioni pubbliche* (Bassano, 1881), modelled on a similar attack, *La sfiducia del pubblico nella S.p.A. Società Veneta* (Genoa, 1890); see also V. S. Breda, *Sulla interrogazione presentata dall'on. Santini . . . il 31 gennaio 1899*, a self-defense. On the scandals of 1904–6, which broke out after Breda's death and the formation of "big steel," see Zannotti-Bianco, *Leopoldo Franchetti*, 40–55.

During the great rearmament period of 1908–14, Terni and its industrial allies finally succeeded in overcoming possible competition from Krupp or Schneider through an understanding with a Piedmontese industrial group headed by Dante Ferraris. The Banca Commerciale backed Terni to the hilt, as Giuseppe Orlando, the firm's chief executive, was willing to testify: see *Rassegna dei lavori pubblici*, 25 Mar. 1913, 198 and 8 Dec. 1914, 628; concerning Vickers-Terni armaments, see the note in ibid., 27 May 1913, 350. On Terni's mining interests, see the Turinese labor paper *Il Metallurgico*, 30 July 1914. On Terni's arms contracts in 1914, see *Il Sole*, 8 Feb. and 27 Mar. 1914.

Concerning the Piombino steel works, which had a close tie with French industrial interests, see in particular the company's annual report in *Il Sole*, 23 Apr. 1914; the account of the stockholders' meeting in ibid., 20–21 Apr. 1914; and the anonymous reports about new French backing for the firm, which was seeking closer working relations with the other participants in the Ilva trust, ibid., 14 Mar. 1914; and, more specifically, *La Metallurgia italiana*, 31 May 1914, 312.

5. *Atti parlamentari*, 9395.

6. For Orlando's speech in full, see *Atti parlamentari*, 9380–9385.

7. See G. Roletti, *Porti cantieri e navi* (Brescia, 1934), 659 et seq.; Primo Levi, *Luigi Orlando e i suoi fratelli* (Rome, 1898); Antonio Tosi, *Gli Orlando e il cantiere* (Leghorn, 1904); Salvatore Orlando, *Per il nuovo assetto marittimo* (Leghorn, 1905). For the complex linkage amng Crispi, Florio, the Orlando brothers, and the Rubattino-Balduino shipping interests of Genoa and the resulting formation of the Navigazione Generale Italiana, see Codignola, *Rubattino*.

8. On this Sicilian success story, see Augusto de Marsanich, "I Florio," in *Confederazione fascista Parte II* (Urbino, 1939), 7–30.

9. There is no biography of Benedetto Brin, and we must wait for the relevant volume of the *Dizionario biografico degli italiani* to read a decent biographical article on him. Meanwhile, see the solid article on Admiral Bettolo in the *Dizionario*

biografico and the many references to Brin and Bettolo in the excellently indexed Farini, *Diario*, which give us an inside view of the two men. During the hard times of the 1890s, Bettolo won much favor among economy-minded moderates by proposing to reduce naval costs without lessening Italy's war potential: this was to be done by having warships and motors built in private shipyards, rather than in state arsenals. These proposals were part of the Brin-Bettolo plan, which envisaged a self-sufficient iron and steel industry based at Elba, Savona, and Terni. See in particular Farini, *Diario*, I, 418.

10. *Rassegna dei lavori pubblici*, 8 Dec. 1914, 628.

11. See *Rivista delle Società Commerciali*, 20 Aug. 1913, 3. In connection with German steel dumping, see Lanino, *La nuova Italia*, I, 17–18 and the relevant sections of Bachi, *Italia economica* for the years 1912 through 1914.

12. See the first two notes of this chapter for sources. In addition, I have consulted the financial agreement dated 7 Aug. 1911, signed at Rome by Bonaldo Stringher of the Bank of Italy; Edoardo Rivoli of the Cassa di Risparmio delle Provincie Lombarde; Marquis Ferrero di Cambiano of the Cassa di Risparmio of Turin; Enrico Silvani of the Cassa di Risparmio in Bologna; Count Franchini Stappo of the Cassa di Risparmio of Verona; Eduardo Varvaro of the Cassa Centrale di Risparmio Vittorio Emanuele per le Provincie Siciliane in Palermio; Mario Ciani of the Monte dei Paschi di Siena; Giacomo Ferretti and Hermann Bohn of the Banca Commerciale Italiana; G. Pfizmaier and Guido Goetz of the Credito Italiano; Roberto Calegari of the Società Bancaria Italiana; Enrico Jacomoni and F. S. Benucci of the Banco di Roma; Luigi Della Torre of the banking house Zaccaria Pisa (Milan); Attilio and Odero, Marquis Durazzo-Pallavicini, R. Bettini of Michele Terni; Marquis Luigi Medici del Vascello, Vittorio Rolandi-Ricci, Zauli, and Lenci for Ilva; Falconi and Marchese Vittorio Garroni (son of Senator Camillo Garroni, Giolitti's prefect at Genoa) for Elba; Bruzzone and Moresco for the Società Siderurgica di Savona; B. Loleo for the Società Ligure Metallurgica; and Davide Viale for the Società delle Ferriere Italiane at Rome. This document was drawn up on tax-stamped paper in twenty-eight copies, one of which I consulted through the courtesy of the Banca Commerciale Italiana, 31 Aug. 1912, 503–510.

13. Terni's failings became a public scandal in 1913. See Giorgio Molli, *La politica industriale e gli armamenti navali* (Milan, 1913).

Between 30 April and 30 November 1914, the *Rivista delle Società Commerciali*, Italy's outstanding big-business journal, published a series of notes and articles by the engineers R. Ridolfi and L. Allievi, as well as an essay by the economist Pasquale Iannacone (30 June 1914, 492–507) and a number of editorials, all defending the steel industry in Italy. The sum of what they had to say is this: free-trade was no protection against monopoly in a situation where one or two producers controlled the world market, and if Italy had not set up tariffs and attempted to compete with German-organized steel cartels, the Italians would have had to pay 30 to 40 percent more for steel products. The Germans had set up a vertical economic system, in which steel, fuel, and machinery producers were all integrated. Any country that wanted to face Germany, even in its own domestic markets, would have to integrate vertically as well. Molli was not the only doubting Thomas among those who knew the real state of the Italian naval industries. *La Marina mercantile italiana*, 10 Apr. 1913, noted that two Italian battleships, the *Giulio Cesare* and the *Leonardo Da Vinci*, were delayed two years because Terni (or Vickers-Terni) was failing in its contractual obligations; the same journal, perhaps at Ansaldo's prompting (*La Marina mercantile italiana* came out at Genoa), returned to the attack in its issue of 10 Feb. 1914, and Captain Ettore Bravetta brought up other delays due to Vickers-Terni's incompetence in the authoritative Lega Navale

Italiana, *Annuario Navale 1915*, (Rome, 1915), 18. None of these critics, though, drew the conclusion that perhaps Italy should not have tried for military self-sufficiency and great-power status in the arms race. They simply blamed Terni, at the evident instigation of Terni's rivals on the Ligurian coast.

14. See *Il Pensiero militare*, 23 May 1909, denouncing Krupp; *La Preparazione*, Feb.–Apr. 1911, passim; and Gen. Carlo Montu', *Storia dell'artiglieria italiana* (Rome, 1941) VII, 1375, 1406–1409, 1616–1618. Concerning the new Turinese armaments production, see Scagnetti, *La siderurgia in Italia*, 215–216.

15. See the pamphlet by Pio and Mario Perrone, *L'Ansaldo, la guerra, e il problema nazionale delle miniere di Cogne* (Genoa, 1932), passim.

2. The Nontrust Industries

1. Concerning the executives of Ansaldo and their political and journalistic connections, see Farini, *Diario*, II, 1168–69, 1175, 1187. On the Bombrini family, see Alfredo Rota, *Bombrini* (Genoa, 1951); Giovanni Bombrini, *Discorso pronunciato in occasione del varo del Cristobal Colon* (Genoa, 1896); and *Il gruppo industriale Bombrini–Parodi-Delfino, edito a cura del gruppo industriale B. P. D.* (Milan, 1962), in addition to the Bombrini articles in the *Dizionario biografico*.

On Ansaldo itself, see Emanuele Gazzo, *I cento anni dell'Ansaldo (1853–1953)* (Genoa, 1953); Perrone and Perrone, *L'Ansaldo*; on Ansaldo's special preference for Schneider over Krupp, see a letter of Pio Perrone, "Sui sistemi di fabbricazione dei cannoni Krupp e Schneider," in *Rivista marittima*, Feb. 1913, 309–311. On Ansaldo's links with Nobel, see *Il Sole*, 5 Sept. 1913; 29 Mar. 1914; *Rivista del servizio minerario 1914* (an Italian government publication), 186–187; *Rassegna dei lavori pubblici*, 3–10 Nov. 1914, 600. Concerning Ansaldo's contracts and balance on the eve of the War, see *Il Sole*, 30–31 Mar. 1914, 4. On Ansaldo's operations in Turkey, there is no published source, but see the exchange between the Nationalist deputy Piero Foscari and the foreign minister in *Atti parlamentari, Tornata dell' 8 giugno 1911*, 15414; and ibid., *Tornata del 9 giugno*, 15452. Concerning Ansaldo's financing, see Giorgio Mori's remarks in *Annali dell'Istituto G. Feltrinelli, Anno Secondo* (Milan, 1959), 318; Ansaldo's special relation with the Banca di Sconto and the French industrial-financial world comes out in Cesare Rossi, *L'Assalto alla Banca di Sconto, colloqui con Angelo Pogliani* (Milan, 1950); see also R. Bachi, *L'Italia economica nell'anno 1911* (Turin, 1912), 37; Umberto Bava, *Quattro maggiori istituti italiani di credito* (Genoa, 1926), 140–144. Concerning the French industrial financier and statesman Senator Paul Doumer, see M. Karolyi, *The Memoirs of Michael Karolyi* (New York, 1957), 49. Concerning Ansaldo's leadership in the Italian armaments industry, see Lanino, *La nuova Italia*, I, 23–24.

Gazzo's *I cento anni*, which is based on company reports and statistics, is the source for most of the information on output and company guidelines furnished in this chapter, as well as for the quoted statements.

2. See Farini, *Diario*, II, 1168–1169. These indiscretions came out in the course of an audience granted to the president of the senate.

3. According to Vickers' official historian, Armstrong lost money through its Italian operations. Vickers, on the other hand, expected to make profits from its affiliation with Terni after 1905, expectations that grew with the setting up of a big plant at La Spezia. Both British firms then decided to join forces in operating Ottoman shipyards and naval arsenals, a deal that was probably years in the making. Under such circumstances it is probable that Armstrong welcomed its

divorce from Ansaldo. It was just as well for Italy, though, that Ansaldo could never mobilize anywhere near enough capital and influence to wrest for itself the Ottoman naval contracts. The British companies, seeming winners, lost heavily in their venture; to judge from their debts and losses, the Constantinople undertaking would have cost well over 25 million lire, a prohibitive figure for any private group in Italy. (A state guarantee, of course, would have changed things, but it is hard to imagine that Giolitti and Stringher would have committed themselves.) See J. D. Scott, *Vickers: A History* (London, 1962), 84–86, 91.

4. *Rassegna dei lavori pubblici*, 1 Apr. 1913, 212–213.

5. See *Rassegna dei lavori pubblici*, 3–10 Nov. 1914, 600; and *Il Sole*, 5 Sept. 1913, which reports the formation of the Italian Nobel company.

In a parliamentary speech of 24 June 1914, Eugenio Chiesa accused Nobel of tax evasion. The firm had no capital but held foreign bonds that the Italian tax authorities could not touch. To this strange firm, he charged, the Italian government had advanced 3 million lire for dynamite manufacturing. See Chiesa, *Discorsi*, 332. By 1919 more than half of Nobel-Avigliana's capital was in Italian hands, and the rest was in French; Pio Perrone was the president. Italian Nobel's technicians worked closely with their opposite numbers in the Ansaldo plants; Paul Clemenceau actually ran the firm, to judge from a letter sent by Pio Perrone to Giuseppe Toeplitz from Rome, 26 May 1919, Banca Commerciale Italiana (hereafter cited as BCI) Archives, Segreteria Amministrato i delegati, 1919.

6. Ferdinando Martini, *Diario 1914–1918* (Milan-Verona, 1966), 81.

7. See Armando Frumento, *Impresse lombarde nella storia della siderurgia italiana. Il contributo dei Falck* (Milan, 1952), an official history. On Gregorini, see *Il Sole*, 20 Sept. 1913 and *La Metallurgia italiana*, 31 Jan. 1913, 73.

8. At the Parma center of the Banca Commerciale, these papers were in Casse 6 and 9 when I consulted them in 1967. At that time the Commerciale's archives were not yet organized; the correspondence relating to Franchi is voluminous and very revealing, offering the materials for a short company history.

9. See *Il Sole*, 14 Feb. 1914, 3, quoting the German trade journal *Stahl und Eisen*, no. 6, 5 Feb. 1914, reviewing the year 1913.

10. See *Il Sole*, 20 May 1914, 2; ibid., 1 June 1914, 4; *La Metallurgia italiana*, 30 Sept. 1915, 595. For facts and figures on little steel in Italy, see the mining review put out by the Italian government (Ministero AIC, *Ispettorato delle miniere*); *Rivista del servizio minerario*, 1912 through 1914. It seems that little steel made about 40 percent of all steel produced in Italy. On the achievements and problems of little steel in North Italy, see A. Stromboli, "L'industria siderurgica in Italia," *La Metallurgia italiana*, 31 July 1915, 424–437; G. E. Falck, "I forni elettrici nella industria metallurgica," ibid., 31 Dec. 1915, 751–755; Mario Borghesi, "Le industrie elettrometallurgiche nella Lombardia e nel Veneto," ibid., 31 Dec. 1915, 778–781; and Ingegnere G. Chierici, "I minerali di ferro di Cogne," ibid., 30 Apr. 1915, 235–242. Concerning German dumping practices in Italy *after* the agreement of 1913, see R. Ridolfi, "La Siderurgia italiana e la protezione doganale," *Le Metallurgia italiana*, 31 June 1914, 350 et seq.; and idem, "Un caso tipico di dumping," *La Riforma Sociale*, Fascicolo II, 1914, 277–291. Ridolfi, an engineer, was the head of the Italian steel industry's sales organization, S.A. Ferro ed Acciaio.

11. I have followed closely the trade journal *La Metallurgia italiana* for the years 1914 and 1915; see in particular the issues 30 Sept. and 31 Dec. 1914, in which Falck and other steelmakers discuss in detail their wartime difficulties, spelling out the attitudes of Germany and Britain.

12. See Lanino, *La nuova Italia*, II, 10–18, 77–79; F. Bonelli's article on Riccardo Bianchi in the *Dizionario biografico*; the Italian government publication,

La questione di stato delle ferrovie italiane (1905–1955). Monografie (Rome, 1956); Luigi Luzzatti, "La costruzione del materiale ferroviario," *Il Sole*, 26–27 Jan. 1914, 1.

13. See the business news in *Il Sole*, 14 Feb. 1914, 3; ibid., 16 Mar. 1914 2; "Informazioni," *Rassegna dei lavori pubblici*, 6 May 1913, 296; 17 June 1913, 392; 15 July 1913, 464, giving statistics on the Rumanian contract awarded to Breda. (Out of 1,850 railroad cars ordered by the Rumanians, Breda was to build 625, the others being contracted to foreign firms, German for the most part.) For Rumanian locomotive orders, see *Il Sole*, 13 Dec. 1913, 3; Rumania was to order twenty-four big locomotives from Miani-Silvestri of Milan at a cost of about 2.5 million francs. *Il Sole* provides a sort of running account of the rail industry's hardships and progress during the years 1913 and 1914, while the *Rassegna dei lavori pubblici* functioned as a trade journal.

14. In addition to Lanino, *La nuova Italia*, II, 77 et seq., see Michelangelo Novi, "La trazione elettrica sulle ferrovie in Italia," *La Nuova Antologia*, Nov.–Dec. 1916, 31–60. When big rail shops, especially Officine Meccaniche (Miani-Silvestri) of Milan and Naples, ran into the red because of insufficient railroad orders, they began furnishing turbines and naval engines to the Italian navy, driving out foreign competitors. Rearmament really saved such firms. See *Il Sole*, 24 Oct. 1913, 3; 10 Nov. 1913, 5; and 5 Dec. 1913, 3.

Concerning Marelli's export of electric fans, see *Atti dell'XI Congresso nazionale fra commercianti industriali ed esercenti, Venezia 8–13 giunno 1913,* (Venice, 1913), 62. But Marelli also had many Italian naval contracts as well as rail work.

15. On the development of the Italian machine and motor industries, see the following company histories: *La Società italiana Ernest Breda per costruzioni meccaniche* (Verona: Mondadori, 1936); *Franco Tosi S.p.A. 1876–1956* (Legnano-Milan, 1956), *I cinquant'anni della Fiat* (Verona, 1950); and *I cinquant'anni della RIV* (Milan, 1956). Concerning Italian mechanical exports, see in particular: United States Tariff Commission, *Tariff Information Surveys on the Articles in Paragraphs 119–122 of the Tariff Act of 1913* (Washington, D.C., 1921), and Ausonio Franzoni, "Appunti sul commercio italo-argentino," *Rivista delle Società Commerciali*, May 1914, 429–441; as well as Bachi, *L'Italia economica*; Lanino, *La nuova Italia*, II, 21–26; and "Note statistiche," *La Metallurgia italiana*, 31 Dec. 1915, 793, which gives the value of automotive imports and exports for the months January-July 1914. See also Ernesto Tornquist & Co., Ltd., *The Economic Development of the Argentine Republic* (Buenos Aires, 1919), 149, 155–164.

16. See *Rassegna dei lavori pubblici*, 5 May 1914, 300, an anonymous note reporting Fiat's success in building submarine engines for Britain and Germany and observing that Fiat had come through because of the faith put in it by "exclusively Italian capitalists."

17. See G. Arfè's biographical article on Giovanni Agnelli in the *Dizionario biografico*; Silvio Pozzani, *Giovanni Agnelli, storia di un'industria* (Milan, 1962); as well as the previously cited company histories of Fiat and RIV.

18. Bachi, *L'Italia economica 1913*, XI, 150–151, 153. Bachi does not draw political conclusions from the facts that he presents so clearly.

19. See Angelo Pogliani's report in *Il Sole*, 10 Mar. 1914.

20. See B. Borgatta, *Quadro delle società azionarie italiane alla vigilia della crisi europea. Supplemento alla Rivista delle Società Commerciali* (Rome, 1916), 60 et seq.

21. While Fiat-San Giorgio, the war producer, made a net profit in 1913 of 50,405.72 lire, right at the start of its operations, the bus line Sita, a Fiat

auxiliary, registered a net loss of 29,032.93 lire in the same year; *Il Sole*, 7 May 1914, 2, 4. According to Paolo Spriano, Fiat tended toward a vertical organization, buying up garages, chassis, and body workshops and furnishing public transportation services, which were heavily subsidized by the government: in the two-year period 1910–11 the state contributed 16,460,000 lire for such lines. See Spriano, *Socialismo e classe operaia a Torino dal 1892 al 1913* (Turin, 1958), 272–273, as well as his remarks about the precariousness of Fiat's first big operations, ibid., 209. To say the least, war orders and subsidies helped to smooth out the harsh ups and downs of international business cycles.

22. For precise information about the interlocking directorates of the Italian armament firms, see *La Metallurgia italiana*, 31 Jan. 1913, 74–75; ibid., 30 Apr. 1913; "Società industriali," 329; *Il Sole*, 2 Apr. 1914, 2; ibid., 20 May 1914, 4; on Gilardini's armament business, see the report in *Il Sole*, 1 Oct. 1913, 2. Machine shops and munitions firms also interlocked; see *Il Sole*, 29 Apr. 1914, 4; this led to cartels, ibid., 2 Apr. 1914, 2.

23. See *La Metallurgia italiana*, 31 Jan. 1913, 74–75; and 21 Dec. 1913, 4. Here again we see a link between Alessandro Centurini and the Parisi clan.

24. Martini, *Diario 1914–1918*, 164–164, 168.

My information on Fiat's wartime dealings in Russia comes for the most part, from the previously cited records of the Banca Commerciale's committees, but I am indebted to Dr. Helju Bennett for the facts concerning Fiat-San Giorgio's contract with a Russian naval trust. Dr. Bennett consulted K. F. Shatsillo, *Inostranny kapital i voenno-morskie programmy Rossii nakanune pervoi mirovoi voiny*, Akademia Nauk SSSR, Istoricheskie Zapiski (Moscow, 1961), vol. 69, 73–100; see especially 89–90.

25. See the already cited Tosi company history, 17; and *Rassegna dei lavori pubblici*, 28 Apr. 1914, 282.

26. *Rivista delle Società Commerciali, 1912, Supplemento, Bilanci delle Società Italiane per Azioni*, 1180.

27. See Riccardo Gualino, *Frammenti di vita* (Milan-Verona, 1931), a work which throws an interesting sidelight on Giovanni Agnelli as well. This is a rare personal account: most Italian business innovators have not told us much about themselves and their times. On his operations, see the report from Bucharest published in *La Rassegna Italiana* (Constantinople), July 1913, 121; "Note e Informazioni," *Il Sole*, 16 Mar. 1914, 3; report on the stockholders' meeting of the Società Bancaria held 23 March 1914 in ibid., 23–24 Mar. 1914. (This report is also interesting because it shows the degree of Parisian "presence" in the Società Bancaria: note especially the minister plenipotentiary Laurence de Lalande, Louis Dreyfus, and the engineer Nathan Suss, all of the Legion of Honor, and all a graceful accompaniment to the Italian majority, which consisted of five members, three of whom were senators.) See Gualino's 1912 statement in *Rivista delle Società Commerciali, 1912, Supplemento, Bilanci*, 376. Gualino also had some connections with the Banca Commerciale. His firm received 650,000 lire, a loan secured by 13,000 shares of Unione Cementi, in order to carry out its lumbering operations in Hungary, Russia, and Sardinia; the deal was arranged by Toeplitz. See BCI Archives, *Verbali Comitato Locale*, 7 Mar. and 14 Nov. 1911.

28. See Dr. Mario Luzzato, "The Italian Rubber and Insulated Wire Industry." *The India Rubber Journal*, 26 July 1924, 151 et seq.; Alberto Pirelli, *La Pirelli, Vita di una azienda industriale* (Milan, 1946); *Rivista delle Società Commerciali, 1912, Supplemento, Bilanci*, statements on pp. 328 and 693; report on Pirelli's operations in *Il Sole*, 30 Jan. 1914; ibid. 16 Mar. 1914, 4; ibid., 23 Mar. 1914, 3.

29. See Franzoni, "Appunti," 436.

30. For information concerning French investment and executive participation in this branch of Italian industry, see the Italian government publication Ministero AIC, *Bollettino ufficiale delle S.p.A.*, 1913, Anno XXXI, Fascicolo XXXIII, 24–29; concerning the foundation of the Società per lo sviluppo dei superfosfati e prodotti chimici in Italia, 1–10 July 1913. The company's purpose was to manufacture and sell sulphuric acid, fertilizers, and other chemical products. For further facts on the composition of the Montecatini board of directors, which included five French representatives of four different French companies, as well as executives of the Banca Commerciale and the Credito Italiano, see *La Metallurgia italiana*, June–July 1913, 323, under the heading "Società industriali." See also *Il Sole*, 27 Mar. 1914, 4, concerning Montecatini's vertical holdings; see ibid., 27 May 1914, 3 for some corporate information about the links between French enterprises in Tunisia and the Italian chemical firms. The Donegani brothers, chief executives of Montecatini, were also involved in the formation at Paris of the Societé Générale des lignites en Italie in February 1912. This interest in Italian lignite and coal brought them into close financial relations not only with Paris, but also with the Ilva steel trust, one of whose constituents, the Ferriere Italiane, took a share in the new firm, which was to develop some of the Ilva partner's mines in the Piombino-Grosseto area. See *La Metallurgia italiana*, 30 Apr. 1913, 312.

31. In addition to Molli, *La politica industriale*, see Lega Navale Italiana, *Annuario Navale 1911* (Rome, 1911) for a general idea of the way in which Italian shipyards and machine shops divided up state orders, so that in one case Ansaldo furnished the machinery while Odero built the boilers; see also the *Annuario Navale 1915*, 19–20, which has some remarks by Captain Ettora Bravetta that corroborate Molli's findings. The important military paper *La Preparazione* evidently received some private tips from the Perrone brothers, as can be conjectured from the information, 27 July and 1 Aug. 1911, concerning Italy's battleships and the ruinous effects of competition in the nation's arms industry. It is clear that the references and innuendos touch on the Banca Commerciale and its foreign executives.

3.   The Shipping Industry

1. See Epicarmo Corbino, *Marina mercantile italiana* (Milan, 1919); idem, *Industria delle costruzioni navali, Estratto dal Giornale degli Economisti, dic. 1918*; Lanino, *La nuova Italia*, II, 33–39; Einaudi, *Cronache*, II, 346 et seq., 534, 681–697, 700, 772–773; ibid., III, 346, 427–445.

2. See R. Ridolfi, "La siderurgia italiana e la protezione doganale," *La Metallurgia italiana*, 31 July 1914, 395–397.

3. See "Informazioni e notizie," *Rivista marittima*, Apr.–May 1914, 143–146; "Per le costruzioni navali," *La Marina mercantile italiana*, 25 June 1913, 4109; "Informazioni particolari," ibid., 10 Apr. 1914, 4438; shipbuilding statistics in "Informazioni e notizie," *Rivista marittima*, Apr.–May 1914. See also "Informazioni e notizie," ibid., July–Aug. 1913, 116–117, and "Prospetto delle navi a vapore, rimaste in costruzione nei cantieri del Regno al 10 luglio 1912," ibid., July–Aug. 1912. Aside from their construction for subsidized shipping lines, the Italian shipyards were also building two ships for the *Società italo-americana per il petrolio*, directed by two Germans and Walter Teagle of Standard Oil; *Il Sole*, 30 Apr. 1914, 4.

4. See "La costruzioni nei Cantieri Navali Riuniti," *La Marina mercantile italiana*, 25 June 1913, 4102; ibid., 10 Apr. 1914, 4438; "Relazioni," ibid., 10 May 1913, 4062.

5. See "I lavori nei cantieri Odero," *La Marina mercantile italiana*, 10 July 1913, 4121.

6. See Ministero AIC, *Bollettino ufficiale delle S.p.A.*, Fascicolo XI, 42 et seq., for the *atto costitutivo* of Sitmar; also "Informazioni," *Il Sole*, 27 Apr. 1914, 3; ibid., 1 May 1914, 3; ibid., 2 May 1914. See also the Navigazione Generale's position; ibid., 29–30 Sept. 1913.

7. See the pamphlet *Società veneziana di navigazione a vapore, A.S.E. il ministro delle Poste e Telegrafi, Alle Rappresentanze Amministrative, Commerciali e Politiche di Venezia, Notizie sulla linea Venezia-Calcutta*, Mar. 1904.

8. See the report from Bari in *Il Sole*, 25 Sept. 1913; "Informazioni e notizie," *Rivista marittima*, Nov. 1913, 372–373.

9. See the articles of incorporation (*atto costitutivo*) in Ministero A.I.C., *Bollettino ufficiale delle S.p.A.*, Anno XXXI, Fascicolo XIII, 3–12.

10. See *Rivista marittima*, Nov. 1912, 347, 350, concerning subsidized navigation and a proposed exclusive line between Italy and Brazil; Lloyd Sabaudo statement, ibid., July–Aug. 1913, 118; ibid., Nov. 1912, 349; ibid., Aug. 1914, 312. All of these are under the heading "Informazioni e notizie." It is clear from them that Lloyd Sabaudo used mostly British-built vessels in spite of its patriotic declarations. See ibid., June 1914, 351–355 for an overall view of the subsidies furnished by the Italian government to the shipping lines. See also the statistics in ibid., *Annesso al fascicolo febbraio 1914*. By 1914, with constant jacking up since the basic law of 1910, the state was paying almost 30 million lire a year.

11. For details concerning interlocking directorates, see *Il Sole*, 19 Mar. 1914, 4; 27 Mar. 1914, 2; 18 Apr. 1914, 4; and "Assemblee e dividendi," *La Marina mercantile italiana*, 25 Mar. 1914, 4432; and 10 Apr. 1914, 4447.

12. Codignola, *Rubattino*, is a good book, which should be supplemented by the articles on the Balduino banking clan in the *Dizionario biografico*. For Triestine competition, see the special centennial publication *Sul Mare: Rivista del gruppo armatoriale Italia-Cosulich-Lloyd Triestino*, October 1936.

13. Carocci, *Agostino Depretis*, 381. Note the close business ties between Florio the ship operator and Giuseppe Orlando the shipbuilder, both Palermitans. See also the material on the Florio family cited in the notes to Chap. 1. It is worth noting, again, the ties that seem to hold this speculative "community" together. The Sicilian "Garibaldini" constitute one family, while the Ligurian "Garibaldini," symbolized by Nino Bixio, make up another. The Garibaldian epic brought together not only romantics and idealists, but also prospective captains of finance and industry: the making of Italy was their single common goal. Once Italy was made, however incompletely, the romantics and idealists spun off into radical republicanism and, eventually, socialism, while the captains and operators settled down to the building of an economic power structure. However, the noneconomic motives, the idea of Italy as a great power with a unique destiny, still lay at the root of this whole process. Megalomania was not peculiar to Crispi but beset his generation and his political friends, from Bixio to Baratieri and Scarfoglio (the latest offshoot). See Roberto Battaglia, *La prima guerra d'Africa* (Turin, 1958), which contains some remarkable observations on the rhetorical dimension of Italian political life in Crispi's era. Though Battaglia belongs to the Marxist Left in Italy, he writes a history of Italy's first colonial venture without any reference to concrete profit motives, except for a reference to the "big coup" that the Navigazione Generale Italiana made in 1887 by leasing sixteen steamships to the first Italian army sent to East Africa (287) and a short, comical account of the little iron forts prefabricated in Italy by the new Terni plant and shipped to East Africa, where they proved to be ovens for the hapless Italian soldiers that they were designed to protect

(303–304). In fact, the Navigazione Generale was the only big Italian industry (if one may call it that) which had anything to gain from the sterile East African colonial ventures of 1885–96.

14. Report of stockholders' meeting and list of directors, *Il Sole*, 29 Sept. 1913.

15. Ibid., 317–318.

16. See *Rivista marittima, Annesso al fascicolo febbraio 1914*, as well as the shipping firms' statements in *Rivista delle Società Commerciali, 1912 Supplemento, Bilanci*.

17. See the 1913–14 editorial articles in every issue of *La Marina mercantile italiana*; in particular, "La Marina mercantile nel discorso di S.M. il Re," 25 Nov. 1913, 4288; "Sulla decadenza della nostra marina mercantile libera," 10 Nov. 1913, 4252–4254; "La Marina mercantile nella relazione dell'on. Di Palma," 25 Apr. 1914, 4470.

18. See centennial publication *Sul Mare*.

19. See "Informazioni e notizie," *Rivista Marittima*, Feb. 1913, 353–354.

20. See the remarks of the *Ufficiale di porto* Gino Albi, "Informazioni e notizie," *Rivista marittima*, Apr. 1914, 196–213. Concerning the competition between Austrian and Italian shipping agents and ticket salesmen, both trying to enlist emigrants, see "Contro la linea diretta per il Brasile," *La Marina mercantile italiana*, 10 Jan. 1913, 3907–3908; "Il governo austriaco e l'Austro-Americana," ibid., 10 Dec. 1913, 4292; "Nuova linea fra il Cile e il Mediterraneo," ibid., 10 Aug. 1913, 4160; and the indignant sequel, reporting Austria's ceaseless, insidious campaign against Italian industry and business, ibid., 25 Sept. 1913, 4195. New York importers ordered Italian goods from Messina, Palermo, and Naples on British ships because the Mediterranean shipping pool charged too much; ibid., 10 Mar. 1914, 4414.

21. For reports on new Italian shipping service, see *La Ressegna Italiana* (Constantinople), July 1913, 111–112 and Aug. 1913, 131; Giuseppe Bevione, *L'Asia Minore e l'Italia* (Turin, 1914), 79–81.

22. See export statistics in the *Annuario Statistico 1915*; "Un Successo dell'Industria Tessile in Turchia," *La Rassegna Italiana* (Constantinople), May–June 1913, 83. The last cited publication was the official organ of the Italian Chamber of Commerce in the Ottoman capital.

23. *Rivista Coloniale*, 30 Apr. 1914, 238; "Informazioni, Curiose manovre austriache," *Rassegna dei lavori pubblici*, 18 Mar. 1913, a note referring to Austria's efforts to acquire a controlling interest in the Ottoman rail lines traversing the Balkan peninsula; *Rivista delle Società Commerciali*, 30 Apr. 1914, 352.

24. This was the lead article in *La Marina mercantile italiana*, 10 Mar. 1913.

4. Industrial Financing and the Banca Commerciale

1. See Ludovico Toeplitz, *Il Banchiere* (Milan, 1963) and Conti, *Dal taccuino*, both based on extensive personal reminiscences. A little more can be gleaned from Joel's papers, concerning which see the following notes.

2. The published material on the Banca Commerciale Italiana is spotty, and much of it stems from the panic over foreign tentacles in Italy that swept the country's public during the First World War. In this connection see Giovanni Preziosi, *La Germania alla conquista dell'Italia* (Florence, 1915), which seems to have drawn some inspiration from Pacelli's Banco di Roma, and F. S. Nitti, *Il*

capitale straniero in Italia (Bari, 1915), a much more serious and balanced work. However, it seems likely that Nitti, too, was somewhat influenced by the Commerciale's enemies, though, in his case, it was more probably the Ansaldo group than the "papal bank" that affected him. His remarks (58) about the failure of Italy to support her "industries" at Constantinople against the combined forces of British and German industrial finance can only refer to Ansaldo's misadventures and resentments. For further material on Nitti's close personal relation to the Perrone brothers, see Alberto Monticone, *Nitti e la grande guerra* (Milan, 1961), a work which, particularly in pp. 200 et seq., throws much light on the Ansaldo executives. Neither these works nor Bava's *Quattro maggiori istituti*, which is later, more impartial, and more factual, really offer anything like a historical reconstruction of the bank's development up to 1915; they amount, at best, to an elaboration or correction of the case *against* the Banca Commerciale, based on suspicion, innuendo, and rivalry, which Bachi soberly and cautiously summed up in his *Italia economica 1914*, 248–249. At least Bachi was free of the conspiracy mania of those years, and when he reported what people were alleging against the Commerciale, he added some objective remarks to the effect that Italian tax law made it hard for foreign banks to operate under their own name in Italy, thus necessitating mixed organizations; that Italian industrial enterprises were often set up with insufficient founding capital; and that they could only get necessary long-term credit by going to big banks that had ostensibly short-term commercial credit funds that they could in fact channel into industry. Hence, Bachi notes, the power and industrial hegemony of a few big banks was really due to the hard realities of Italian economic development.

A reconstruction of the Banca Commerciale's history must take its start from the great bank's archives, with frequent side glances at the published and unpublished materials from Giolitti's correspondence.

When I consulted the Commerciale's archives in 1967, the materials were dispersed between Milan and Parma without a regular organization. However they were scheduled to be classified and arranged in accordance with the standard practices of Italian archives. Therefore I will not cite exact locations, which by now would be out of date and useless, but will give the general character of the documents; their date, category, or correspondence headings; and any other identifying marks.

The archival materials consulted fall into different basic categories. Most important of all, for the general policy lines of the bank, were the minutes (*verbali*) of the central committee (Comitato Centrale) and local committee (Comitato Locale) of the bank's Milan headquarters. The minutes of the central committee (henceforth cited as *Verbali CC*) run from 1901 to 1916; the local committee records (hereafter cited as *Verbali CL*) start in 1908 and go on through the war years. These committees screened all credit applications before sending them up to the full board of directors (Consiglio d'amministrazione), which met infrequently and, in the earlier years, often outside of Italy for the sake of the foreign members. These committees made most of the real decisions of the bank, and their records contain the summary of Joel's policy lines, as well as the substance of the steps that he recommended: in effect, they were the bank's presidium.

The second category is Joel's correspondence, which includes letters from 1907 to 1913. This material falls into dossiers: Rolandi-Ricci, 1908–13; U. Rattazzi, 1907–10, Stringher, 1911; and Volpi, 1912. Included in this collection are two letters regarding the Heraclea mines from Stringher to Senator Mangili, president of the Commerciale, dated 14 and 23 May 1908.

The third category of materials consulted is business correspondence: the letters received or sent by the bank's directors, especially Toeplitz, between 1915 and 1931, as well as some letters relating to North Italian steel firms (Franchi-Gregorini) for the years before the First World War. Much of these letters and memoranda throw a retrospective light on what the Commerciale was doing *before* the war; of special interest is the voluminous and revealing correspondence of Giuseppe Volpi. The Volpi letters, of course, have to be integrated by consulting his correspondence in the Ministry of Foreign Affairs and in the Bank of Italy, which I have done to the best of my ability. In general, I maintain that the aims and mentality of both Volpi and Toeplitz come out during the war, when they were on their own, without Joel, and faced unusual risks, as well as chances to build empires.

My account of the special "deals" that preceded Giolitti's return to power in 1911, the refinancing of the steel trust, and the salvaging *in extremis* of the *Tribuna* draws not only on Joel's letters but also on later material in the postwar business correspondence of his successor, Toeplitz. It was integrated with reference to Giolitti's own letters, both published and unpublished, in the ACS.

3. Rolandi-Ricci to Joel, 8 Mar. 1913, in response to Joel to Rolandi-Ricci, 2 Mar. 1913. The most important single foreign director of the Banca Commerciale was Edouard Noetzlin of the Banque de Paris et des Pays-Bas, who was also head of the "Russian syndicate" that the French banks had formed in order to negotiate with the Russian Ministry of Finance. See Kokovtsov, *Out of My Past*, 42–43, 62–65. It is interesting to note that Noetzlin's basic contact in Russia was the finance minister, not private bankers like Joel. In parallel fashion, Nationalist papers in Italy were financed by industrialists, but in Russia they took their funds from the ministers of state: see ibid., 284–285.

4. The Commerciale's management first reported on Terni's new combine at the Comitato Centrale meeting of 9 May 1903, when Joel described how Terni, Savona, and Elba had formed a link, the latter two firms being now largely owned by Terni, for the purpose of creating a self-sufficient domestic steel industry. The directors on the Comitato Centrale authorized an initial credit of 2 million, with the understanding that the new steel combine would become one of the bank's regular customers; one of the directors, Pollone, who was on the board of Terni, abstained from voting as a matter of course.

Relations with the Terni-Savona group (it should be remembered that Savona was at first headed by Edilio Raggio, a prominent Genoese politician-promoter) soon became tense. Later, in 1903, Joel wished to limit speculation in Terni shares and proposed certain steps which met with the favor of the Milan Stock Exchange's syndics, as well as that of the city's Chamber of Commerce, but he found that the Terni executives themselves would not agree. Consequently, with Noetzlin's approval, he decided to back no more stock issues of Terni: see *Verbali CC*, Nov. 1903. Later, in 1906, the Commerciale was actually raising its credits to the steel and shipbuilding combine, the Terni group and its Orlando associates, from 5.4 million to 8 million lire; in justifying this move, Joel argued that the combine's credits, especially with the government, vastly exceeded its debits. However the bank's management did underline the fact that it was cutting down on the amount of Terni securities that the bank was carrying as margin or collateral: see *Verbali CC*, 19 July 1906.

5. See *Verbali CC*, 11 July 1908, from which it appears that Fiat was reducing its indebtedness to the Commerciale in regular installments: at that date, Fiat owed the bank 240,000 lire out of an initial 600,000. At the time Terni had a debt that had risen during the depression period to 15 million; in addition, the Terni group wanted advances and extensions that would have raised its total indebtedness to 23 million. The central committee allowed an additional indebtedness

of 3 million lire but wanted collateral in securities that the bank management would approve of, as well as a survey of the whole industry, in order to avoid future credits of this scale. In fact, the steel industry was moving toward a trust organization and total refinancing. For Ansaldo's much more modest long-term credits obtained from the Commerciale, see *Verbali CL N. 12*, 7 Apr. 1914; between May 1910 and April 1914 they rose from 2 million to 2.5 million lire. (Nobel-Avigliana, the emanation of Perrone and Clemenceau, received a loan of 200,000 lire in Italy: see *Verbali CL* [Milan], 9 Mar. 1910.) In contrast, the total credits allowed to Terni-Orlando had risen by the autumn of 1912 to 27 million. In December of the same year Ilva had obtained, over and above a previous credit of 3 million, another 1.5 million lire advanced against receipts issued by the war and naval ministries for items already delivered; this was in addition to short-term drafts of 500,000 lire. When some directors raised questions about the bank's tying up capital in this kind of long-term credit—often disguised as advances against future government re-mittances—the bank's management answered that the public was shy of investing in, or lending to, private industries after the crash of 1907, and the bank had to make up for the public's absence: see in particular *Verbali CC*, 4 Oct. 1912.

6. See *Verbali CC*, 3 July 1905, 21 Oct. 1905; *Verbali CL N. 4, (1903–1907)*, 29 Sept. 1905; but with regard to Florio, see especially the Comitato Centrale's meetings during November 1908.

7. See in particular *Verbali CC*, 11 July 1913.

8. After the crisis of 1907, the Italian economy did not succeed in breaking out of the vicious cycle that checked its further growth. Wages, purchasing power, and domestic demand all stayed stationary in a situation of general stagnation. Industrial enterprises had to live by bank loans, constantly renewed, instead of by long-term bond issues, which the Italian public would not buy. This fact helps to explain the patriotic industrialists' resentment against bankers, who were so often foreign. The banks, in their turn, were caught by the need to keep their capital potentially liquid in order to meet the possible demands of their depositors. The banks were, after all, tying up their depositors' money in industries which many of their depositors would not have chosen to sink money into. Both bankers and in-dustrialists were trapped, and willingly or not, the Italian state became the real arbiter of the situation. The Italian state with one hand drained the money market of available capital but with the other hand favored certain industries, mostly con-nected with arms or public transportation, by special orders and financial salvage operations. These decisions on the part of the government indicated to every Italian banker the guidelines he was to follow: little wonder, then, that Joel and Toeplitz advocated the decisions they did in the minutes of the central committee between 1908 and 1915. See Franco Bonelli, "Osservazioni e dati sul finanziamento del-l'industria italiana all'inizio dell secolo XX," in *Annali della Fondazione Luigi Einaudi* (Turin, 1969), II, 257–286.

9. Our account of these matters is based on the correspondence of Joel with U. Rattazzi and with Rolandi-Ricci. In the Rolandi-Ricci letters there is a most curious note from Rolandi-Ricci dated 21 Feb. 1907, on Terni's executive stationery, in which it appeared that the Terni management group, especially Odero, were very worried about the possibility that the Parisi bank of Genoa might try to take over Terni at the next stockholders' meeting. The Parisis were connected by marriage, and apparently by business interests, to the Perrone brothers, as Giolitti later established: see *Dalle carte di Giolitti*, III, 287. Rolandi-Ricci wanted the Commerciale to support him and the Orlando-Odero group that controlled Terni; to judge from the sequel, Parisi's surprise attack never materialized. In the cited letter, Rolandi-Ricci mentions the possibility of this "surprise," linking

Parisi to Centurini. Alessandro Centurini was a Roman financier of known clerical associations; however, there is no real evidence, at this point or later, of any alliance between Genoa and Rome against the Commerciale, though Rolandi-Ricci's note is tantalizing.

10. Fenoglio dealt with the Ferraris group, which included the Terni combine, Breda, Fiat motors, and most of North Italy's modern machine shops. Dante Ferraris had a 32 million lire order from the government. See *Verbali CL*, 10 Dec. 1912. The dealings with Whitehead torpedoes, which had one branch corporation at Fiume and another at Naples, appear in ibid., 17 Apr. 1914. For Cantieri Riuniti, see *Verbali CC*, 11 July 1913.

11. Concerning the Commerciale's French ally, see Robert Aron, *Une grande banque d'affaires: La Banque de Paris et des Pays-Bas* (Paris, 1959). The *Verbali CC* during 1908 and 1909 are full of reports on the Franco-Italian ventures in São Paulo and Tunisia: the Commerciale employed in Brazil a Swiss director named Dapples, with good results. During the boom years he had kept away from the small Italian firms in Latin America: consequently the bank's affiliate in Brazil did not suffer from the crash of 1907.

As the fatal year 1914 drew nearer, the bank's operations abroad grew, but they did not necessarily coincide with any lines of political or military expansion. For example, the Comitato Locale in the course of 1909 allowed credits to a Savona engineering firm, Ottorino e Nicola Zanelli, that was developing mines in Morocco. More important was the opening of a branch in London with two directors: one was an Italian named Carmine with experience in that city, and the other, Siegfried Bieber, who had a background with the Credit Lyonnais and the Diskontogesellschaft. The London branch had a big Italian customer, Pirelli, whose British affiliate had debits and drafts of 60,000 pounds (1.5 million lire) outstanding there. These facts suggest that much of the bank's operations abroad were stimulated by the expansive, world-girdling character of modern Italian industry, that they were a consequence of the way in which modern productive systems work and grow: see *Verbali CC*, 4 Oct. 1912.

12. *Verbali CC*, 9 Jan. 1904. According to an updated memorandum in the BCI Archives file "Impegni Disponibilità dell'Estero" headed "Annotazioni sulle principali variazioni inerenti al lavoro straordinario della Banca negli esercizi seguenti," which is a list of losses suffered by the Commerciale, entered as *svalutazioni* on the bank's yearly balances, we find that the Commerciale listed 1,142,000 lire worth of equity in the Baghdad railway as a loss in the balance of 1917. This memorandum (hereafter cited as "Annotazioni"), gives a list of losses written off by the bank during the First World War. Given the enormous sums invested in the Baghdad line, the Italian losses were slight and show how little Italian capital was ever involved. The question came up over and over again. In 1907 and 1908 the Germans took up the matter with the Italian foreign ministry. As the line spread from Anatolia to Syria and Mesopotamia, the Germans, eager for new capital, offered to name an Italian director in a reorganized executive. Five hundred million francs were needed, of which Italian capitalists were to lay out between 30 and 60 million, with the further understanding that Italian-held shares would not be sold to third parties. The Italian foreign ministry, then headed by Tittoni, thought that Italy should go in only on condition that the Baghdad line became truly international, with all great powers sharing in funding and management. This seemed momentarily possible, but it soon became clear that the Germans did not wish any such internationalization. They preferred to go slowly, financing the line stage by stage without recourse to massive foreign loans or refinancing. Of course, when the line reached the Persian Gulf, the Germans, so

the Italian foreign ministry thought, would come to terms with Britain, since British engineers had prepared plans for large-scale river control and land reclamation in the Tigris-Euphrates delta area. At any rate, short of thoroughgoing internationalization, there was no reason for Italy to take any political interest in the way the Baghdad railway was being financed. Tittoni was more interested in an understanding with the Deutsche Bank over Albanian-Macedonian rail lines, in which Italy could go halves with the Germans. See Archivio Esteri (hereafter cited as AE), Archivio Riservato, 1909, Casella 4, Fascicolo 176. What is the point of all this? That Italian capital entered into massive long-term investments in the eastern Mediterranean only when it had political or military underpinning from Rome.

13. Lanino, *La nuova Italia*, III, 99; II, 67 et seq.; F. Carli, "L'indipendenza economica dell'Italia e le industrie meccaniche e chimiche," *Rivista delle Società Commerciali*, Sept. 1915, 761–769 (the quotation is from p. 767); Lanino, *La nuova Italia*, II, 71.

14. See M. Alberti, "I piu' recenti aspetti del capitalismo moderno; le società di finanziamento e partecipazione," *Rivista delle Società Commerciali*, Aug. 1914, 113 et seq.

15. See *Il Sole*, 18 Apr. 1914. In fact, electrical companies in Italy were underpinned by Austrian, Hungarian, and Swiss investing firms, as well as by German firms. See *Verbali CC*, 24 Feb. 1907 and 28 Feb. 1910: the Swiss holding companies became especially important later on.

16. Lanino, *La nuova Italia*, II, 70–77.

17. The Mannesmann firm aimed at filling all domestic needs and eventually entering foreign markets; its first principal customers were the state rail system and the navy. See *Il Sole*, 9 Jan. and 14 Feb. 1914. Concerning the firm's italianization during the War, an operation masterminded by Toeplitz, see the correspondence between Toeplitz, Ghisalberti, and Attilio Franchi of Brescia in the BCI Archives, correspondence files headed "Franchi-Griffin": the principal letter from Franchi to Toeplitz is dated 1 Aug. 1917. The Officine meccaniche di Saronno, also set up before the War in northern Italy, belonged to the Maschinenfabrik of Esslingen, and its staff was partly German. Like Mannesmann, its principal customers were the state railroads and the navy, since it specialized in heavy metal parts and locomotives. It, too, was italianized during the War through the Banca Commerciale: see *Verbali CC*, 20 Nov. 1916. Toeplitz got special recognition and reward (2,000 shares at par value) for arranging the purchase of Mannesmann on behalf of the Franchi-Gregorini steel firm: *Verbali CC*, 12 Oct. 1917. What interests us here is the strategic character of these firms. They were highly specialized, set up by parent concerns in Germany to control a specific foreign market of a technologically advanced sort. This kind of operation attracted much less public attention than dumping did and aroused much less resentment.

18. See *Verbali CL*, 26 Sept. 1908 and 23 Mar. 1910.

19. The Commerciale archives have two files dealing with the Merkurgewerkschaft and Monte Amiata; the correspondence in them runs from 1919 to 1926 and includes an interesting effort by the Commerciale executive and mining engineer B. Nogara to get the Amiata corporation to take an interest in Anatolian mining during the years 1920–22. In the postwar "Annotazioni," the Commerciale figured that it had lost 900,000 lire through its shares of the Merkurgewerkschaft but had gained, in recompense, 2,405,000 lire through acquisition of the Monte Amiata mines.

20. See Henry Wickham Steed, *Through Thirty Years* (Garden City, 1925), 353. This book is a mine of information about the sinuous and murky world of pre–First World War journalism, especially in its international sides. When one

thinks of the oceans of ink that have been spilled over the arms makers, merchants of death, and so on, one sees how the newshawks have been slighted. Many of them were at least as sinister as Maxim, Zaharoff, and others, and their responsibility for the European tragedy is greater.

21. See *Dalle carte di Giolitti.* See in particular vol. II, 375 and 430 for Joel's letters to Giolitti on the occasion of his talk with Chancellor Bülow and on his collaboration with Giolitti in working out the conversion of the Italian public debt. These letters were sent 22 Apr. 1905 and 29 June 1906.

The rift between the Giolitti government and the Banca Commerciale over the organization of subsidized shipping lines presents some real problems. The minutes of the Banca Commerciale's committees, on which I have usually relied, are un-accustomedly reticent on this delicate matter. They contain, to be sure, plenty of information on the way in which the Commerciale's management acquired German-owned shipping lines, consolidated Genoese and Palermitan shipping lines, and made every effort to centralize and coordinate the Italian merchant marine, but there is nothing about the main question of government subsidies: see *Verbali CC,* 13 July 1905 and 21 Oct. 1905. The complex arrangements made to keep Ignazio Florio's 11 million lire in Navigazione Generale shares from passing into public ownership are explained in the November 1908 meetings of the Comitato Centrale. Senator Erasmo Piaggio resigned from the directorship of the Banca Commerciale 19 March 1909; President Mangili, announcing the fact ten days later, simply stated that Piaggio's reasons for quitting were of such a nature that the president did not think he should insist on Piaggio's remaining; *Verbali CC,* 29 Mar. 1909.

We have filled in this lacuna by using Giolitti's published correspondence, which is quite clear, and Senator Erasmo Piaggio, *Lo Stato e le convenzioni marittime* (Genoa, 1910). It appears that Joel operated in this matter with Federico Weil, the bank management's specialist in shipping and that Weil acted crudely: see Rolandi-Ricci to Joel, 16 Nov. 1909. The Piaggio interests finally had their revenge, for they eventually got the Cantieri Riuniti away from Orlando-Odero-Terni and installed a new management there: see Rolandi-Ricci to Joel, 21 Jan. 1913, in which he complains on behalf of the old Terni management that the Commerciale had bypassed Terni altogether, leaving Terni with 20,000 shares in the Cantieri Riuniti, a minority interest, while selling to Piaggio a controlling interest through other shares bought by Toeplitz in Turin; was this any way to treat old friends? In fact, Rolandi-Ricci's letter shows that Piaggio—and Fiat, which took over the shipyard at Muggiano at the same time—had better industrial talents than the Terni group, now supplanted, and that the Commerciale realistically recognized this fact. On 8 March 1913 Rolandi-Ricci wrote Joel again, to complain about the high-handed way in which Fiat was reorganizing the Muggiano yards. In reality the Commerciale in 1913 had managed to heal the old breaches with Piaggio, just as it had ceased underestimating Fiat.

The main thread of the *Tribuna*'s refinancing can be picked up through a close reading of Giolitti's correspondence in its published form. I have integrated these sources by reference to an unpublished letter from Rattazzi to Giolitti 28 Oct. 1910; Rolandi-Ricci to Giolitti, 19 Oct. 1910; and Joel to Giolitti (announcing that he had been awarded Italian citizenship), 15 Aug. 1910; see ACS, "Carte Giolitti," Fondo Cavour, Scatola 7, Fascicolo 20, Sottofascicoli 3 and 4, as well as Fascicolo 21, Sottofascicolo 8. My other principal source is Joel's correspondence in the Commerciale Archives, especially with Rattazzi and Rolandi-Ricci: this material includes some letters that passed between Giolitti and Rattazzi and were sent by the latter to Joel for his information. Included in the Joel correspondence is a typewritten memorandum, unsigned and undated, giving the 1910 ownership of *La*

Tribuna, together with Maraini's proposed plan for new ownership and some hand-written notes.

Concerning the personality and background of Camillo Garroni, I was able to consult the marquis's *fascicolo personale*, kept in the ACS. My information on Olindo Malagodi's career and relations with the Commerciale comes, in large part, from the 1923 correspondence between him and Fenoglio and Toeplitz in the Commerciale archives. The character and connections of Andrea Torre appear vividly in the correspondence (with Wickham Steed and others) that is kept in ACS, "Carte Andrea Torre," Busta 1, Fascicolo 4. Of special retrospective interest is a letter from the engineer Pietro Lanino, on Comitato di difesa interna stationery, undated but obviously of 1917 or 1918. Lanino warns Torre that by paying its arms suppliers so tardily, the government is driving Italian industry into the waiting arms of the Banca Commerciale; Lanino reminds Torre of the bank's origins and its remaining close ties to Giolitti. Lanino was not only a Nationalist industrial expert but also, at that moment, an active home-front vigilante.

22. Rolandi-Ricci to Joel, 16 Jan. 1910; and telegram, Rolandi-Ricci to Joel in Berlin, 23 Mar. 1910. In January 1910 Rolandi-Ricci was working to put together a new shipping combine to operate the government's subsidized lines and was even feeling his way toward a reconciliation with Senator Erasmo Piaggio, whose wrathful denunciations of shipping monopolies had finally recoiled on his own head. Piaggio, had, after all, been one of the principal executives of the Navigazione Generale from 1896 to 1903, during which years, he now claimed, there had been some misleading items in the line's corporate balance. Rolandi-Ricci held that by dragging things into the open, Piaggio had made a false move, putting himself in the wrong. As an interest-broker, Rolandi-Ricci was concerned with reaching an equitable settlement for all concerned, and he moved from the shipping combine to the *Tribuna* refinancing, the steel-trust salvage, and the question of longer credit terms for Terni, all with the same air of mixed deference and self-assurance.

23. See AE Archivio Gabinetto, 1911, Titolo III, Fascicolo 408, "Turchia, posizione generale 1910–1914," dispatch from Italian embassy to Di San Giuliano, 13 Mar. 1911. The Italian embassy thought Ansaldo unreasonable. The memoranda and promotional ideas emanating from the Perrone brothers are all to be found in this section of the AE, and they shed much light on the early, high-vaulting ambitions of the Ansaldo executives years before the First World War made them into Italian public figures.

24. See *Verbali CL*, 3 Jan. 1911, and 14 Feb. 1911. The Banca Cattolica S. Liberale of Treviso, on the latter date, received a loan from the Commerciale secured by Austro-Hungarian state bonds *in toto*; the sum involved was half a million. On 28 April 1911 the Associazione nazionale per soccorrere i missionari of Turin got the same sum without putting up security; this credit, to be used for operations in China, was annulled 26 September 1911. The Banca Cattolica Vicentina was the only Catholic institution that regularly recurred to the Commerciale. All of these relations with the Catholic economic world were trivial.

On the origins of the Banco di Roma, see Caracciolo, *Roma capitale*, which is full of material about Catholic economic enterprises, clerical notables like Pacelli and R. Tittoni, and information about the links between the Catholic capitalist world and the larger Italian institutions. Especially interesting are the references to Marco Besso (171, 264), who was a director of the Banca Commerciale, an old associate of V. S. Breda in the Società Veneta, and at the same time director of one of the biggest Roman realestate companies, together with Romolo Tittoni. In the person of this Jewish financier, we find a linkage of interests and influence which should be kept in mind even in discussions of rivalries between banking groups: the balance between competition and cooperation was always delicate. See also Bava, *Quattro maggiori istituti*, 113–121 and Volpe, *Italia moderna*, III, 315–440, which has some important details concerning the Banco di Roma in Libya. See also *Annuario Navale 1911*, 318 for the shipping subsidies collected by the Banco di Roma from 1910 on. Chiesa, *Discorsi*, 184–185 offers a muckraker's view of the Banco di Roma, but see also Bachi, *Italia economica 1914*, 60–62; *Il Sole*, 4 Apr. 1914; *Rassegna dei lavori pubblici*, 1 Apr. 1913, 212–213; and, most caustic of all, Alberto De'Stefani, *Baraonda bancaria* (Milan, 1960), 19–20. Lodi, *Venticinque anni*, 152 reports unfavorably on Pacelli's policies in Libya, and Martini, *Diario 1914–1918*, 229, 238, 539, gives some generally unsavory details on the tangled relations between Pacelli, the khedive of Egypt, and the Italian government. All of my account later in this chapter is based on the foregoing materials, but my explanation of Salandra's moves toward settling the dispute between the government and Pacelli is drawn from the papers in ACS Fondo Salandra, Scatola 8, Fascicolo 63, which contain letters and memoranda, mostly from the Italian foreign ministry, concerning the Banco di Roma.

25. See *Il Sole*, 8 May 1914, 1.

26. See Volpe, *Italia moderna*, III, 322. It seems that the project of a united front of Italian banks and industries with the goal of penetrating the Ottoman Empire first sprang in early 1909 from the Perrone brothers; but it appears again in 1910, this time from the foreign minister himself, who wanted to join together the Società Commerciale d'Oriente and the Banco di Roma. This was connected with Pacelli's plan, during the same year, to raise his bank's capital from 80 to 100 million lire, for which he wished the Bank of Italy's backing. Who was dragging his feet? First of all, the Bank of Italy's general manager, Bonaldo Stringher, whose reluctance to move, to call meetings, to put pressure on the North Italian banking powers was quite clear to the ministry of foreign affairs. Second, in all probabiliy, Joel and Volpi, whose correspondence of 1912 shows anything but esteem for Pacelli's business methods: Joel on 30 July 1912 wrote sarcastically to Volpi about Pacelli's "artistic" style in his dealings. However, one of the Commerciale's big textile customers, Silvio Crespi, was much interested in setting up an all-Italian bank in the Ottoman Empire. See the already cited papers in the AE concerning Ansaldo in Turkey, as well as AE Archivio di Gabinetto, 1910, Titolo III, Casella 21, Fascicolo 130.

27. AE, Archivio Gabinetto, 1911, Titolo III, Casella 22, Fascicolo 184.

28. *Verbali CL*, 3 Oct. 1911.

29. The correspondence between Stringher and Joel on this painful subject to be found in Joel's papers in the Commerciale's archives in Milan, runs from October through December 1911. In Stringher's letter to Joel, 15 Oct. 1911, the Bank of Italy's manager warns the Commerciale against setting up some sort of counter-altar (as he puts it) to the Banco di Roma in Libya, since the latter institution had the merit of being a pioneer in that zone. On 17 October Joel assured Stringher that he would act in unison with the Banco di Roma, as he had with regard to Constantinople, a remark which suggests that just before the Libyan War some sort of agreement had finally come out of the three years of desultory discussion. This bears out the information that the Ottoman Embassy at Rome wired to Constantinople on 18 March 1911 concerning a merger beween the Società Commerciale d'Oriente and the Banco di Roma. See n. 7, chap. 8. The understanding between the two banks, limited and precarious in any case, did not survive the Libyan War, and it left no trace in most records or sources.

30. *Rassegna dei lavori pubblici*, 1 Apr. 1913, 212. For the stockholders' meeting of the next year, see *Il Sole*, 4 Apr. 1914.

31. See *Rivista italiana di ragioneria*, 30 Apr. 1913, 145–152; *Atti dell'XI Congresso*; statement of the Navigazione Generale directors denying the Syndicalists' accusation of German control, *Il Sole*, 23 Jan. 1914, 3. The *Rassegna* went so far as to accuse the foreign-dominated banks of subsidizing socialists and radicals, a charge taken up again by the Perrones after the war.

32. The Russians were pleased to learn that Andre Luquet, *Directeur du Mouvement des Fonds* at the French ministry of finance, was fighting staunchly against "cosmopolitanism" in the Parisian banking world: see the letter from the Russian chargé d'affairs to his foreign minister, 9 Oct. 1913, in Marchand, *Un livre noir*, II, 158.

33. French authorities were always worried about Italian big business. France's ambassador at Rome, Barrère, called Joel a "German agent," while Cambon at Paris kept an eye on Joel's relations with Gwinner of the Deutsche Bank. The French military attachés at Rome, anxious to have Deport and the Schneider-Creusot interests edge out Krupp in supplying Italy with artillery models, considered Ansaldo a firm ally, suspected Terni of subcontracting to Krupp; and were convinced that the Banca Commerciale, with all its tentacles in the shipping and steel combines, was working in the interests of Germany. Early in 1914 Lieutenant Colonel de Gondrecourt, acquainted with Italian business journals, thought that French bankers and industrialists, with their many holdings in the Italian banks that were later to join in the Sconto, had a good chance of dislodging Germany from its key economic positions in the peninsula. Italian nationalism could serve French political interests in the long run. See Ministère des Affaires Etrangères, *Documents Diplomatiques Français (1871–1914)* (hereafter cited as *DDF*) (Paris, 1929), 2e Série, X, 101 (dispatch by Barrère, Rome, 24 May 1906); ibid., XII, 481 (letter by Lt. Col. Jullian, 5 Oct. 1909); and ibid., 3e Série, III, 283–284 (dispatch by Cambon, Berlin, 22 July 1912); ibid., X, 150–158 (letter by Lt. Col. de Gondrecourt, Rome, 9 Apr. 1914).

5. Industrial Labor and Management Conflicts

1. *Il Metallurgico* (Turin), 1 May 1914.

2. "La nostra Federazione nel 1913," *Il Metallurgico*, 15 June 1914. In the same labor paper, 30 July 1914, 3, a little column quoted Veblen on the criminality and brutality of decaying capitalist classes.

3. See Spriano, *Socialismo e classe operaia*, which contains a complete account of these events.

4. I have followed De Felice, *Mussolini il rivoluzionario*, 162–176 and especially, Yvon De Begnac's substantial biography of Corridoni, *L'Arcangelo sindacalista* (Milan: Mondadori, 1943), which contains in its central portions a detailed account of the labor troubles at Milan, the analytic remarks of the deputy Eugenio Chiesa, and the tactics followed by syndicalists, reformists, and industrial management groups; Chiesa is cited *in extenso*, 379–382.

5. I have based my account on *Il Metallurgico*, organ of the reformist FIOM, for general remarks. Specifically, I have discussed the 1911 strikes with reference to *Il Metallurgico*, 8 July and 9 Aug. 1911, with Buozzi's remarks; and *La Fiamma, Organo della federazione socialista del Collegio di Volterra*, a weekly paper that provides a running account of the strike at Elba-Piombino between June and December 1911.

6. Chiesa, *Discorsi*, 207.

7. Debate between the reformist Colombino and the revolutionary syndicalist Zocchi, *Il Metallurgico*, 28 Feb. 1912, 4.

8. We have relied on the detailed reporting of Terni's local labor paper, *La Turbina, Giornale settimanale delle sezione socialista "Luigi Riccardi," Organa della federazione socialista umbra*. This was an unusually well-put-together journal, which provided, in addition to labor news and political commentaries, a running critique of the industrial operations of Terni, often supplementing or correcting the reporting of Italian business and trade papers. A student of the Italian steel industry cannot ignore *La Turbina*, the reporting of which sheds so much light on the technical-managerial failures of Terni, its fear of Ansaldo's competition, and its political wire-pulling.

9. *La Turbina*, 16 Aug. and 6 Sept. 1913.

10. In addition to the columns of *Rivista marittima and La Mercantile*, see also the information in Bachi, *L'Italia economica 1914*; our principal source is G. Giulietti, *Pax Mundi* (Naples, 1945), 27–61, a firsthand account by one of the chief protagonists in the whole maritime labor dispute, who offers documents as well as reminiscences.

11. See in particular Bachi, *L'Italia economica 1913*, 249–250.

6. Italy's Drive to the East

1. See E. M. Earle, *Turkey, the Great Powers and the Baghdad Railway* (New York, 1923), and Donald C. Blaisdell, *European Financial Control in the Ottoman Empire* (New York, 1929).

2. See dispatch, Ambassador Imperiali to Tittoni, Constantinople, 18 Feb. 1907, AE, Archivio Riservato, 1909, Casella 3, Fascicolo 135.

3. See an Italian engineer's private report, transmitted to Tittoni in August 1908 by the Italian legation at Bucharest, ibid., Casella 1, fascicolo 112.

4. Telegram, Cucchi to Tittoni, Sofia, 18 Feb. 1908, ibid., Fascicolo 106.

5. Report in AE, Archivio Gabinetto, 1911, Titolo III, Casella 22, Fascicolo 173; ibid., 1913–14, Titolo III, Casella 30, Fascicolo 408, "Turchia, posizione generale."

6. Quoted in *Rivista Coloniale*, 30 Apr. 1914, 238.

7. AE, Archivio Gabinetto, 1911, Titolo III, Casella 22, Fascicolo 179, "Turchia, Documenti riservati."

8. Because of his naval background, Vannutelli took a special interest in the Heraclea-Zongulzak coal mines on the Black Sea coast of Turkey. Forty percent of all the coal produced there was used by Italian shipping lines. See L. Vannutelli, *In Anatolia* (Rome, 1905); and Paolo Revelli, *L'Italia e il mar di Levante* (Milan, 1917), 198–200.

9. Gino Damerini, *D'Annunzio e Venezia* (Milan-Verona, 1943).

10. Armondo Odenigo, *Piero Foscari, una vita esemplare* (Rocca San Casciano, 1959); see also our previous citations from the BCI Archives.

11. See Toeplitz, *Il Banchiere*. Concerning the references to Volpi, through the personal courtesy of Professor R. De Felice, I was able to consult a biography of Volpi in a manuscript by Oreste Mosca, which supplemented Oreste Mosca, *Volpi di Misurata* (Rome, 1928), as well as the commemorative volume, Vittorio Cini et al., *Giuseppe Volpi, Ricordi e testimonianze. A cura della Associazione degli industriali*

nel 40° anniversario di Porto Marghera e del Rotary Club di Venezia nel 35° anniversario della sua fondazione (Venice, 1959). See also Lodi, *Venticinque anni*, 157.

12. These interchanges were in the BCI Archives in Parma, Cassa 548, Raccolta 521.

13. See the company historical work, *Impianti della Società Adriatica di Elettricità, Pubblicazione edita in occasione del cinquantenario della società 1905–1955* (Venice, 1956), as well as *Verbali CC*, 24 Feb. 1907. See also the *SADE* statement in *Rivista delle Società Commerciali, 1912, Supplemento, Bilanci*, with special attention to the makeup of the directorate.

14. The Baldacci reports constitute a sort of counter-altar to the eulogistic writings of Oreste Mosca, and it is hard at this distance to assess either with perfect assurance. To form some idea of Antonio Baldacci's character as a scholar and writer, see the collection, A. Baldacci, *Scritti adriatici* (Bologna, 1943). Baldacci, one of Italy's few Balkan specialists, felt keenly his country's inferiority to Austria in this field. However, one is tempted to question his capacity for critical and objective writing when (in 1919, to be sure) he asserts the authenticity of Abraham Lincoln's letter to Macedonio Melloni concerning Italy's rights in Dalmatia. At any rate, his criticisms of Volpi's Balkan undertakings do turn up in print, as well as in the poison-pen letters to Rome: see his *Scritti adriatici*, 364–374. His reports to the foreign ministry at Rome are in AE, Archivio Riservato (Gabinetto del Ministro), 1910, Titolo III, Fascicolo 136.

15. See Ministero AIC., *Bolettino ufficiale della S.p.A.*, Anno XXI, Fascicolo XXXIV (20 Aug. 1903). The "Regia cointeressata dei tabacchi del Montenegro" was officially constituted on 15 July 1903, At Venice. By the terms of the contract with the Principality of Montenegro, the Italian concession-holders had the right to take a 5 percent interest on both capital invested and credits advanced to local tobacco growers before any profits were divided. The remaining proceeds would be divided between the Montenegrin government and the Italians, with the government taking 80 percent of the profits within the principality and the Italians, 80 percent of the export profits. See *Regolamento di amministrazione e contabilità del Monopolio dei Tabacchi nel Principato di Montenegro* (Venice, 1906).

16. Volpi appears to have overestimated the mineral wealth of the lower Adriatic coastal areas. He also thought that the Drina, as it debouched from Lake Ochrida, offered remarkable hydroelectric possibilities. See the reminiscences about him in Francesco Jacomoni di San Savino, *La political dell'Italia in Albania* (Rocca San Casciano, 1965), 25–30. Jacomoni is the son of a high officer of the Banco di Roma.

17. See the brochure by Vico Mantegazza, *Compagnia di Antivari* (Milan, 1910), describing in detail the founding, financial backing, and accomplishments of the firm.

18. The ministerial correspondence, as well as drafts of the contract between the Antivari Company and the Italian state, were copied four years later, when the whole matter came up for revision, and they are in AE, Gabinetto Archivio Riservato 1913, Titolo III, Fascicolo 334.

19. My account of the Antivari Company is drawn, for the most part, from the reports written by the Commerciale staff after the war, BCI Archives, Milan, Cassa 3 (unarranged). The *Verbali CL*, 1 Oct. 1912, register an unsecured credit of 20,000 lire to Count Piero Foscari, as administrator of his wife's properties. It is clear from the above cited reports that Foscari was useful to the Antivari Company in other respects, too, particularly through his contacts with Admiral Bettolo and the naval ministry at Rome.

20. In Trieste, where an Italian middle class was struggling to maintain the city's Italian nationality, there were no fewer than nine Slavic banks operating.

Writing in *L'Economista d'Italia* (a Roman business daily) 10 Apr. 1913, the Triestine patriot and economics expert Mario Alberti urged Italian businessmen dealing with Austria-Hungary to use Trieste as a channel and never to turn to Slavic banks or lawyers. If they had to use non-Italians, he said, let them use the services of the neutral Viennese Jewish banks rather than the Czech-Croat-Slovene financial combines. During these years Alberti and other Italian patriots of the Venezia Giulia felt that the empire was becoming Slavized because of universal suffrage. See Alberti, *L'Irredentismo senza romanticismi* (Como, 1936), especially 288 et seq.

21. See Ingegnere Giacomo Buonuomo, *La ferrovia transbalcanica italiana* (Naples, 1924). There was a stream of articles and reports in the Italian business press—as well as in other journals—concerning these railway projects and Italy's future leadership in the Balkans. See especially "Informazioni," *Rassegna dei lavori pubblici*, 4 Mar. 1913, 152; and "Cronache delle provincie," ibid., 30 June 1914, 427 for the resolution of the Venetian Chamber of Commerce; Vico Mantegazza, *Questioni di politica estera, Anno VIII (1913)* (Milan, 1914), 8–9 and 292–293; a little earlier one of the Foscari group's experts, Battista Pellegrini, wrote a tract, *Verso la guerra? Il dissidio fra l'Italia e l'Austria* (Rome, 1906), in which much space was devoted to railroad questions and the persistent "legitimate" interests of Italian business in the Balkans; see especially the resolutions of the Congresso dei commercianti italiani, a convention held at Milan 19 May 1906, concerning harbor and rail construction on the Albanian Adriatic coast. When the great powers decided that Serbia might have a neutralized corridor to the sea through Albania, which would thus reopen the whole railway-harbor issue, Milanese businessmen told Di San Giuliano that the Balkans were Italy's natural commercial outlet and urged him to work for a concrete and satisfactory outcome. Edoardo Scarfoglio spelled the matter out in an interview granted to the *Gaulois* of Paris: Italy's aim in these negotiations should be the construction of a rail system linking the Adriatic harbors of Albania with the Balkan hinterland. See *La Nazione Albanese* (Rome), 15 May 1914. For a broader view of Italy's prospects in the Balkan peninsula, see A. Caroncini, "L'Italia e la futura economica balcanica," *Rivista delle Società Commerciali*, June 1913, 285 et seq.

22. My account of the diplomatic background of the trans-Balkan railway is drawn from the correspondence in AE, Archivio Riservato, 1908, Titolo III, Casella 1, Fascicoli 106–112. These documents, awaiting eventual publication, cover the months January through July 1908; they include not only the letters and dispatches passing between the foreign minister and the Italian embassies, but also the exchanges between Tittoni and Stringher. In Fascicolo 112, Dossier 2 there is a memorandum in French, evidently drawn up by a Serbian official in 1906, setting out the possibilities of Serbia's forests and mines. According to this prospectus, a modern rail line would allow goods and passengers to move in only eleven hours from the Rumanian frontier to the Adriatic coast. Fascicolo 112 also contains long telegrams from Tittoni to the Italian embassies at Berlin and Constantinople, 20 and 23 Mar. 1908, giving the whole background of the rail project from 1893 on.

23. See Imperiali's report to Tittoni, 17 Mar. 1908, ibid.

24. See *Verbali CL*, 10 Dec. 1912, concerning Joel's project to reorganize and re-finance Volpi's original company. Among the Joel papers there are three letters from Stringher to Senator Mangili, president of the Banca Commerciale; these letters, dated 14 May 1908, 23 May 1908, and 25 May 1908, fill out the picture given in Stringher's letter to Tittoni of 27 May 1908 in AE, Archivio Riservato, Titolo III, Casella 1, Fascicolo 112. Evidently Volpi hoped to link a satisfactory settlement of his claims on Heraclea to a general agreement concerning the future Balkan rail

line. As recompense for yielding in Anatolia, he and Paganini hoped to be dealt into the forthcoming rail syndicate; it cannot be said that the Bank of Italy's manager gave them any encouragement. Evidently he thought they were lucky to get any compensation at all from the obdurate French.

25. Volpi got in touch with the Italian government in the best possible way. Joel appealed to Rattazzi to champion Volpi's interests, and Rattazzi, of course, had direct access to Giolitti. It turned out that Volpi and Joel had to tread carefully. Rattazzi pointed out to Joel that the Commerciale was disliked by France because of the bank's German background. The government, it turned out, could give some help to Volpi's Montenegrin corporation, but only in the modest form of a postal subsidy. Italy had to avoid any appearance of preparing a naval base on the opposite shore of the Adriatic. In addition to all this, Stringher, not Joel or Volpi, had to head any future Italian rail syndicate in the Balkans, since the Italian government was putting itself behind the venture. See BCI Archives, Joel Papers, Joel to Rattazzi, 2 Mar. 1908; Rattazzi to Joel, 11 Mar. 1908; Rattazzi to Joel, 17 May 1908; and Joel to Rattazzi, 22 July 1908.

26. This account of the final railroad pacts is drawn from the dispatches that passed between Tittoni and Stringher April–July 1908, as well as from the foreign minister's correspondence with the Italian embassies. All of this material, together with the exchange between Tittoni and the Italian legation at Belgrade concerning Vesnic, is in AE, Archivio Riservato, Titolo III, Casella 1, Fascicolo 112.

27. This narrative of the trans-Balkan rail project as it unfolded between 1908 and 1914 follows the collection of reports, maps, letters, and memoranda kept in the Bank of Italy archives in a dossier headed "Ferrovia Danubio-Adriatico." This file includes, apparently, every paper connected with the project that crossed Stringher's desk during his tenure at the Bank of Italy. In addition it contains the lively correspondence of Giuseppe Volpi, cited in the succeeding pages, as well as the minutes of meetings that Stringher chaired. The latter tell us much about the Italian industrialists' point of view. The dossier has no archival classification or subdivisions.

28. For this deal among Ghisleri, Volpi, and the German rail concern, see *Verbali CL*, 21 Dec. 1909.

29. See preceding notes on the Joel-Rattazzi letters of 1908, with the Mangili correspondence.

30. These letters are in the above-mentioned dossier in the Bank of Italy's archives.

31. These reports are in AE, Archivio Riservato, Titolo III, Cassella 1, Fascicolo 112; see especially Stringher to Tittoni, 7 July 1908.

32. This account is based on Volpi's letters to Stringher, which run from 1908 to 1911; they are in the previously cited dossier in the Bank of Italy's archives. Theodoli represented the Italian holders of Ottoman bonds, most of whom appear to have been Roman. The Theodoli family was prominent in the city's "black" social and financial elite: see Caracciolo, *Roma capitale*, 46, 128, 183.

33. See the memoranda in AE, Archivio Gabinetto, 1911, Titolo III, Casella 22, Fascicoli 173 and 182; also ibid., 1910, Titolo III, Casella 21, Fascicolo 130.

34. See references to the AE documents on Ansaldo at Constantinople in the notes to chap. 4. These foreign ministry documents, mostly letters received by Primo Levi allowed me to reconstruct the negotiations of 1908–11 concerning an Italian industrial offensive at Constantinople; of special interest is the correspondence between Levi and the lawyer Carlo Scotti, who was in contact with Joel and Volpi.

35. See the archival material cited in the notes to chap. 3.

7. On the Eve of the War

1. See *La Preparazione*, 21 Dec. 1911. Concerning possible Italian atrocities against the Arab snipers, see ibid., 14 Dec. 1911. Barone was much superior in mind to most Nationalists. It is easy to dismiss Federzoni or Corradini as lower middle-class politicians with a flair for rhetoric and others as sufferers from political or literary hallucinations. Barone, though, offers a real intellectual challenge. The fact that a man of his clear and penetrating brain worked with the Nationalists gives us some clue about how that movement developed a consistent and realistic doctrinal thrust. Among the Nationalist leaders, only Rocco comes close to Barone in mental clarity. While Rocco elaborated a politico-historical theory of Nationalism, Barone offered a cogent economic doctrine of what he called "syndicates" as the highest stage of capitalistic production. Briefly, Barone argues that modern industries, with their high initial costs, have reached the stage in which coalitions, mergers, and long-range planning have superseded the old systems of free competition: given modern methods of production, "syndicates" benefit the consuming public as well as the national economy as a whole, because in a system of free competition the losers' sacrifice of capital and assets is passed on to a broader public, with unpredictable evils. Rationally planned mass production will so reduce costs that the public, even while paying an extra tribute to the syndicate, will still be able to buy at a price lower than what would prevail in a situation of unlimited competition, with all the disadvantages that go with undersized plants, sudden market fluctuations, and other concomitants of the old free-enterprise anarchy. And through lowering production costs, rationally managed industrial syndicates can pay their workers better than they could in a situation of cutthroat competition; and hence they can resist unreasonable union demands. These theoretical constructions, however far they might have been from the often inefficient realities, fitted perfectly the Italian business mentality at its higher levels. In the years just before the First World War, Italian industrialists and capitalistic farmers were forming all kinds of lobbying groups, marketing syndicates, and leagues of resistance to labor unions. The convergence between Italian business practices and Nationalist theory was clear. See Enrico Barone, *Principi di economia politica*, 4th ed. (Rome, 1919); and concerning *le leghe padronali*, see Bachi, *Italia economica 1913*, 249–250.

2. See the letters from Croizat and others in AE, Archivio Gabinetto, 1911, Titolo III, Casella 24, Fascicolo 226, headed "Richieste per la Tripolitania."

3. See "Costituzione della S.A. Elettrica Coloniale Italiana in Milano 19–23 Diaggio 1913," *Bollettino ufficiale delle S.p.A.*, Anno XXX, Fascicolo XXIV, 19–23.

4. See BCI Archives, Joel Papers, express letter, Joel to Volpi, Milan, 4 Jan. 1913.

5. See Cantalupo, *Vita diplomatica di Salvatore Contarini*, 47. Giolitti had some unspecified personal grievance about Contarini's conduct in the ministry. In general the premier appears to have disliked diplomats and generals equally.

6. I have based my account of Volpi's plans to deal with Montenegro and Heraclea on the correspondence between Joel and Volpi covering the period 8 June 1912 to 4 January 1913, in BCI Archives, Joel Papers.

7. Volpi to Joel, Ouchy-Lausanne, 19 Sept. 1912; *Verbali CL*, 10 Dec. 1912.

8. I have followed the firsthand account of a Zionist executive who lived and operated in Constantinople under the Young Turk regime: see Richard Lichtheim, *Sh'ar Yashuv* (Tel-Aviv, 1953), 189 et seq.

9. I have followed here Oreste Mosca's unpublished biography of Volpi, consulted through the courtesy of Professor De Felice. Also, see Joel to Volpi, 30 July 1912.

10. Stringher's resentment of Volpi comes out in a memorandum of 1913 that wound up on the premier's desk: *Dalle carte di Giolitti*, III, 96–97. Also two letters from Stringher to Di San Giuliano dated 20 June 1913 in AE, Archivio Gabinetto, 1913, Titolo III, Casella 28, Fascicolo 364. Concerning Volpi's attitude toward Stringher, whom he considered a small man with big pretensions, see Volpi to Joel, Montreux, 22 Aug. 1912, in the BCI Archives, Joel Papers.

11. For these details concerning the Ottoman Public Debt Council, see the previously cited work by Blaisdell, which does not identify Tittoni or distinguish him from his brother.

12. See this and other documentation in AE, Archivio Gabinetto, 1913, Titolo III, Fascicolo 402, "Eventuale liquidazione della Turchia asiatica ed equilibrio del Mediterraneo"; this dossier contains the minister's January 1913 wires to Garroni.

13. I have based my account on the dispatches and memoranda in ibid., Fascicolo 411, which has communications from Constantinople, Paris, and the capitals of the Central Powers: there is documentation on British attitudes in ibid., Fascicolo 404.

14. The Italian navy's reports to the foreign ministry concerning Anatolian coastal opportunities are to be found in ibid., Fascicolo 418B.

15. See Biagio Pace, *L'Italia e l'Asia Minore* (Palermo, 1917); T. Sillani, *Capisaldi* (Milan, 1918); and Mario Toscano, *Gli accordi di San Giovanni di Moriana* (Milan, 1936).

16. These corporate arrangements and the arrangements with the Italian government to follow the pattern set by the Antivari Company contracts of 1909 have left an abundant documentary trail. See AE, Archivio Gabinetto, 1913, Titolo III, Fascicolo 334, 335, and 418. This material includes memoranda and reports from Nogara himself, as well as correspondence with Joel and the Italian authorities; it also illuminates the contractual ties between the Antivari Company and the Italian state, since they were taken as a model. See also reports in *Il Sole*, 29 and 30 Nov. 1913, concerning Nogara's financial operations in Constantinople; and a story, ibid., 4 Dec. 1913, about Garroni's "brilliant" success in obtaining rail concessions in the Adalia region.

17. See the previously cited sentence of the Milan court, reported in *Rivista delle Società Commerciali*, 5 July 1913, 530.

18. See Di San Giuliano to Garroni, 20 Mar. 1914, with enclosures, in AE, Archivio Gabinetto, 1913–14, Titolo III, Fascicolo 418.

19. See Telegramma in arrivo n. 3374, Legazione Bucharest, 18 aprile 1913, AE, Archivio Gabinetto, 1913, Titolo III, Casella 27, Fascicolo 348. The German historian Fritz Fischer notes that Italy's successes in Rumania made the German authorities nervous: see the section on the "Crisis of German Imperialism" in the introduction to his book *Griff nach der Weltmacht*; in the Italian edition, F. Fisher, *Assalto al potere mondiale* (Turin 1965), 42–43.

20. My account of the relations between Italy and Germany—and particularly the exchanges between the Italians at Berlin and Zimmermann and Rosenberg—is based on the reports in AE, Archivio Gabinetto, 1973, Titolo III, Fascicolo 411, which run up to the end of 1913. I have also drawn on the German government publication *Die Grosse Politik der Europäischen Kabinette* (Berlin, 1926), vol. 37, part II, 641 et seq., weaving together that material with the dispatches in AE, Archivio Gabinetto, 1913, Titolo III, Fascicoli 402 and 404.

21. I have based my account of the Turkish loan negotiations on the correspon-

dence between the foreign minister and the Italian bankers (with some material from the Italian embassy at Constantinople) in AE, Archivio Gabinetto, 1913, Titolo III, Casella 28, Fascicoli 335, 363, and 364. This collection runs from 5 January 1913 to 24 March 1914 and seems to include all the memoranda, copies, and summaries concerning the loan that passed over Di San Giuliano's desk during that period.

22. In ibid., Fascicolo 363, there is an important memorandum sent by Stringher to Di San Giuliano in January 1913 concerning the attitude of Italian businessmen toward a Turkish loan; I have summarized it here. All of my narrative on the following pages is based on the foreign minister's correspondence in the above-mentioned file. The original documents are awaiting publication by the Italian government.

23. Primo Levi's report, 29 Sept. 1913, is in ibid., Fascicolo 418: see also the commercial information furnished by the new Italian vice-consul at Adalia, ibid., Fascicolo 408.

24. See the correspondence and reports concerning Italian automobile lines in Asia Minor in ibid., Fascicolo 418D, running up to 19 Nov. 1914.

25. The differences in mentality between the ambassador and the foreign minister come out well in the letters they exchanged on 20 June and 10 Sept. 1913, in ibid., Fascicolo 409.

26. Garroni and Nogara reported continually to Rome on their engineering-prospecting activities: see the memoranda in ibid., Fascicolo 407B and Fascicolo 418. In Fascicolo 409 there is important correspondence concerning railroad projects and authorizations.

27. The engineer's report is in ibid., Fascicolo 418.

28. See the voluminous correspondence and reports concerning "la tenuta di Gemal Bey" in ibid., Fascicolo 417.

29. There is a memorandum on Italian medical personnel on the khedive's estates in Asia Minor, evidently drawn up in 1911, in ibid., Fascicolo 408, "Turchia, posizione generale." There are two letters from the Italian diplomatic agency at Cairo, addressed to Di San Giulino and shown by him to Joel, dated 19 and 22 Dec. 1913 in ibid., Fascicolo 418. In addition, there is a special file, containing letters from Senator Lustig and detailed engineers' reports, all in 1912 and 1913, in ibid., Casella 30, Fascicolo 418C. There is more correspondence concerning Italian engineers on the khedive's properties in ibid., Fascicolo 409A, referring to August 1914.

30. See the telegram from Nogara to his Greek agent, Telioudis, 21 Mar. 1914, which was copied and sent to Rome by the Italian vice-consulate at Adalia, in ibid., Fascicolo 418.

31. The mining projects of Garroni and Nogara are summarized in their 1914 correspondence with Rome; ibid., Fascicolo 407B.

32. See especially the voluminous reports, from naval consular and other sources, in ibid., Fascicolo 418B.

8. The End Play in the Balkans, 1913–14

1. Aside from the article already cited, see the posthumous collection, A. Caroncini, *Problemi di politica nazionale* (Bari, 1922).

2. Nitti's memorandum, dated 28 Mar. 1913, is part of a collection of official

papers concerning the Danube-Adriatic railway question that passed through Stringher's office. This particular collection, running from March through the end of October 1913, is in the previously cited dossier "Ferrovia Danubio-Adriatico," Bank of Italy archives.

3. See Mantegazza, *Questioni di politica*, 292–293.

4. See the reports in *Il Sole*, 21 Sept. and 7 Nov. 1913; and ibid., 26 Jan. and 25 June 1914. Also Revelli, *L'Italia e il mar*, 208.

5. See the previously cited dossier on the Antivari Company in the BCI Archives at Milan.

6. Aside from the well-known works by Skendi and Swire, I have used the cited Baldacci reports in the AE, which contain some "tips" on the political situation in Albania as well as in Montenegro. For the crisis of 1913–14, I have followed the detailed accounts of the bimonthly Albanian paper *La Nazione Albanese*, published at Rome. The economic prospects of Albania formed the subject of special surveys and reports in *Il Sole*, 8 Sept., 19 Sept., 24 Sept., 27 Nov., and 12 Dec. 1913; and 5 Mar. 1914.

7. See *La Nazione Albanese*'s stream of reports during the spring and summer of 1913.

8. See R. Cantalupo, *Fuad primo re d'Egitto* (Milan, 1940), 56, 70–75, 86–87, 93–99.

9. See Volpi to Stringher, 11 Oct. 1909, in "Ferrovia Danubio-Adriatico," Bank of Italy archives; see also the exchanges among Tittoni, Ambassador Imperiali at Constantinople, and Stringher, 4 Oct. to 6 Dec. 1909, in AE, Archivio Riservato, 1908, Casella 1, Fascicolo 112, Dossier 2. See also a highly slanted report on Vismara's patriotic role in *La Nazione Albanese*, 15 Sept. 1913.

10. See Revelli, *L'Italia e il mar*, 208.

11. See documentation in AE, Archivio Gabinetto, 1911, Titolo III, Caselle 23–24, Fascicoli 215, 216.

12. In addition to the stream of reports in *La Nazione Albanese*, see the foreign ministry memoranda in ibid., Fascicolo 286.

13. Società italiana per il progresso delle scienze, *Relazione delle Commissione per lo studio dell'Albania*, 2 vols. (Rome, 1915).

14. My account of the Albanian fiasco rests on *La Nazione Albanese*, Jan. through July 1914.

15. My account of the 1913 negotiations between Italy and the other powers concerned over Balkan railways, as well as the vexed question of Italian representation at the Paris conference, is drawn from Giolitti, *Dalle carte di Giolitti*, III, 85–89 (covering 10 through 16 Apr. 1913), and the diplomatic papers and ministerial memoranda in AE, Archivio Gabinetto, 1911, Titolo III, Casella 28, Fascicolo 364, which I have supplemented with the Stringher papers of 1913, in a dossier in the Bank of Italy archives. The AE file does not take us beyond June 1913, while the papers transmitted by the foreign minister to Stringher, mostly dealing with Volpi's reports on Serb railroad policy and with the unofficial sounding and probing missions entrusted to Volpi by Di San Giuliano, end with 31 Oct. 1913.

16. In AE, Archivio Gabinetto, 1911, Titolo III, Casella 28, Fascicolo 364, see Tittoni's wire to Di San Giuliano, 26 May 1913, and Volpi's wire from Venice, 2 June 1913, as well as copies of two telegrams from an Italian emissary signing himself "Alessandro." These telegrams, sent from Vienna 23 June 1913, refer to private contacts with Austrian bankers and with Berchtold himself concerning an international trans-Balkan rail line: at Paris the emissary had imparted guidelines to Volpi, whom he praised for his adroitness. These communications, sent to Di San

Giuliano, are signed with the conventional name "Alessandro," but they appear to be from Joel or someone acting with his authority.

17. See the final copies of ministerial letters and memoranda in the Stringher papers of 1913 in "Ferrovia Danubio-Adriatico," Bank of Italy archives. These end 31 Oct. 1913, and the rest of Volpi's operations to the outbreak of the First World War must be reconstructed from other sources.

18. Concerning Volpi's new operations in Montenegro—alternating the carrot of financial advances and the stick of railroad concessions—see the French diplomatic reports and exchanges between the French legation at Cetinje and the French foreign ministry in *DDF*, 3e Série (1911–1914), IX, 342, 381, 392–393, 475–476, 523–524; X, 389, 463–464, 616–617. These cover the period 11 Feb.–23 June 1914. The French had reason to believe that the Italians were working in Montenegro with an eye toward Serbia, the "heir presumptive" to the unviable little monarchy.

19. See *DDF*, VIII, 866–868, a dispatch from Barrère at Rome, 29 Dec. 1913, reporting Italy's dissatisfaction over the fact that French bankers were dealing directly with Vienna in Balkan railroad matters in an attempt to freeze out the Italians. A little later Tittoni took up the matter directly at Paris, in a note to the French government, 29 Jan. 1914: ibid., IX, 225–226. The Serbs, under heavy pressure from several great powers, still wanted to keep a free hand in arranging for the construction of a Danube-Adriatic rail line, as the French minister at Belgrade reported, 20 Mar. 1914: ibid., X, 16–18. One suspects from these exchanges that the French ministries and bankers were following two tracks. They were willing to cooperate with the Italians in Montenegro, but this may well have served as a means of pressuring the Austrians to come to a general Balkan agreement which would have excluded the Italians. One may further surmise that if there had been no general war in 1914, the French would have worked to draw Austria away from its close dependence on Germany by projecting a trans-Balkan rail line under joint Austro-French auspices, with only token concessions to Italian interests. Certainly Volpi was well aware of such possibilities. Isvolsky reported that Volpi threatened to get Serbia to refuse any arrangements in which Italy was not given her share of control and contracts. Volpi also allegedly said that he would invoke the Germans. See the editorial notes quoting Russian reports, 10 Feb. 1914, in ibid., IX, 226.

Conclusion:
The View from Trieste

1. In addition to Slataper's political writings, see his letters to Amendola in the *Epistolario* (Milan, 1950), 292 et seq.

2. See Virginio Gayda, *La crisi di un impero* (Turin, 1913) and *L'Italia d'oltre confine* (Turin, 1914), written under irredentist inspiration; M. Alberti, *L'Irredentismo*. See also the standard histories of Trieste and Fiume, written from an irredentist point of view, by Attilio Tamaro and Riccardo Gigante.

3. See notes to chap. 6.

4. There is a sizable dossier on Foscari in AE, Archivio Riservato, 1909, Titolo III, Fascicoli 172 and 194.

Index

Abbas Hilmi Pasha (Abbas II, khedive of Egypt), 199; Italian relations with, 159, 204, 242, 281, 292; negotiations over properties of, 299–304

Abdul Hamid II, 199–200, 219–220, 223, 225, 238, 315

Abdul Hamid Shedid, 300–301

Abruzzi, duke of the, 261, 299–300, 317

Adalia, 278; Italian interest and activity in, 119, 261–262, 264–267, 270–272, 274, 277, 280, 282, 286–294, 299, 305, 309; Austrian interest in, 306–308

Adowa, 5, 22, 62

AEG, 138–140

Africa: Italian imperialism in, 5, 22, 29, 32, 113–116, 159, 191, 195, 203, 237; shift away from, in Italian foreign policy, 333. See also Egypt; Libya

Agnelli, Giovanni, 95, 98, 99, 123–124

Agriculture: modernization of, 8; in Lombardy, 11; under protectionism, 16; taxation of, 46; position of, in Italian economy, 47; issue of colonies for, 199–200; more applied science needed in, 344–345 n. 8

Alaja, 272–276, 278, 288, 292, 307

Albania, 194; Italian interest and activity in, 77, 111, 119, 203, 317–319, 324–325, 328; and trans-Balkan railway project, 218, 221, 238; revolts in, 251; and Italo-Austrian competition, 257, 279, 311–314, 317, 324–326; social and economic characteristics of, 315–316; political situation of, 316–318, 321–322; Italian studies of economic potential of, 323–324

Albano-Trezza, 136

Alberti, Mario, 139, 336–337, 371 n. 20

Albertini, Alberto, 146

Albertini, Luigi, 146–147, 149, 180, 346 n. 14

Albini, Admiral, 81

Allievi, Lorenzo, 67–68

Aluminum industry, 141–142

Amendola, Giovanni, 29

Anarchists, 24

Anatolia (Asia Minor), 30, 35, 73, 135, 156, 192, 200, 256–280, 289, 304–305, 309. See also Adalia; Alaja; Ottoman Empire

Angeli, Angelo, 241–242

Ansaldo, 62, 63, 88, 91, 93, 100, 104, 107, 366 n. 23; development of, 76–86; and Banca Commerciale, 132–133, 151; a competitor of Terni, 176; and Ottoman Empire, 204, 239–242; relations with Armstrong, 354

Antivari (city), 212, 214, 216–218, 223, 224, 233, 239, 315, 319, 331

Antivari Company, 212–216, 232–234, 239, 248–249, 254, 314–315, 330, 370 n. 19

Aosta, duke of, 339

Arabs, 251; hostile to Italians, 156, 244–245; nationalism of, 301. See also Moslems

Argentina, 79, 98; Italian trade with, 50, 51, 80, 103, 124

Armenians: in Ottoman Empire, 195–196, 202–203, 251, 261, 273; confidants of Volpi, 237

Armor plate: made by Terni, 55, 56, 57, 59, 73, 176; made by Ansaldo, 81–83, 176

Armstrong, 56, 62, 81, 353–354 n. 3

Artillery: manufacture of, 73–74, 81–83, 133

Assab, Bay of, 113–114

Associazione fra le società italiane per azioni, 187

Austria-Hungary, 144, 178, 270; rivalry with Italy, 41–42, 85–86, 91–92, 213, 217–218, 266–267, 278, 296; competition of Italian shipping with, 106, 120–124, 197, 257, 262; shipping industry of, 108, 112, 274; Bosnia-Herzegovina annexed by, 193, 215; and Ottoman Empire, 195–196, 199, 219–220, 271–276, 291, 306; and Balkans, 195–197, 203, 212, 265, 311–314, 377 n. 19; imperialist aims of, 265; and Albania, 317–319, 321–322,

324–325; growing rift with Italy, 326, 328–329, 333–336; minorities in, 334–335, 337

Autarky, 60, 76, 163, 167, 188; sought in naval production, 59, 61–63, 73, 104–105, 107, 120, 176; and Banca Commerciale policies, 129, 136, 141; lack of alternatives to, 144; in Fascist policy, 337

Automobile industry, 49, 51, 95–98, 130; problems of, 169; workers in, 171–172; criticized, 173. *See also* Fiat *Avanti!*, 176

Azzarita, Leonardo, 322

Bacchelli, Riccardo, 24
Bachi, Riccardo, 97–98, 186, 360 n. 2
Baghdad railway, 193, 197–198, 265, 266, 272, 277; Italian involvement in, 137, 201, 278–279, 363–364 n. 12
Bagnoli: steel plant at, 94, 177
Baldacci, Antonio, 209–211, 214–215
Baldacci, Giovanni, 209
Balduino, Cesare, 110, 118
Balkans, 26, 258–259, 269, 279; Italian interest and activity in, 5, 33, 91–92, 135, 158, 192–195, 200, 203, 208–209, 231, 256, 309–311; Italian problems in, 217–218; Italian foreign policy toward, 220, 311–313, 333; Italo-Austrian rivalry in, 335–336. *See also* Balkan railway project; Balkan Wars
Balkan railway project, 91–92, 156, 196–197, 218–222, 229–230, 234–237, 254; Italian interest in, 203–204, 217–218, 224–229, 238–239, 259, 311–313, 315, 326–330, 364 n. 12, 371 nn. 21, 22, 371–372 n. 24; ended by World War I, 332
Balkan Wars, 203, 217, 238, 244, 247
Banca Commerciale, 255, 290, 366 n. 24; and heavy industry, 59, 65, 66, 69, 73, 75, 76, 87–89, 134–136, 354 n. 4, 361 n. 4, 362 n. 9; rivalry with Ansaldo, 76, 242, German influence in, 86; and auto industry, 95, 99, 316 n. 5; and lumber industry, 102; and chemical industry, 104, 357 n. 30; shipping ties of, 109, 110, 111, 112; and interlocking directorates, 112; operations in East, 121, 154, 156; importance of, in industrial financing, 126; policies pursued by, 127–136; relations with German business, 137–143, 198; patriotism of, 144, 162; relationship with government, 144–148, 151, 154, 158, 253, 365 n. 21, 366 n. 21, 372 n. 25; and reorganization of *La Tribuna*,

147–150; interests in Libya, 158, 246–247; public campaign against, 160–161; and Ottoman Empire, 204, 224, 264; and Giuseppe Volpi, 206–208, 232, 250, 326, 327, 332; interests in Montenegro, 209, 211, 213, 216, 331; and Antivari Company, 216, 217, 249, 314; interest in trans-Balkan railway project, 230, 231, 233, 234; and Banco di Roma, 243, 254; increased involvement in foreign policy, 248; and Baghdad rail line, 278, 363 n. 12; and Turkish loan question, 283; expansionism of, 290, 338, 363 n. 11; and Italian interest in Albania, 319, 321, 322; archives of, 360–361 n. 2; interest in Brazil, 363 n. 11; and mercury industry, 364 n. 19

Banca di Busto Arsizio, 85
Banca di Genova, 77
Banca Generale, 126
Banca Italiana di Sconto, 86
Banca Nazionale, 20, 21, 77
Banca Romana, 20, 21
Banca Tiberina, 19–20
Banco di Roma: and the refinancing of the steel industry, 69; shipping interests of, 110–111; and *La Tribuna*, 149–150; origin and development of, 152–153; interests in Libya, 154–155, 242, 244, 246, 367 n. 29; effect of Libyan War on, 156, 243; setbacks of, 156–159; and Ottoman Empire, 201; relations with khedive of Egypt, 204, 242, 300–301; and Antivari Company, 216, 248–249, 254, and trans-Balkan railway project, 231; and Turkish loan question, 281–282. *See also* Pacelli, Ernesto

Bank of Abyssinia, 152
Bank of Albania, 322, 324
Bank of Italy, 154; role in banking system, 25; and steel industry, 60, 69–70; and Banca Commerciale, 127, 131–132, 134, 155; and *La Tribuna*, 149–150; and trans-Balkan railway project, 227; and Ottoman Empire, 237, 242; and Giuseppe Volpi, 254, 328; interest in Adalia, 264; and Turkish loan question, 285; and Antivari Company, 314; interests in Albania, 320–321. *See also* Stringher, Bonaldo

Bank of Naples, 79
Banks: reliance on French, 6; inadequacy of Italian, 17–19; government intervention in, 19–21, 25, 60; and parliamentary system, 36; rate of return in, 48; and steel industry, 59–60,

94; scandal involving, 79; connections with shipping industry, 106–107, 110–112; German influence in Italian, 126; in Rome and Alexandria, 152; and European politics, 162; role of, in Italian economy, 362 n. 8; foreign-dominated, 368 n. 31. *See also* Turkish loan issue

Banque de Paris et des Pays-Bas (Paribas), 127, 134, 136, 137, 332

Banque Russe-Asiatique, 331

Bardy, Charles, 85

Barone, Enrico, 73–74, 245–246, 373 n. 1

Barrère (French ambassador), 226–227, 229, 277, 368 n. 33

Beet growing, 16. *See also* Sugar refining industry

Belgium: Italian business relations with, 41, 51, 64, 136; and Stahlverband, 72; interests in Ottoman Empire, 198

Benucci (bank official), 111, 249

Berchtold, Leopold, Graf von, 271–272, 326, 376 n. 16

Berlin, Congress of, 212, 215

Bertolini, Pietro, 248

Besanzanica, Ernesto, 200

Besso, Marco, 139, 366 n. 24

Bethlehem Steel, 176

Bethmann-Hollweg, Theobald von, 280

Bettolo, Admiral, 57–58, 183, 351–352 n. 9, 370 n. 19

Biancardi, Dionigi, 112

Bianchi, Feliciano, 296–299

Bianchi, Riccardo, 90–91

Bismarck, Otto von, 126

Bixio, Nino, 113–114, 116

Bleichroeder Bank of Berlin, 126, 139, 142

Bombrini, Giovanni, 77, 80, 104

Bombrini family, 77–78, 81

Borgatta, Gino, 98, 187

Bosnia-Herzegovina, 193, 215; Italian labor in Bosnia, 200

Bourgeoisie: the term, 343–344 n. 6. *See also* Middle class

Boxer rebellion, 194

Braida, Nicola, 210

Brazil, 50–51, 98, 136–137

Breda, Ernesto, 53–54, 104, 108–110, 117, 213, 363 n. 10

Breda, Vincenzo Stefano, 19, 53–55, 57, 65

Breda firm, 53, 75, 91, 135, 171–172, 208, 247–248, 287, 355 n. 13

Briand, Aristide, 277

Brin, Benedetto (admiral), 54, 55, 57, 61–63, 104, 351–352 n. 9

Brunelli, Domenico, 112

Bulgaria, 91, 193, 194, 203; Italian labor in, 200; Italian interests in, 231, 247–248, 250, 269–270

Business class: views of, 187, 338; in Asia Minor, 289

Cadorna, Luigi, 84

Cantieri Navali Riuniti, 109, 365 n. 21

Capital: German shortage of, 137, 143–144, 198, 241, 270; Italian shortage of, 137, 243, 279, 314

Caprioglio (engineer), 290–291

Carducci, Giosuè, 62

Carli, Filippo, 138–139

Carnegie Steel Company, 73, 76

Carocci, G., 116

Carol I (king of Rumania), 270, 313

Caroncini, Alberto, 310–311, 337

Catholics: in North Italy, 10; and Giolitti's government, 24, 26–27, 34–35, 345 n. 10; Salandra supported by, 160; voting strength of, 167; and Italian conservatism, 177; in Albania, 316, 318, 324, 325

Cavour, Camillo, 8, 63, 113

Celesia, Baron, 182

Cellina electrical company, 207

Central Powers: and Italy, 90, 125, 195, 269, 328; imperialism of, 196–197, 244; and declining Ottoman Empire, 218–219; interests in Balkans, 247. *See also* Austria-Hungary; Germany; Triple Alliance

Chamber of Deputies, 3, 73; held in low esteem, 4, 346–347 n. 14; and power of king, 9; and protectionism, 15; and failure of parliamentary system, 22; and colonialism, 33; and Terni, 59. *See also* Parliamentary system

Chauvet, Costanzo, 81

Chemical industry, 77, 104, 127, 129, 136, 357 n. 30

Chemins de Fer Orientaux, 312

Chiesa, Eugenio, 69–70, 172–173, 175, 354 n. 5

Child-labor legislation, 33

Cines film manufacturer, 153

Class system: in steel trust complex, 173. *See also* Middle class

Clemenceau, Paul, 85, 354 n. 5

Collective bargaining, 24, 170; lack of, 172, 175

Colonialism, 116, 153, 341 n. 1; Giolitti's pursuit of, 24, 27–29; of Di San Giuliano, 32–33; and economic system of a state, 192–193. *See also* As-

382   *Index*

sab, Bay of; Adalia; Alaja; Anatolia; Eritrea; Imperialism; Libya
Colonies, Ministry of, 159, 300
Comitato nazionale per le tariffe doganali e per i trattati di commercio, 187
Commercial Museum of Venice, 313
Commune of 1871, 9
Constans (French ambassador), 222, 226
Constantinople: Italian interests at, 239–242; methods of diplomacy at, 252, 265. *See also* Ottoman Empire
Contarini, Salvatore, 248
Conti, Ettore, 27, 246, 343 n. 4
Corbino (economist), 107
Corinaldi, Amadeo (count), 213, 223
Cornaggia, Carlo Ottavio (marquis), 140
Corradini (author), 39, 373 n. 1
Corridoni, Filippo, 172, 173
Corriere della Sera, 146–147, 149, 180
Corruption: in Naples, 34; in Ottoman Empire, 201–202, 252–253; Volpi's enterprises charged with, 214
Coulant (engineer), 290–291, 305
Credito Italiano, 64–65, 69, 99, 104, 110, 132, 134, 230–231, 233, 357 n. 30
Credito Mobiliare, 18, 126, 129
Credito Provinciale, 98
Crespi, Silvio, 130, 367 n. 26
Crispi, Francesco, 5, 12, 13, 78; and Giolitti, 20–23; supporters of, 61, 62; African expansion policies of, 64; and 1897 bank scandal, 79–80; and founding of Banca Commerciale, 126; and royal line, 342 n. 3; attitude toward labor, 344 n. 6
Cristobal Colon, 80
Croatians, 214, 218, 335
Croizat, Vittorio, 246
Cyprus, 198

D'Annunzio, Gabriele, 204–205, 348
Dardanelles, 245
Darmstaedter banks, 139
De Felice-Giuffrida, 31
Deffès, M., 235–236
Del Buono, Pilade, 66
De Martino (foreign minister), 301
Denmark: sales to, 100
Depretis, Agostino, 12–13, 61
Deutsche Bank, 139, 218, 265, 270, 312, 328
Deutsche Orient Bank, 241
Diatto, Vittorio, 98; and brother, 99
Di San Giuliano (marquis), 29, 117, 337, 347–348 n. 15; background and career of, 30–31, 33–35; interest in

East Africa, 32; and Italian penetration of Libya, 153–154; relations with banks, 154–155, 159; and Ottoman Empire, 201; foreign policy of, 221, 222, 256–261, 276, 277–278, 280, 290; and Italian interest in Balkans, 229, 311–312, 321, 326–330, 371 n. 21, 376 n. 16; and Anatolia, 264–265, 267–270, 272, 275, 289, 293, 296–299, 306, 308; and Turkish loan question, 281–284
Diskontogesellschaft, 139
Ditta Zaccaria Pisa, 230
Djavid Bey, 239, 309
Djemal Bey, 73, 292–299
Doci, Primo (abbot), 316, 321
Doda, Prenk Bib, 316, 321
Dodecanese Islands, 203, 245, 278, 309
Donegani family, 104, 129, 136, 357 n. 30
Doumer, Paul, 85, 330
Dresdener Bank, 139, 141
Dreyfus, Louis, 86
Dreyfus Bank. *See* Louis Dreyfus Bank of Paris
Dumping: practiced by Germans, 67–68, 72, 87, 89
Dynamite Nobel, S.A., 84

Economista d'Italia, L', 336
Economy: nineteenth-century, 5–8, 13; crisis of 1898, 22; crash of 1907, 26, 66, 81, 95, 131; problems of, 42–45, 362 n. 8; imbalance of, 49
Edison electrical workers, 171
Education, 45. *See also* Engineering profession; Illiteracy
Egypt, 191, 198; Italian interest in, 113–114, 159; khedivial house of, 315. *See also* Abbas Hilmi Pasha
Einaudi, Luigi, 46, 107, 147, 187–188, 190, 346 n. 14
Elba company, 64–68, 70, 72–73, 116, 148, 151, 173
Elba Island: iron mines of, 52, 64
Electrical industry, 95, 129–130, 137–140, 158, 207–208, 246, 345 n. 10, 364 n. 15; reliance on hydroelectric power, 7, 18, 66, 86, 89, 92, 136
Elena (queen of Italy), 209, 342 n. 3
Emigration, 5, 27, 32; and Italian economy, 43–44, 345–346 n. 12, 347 n. 14; statistics on, 49; and Italian shipping, 119–120, 122, 160–161
Employment: figures on, 47
Engineering profession: development of, in Italy, 11, 343 n. 5
Entente. *See* Triple Entente

Eritrea, 30, 33, 122, 191
Essad Pasha Toptani, 316, 322, 324–325
Esterle, Carlo, 137, 246
Ethiopia, 32, 35, 152, 159

Facta, Luigi, 28
Falck, 87, 89, 93
Farini, Domenico, 79
Fascism, 3, 4, 19; origin of, 39, 167–168; policies of, 337; class roots of, 338–339; Nationalism distinct from, 348–349 n. 17
Fauro, Ruggiero, 336
Favilla, Luigi, 79
Federazione Marinara. *See* Marine Federation
Fenoglio, Pietro, 127, 246, 250–251, 363 n. 10
Ferrante, Marquis, 287
Ferraris, Dante, 74–75, 91, 98–99, 133, 246, 286, 339, 351 n. 4, 363 n. 10
Ferraris, Federico, 99
Ferriere del Vesuvio, 177
Ferriere di Voltri, 89
Ferriere Italiane, 64–65, 68, 357 n. 30
Ferriere Piedmontesi, 87, 89
Fiat, 355 n. 16, 355–356 n. 22, 363 n. 10; origin and development of, 95–100; tie with shipbuilding, 109; financing problems of, 130; relations with Banca Commerciale, 133, 365 n. 21; labor troubles of, 170; interest in Anatolia, 288–289; indebtedness of, 361 n. 5
Financial, Commercial, and Industrial Society, 262–263
FIOM (Italian Federation of Metal Workers), 169–171
Fiume, 106–107, 197, 335; and Italo-Austrian maritime rivalry, 121, 213, 334; Italian irredentism in, 336
Florio, Giulia, 117–118
Florio, Ignazio (senator), 64, 109–110, 115–117, 131, 145; 365 n. 21; family of, 62, 111, 115, 118, 130
Florio, Vincenzo, 115
Flotow (German ambassador) 267–268
Flour milling, 16, 130, 152
Food: high cost of, 16
Foreign policy: and Giolittian system of government, 36; related to marginality of Italian economy, 41–43; aimed at achieving great-power status, 47, 194; and Italy's trade relations, 51; and shipping industry, 106; and Adriatic provinces, 106–107; and Banca Commerciale, 156, 248; and needs of industry, 159, 167, 194, 279, 283, 314, 321, 332; interventionist, 161; re-

lating to new nations, 194–195; trends in, 204; toward Anatolia and Balkans, 221–222, 247; businessmen as agents of, 252, 255–256; basic shift in, 333; and Trieste and Fiume, 334; expansion of, 341 n. 1. *See also* Colonialism; Di San Giuliano; Imperialism
Fortis, Alessandro, 25, 26, 79–80
Fortunato, Giustino (senator), 345–346 n. 12, 347 n. 14
Foscari, Countess, 205–206, 216
Foscari, Piero (count), 131, 207, 210, 213, 370 n. 19; background and career of, 205–206; Montenegrin operations of, 212–213, 216–217; interest in Trieste, 337
France, 312; Italian dependence on financing from, 6, 8, 64; Italian heavy industry links with, 41, 72, 81, 88, 104–105; Italian exports to, 50–51, 87, 91; interests in Italy, 85–86, 103–104, 368 n. 33; technicians from, 89; imports from, 96; auto exports of, 97; subsidized merchant shipping of, 115; Italian shipping rivalry with, 120; financiers of, and Banca Commerciale, 128, 136–137; loans from, to German banks, 143; foreign influences in banks of, 161–162; and Balkans, 195, 321, 324, 329, 332, 377 nn. 18, 19; and Ottoman Empire, 195, 196–200, 203, 219–220, 223–224, 231, 236–237, 259, 268, 272, 277–278, 284; interest in trans-Balkan railway project, 222–228, 234–235. *See also* Morocco; Tunisia
Franchetti, Leopoldo, 29–30
Franchi, Attilio, 87–89
Franchi, Camillo, 87
Francis Ferdinand (archduke), 219, 335
Franco Tosi firm, 100–101, 109
Frassati (senator), 28
Free trade, 7–8
Fuad (prince of the Egyptian khedivial dynasty), 318
Fusinato, Guido, 248

Garibaldi, Giuseppe, 113
Garroni, Camillo (marquis), 73, 273, 291; and reorganization of *La Tribuna*, 148–149; and Italian aims in Anatolia, 151, 254, 258, 261, 264–265, 276, 288–289, 297, 305, 307, 309; and Turkish loan issue, 281, 284–285; acquainted with industrial problems, 290
Garroni, Vittorio (marquis), 73, 151
General Electric, 103

Genoa, 94, 113, 120
Germans: in Austria-Hungary, 336
Germany, 9, 193; and Italian industry,
41–42, 59–60, 67, 88–92, 96–97, 103,
352 n. 13; Italian exports to, 50, 51,
100; Italian imports from, 50, 67, 72,
89, 140; and Banca Commerciale, 86,
128, 131, 136, 141–142, 161; rivalry
with Italy in Argentina, 103, 124; and
Italian shipping, 108–109, 121, 287;
economic influence in Italy, 118–119,
137–143, 178, 364 n. 17; Fiat contracts with navy of, 133; industrial position of, 137; capital lacked by, 137,
143–144, 198, 241, 270; press of, 154–
156; rise of Fascism in, 168; and Balkans, 195, 247–248, 266, 314, 317,
328; and Ottoman Empire, 195, 196,
199–200, 236, 250, 258, 261, 266–
269, 273–275, 279; on collision course
with other powers, 197, 269–270; and
Baghdad railroad, 197, 265, 278, 363–
364 n. 12; and Italian foreign policy,
259; and failure of Triple Alliance,
280. *See also* Central Powers; Triple
Alliance
Gini, Corrado, 39
Giolitti, Giovanni, 79, 127, 204, 256,
373 n. 5; government of, 12, 13, 22–
28, 35–36, 86, 147, 150–151; and
transformism, 14; and bank reform,
20–21; election-fixing of, 21; party of,
28–29; opposition to, 39; and sugar
industry, 48; and Terni mills, 58; and
Navigazione Generale, 117, 123; relations with Banca Commerciale, 144–
148, 151, 154, 158, 160–161, 253–
254, 365 n. 21; and the reorganization
of *La Tribuna*, 147–149; and Salandra, 160, 161; and labor, 170, 172,
175, 180–182; relationship with Giuseppe Volpi, 206, 327, 372 n. 25; and
Ottoman Empire, 244–245, 248; and
Turkish loan issue, 282–284; and
House of Savoy, 342 n. 3; relations
with Catholic leaders, 345 n. 10; criticisms of, 346–347 n. 14
Giovanni Gilardini firm, 99, 135, 286
Giulietti, Giuseppe, 118, 178–185, 339
Goria-Gatti, Cesare, 320
Grain: protective tariffs for, 16
Gramsci, Antonio, 12
Grandi, Dino, 39, 349 n. 17
Great Britain, 8, 57, 97; business and in-
dustrial connections with Italy, 41,
102–105; trade with Italy, 50–51, 64,
89, 91, 100, 108–109; Italian compe-
tition with, 90; war with Turkey, 159;

and Balkans, 195; and Ottoman Empire, 195, 198–199, 267, 271, 276–
278, 287; colonialism of, 197; and
trans-Balkan railway project, 229;
competition with Italian shipping, 287;
relations with khedive of Egypt, 301
Greece, 123, 194, 268–269, 317
Greeks, 244; in Ottoman Empire, 195,
196, 202–203, 261, 294
Gregorini firm, 87
Gualino, Riccardo, 102
Guarneri, Felice, 43–44
Guiccioli (Italian minister at Belgrade),
229–230
Guppy shipyard, 62–63

Halagian, Aram, 262, 265
Halagian, Bedros, 237
Helfferich (German financier), 253, 327
Heraclea, 223–226, 231, 250, 264, 371 n.
24
Herzegovina (Austrian vessel), 325
Herzog, Peter (baron), 307
Hilferding, Rudolf, 4
Hoetzendorf, Conrad von (field mar-
shal), 335
House, E. M., 144
Humbert I (king of Italy), 33, 79, 341
n. 3. *See also* Savoy, House of

Iannacone, Pasquale, 68
Idea Nazionale, L', 337
Illiteracy, 6
Ilva. *See* Steel trust
Imperiali (Italian ambassador), 201,
219, 221, 222, 226, 232, 252, 277, 320
Imperialism, 341 n. 1, 346 n. 13; causes
of, 3–5, 46–47, 51–52, 144, 191–192,
280; aimed at East, 26–27, 30, 124,
135, 179, 193–197, 220, 244, 321, 334;
and Di San Giuliano's policies, 35;
supporters of, 40; and regional gap
between North and South, 95; and
shipping industry, 106–108, 118, 121,
124–125; role of banking in, 152, 159;
and fascism, 167–168, 337; popular
appeal of, 177; and national interest,
186; and the welfare of Italian workers, 187; varieties of, 192–193; in
Montenegro, 213; supported by business groups, 338; Italian switch from
colonialism to, 341 n. 1. *See also* Colonialism
Industrialization, 5–9, 25, 32, 347 n. 14;
economic effects of, 43–46, 72; implications of, 144; problems of, related to
rise of fascism and socialism, 168;

costs of, 185–186; impossible for Turkey, 195

Industry: and Italian imperialism, 4, 194, 203–204, 222, 247, 280, 338; nascent, of North Italy, 5, 15; effects of protective tariff system on, 16–17; relations with labor, 24, 42, 167–190 (*see also* Labor); Giolitti's plans for, 26; and parliamentary system, 36; imbalance of, 41–44, 48; position of, in Italian politics, 41, 47; problems of, 48–49, 52–53, 243, 287–288, 326 n. 13; vertical organization of, 67–68, 83, 84, 104, 352 n. 13; and military orders, 71, 97–98, 133; at Puzzuoli, 81; and goal of autarky, 104–105; heavy, and shipyards, 107; financing of, 126–163, 362 n. 8; and Italian foreign policy, 282–283, 286, 332; and rise of Fascism, 339; and Nationalism, 349 n. 17. *See also* Aluminum industry; Automobile industry; Chemical industry; Electrical industry; Industrialization; Machine industry; Mercury industry; Rubber industry; Shipbuilding industry; Shipping industry; Steel industry

Iron ore, 7, 8, 52, 89; and protectionism, 61

Irredentism, 85–86, 106–107, 218, 334–335

Istituto italiano per l'espansione commerciale e coloniale, 313

Isvolsky papers, 51, 377 n. 19

Italo-Turkish War, 3, 100, 153, 154, 170, 238–239; 244; effects of, 179, 182, 247; settlement of, 250–252, 254

Jacomoni (bank officer), 154

Jagow (German foreign minister), 270, 272, 280

Jakobovics, Joseph, 307

Japan, 168

Jews: in financial world, 161, 162–163; in Ottoman Empire, 195, 261

Joel, Otto, 240, 248, 249, 280, 286, 287, 367 nn. 26, 29, 368 n. 33; background and personality, 126–127; director of Banca Commerciale, 127–129; and steel industry, 132–135, 361 n. 4; and electrical industry, 139; relations with Giolitti government, 145, 253–254; letters to, from Rolandi-Ricci, 147, 150–151; and reorganization of *La Tribuna*, 148–150; criticism of, 151, 154–155, 161; patriotism of, defended, 155–156; and trans-Balkan railway project, 156, 231, 233–234, 238–239;

relations with Volpi and Antivari Company, 215–216, 249–250, 254, 332, 372 n. 25; and projected naval syndicate, 240–241; and Società Commerciale d'Oriente, 250–251; in business negotiations over Anatolia, 277; and Turkish loan issue, 283–284; and Italian foreign policy, 326; correspondence of, 360–361 n. 2, 365 n. 21

Jonction-Salonica, 198, 224–225, 228–229, 237–238

Kiel agreement, 270–273, 278

Kreditanstalt, 126

Krupp, 56–58, 74, 84, 87, 270

Labor: in nineteenth century, 7; low wages of, 16; and Giolitti government, 24, 26–27, 36; relations with management, 42, 167–190; lack of legislative progress for, 45; and imperialism, 168; Italian, abroad, 200–201; and Italian liberalism, 344 n. 6. *See also* Marine Federation; Strikes

Lalande, Laurence de, 86

Lancia, 170

Lanino, Pietro, 136, 140, 366 n. 21

Latin America, 103, 194. *See also* Argentina; Brazil

Lawyers: in nineteenth-century Italy, 8–9

Left, 245; government of, 12–13, 15; and Giolitti, 26–27, 36; disarray of, 39–40; and Italian shipping lines, 114–116; unable to solve basic economic problems, 168; imperialism of, 337–338

Lepanto, 61

Lerda, Giovanni, 174

Levi, Primo, 240, 286–287, 314

Liberal: term, 19

Liberalism: and nationalism, 11–12; political system of, 23, 36; 1908 crisis faced by, 26, 194; and Nationalist movement, 37, 349 n. 17; decline of, 186–187; term, in an Italian context, 343–344 n. 6; and transformism, 344 n. 7; and Fascism, 346 n. 13; criticized, 346 n. 14; failure of, 347 n. 14

Libya: Italian interest and activity in, 30, 80, 191, 203, 238–239, 244, 246–247, 299; Banco di Roma's involvement in, 152–153, 156–159, 242, 281; Banca Commerciale's investment in, 234. *See also* Libyan War

Libyan War, 35, 39, 45, 100, 101, 150, 151, 156–157, 176, 243, 244–245, 321; supported by Einaudi, 188; effect on

Italian enterprises in Ottoman Empire, 249–250
Ligure-Brasiliana line, 109
Liguria, 24, 66
List, Friedrich, 189
Lloyd shipping lines, 111–112, 121–122, 145–146
Locomotives: Italian manufacture of, 77–78, 81, 83, 90, 93, 140; exported to Rumania, 135; government orders for, 171–172; Bulgaria in market for, 247–248
Lombardy, 8, 11, 24, 52, 86–87
Louis Dreyfus Bank of Paris, 86, 102
Lustig, Enrico (senator), 301–302
Luzzatti, Gino, 26, 35, 143, 146, 149, 175

Macedonia, 193, 203, 218, 221, 234–236
Machine industry, 25, 76, 78, 90–92, 130; in Milan, 100; in Saronno, 140
Malagodi, Olindo, 149–150
Mangili, Cesare, 131, 231, 320
Mannesmann firm, 89, 93, 140, 364 n. 17
Mantegazza, Vico, 248, 313
Marina mercantile italiana, La, 124–125
Marine Federation (Federazione Marinara), 118, 177–184
Marittima Italiana, 112
Marseilles, 115, 120
Martini, Ferdinando, 29, 246
Masonic lodges, 335, 336
Maurici, Joseph, 300–301
Mazzini, Giuseppe, 12
Meccanica Lombarda, 101–102
Medici, Giacomo, 73
Medici, Luigi (marquis), 73, 112, 233
Mehmed Ferid Pasha, 220–221
Menada, Emilio, 109, 110, 286
Menada shipping interests, 121, 181, 182
Merchant marine. *See* Shipping industry
Mercury industry, 141–143, 364 n. 19
Mesopotamia, 200, 277
Messagero, Il, 76
Mexico, 109
Michel, Charles, 104
Middle class, 5, 8–11, 343 n. 4; and Nationalist movement, 38–39, 349 n. 17; in Ottoman Empire, 195; and origins of Fascism, 338–339
Milan, 10, 94; engineering education in, 11; labor trouble in, 168, 171–173
Millo, Admiral, 180, 182
Mirabello, Carlo (admiral), 58–59
Mirdites, 316; leaders of, 321
Molli, Giorgio, 104–105, 352 n. 13
Moltedo, Captain, 325–326

Monarchists, 177
Monte Amiata mines, 142–143, 364 n. 19
Montecatini firm, 104, 129, 136, 357 n. 30
Montenegro, 194, 203, 212, 283, 322; Italian trade with, 135; Italian interests and operations in, 154, 156, 193, 208–218, 234, 239, 247–249, 254, 257, 311, 314–315, 327, 329–331, 370 n. 15, 372 n. 25, 377 n. 19
Morocco, 191, 199, 203, 244
Moslems: in Ottoman Empire, 195, 251; in Albania, 315, 324, 325
Motor industry, 90, 93, 95, 96
Mougeot, Leon (senator), 104
Muricchio, Lieut. Col., 325–326
Mussolini, Benito, 23, 345 n. 10; and Nationalism, 37, 348–350 n. 17; as editor, 172, 176; relations with Volpi, 206; fascism of, 338

Nani-Mocenigo, Count, 273–274, 276, 288, 302
Naples: urban renewal of, 18; corruption in, 34; lack of sufficient industry at, 65–66, 94–95, 97
Nase Jedinstvo, 214
Nationalism: in economic assumptions, 19; reaction against German marketing practices, 67; in Banca Commerciale policies, 129, 133–136; and Libyan War, 151; and European Jews, 161–163; of Italians in Trieste, 336–337
Nationalist movement: Fascist adoption of ideas of, 4; ideology of, 37–40, 190, 338; deputies representing, 73, 112; connection with shipping industry, 106; sponsored by Terni, 177; and Trieste, 336–337; professionals and intellectuals in, 338, 373 n. 1; and emigration of unskilled labor, 346 n. 12; origin of, 348–350 n. 17; newspapers of, 361 n. 3. *See also* Rocco, Alfredo
National-Liberals, 4, 40
Navigazione Generale Italiana, 148, 366 n. 22; and subsidization, 61, 64, 119; formation of, 62, 115–116; Ansaldo contract with, 83; vessels ordered by, 109–110; importance of, in industrial development, 116–117; power of, 117, 123; charges of German influence in, 118–119, 160–161; Banca Commerciale connections with, 130, 131, 145; troop transport lucrative to, 191. *See also* Florio, Ignazio

Navy, 125, 261, 350–351 n. 4, 370 n. 19; relations with industry, 30, 54–58, 73, 76–78, 85, 87–88, 101, 107–109, 133; expenses for, 45, 104–105; and 1913 naval law, 120

Negos, Danilo (prince of Montenegro), 208–211, 214, 249

Negos, Mirko (prince of Montenegro), 214

Negri, A. O., 240

Nicholas I (king of Montenegro), 314

Nitti, F. S., 36, 59, 65–66, 312–313, 328, 347 n. 14, 359–360 n. 2

Nizami, Osman, 276

Nobel-Avigliana. *See* Società Nobel-Avigliana

Noetzlin, Edgar, 134, 361 nn. 3, 4

Nogara, Bernardino, 327; in negotiations with Turks and Balkan powers, 158; and trans-Balkan railway project, 232–233; as Volpi's agent in Constantinople, 253; on Ottoman Public Debt Council, 255–256, 274; and Italian aims in Anatolia, 261–267, 271, 277, 279–280, 288, 290–291, 293, 297, 301, 305–307, 309; and Turkish loan issue, 285–286

Noradunghian, Gabriel Effendi, 237

North Italy: early industrialization of, 5–8, 15; contrasted with South, 10–12, 15; political leaders from, 12; and national politics, 15; more advanced, 27; opposition to Giolitti regime in, 36; unable to absorb South's labor surplus, 49; widening gap with South, 94–95

Obrenovic, Alexander (king of Serbia), 200

Obrenovic dynasty, 208

Odero, Attilio, 99, 241, 305. *See also* Oderos

Oderos (shipbuilders), 61–66, 107, 109–110, 133, 145, 213. *See also* Odero, Attilio

Officine Galileo, 208

Oil, 110; in Mesopotamia, 197–198, 265

Oliva, Giuseppe, 231

Olivetti, 93

Oriani, Alfredo, 62

Orlando, Giuseppe, 73–75, 99, 108, 116, 132, 145, 175, 176, 351 n. 4

Orlando, Luigi (senator), 61, 286

Orlando, Salvatore, 60, 63, 178

Orlandos (shipbuilders), 61–66, 78, 104, 107, 121, 133, 208, 213

Ottina, Cavaliere, 305

Ottoman Empire: Italian interest and operations in, 5, 124–125, 133, 135, 151, 154, 158, 193–194, 196, 199–204, 219–220, 243–244, 367 n. 26; and Italian shipping, 80, 119, 121; Italian interest in partitioning of, 107, 194, 256–260; and Banca Commerciale, 135; war with Britain, 159; army of, 195, 197–198, 201, 251; and European powers, 195–203; decay of, 201–202, 255, 301; methods of doing business in, 202–203; and trans-Balkan railway project, 218, 226, 238–239; French influence in, 229; hostile attitude toward Italy, 236–238, 249–250; politics in, 251; slight improvement of, 283; and World War I, 288; landholding practices in, 293–294; Albania under, 315–316. *See also* Adalia; Alaja; Anatolia; Constantinople; Italo-Turkish War; Ottoman Imperial Bank; Ottoman Public Debt Council; Turkish loan issue

Ottoman Imperial Bank, 156, 198, 224–225, 228, 229, 233, 234, 235–236, 238, 285

Ottoman Public Debt Council, 195–196, 198, 202, 229, 234, 235, 237, 255, 271, 274, 320, 326, 327

Pacelli, Ernesto, 152–155, 157–158, 238, 240, 242–243, 249, 281, 300, 367

Pacelli, Eugenio, 153

Paganini, Roberto, 210, 249

Paganini, Vittorio, 212–213, 215, 217, 223, 239, 372 n. 24

Pan-Germanism, 336

Papadopoli banking interests, 131, 207, 210, 213

Pareto, Vilfredo, 17

Paribeni, Roberto, 291, 293–294, 296

Paris conference (1913), 326–327

Parisi, Saverio, 99; family and connections of, 99, 362–363 n. 9

Parliamentary system: problems of, 3–4, 22, 346–347 n. 14; functioning of, 5, 9, 12–13, 26; transformist, 13–15; and liberalism, 19, 23, 344 n. 6; and bank reform, 21; under Giolitti, 24; Nationalists' views of, 37; and industrialization, 72; and emergence of imperialism, 168. *See also* Chamber of Deputies

Parodi, Emanuele, 178, 181, 184

Parodi-Delfino, Leopoldo, 77

Parodi firm, 121, 182

Peasants: hurt by protectionist policies, 16; Sicilian, 29–30

Perrone, Fernando Maria, 79–80. *See also* Peronne family

Perrone, Pio, 84–85, 240–241, 354 n. 5. *See also* Perrone family

Perrone family, 76, 81, 84, 99, 133, 239–241, 357 n. 31, 362–363 n. 9, 367 n. 26

Pesso, Sergio, 302

Piaggio, Erasmo (senator), 145–146, 148, 160, 178, 213, 234, 365 n. 21, 366 n. 22

Piaggio interests, 80, 109, 111, 145, 365 n. 21

Pichon (French foreign minister), 222, 225, 226

Piedmont, 8; labor unions in, 24; iron deposits in, 52

Piombino: steel plant at, 67, 68, 72; living conditions for labor at, 173; right to strike at, 175

Pirelli, G. B., 93, 99, 102–103, 123–124, 191, 286

Pirelli-General Cable Works, Ltd., 103

Pisacane (revolutionist), 113

Pius X (pope), 24, 35. *See also* Pope

Pius XI (pope), 95. *See also* Pope

Pogacnik (engineer), 322

Pogliani, Angelo, 85–86

Politecnico. *See* Reale Politecnico di Milano

Ponti (senator), 130

Pope: power of, in Italy, 10; electoral boycott of, 35. *See also* Pius X; Pius XI

Popovic, Ivan, 208

Population: pressure of, 5, 7. *See also* Emigration

Portugal, 100

Po Valley: agriculture in, 11

Preparazione, La, 73–74, 357 n. 31

Press: Italian, 36, 42, 48, 76, 80, 85, 124–125, 160, 169, 176, 247, 260, 276 (see also *Corriere della Sera; Preparazione, La; Rivista della Società Commerciali; Sole, Il; Stampa, La; Tribuna, La*); Austrian, 124; German, 154–156; Slavic, 214; British, 229–230; Turkish, 253, 309; French, 277; Nationalist, 337, 349 n. 17, 361 n. 3; pre-World War I, 364–365 n. 20

Pritsch (delegate to Ottoman Public Debt Council), 327

Protectionism, 8, 13, 15–16, 24, 49, 90, 167; effects of, 16–17, 25, 71, 78; a Nationalist ideal, 38; and shipbuilding, 61, 108; and Banca Commerciale investment policies, 129; criticized by Einaudi, 147; and flour mills, 152; defended, 187–189

Quilici, Nello, 343 n. 4

Raggio, Carl, 233–234

Raggio, Edilio (count), 66, 361 n. 4

Railways: state involvement in, 6, 25, 42, 71; conventions of 1885, 53–54, 71, 77, 90; manufacture and sale of items for, 64–65, 71, 87, 90, 130, 231; of the Salento, 77–78; aftermath of nationalization of, 78, 90; modernization of, 90–93, 345 n. 11; unemployment of railroad-car workers, 171–172; built in Balkans with Italian know-how, 200–201; built in Montenegro, 213–214; competition over franchises for in Balkans, 313–314, 317; importance of, in Italian foreign policy, 332. *See also* Balkan railway project

Rappaport, Leo, 86

Rassegna dei lavori pubblici, 85, 160

Rathenau, Emil, 139

Rathenau, Walther, 112, 139

Rattazzi, Urbano (senator), 20, 28, 35, 80, 132–133, 148, 232, 342 n. 3, 372 n. 25; family of, 81

Ratti family, 95

Ravà, Enrico, 233–234

Reale Politecnico di Milano, 11, 38, 343 n. 5

Real estate: speculation on, 18; slump in, 20; bank involvement in, 21, 130, 152

"Red cooperatives," 24–25

Régie des Chemins de Fer, 198, 234, 237

Régie générale, 331

Regionalism, 10, 13–15, 27. *See also* North Italy; South Italy

Reichspost, 124

Republicans, 177

Revedin, Ruggero (count), 208–210; family of, 131, 207

Rezzonico, Elisabetta Widmann, 205–206

Rhodes, 203, 244–245, 258, 261, 278

Ricciardi, Adelchi, 286

Right: aims of, 6, 12; Giolitti regime opposed by, 36; expansionism of, 40; and steamship industry, 113; unable to solve economic problems, 168; and Adriatic irredentism, 334; extremism of, 339

Risorgimento, 9, 10, 12, 13, 16; departure from ideals of, 61–63; and Adriatic Italians, 334–335

RIV, 96

Rivista della Società Commerciali, 187, 188, 190, 336

Rocco, Alfredo, 4, 39, 188–190, 338, 373 n. 1
Rolandi-Ricci, Vittorio (senator), 213, 362–363 n. 9, 365 n. 21, 366 n. 22; and steel trust, 69–70, 132, 150–151; and *La Tribuna*, 146–150
Rome, 10, 18; Chamber of Commerce of, 255
Rosano, Pietro, 79
Rosenberg, Friedrich (baron), 274
Rossi-Martini, Gerolamo (count), 112, 139
Rothschilds, 126, 162
Rotten boroughs, 28
Rubattino, Raffaele, 62, 112–116
Rubber industry, 50, 51
Rubini, Giulio, 87
Rumania, 194, 283; Italian commercial relations with, 91, 101, 135, 270, 355 n. 13; Italian interest in, 283, 311, 313, 328; and European powers, 312–313
Russia, 57, 92; Italian exports to, 50, 51, 101; Fiat's contracts with, 98–100; Italian business interests in, 102; and French banking, 161; and Balkans, 195, 203, 329; conflicting interests of, with Germany, 197; and Ottoman Empire, 199, 220, 255; and trans-Balkan railway project, 22, 226–227; relations with, 259, 312; and Turkish loan issue, 284; relations with French banks, 361 n. 3

SADE network, 139, 207–208
Sahadun, Giuseppe, 233, 250–251
Salandra, Antonio, 12, 35, 87, 281, 346 n. 14, 349 n. 17; political views of, 36; and banking industry, 86, 158–159; and Giolitti, 160–161; and auto workers, 170; and labor conflict in shipping industry, 182–185; and Italian interest in Albania, 320–321
Salonika: Italians in, 200–201
"Salvaging" of businesses, 18, 20, 25, 366 n. 22
Salvemini, Gaetano, 337, 346–347 n. 14
San Giorgio firm, 98
San Pietro (lawyer), 319–320
Sapeto, Giuseppe, 114
Sarajevo, 3, 204
Savona steel company, 68
Savoy, House of, 3, 9–10, 15, 20, 33, 62, 117, 261, 339, 341–342 n. 3; Giolitti's relations with, 24; and foreign policy, 35–36, 161, 204, 256; and Nationalists, 38; connections with Montenegrin royal house, 209, 214–215; relations with khedivial prince Fuad, 318

Scalea, Giuseppe Lanza di, 111
Scalea, Pietro di (prince) 117–118, 246
Scalea family, 131
Scalea-Trabia, Francesco Lanza Spinelli, prince of, 117–118
Scarfoglio, Edoardo, 29, 202, 371 n. 21
Schanzer (minister), 145
Schmitt, Carl, 189
Schneider interests, 54, 64, 65, 66, 74, 104; Ansaldo's ties with, 81–82, 84
Schwabach (bank officer), 327
Science: application of, 344–345 n. 8
Sconto, Banca Italiana di, 86
Sconto e Seta banking firm, 19
Scotti, Carlo, 211
Scutari: shipping at, 213–214; and Anti-vari Company, 216, 217, 319; and trans-Balkan railway project, 232–233, 238; Catholics of, 316; Italo-Austrian competition at, 318; rail plans involving, 322, 331
Seccia, Pasquale, 294–295, 297–298
Secolo XIX, Il, 76, 80
Seminati, Arturo, 297–299
Senussi, 245, 299, 300
Serbia, 194, 253, 283; and Ottoman Empire, 203, 220; Giuseppe Volpi's contacts with, 208, 209; Italian interest in, 217, 311–314; and trans-Balkan railway project, 218, 220–221, 227, 229–230, 238, 371 n. 22, 377 n. 19; Austrian policy regarding, 317; and Italo-Austrian competition in the Balkans, 328–330
Serra, Attilio, 299–300
Servizi Marittimi, 109, 110, 117, 119, 123
Sforza, Carlo (count), 209
Shipbuilding industry: subsidized, 42, 61, 71, 77, 107–108; and goal of self-sufficiency, 63–64; sales abroad, 80, 101; lack of orders, 81; customers of, 108–110. *See also* Ansaldo; Oderos; Orlandos; Shipping industry
Shipping industry, 42, 64, 77, 287; linked with government-military-industrial complex, 106–112, 127; and Italian imperialism, 112–125; owners' coalition, 181–185; Italo-Austrian competition in, 197, 279; at Lake Scutari, 213; in eastern Mediterranean, 261–262. *See also* Florio, Ignazio; Marine Federation; Navigazione Generale Italiana; Sicilia line
Sicilia line, 111, 117, 158
Sicily: peasants of, 29–30; politics of, 31; emigration from, 49
Siemens Schuckert, 140

Sigismondi (engineer), 56–57
Silvestri (industrialist), 231, 233, 286; company of, 355 nn. 13, 14
Sinigaglia, Oscar, 68
Sitmar shipping company, 180
Slataper, Scipio, 333–334
Slavs: rivalries with Italians in Austria, 85, 244, 334–336; banks run by, 85, 370–371 n. 20
Slovenes, 218, 334, 335
Smyrna, 119, 123, 262
Smyrna-Aidin rail line, 266, 270, 271, 276, 277, 299, 306
Socialism: theory of fascism as a reaction to, 168
Socialists, 34–35; repression of, by Crispi, 22; and Giolitti, 24, 36, 39; in Sicily, 31; Neapolitan, 34; voting strength of, 167; motor workers as, 169; and labor troubles, 170; and strikes at Elba-Piombino, 173–175; and Terni, 175–177; and Chamber of Deputies, 179–181, 183–185; programs of, 186; converted to imperialism, 338
Social welfare, 28, 39
Società Anonima Bauchiero, 101
Società Bancaria Italiana, 19, 25, 69, 86, 91, 102, 111–112, 132, 231
Società Commerciale d'Oriente, 154, 201; interests in Albania, 111, 322; interests in Heraclea, 223–226; and trans-Balkan railway project, 230–233; operations in Constantinople, 242, 252–253, 262; operations in Libya, 247; financial troubles of, 248–250; reorganized, 250–251; loan to Turks by, 282; and Turkish loan issue, 285–286; interest in khedivial properties, 300; participation in loan to Montenegro, 331
Società delle Foreste Rumene, 102
Società del Linoleum, 103
Società di Credito Provinciale, 85, 86
Società Geografica Italiana, 202
Società italiana per il progresso delle scienze, 323
Società Italiana per imprese Elettriche, 139–140
Società Italiana per la fabbricazione dei proiettili, 99
Società Italiana per le Strade Ferrate del Mediterraneo, 231
Società Italiana Westinghouse, 93
Società Maremanna, 104
Società Metallurgica Italiana, 99, 286
Società Nobel-Avigliana, 81, 84–85, 354 n. 5

Società Pirelli, 102–103
Società Veneta per costruzioni ed imprese pubbliche, 53–55, 208
Società Veneziana di navigazione a vapore, 111, 121, 122
Sole, Il, 100, 279, 322
Sonnino, Sidney, 26, 29, 35, 36, 146, 147–148, 288
Soubhi Bey, 288–289
South America. *See* Latin America
South Italy, 5, 346–347 n. 14; contrasted with North, 11–12, 15; corruption and election abuses in, 14, 27; social and economic problems of, 27, 31–32, 49; Giolitti regime opposed by, 36; widening gap with North, 94–95
Spain, 79, 80, 101, 103, 143
Stahlverband, 67, 72
Stampa, La, 28, 147
Standard Oil: Italian subsidiary of, 109–110
Steed, Wickham, 143–144
Steel industry, 91, 134, 173, 354 n. 10, 361–362 n. 5; protected, 16, 25, development and problems of, 41–71; and foreign competition, 72–75; relations with French business, 86; specialities of, 89; profits in, 98. *See also* Steel trust
Steel trust (Ilva), 91, 112, 123, 305, 357 n. 30, 362 n. 5; "salvaged," 25, 69, 71, 150–151, 175; scandal involving, 30; background to formation of, 41–59; formation of, 59–71, 78; operations of, 71–75; Ansaldo a competitor of, 76, 78, 82–84; problems of, during World War I, 89; connections of managers of, 99–100, 110; connections with shipping industry, 106–107; and Banca Commerciale, 132–135; politics of, 147; and strikes at Elba-Piombino, 173–175
Strade Ferrate del Mediterraneo, 322
Strausz, Joseph, 208
Strikes, 36; government policy toward, 24; of auto-workers, 169–170; in Milan, 172; of Elba-Piombino, 173–175; at Terni, 175; opposed by Socialists, 175–177; at Ferriere del Vesuvio, 177; of Marine Federation, 179; ineffectiveness of, 186; in Montenegro, 211. *See also* Labor
Stringher, Bonaldo, 367 nn. 26, 29; director of Bank of Italy, 25, 44, 70, 146, 150; relations with Otto Joel and Giuseppe Volpi, 155–156, 254, 280; and trans-Balkan railway project, 226, 227–228, 230–238; and Italian in-

terests in Ottoman Empire, 240, 242–243, 306; and Turkish loan issue, 281–285; and Italian interest in Albania, 320, 323; and Italian interests in Balkans, 328, 331; and Italian interests in Montenegro, 372 n. 25

Subsidization: policy of, 13; of machine industries, 16; of bus lines, 25; of shipping, 25, 108, 119–120, 145–146; and steel industry, 71; of Antivari Company, 249

Suez Canal, 113–114, 122–123

Suffrage: universal male, 4, 26–28, 37, 150, 335, 345 n. 10, 371 n. 20

Sugar refining industry, 16, 48, 130, 147

Sulphur producers, 25, 208

Süss, Nathan, 86

Sweden, 96, 100

Switzerland: business relations of, 51, 128, 136

Syndicalists, 24, 36, 175; appeal of Nationalist ideals to, 38; and labor, 118, 170, 174, 178, 181, 186; converted to imperialism, 338. *See also* Corridoni, Filippo

Syria, 159

Talaat Pasha, 276

Tamaro, Attilio, 336

Tani, Cavaliere, 210

Tanlongo, Bernardo, 20; son of, 21

Tasviri-Efkiar, 307

Taxes: nineteenth-century, 6; consumer, 12, 46, 185; regressive structure of, 45–46, 347 n. 14; effect on banks, 360 n. 2

Tecnomasio italiano Brown-Boveri, 93

Tedesco (minister of the Treasury), 283, 284

Telioudis, Alexander, 293, 296, 305

Terni foundry and steel mill, 53–60, 62, 65–66, 87, 104, 351 n. 4, 363 n. 10, 369 n. 8; connected with shipbuilding interests, 70, 73, 107; production of, 82; 1913 report of, 83; board of managers of, 110; and Banca Commerciale, 129, 361 n. 4, 362 n. 9; labor relations, 175–176; inefficiency of, 176–177; criticized, 352–353 n. 13; indebtedness of, 361–362 n. 5, 366 n. 22

Textile industry, 5, 8, 11, 19, 61, 124, 130, 286

Theodoli, Marquis, 237, 255, 320

Tientsin: Italian concession in, 194

Times (London), 229–230

Tittoni, Romolo, 110, 111, 152, 154, 249, 255, 366 n. 24

Tittoni, Tommaso (senator), 201, 229–230, 363–364 n. 12, 377 n. 19; as prefect, 24, 34; political views and career of, 34–35; connections with Catholic political world, 152–153, 345 n. 10; and Antivari Company, 215; and Ottoman Empire, 219–220; and trans-Balkan railway project, 221, 226–227, 232, 236; foreign policy of, 222, 225, 264, 277–278; effort to establish Italo-Ottoman bank, 242; accused of collaboration with underworld, 348 n. 16

Tobacco monopoly in Montenegro, 209–216, 231

Toeplitz, Giuseppe, 109, 126–127, 129, 140–143, 161, 206–207, 360–361 n. 2, 364 n. 17, 365 n. 21

Tonietti, Ubaldo, 64, 65

Torre, Andrea, 149

Tosi. *See* Franco Tosi firm

Tourism, 44

Transformism, 22, 24, 30, 344 n. 7; the term, 13–14; economic system under, 16

Tribuna, La, 145–150, 170, 175, 254, 365–366 n. 21, 366 n. 22

Trieste, 85, 112, 115, 204, 213; Italo-Austrian rivalry at, 121, 123, 197, 334; Italian nationalism and irredentism in, 121–122, 335–336, 370–371 n. 20; comments of Mario Alberti on, 336–337

Triple Alliance, 62; strains in, 60, 124, 274–276; Italy's participation in, 105, 194, 227; and Banca Commerciale, 126; and Italian interest in Asia Minor, 257, 267, 269; and Italian competition with Austria-Hungary, 258–259; failure of, 278–280, 313, 333; and Italy's role in Balkans, 312, 328–330; and Albania, 317; and Adriatic Italians, 335–336

Triple Entente: Italian relations with, 35, 124–125, 194, 222, 276, 326; and Italian industry, 42, 90; and Ottoman Empire, 197, 257; and Italian foreign policy, 259

Tunisia, 199; as French protectorate, 32, 115, 191; Italian interest in, 115, 136

Turin, 94; labor discontent in, 168–171

Turkish loan issue, 280–286, 309

Turks: ethnic, 202; nationalism of, 251, 258; described by Seccia, 294–295

Unification of Italy, 3, 5, 10, 77

Unione Concimi firm, 136

Unione Italiana Cementi, 102

United States, 57; Italian imports from,

50; auto industry of, 96–97; Italian sales to, 96, 100
Unity and Progress Committee, 239–240, 253, 265
Universities: declining financial support for, 45
Urban development, 18
Utilities, 129, 130, 152. *See also* Electrical industry

Vannutelli, Lamberto, 202–203
Veloce, La, 112
Venetian group ("friends" of the Banca Commerciale), 127, 131, 204, 207–208, 313; interests in Montenegro, 209–210, 212–213, 216, 218; and trans-Balkan railway scheme, 230
Veneto: emigration from, 49; electrification of, 207
Venice, 113, 204–205
Vesnic, Milenko, 208–209, 217, 227, 229–230
Vesnic, Mme. (Blanche Blumenthal), 230
Vickers-Armstrong, 104
Vickers-Terni, 73, 74, 352–353 n. 13, 353 n. 3
Victor Emmanuel II (king of Italy), 9, 12, 114, 341 n. 3. *See also* Savoy, House of
Victor Emmanuel III (king of Italy), 34, 209, 260, 341–343 n. 3. *See also* Savoy, House of
Visconti di Modrone, Marquis, 320
Vismara, Giacomo, 319–321
Vitalis, Georges (count), 233, 330–331
Vlora, Ismail Kemal Bey, 316, 321–322, 324
Vlora, Sureya Bey, 320
Vlora family, 319–321
Voinovic, Ivan (count), 208
Volpi, Giuseppe, 254, 280, 286, 339, 372 n. 25; shipping interests of, 111; and Venetian group, 127, 131; and

SADE, 139; career of, 154, 206–210; and Balkans, 158, 231–232, 370, 376 n. 16, 377 n. 19; involved in Italo-Ottoman negotiations, 158, 248, 250, 252–253; activities in Montenegro, 210–213, 216–217, 314; and Antivari Company, 217, 249; operations in Ottoman Empire, 223–224, 262; and Heraclea, 223, 231; and trans-Balkan railway project, 232–233, 239, 254, 371–372 n. 24; knowledge of Ottoman scene, 237; business difficulties of, 250; and reorganized Società Commerciale d'Oriente, 250–251; return to Italy, 253; disliked by Stringher, 254; operations in Serbia, 313; and Italian interest in Albania, 319, 322; and Paris conference, 326–332; and Adriatic question, 337; correspondence of, 361, 367 n. 26

Wangenheim (German ambassador), 265, 266, 272
War, Ministry of, 74, 82, 85, 101, 176
Weil, Federico, 365 n. 21; business positions of, 110, 112, 118, 126–127; efforts to discredit, 161
Wheat, 157, 158; protected, 48, 61
Wiener Bank Verein, 322
William, prince of Wied, 318, 324–326
Wilson, Woodrow, 144
World War I: Italy's entry into, 4, 35
World War II: factors in Italy's intervention in, 89

Young Turk regime, 151, 153
Young Turk revolution, 193, 201, 236–237

Zanzibar, 191
Zara, 106–107
Zinoviev (Russian ambassador), 219
Zionism, 162–163